INFANTRY
IN BATTLE

THE INFANTRY JOURNAL·INCORPORATED
WASHINGTON, D. C.
1939

Printed courtesy of the U.S. Army Center of Military History, Washington, D.C., 1997.

CONTENTS

INTRODUCTION

THIS book treats of the tactics of small units as illustrated
by examples drawn from the World War. It checks the
ideas acquired from peacetime instruction against the experience
of battle.

There is much evidence to show that officers who have received the best peacetime training available find themselves surprised and confused by the difference between conditions as pic-
tured in map problems and those they encounter in campaign.
This is largely because our peacetime training in tactics tends
to become increasingly theoretical. In our schools we generally
assume that organizations are well-trained and at full strength,
that subordinates are competent, that supply arrangements function, that communications work, that orders are carried out. In
war many or all of these conditions may be absent. The veteran
knows that this is normal and his mental processes are not
paralyzed by it. He knows that he must carry on in spite of
seemingly insurmountable difficulties and regardless of the fact
that the tools with which he has to work may be imperfect and
worn. Moreover, he knows how to go about it. This volume is
designed to give the peace-trained officer something of the viewpoint of the veteran.

By the use of numerous historical examples, the reader is acquainted with the realities of war and the extremely difficult
and highly disconcerting conditions under which tactical problems must be solved in the face of an enemy. In so far as there
was material available, these examples pertain to American
troops and have been drawn from the personal experience monographs on file at The Infantry School. The combat experience
of other armies, however, has been utilized to supplement that
of our own.

This work does not purport to be a complete treatise on minor
tactics of infantry. The aim of its authors has been to develop

fully and emphasize a few important lessons which can be substantiated by concrete cases rather than to produce just another book of abstract theory.

GEORGE C. MARSHALL,
Colonel, Infantry.

May 1, 1934.

✔   ✔   ✔   ✔

FIRST EDITION

May 1, 1934.

INFANTRY IN BATTLE was prepared by the Military History and Publications Section of The Infantry School under the direction of Colonel George C. Marshall. Major Edwin F. Harding planned the book and supervised the preparation and edit of the manuscript. Major Richard G. Tindall wrote the original drafts of most of the chapters. Captain John A. Andrews, Captain Robert H. Chance, and Lieutenant C. T. Lanham assisted in the research and the preparation of the maps, and contributed parts of some of the chapters. Captain Russel B. Reynolds drafted the chapter on the fire of machine guns. Lieutenant Lanham edited and revised the manuscript in full.

✔   ✔

SECOND EDITION

September 1, 1938.

The second edition of INFANTRY IN BATTLE is not a mere reprint. The entire book has been extensively revised. Many of the sections have been completely rewritten; much of the tactical doctrine restated; and new maps by Technical Sergeant William H. Brown substituted for those of the first edition. This work was performed by Captain C. T. Lanham, in consultation with Lieutenant Colonel Edwin F. Harding.

Chapter I: *Rules*

Combat situations cannot be solved by rule.

THE ART OF WAR has no traffic with rules, for the infinitely varied circumstances and conditions of combat never produce exactly the same situation twice. Mission, terrain, weather, dispositions, armament, morale, supply, and comparative strength are variables whose mutations always combine to form a new tactical pattern. Thus, in battle, each situation is unique and must be solved on its own merits.

It follows, then, that the leader who would become a competent tactician must first close his mind to the alluring formulæ that well-meaning people offer in the name of victory. To master his difficult art he must learn to cut to the heart of a situation, recognize its decisive elements and base his course of action on these. The ability to do this is not God-given, nor can it be acquired overnight; it is a process of years. He must realize that training in solving problems of all types, long practice in making clear, unequivocal decisions, the habit of concentrating on the question at hand, and an elasticity of mind, are indispensable requisites for the successful practice of the art of war.

The leader who frantically strives to remember what someone else did in some slightly similar situation has already set his feet on a well-traveled road to ruin.

❧ ❧ ❧

EXAMPLE 1. In the early days of August, 1918, the Germans were retiring toward the Vesle River. On the third day of this month the U. S. 4th Division relieved the 42d and advanced. The 39th Infantry, part of this advancing division, moved forward in an approach-march formation with two battalions in assault. All day the troops struggled forward—the slowness of the advance being caused not by hostile resistance but by the difficulty of the terrain, particularly the dense woods that had to be negotiated.

Late in the day resistance was encountered and overcome. The enemy fell back. Orders were now received to form a column with an advance guard, take up the pursuit and drive across the Vesle in order to establish a bridge-head on the slopes to the north.

The 39th Infantry (less one battalion) was designated as the advance guard of the 7th Brigade. After a march of several hours, hostile artillery fire was encountered, whereupon the column halted for the remainder of the night. At dawn the march was resumed, but finding that the proposed route of advance was being shelled by the enemy, the advance guard counter-marched to another road. Some confusion resulted from this, the 2d and 3d Battalions becoming intermingled. Thus, when the movement again got under way, Company H formed the advance party, Companies F, K, and L the support, and Companies I, M, Machine-gun Company, Companies E and G, in the order named, the reserve.

Early on August 4 the column approached the Vesle on the Chéry-Chartreuve—St. Thibaut Road. About 2,000 meters south of St. Thibaut this road passes through a deep defile, 200 meters wide and nearly perpendicular to the commanding heights north of the river. The road runs through the full 1,000-meter length of this defile, then emerges at the northern exit to open terrain, over which it winds smoothly to the little village of St. Thibaut. To reach this village, the open terrain before it has to be crossed, and this lies under direct command of the high ground to the north.

No enemy infantry had been encountered. Company H, in column of twos, approached St. Thibaut without being fired on. At 8:00 a.m. it entered the town. By this time part of the support, marching in column of squads, was well out of the defile. Company H had cleared the town and had nearly reached the bridge over the Vesle when suddenly the Germans on the north-

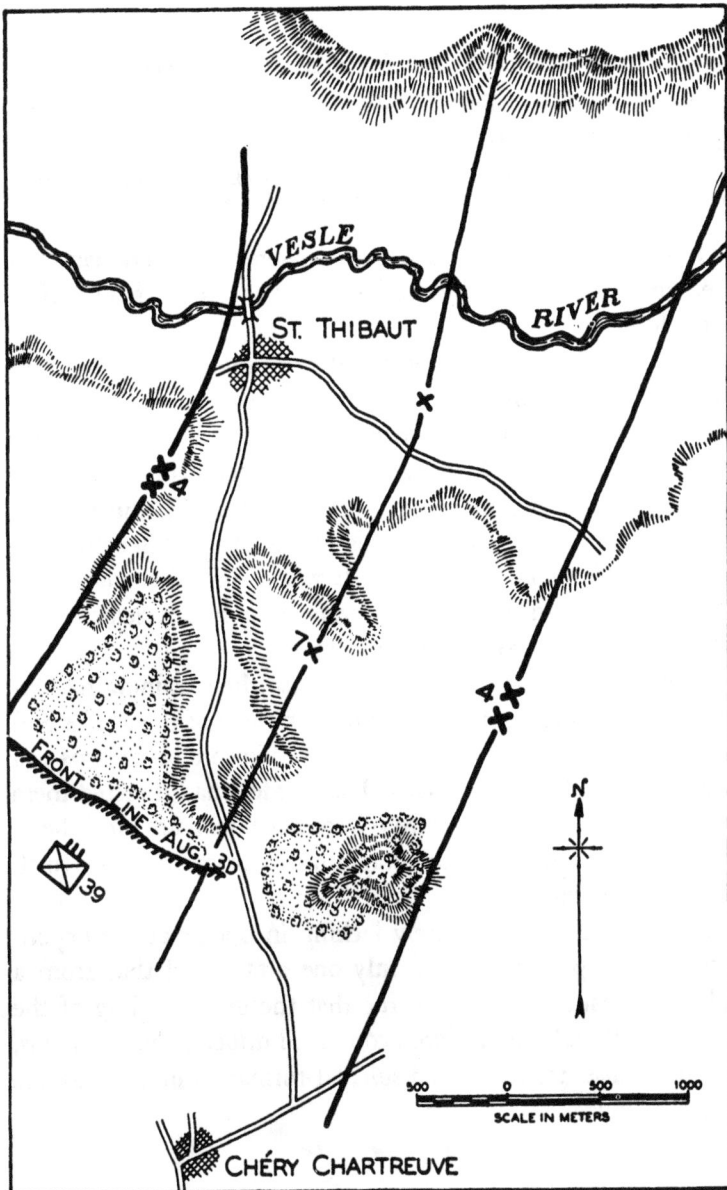

VESLE

ST. THIBAUT

RIVER

X

4

7X

4X

FRONT LINE - AUG. 30

39

N

500   0   500   1000
SCALE IN METERS

CHÉRY CHARTREUVE

Example 1

ern heights opened with machine guns and artillery on the advance party and the support, causing heavy casualties and throwing the support, in particular, into the greatest confusion.

From the personal experience monograph of Major Manton S. Eddy, who commanded the Machine-Gun Company of the 39th Infantry.

DISCUSSION. Here is a perfect example of a command offered up on the bloody altar of *form*. Let us look at that sacrifice more closely.

Until the advance guard emerged from the defile, the terrain had shielded it from hostile ground observation. As it left this friendly protection it came in direct view of the commanding heights to the north. Hostile artillery had been firing from these heights but a short time before, but in spite of this the advance party moved out in column of twos and the support in column of squads. In Major Eddy's words, "It was a sight that must have made the German artillery observers gasp in amazement, for before them lay an artilleryman's dream."

Why was this done? Probably because their training had established it as a custom of the service, as a law of the Medes and the Persians, that an advance party moved in column of twos and a support in column of squads. Their orders had directed them to form an advance guard, they were not under fire, and therefore they adopted one of the diagrammatic formations set forth in training manuals.

True, this unit was entirely lacking in open-warfare experience, having participated in only one attack and that from a stabilized position. It is also true that the intermingling of the 2d and 3d Battalions rendered command difficult. Nevertheless, common sense decried such a suicidal formation in the presence of the enemy.

✓   ✓   ✓

EXAMPLE 2. On October 14, 1918, the U. S. 77th Division attacked the Germans north of the Aire River near St. Juvin.

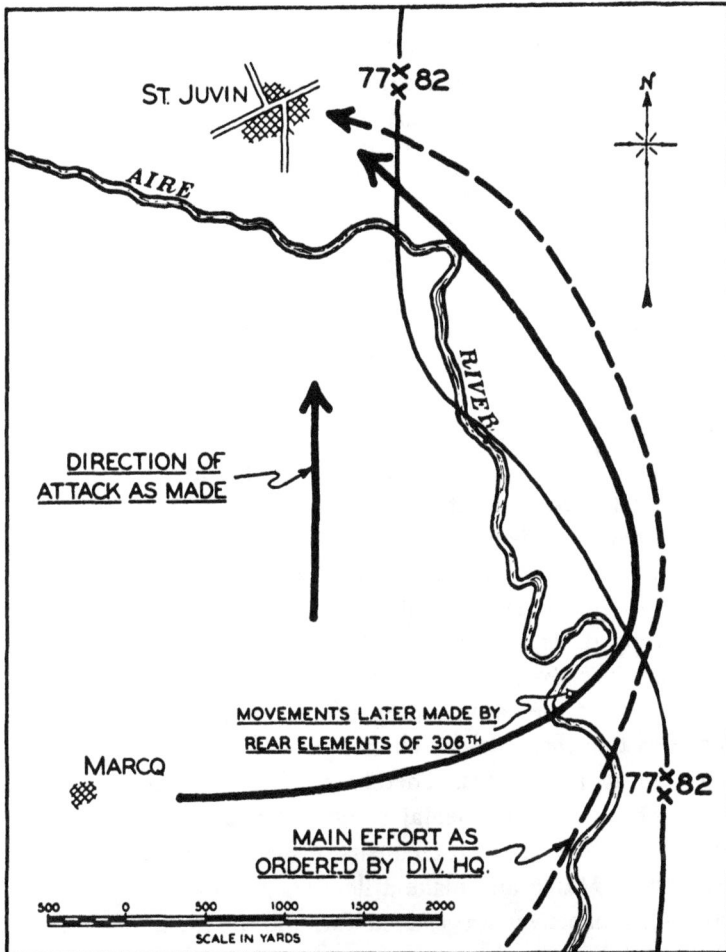

Example 2

The hostile positions in this vicinity were strong, particularly against an attack from the south. Feeling certain that the German barrage and defensive fires were registered south of St. Juvin and the Aire River, the division commander planned to take the village by envelopment from the east and southeast, while one regiment made a frontal demonstration from the south. He decided that, under cover of darkness, troops could cross the Aire well to the south unobserved. This operation would require movement in the zone of the 82d Division on the right, but the position of the 82d facilitated this maneuver. Therefore the 77th Division order specified:

> By maneuvering with its right in the area of the 82d Division it (the 77th Division) will attack St. Juvin from the south and the east.

Unfortunately, this idea of maneuver was not reproduced in the orders of the lower echelons, the troops being sent "straight against St. Juvin from the south," the direction that the division commander had particularly wished to avoid for the real attack.

The 1st Battalion of the 306th Infantry, which the division commander had expected to be directed against St. Juvin from the east, attacked straight from the south with the unfordable Aire between it and its objective. The hostile barrage and murderous machine-gun fire from the slopes north of the Aire swept through the assaulting units in a wave of destruction. The attack stopped. At noon the situation was such that the division commander believed a serious repulse inevitable.

At this time the commanding officer of the 306th Infantry concluded that there was no chance of success if the attack continued along these lines. Therefore, after the failure of the frontal effort, this regimental commander, acting on his own initiative, directed the rear elements of his regiment to cross the Aire east of Marcq and make a flanking movement against St. Juvin. This maneuver was carried out, and the town, the hostile position, and 540 prisoners were captured.

From "Memories of the World War" by Major General Robert Alexander, who commanded the 77th Division.

DISCUSSION. General Alexander emphasizes the fact that the attack, as launched at first, was merely frontal. It failed. Not until the regimental commander, acting on his own initiative, ordered troops to cross the Aire and strike the hostile position in flank, was success achieved.

This division commander states that "evidently the malign influence of trench-warfare doctrine, which in all cases depended upon a barrage and a straight push behind it," still controlled the minds of some of his subordinates.

From beginning to end, the World War is studded with major and minor reverses that resulted from attempts to apply methods that were successful in one situation to another situation.

✓ ✓ ✓

EXAMPLE 3. On November 2, 1918, the 9th Infantry, part of the U. S. 2d Division, was in division reserve southwest of Bayonville-et-Chennery. An American attack, launched on November 1, had achieved considerable success, and the Germans appeared somewhat demoralized.

On the afternoon of November 2, the 9th and 23d Infantry Regiments (3d Brigade) received orders to advance abreast, cross the front line at 8:00 p.m., and under cover of darkness moved forward to the heights just north of the Nouart—Fossé Road. They would then organize this position and prepare for a vigorous pursuit.

The 9th Infantry, in the order 1st, 2d, 3d Battalions, moved out in column of twos along the Bayonville-et-Chennery—Nouart Road to the front line then held by the 4th Brigade. As the regiment came to the outguards of the 5th Marines it was informed that the enemy still occupied the area to the immediate front—information which was soon found true.

The leading company (Company A) sent forward a patrol of several selected men which preceded the column by about 100 yards. Slowly the regiment moved forward. It passed through a long cut in the road. As the head of the column emerged from the cut, it ran into an enemy outguard of seven or eight men. These were promptly killed or captured and the regiment resumed its forward movement, this time protected by a deployed platoon to the front and by small groups from the leading company as flank guards. Heavy fire was now received from the left.

The column at once took cover while Company A deployed, moved against the enemy and drove him off. It was now midnight and the objective was close at hand. Accordingly, a halt was called until 5:00 a.m., at which time the regiment advanced a short' distance and deployed on the designated line, Nouart—Fossé.

An attack was launched from this line and new objectives were reached without encountering serious opposition. Here another pause ensued.

Although German resistance was rapidly crumbling along the entire Western Front, the 9th and 23d found that a definite stand was being made a short distance to their front on the crest along the south edge of the Bois de Belval. Accordingly, American artillery fire was placed on this position and preparation made to take it.

The brigade plan was unusual. The 9th and 23d were ordered to *penetrate the German position by marching in column on the road* through the Bois de Belval and to seize and occupy the heights south of Beaumont. The advance was to be supported by a rolling barrage extending 200 yards on each side of the road.

The 9th Infantry began its forward movement about 4:30 p.m. in the following order of march: 3d Battalion and Machine-Gun Company as advance guard, followed by the 2d and 1st Battalions, each with one company of the 5th Machine-Gun Battalion attached. It soon became dark. As the head of the advance guard approached the edge of the woods a few hundred yards south of Belval, German machine guns opened fire from both sides of the road. Patrols sent to the left and right made short work of silencing these guns. At Belval the road was barricaded. This was cleared up and the regiment, in column of twos, moved on in the darkness and mud. Rain began to fall.

Frequent halts were made to intercept enemy detachments moving along the road and to verify the route. Several German-speaking soldiers were placed at the head of the advance guard to hold the necessary brief conversation with any groups of the

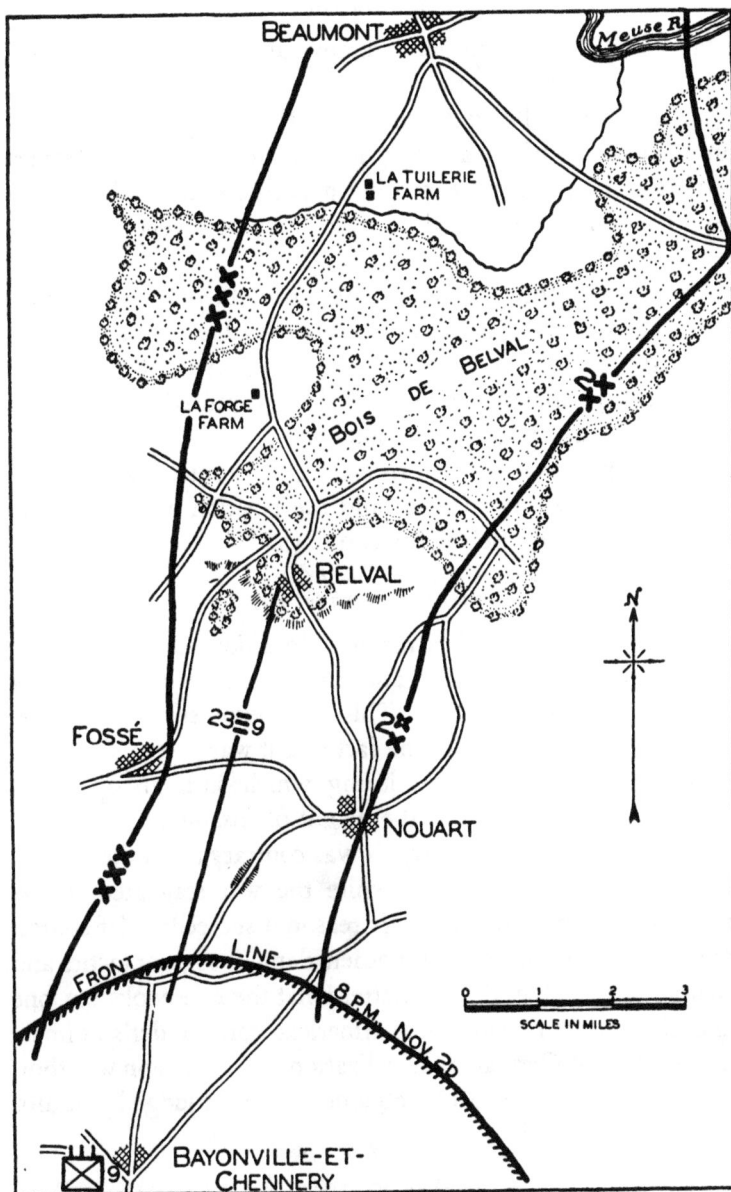

Example 3

enemy that might be encountered. Several of these groups were taken prisoner without firing a shot.

Just north of la Forge Farm the leading company of the advance guard surprised a large detachment of German troops who were industriously preparing a position from which they could cover a clearing in the forest. Sixty or seventy prisoners were taken.

The column continued, surprising a train bivouac and capturing an aid station. It arrived at the north edge of the wood at 10:45. At la Tuilerie Farm the officers and men of a German minenwerfer company were surprised and captured. Dispositions were then made to hold the ground won.

According to reports of prisoners and captured documents, the Germans had intended to hold the position near the south edge of the Bois de Belval for two days.

From the personal experience monograph of Captain Roy C. Hilton, who commanded the Machine-Gun Company of the 9th Infantry.

DISCUSSION. Here is a remarkable action. During a single night a regiment, in column and on roads, marched five miles through the enemy position! This feat becomes still more remarkable when we consider the fact that it was preceded by four years of stabilized warfare during which such an operation would have been classed as the height of insanity.

The plan was revolutionary. It was contrary to all the tedious rules that had been evolved while the war stagnated in the trenches. Perhaps that is the very reason it succeeded. Of course, some praise this operation and others damn it as poor tactics and a dangerous gamble. But no matter what the rule books say, one unassailable fact remains—the American commander's estimate of the extent of German demoralization and confusion was thoroughly upheld by the success obtained. And we judge by results.

✻   ✻   ✻

EXAMPLE 4. On October 29, 1918, the 2d Battalion of the U. S. 61st Infantry held a position south of the Andon Brook.

From the north edge of the Clairs-Chênes Woods the ground—devoid of cover—falls in a long gentle slope to the little brook that skirts Aincreville.

The Germans, in possession of Aincreville, had emplaced their machine guns about 250 yards in front of the town in a semicircular position. In addition, they had prepared an artillery barrage to fall about 200 yards in front of their machine guns.

The Americans could hear voices and the rumbling of wagons in Aincreville, but had no idea in what strength the enemy held the town. Patrols could advance only a short distance before they were driven off, for the Germans signalled for their defensive barrage on the slightest provocation. The signal was a green-star rocket, which brought the barrage down about two minutes later.

Expecting that he would be ordered to capture Aincreville, the battalion commander made his estimate of the situation. His men were very tired. After a succession of long marches, they had taken part in operations from October 12 to 17, and, though suffering heavy casualties, had met with only small success. Following this they had remained under artillery fire in division reserve for several days and then, after receiving a few partly-trained replacements, had relieved elements of the 3d Division in the front line on the night of October 26-27.

In view of the condition of his men, the battalion commander believed that any cut-and-dried attack would have small chance of success. There was no cover. An American artillery preparation would be certain to bring down the German's barrage and cause their machine guns to open. And he was not at all sure that his weary men would advance through this fire over open terrain. He did believe, however, that the Germans were equally tired and that if he could only get close quarters with them the problem would be solved.

On the afternoon of October 29 the expected order arrived. It directed that one officer and 100 men from this battalion attack

and seize the town following a preparatory artillery and machine-gun barrage. The battalion commander immediately proposed an alternative plan which was approved. Only the officer
directly in charge of the action and four or five reliable sergeants
were let in on the plan. This is how the battalion commander
proposed to take Aincreville—

At 2:30 a.m., October 30, Lieutenant R. W. Young and 100
men from Company F would capture Aincreville by surprise.

The attack would jump off without preparatory fire of any
kind. The assault would be made in two waves. The sergeants
who were in on the plan would follow the second wave to insure
that all men went forward at the crucial moment and not back.
The advance would be made silently. The battalion commander
believed that these troops could reach a point within thirty yards
of the line of machine guns before being discovered. When the
hostile machine guns opened up, the attackers were to lie down
and take cover. Lieutenant Young, with a captured German
Very pistol and green-star rocket, would then fire the signal
calling for the German defensive barrage. All of the Americans
knew this signal.

As soon as Lieutenant Young felt that his men realized the
meaning of the green-star rocket, he would yell: "Beat it for the
town!" The battalion commander believed that the assaulting
troops would realize that there was no time to regain their line
before the German barrage came down in rear of them and that,
therefore, their only hope of safety lay in reaching the town.

Arriving in town, they would take cover in the houses and
cellars, wait until morning, and then mop it up. Arrangements
were made to report the capture of the town by rocket.

The unit on the left would place a machine-gun barrage on the
western exit of the town, preventing German escape and diverting attention there. The signal for this barrage would be the
green-star rocket fired by the attacking force.

The plan worked perfectly. The Americans advanced until

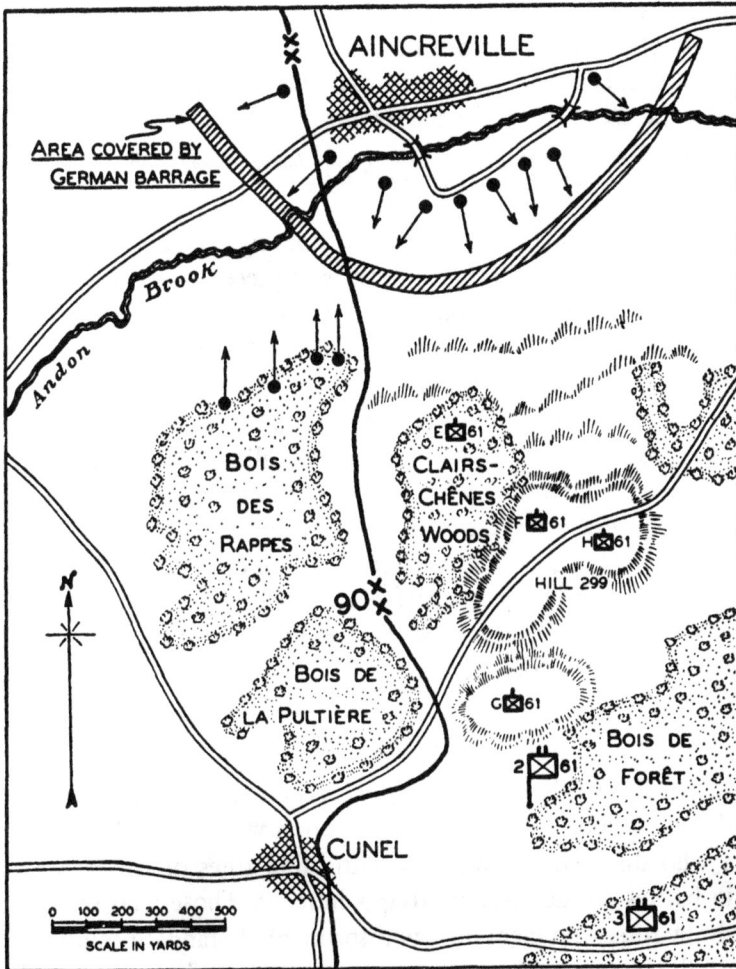

Example 4

halted by fire from one or two machine guns. They were close to
the guns and in a line. The rocket went up and a voice shouted:
"Beat it for the town, it's your only chance!" The men ran over
the machine guns, leaped across the stream and entered the

town, where they were assembled and directed into houses and cellars. There were only one or two casualties.

Lieutenant Young was killed the next morning while supervising the mopping up of the town.

From the personal experience monograph of Major Alexander N. Stark, Jr., who commanded the 2d Battalion of the 61st Infantry.

DISCUSSION. Certainly there is nothing stereotyped about this plan. It is not customary to sit on a piece of ground where the enemy places his barrage and then send up a signal calling for that barrage. It is equally unusual to devise a deliberate surprise for your own troops. This plan worked, however, and that is the criterion by which an action must stand or fall.

It is possible that the town might have fallen before a daylight assault well supported by fire. Perhaps it might have been taken by a night attack more nearly conforming to the book. On the other hand, it is possible that the battalion commander was entirely correct in his estimate of the effort he could expect from his men at this particular time. The result obtained fully justified the means employed.

✓ ✓ ✓

CONCLUSION. Every situation encountered in war is likely to be exceptional. The schematic solution will seldom fit. Leaders who think that familiarity with blind rules of thumb will win battles are doomed to disappointment. Those who seek to fight by rote, who memorize an assortment of standard solutions with the idea of applying the most appropriate when confronted by actual combat, walk with disaster. Rather, is it essential that all leaders—from subaltern to commanding general—familiarize themselves with the art of clear, logical thinking. It is more valuable to be able to analyze one battle situation correctly, recognize its decisive elements and devise a simple, workable solution for it, than to memorize all the erudition ever written of war.

To quote General Cordonnier, a French corps commander:

The instruction given by leaders to their troops, by professors of military schools, by historical and tactical volumes, no matter how varied it may be, will never furnish a model that need only be reproduced in order to beat the enemy. . . .

It is with the muscles of the intellect, with something like cerebral reflexes that the man of war decides, and it is with his qualities of character that he maintains the decision taken.

He who remains in abstractions falls into formula; he concretes his brain; he is beaten in advance.

Chapter II: *Obscurity*

In war obscurity and confusion are normal. Late, exaggerated or misleading information, surprise situations, and counterorders are to be expected.

IN WARFARE of movement even higher commanders will seldom have a clear insight into the enemy situation. Detailed information of hostile dispositions and intentions will ordinarily be revealed only through the medium of combat. Obviously, such information is not available in the initial stages of a battle and experience has shown that little of it ever filters down to front-line leaders as the fight progresses. In mobile warfare, then, small units may expect to fight with practically no information of friend or foe. Theirs, as Captain Liddell Hart expresses it, is the problem of how to guard, move and hit in the dark.

In stabilized warfare more information is usually available, but even here the smaller units will be repeatedly confronted with obscure situations that demand immediate action.

The leader must not permit himself to be paralyzed by this chronic obscurity. He must be prepared to take prompt and decisive action in spite of the scarcity or total absence of reliable information. He must learn that in war the abnormal is normal and that uncertainty is certain. In brief, his training in peace must be such as to render him psychologically fit to take the tremendous mental hurdles of war without losing his stride.

EXAMPLE 1. On September 8, 1914, the German 14th Division, which had been in army reserve during the early stages of the Battle of the Marne, was ordered to force a crossing of the wide swamp south of Joches. This swamp, impassable even to

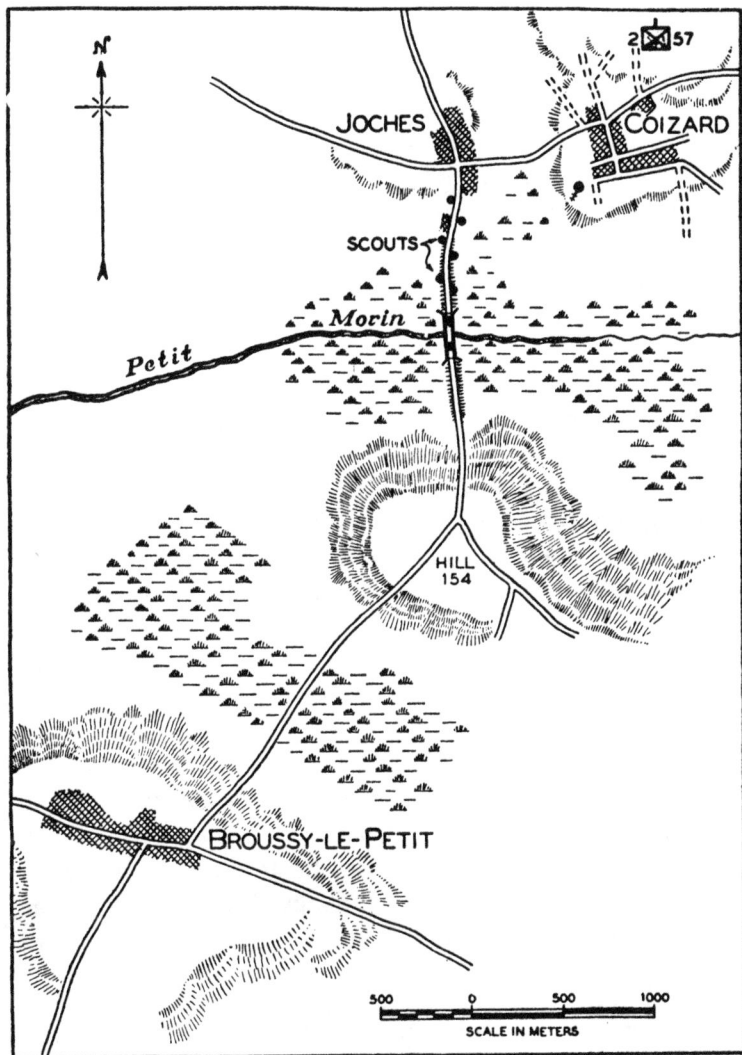

Example 1

foot troops, was bridged by a single road. The French, located south of the swamp, could fire with artillery and machine guns on both Joches and this road.

Marching from the north the 2d Company of the 57th Infantry (temporarily attached to the 53d Infantry) reached the north edge of Coizard at 8:00 a.m., and prepared for action while its commander went forward to the southern outskirts of the village to reconnoiter. From there he could see Joches, the formidable swamp and, beyond the swamp, Hill 154 interlaced by hedges and dotted with sheaves of grain. He could see that the French held this hill, for their red pantaloons were clearly visible in the morning sun. There was no firing; everything was quiet. Behind him he saw a few German batteries moving up. At 9:00 a.m. he saw a group of German scouts leave Joches and start forward to cross the swamp. The French immediately opened fire on the village and the road with artillery, machine guns and rifles. At this point the company commander was called to the rear where he received the following battalion attack order:

> The 2d Battalion of the 16th Infantry starts the crossing of the Petit Morin River. The 53d Infantry will follow, with the 2d Company of the 57th Infantry at the head. The objective is the village of Broussy-le-Petit.

That was all.

The attacking infantry knew neither the enemy's strength nor the location of his front line. They were not told whether or not their attack would be supported by artillery. They had no idea what units would be on their flanks. They only knew that they had to attack and would meet the French somewhere beyond the swamp.

From the personal experience monograph of Captain Adolf von Schell of the German General Staff, who commanded the 2d Company of the 57th Infantry.

DISCUSSION. This example is typical of attack orders that infantry companies may expect in open warfare. Leaders had to be guided by their mission, by the ground in front and by what they could see. Indeed, Captain von Schell emphasizes the fact that the order quoted was the only one he received during the entire day.

In peace these highly-trained troops had been accustomed to orders arranged in a certain set sequence and to elaborate information of the enemy. But when war came there were only fragmentary orders and little or no information of the enemy. To quote Captain von Schell:

> In open warfare on the Western Front and on the Eastern Front, in Rumania and in the Caucasus, it was always my experience that we had the most meager information of the enemy at the start of an attack.

✓   ✓   ✓

EXAMPLE 2-A. On July 14, 1918, the U. S. 30th Infantry held a defensive sub-sector south of the Marne, with its command post in the Bois d'Aigremont. The 1st Battalion, reinforced by an additional rifle company (K), Stokes mortars and machine guns, defended the area north of the Fossoy-Crézancy Road. Companies B and C outposted the river bank from Mézy to the Rû Chailly Farm. The rest of the regiment, with two companies of the 38th Infantry attached, had organized the Bois d'Aigremont in depth.

Communication agencies between the 1st Battalion and the regiment included two independent telephone lines, one buzzer, one TPS (earth telegraphy), a projector, pigeons and runners.

About midnight on the 14th, American artillery opened a violent bombardment. A few minutes later German shells began to burst in the American area. The cannonade increased in violence.

Soon after the German bombardment had gotten under way, it was realized at headquarters of the 1st Battalion that the long-expected German attack had at last jumped off. Signal equipment was tested and found useless. A rocket was sent up calling for artillery fire on the north bank of the Marne. Since it was impossible to tell whether the American artillery was firing there or not, other rockets were sent up from time to time. Runners were sent to Companies A, K, and D, informing them that the expected attack was in progress and directing them to hold their positions.

About 2:10 a.m. an excited runner from Company C arrived at the battalion command post. He reported that at the time he left Mézy the Germans in the town greatly outnumbered the Americans there. He also said that he had passed many of the enemy between Mézy and the battalion C.P. He appeared very calm after a time and was positive that the information he had given was correct.

A few minutes later another runner arrived, this time from Company B. He stated that the Germans had crossed the river opposite the Rû Chailly Farm, had destroyed two platoons of Company B, and that his company commander requested reinforcements. The folly of attempting to move troops through the woods in darkness and under intense artillery fire was realized, and accordingly no movement to reinforce Company B was ordered.

A messenger from Company A now reported that all the officers in his company had been killed.

Runners sent out from the battalion C.P. for information never returned.

At daylight four officers' patrols were sent out. One of these, commanded by a battalion intelligence officer, returned shortly and reported that a hostile skirmish line was only fifty yards in front of the woods.

In view of these alarming reports the battalion commander decided to move his C.P. about 500 yards to the rear in a ravine west of Crézancy. He believed that this location would facilitate control, give a better line on the action, and be more accessible to runners. Messengers were sent to Companies A, K, and D, informing them of the change. The commander of Company D construed this message to mean that the battalion was withdrawing. Accordingly he withdrew his company to the Bois

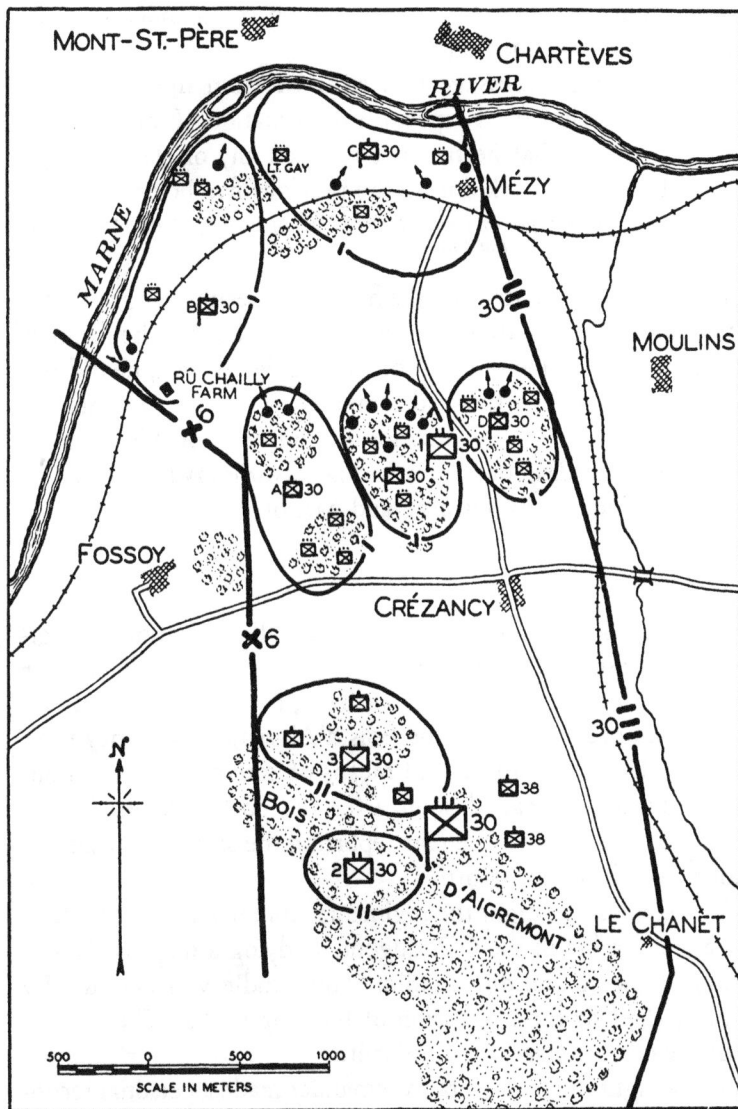

Example 2-A

d'Aigremont via Crézancy. The battalion commander was un-aware of this movement at the time.

At this point a message was received from the regimental commander asking for a report on the situation. From the con-text it was clear that he had not received any of the messages that had been sent back during the previous five hours.

From the personal experience monograph of Major Fred L. Walker, who com-manded the 1st Battalion of the 30th Infantry.

DISCUSSION. Although the battle had been in progress only a few hours, the battalion commander knew neither the location of his own front line nor that of the enemy. In fact, he did not even know if his two forward companies were still in existence. He was unaware of the situation of the units on his flanks— if they were holding or if they had been withdrawn. He had to judge the situation by surmise, and part of that surmise was in-correct.

✓ ✓ ✓

EXAMPLE 2-B. Let us now consider the situation at regi-mental headquarters during this same action. Hour after hour passed, but no word came in from front, flanks, or rear; only re-ports from nearby units in the Bois d'Aigremont that they were suffering heavy casualties. All means of communication within the regiment had failed soon after the bombardment began. Messages were sent to the rear reporting the situation. Runners sent forward did not return.

Throughout the night the regimental commander and his staff sat about a table in the C.P. dugout, studying a map by the un-certain light of one dim candle. This candle was periodically extinguished by the concussion of bursting shells. The roar of artillery made conversation difficult.

At daylight the regimental commander made a personal recon-naissance. Shells were falling everywhere within the area be-tween the Fossoy-Crézancy Road and the Bois d'Aigremont, but except for this he saw no signs of activity.

He returned to the C.P. and there he found that a message had come in from the front line indicating that the Germans had crossed the Marne at two or three places. Apparently it had taken hours to get this information back.

At 5:00 a.m. a runner from the 1st Battalion brought in the following message:

FROM: Portland (1st Battalion, 30th Infantry) July 15, 2:30 a.m.
TO: Syracuse (30th Infantry)

We have had some gas. All groups south of railroad, on line with P.C. are being heavily shelled. Heavy machine-gun fire in vicinity of Mont-St.-Père since 2:00 a.m. Have received no news from front-line companies. I believe all lines are out. Bombardment began at 12:00.

Signature.

P.S. Captain McAllister reports that he needs reinforcements and that his two front-line companies have been driven back. Cannot depend on any method of liaison. Better base your actions from your P.C.

In five hours the regimental commander had learned practically nothing of the situation. The American artillery kept pressing him for targets, but he could designate none. He had no idea where his own troops were or where the enemy was. All he could do was send out more runners in an endeavor to determine the situation; and this he did.

Shortly after 5:00 a.m. an officer came to the C.P. with the report that one of his men had talked to a man from Company C who said that some of his company had been driven out of Mézy. A few minutes later an officer reported in from 1st Battalion headquarters. He stated that the battalion commander had been unable to get any direct news from his forward-company commanders since 2:30 a.m.; that the woods just north of the Fossoy—Crézancy Road had been torn to pieces by shellfire, and that casualties in the headquarters personnel were heavy. Companies A, K, and D had not been engaged. The battalion commander was certain, from what some stragglers had said, that the Germans had crossed the river near Mézy and the Rû Chailly Farm, had passed the railroad and were moving south.

Some time after this the commander of the 1st Battalion reported in person to the regimental command post. He said that his two forward companies (B and C) were totally lost; that every unit of his command had sustained heavy losses; that communication, even with companies nearby, was extremely difficult; and that he had moved his command post slightly to the rear. He then recommended that the artillery, which had prepared defensive concentrations within the position, place fire south of the railroad. He added that the remnants of Companies A, K, and D should be able to hold out a while longer.

A little later another officer came in. He had a message for the regimental commander—"a message from brigade," he said. The colonel reached for it expectantly. Here, at last, would be some definite news—the location of the hostile front line, the enemy's assembly areas, the location of the German boats and bridges. Brigade probably had it from the aviators. He opened the message and read:

FROM: Maine (6th Brigade) July 14, 11:30 p.m.
TO: Syracuse (30th Infantry)

Test message. Please check the time this message is received and return by bearer.

This message, received at 6:35 a.m., was the first word from higher headquarters since the start of the battle at midnight.

From "The Keypoint of the Marne and its Defense by the 30th Infantry," by Colonel Edmund L. Butts, who commanded the 30th Infantry.

DISCUSSION. Here is an instance where the regimental commander knew even less of the situation than the commander of his front-line battalion. Not until the battalion commander went in person to the regimental command post did the colonel have even a glimmering of the situation, and then much vital information was lacking and much was in error. For example,

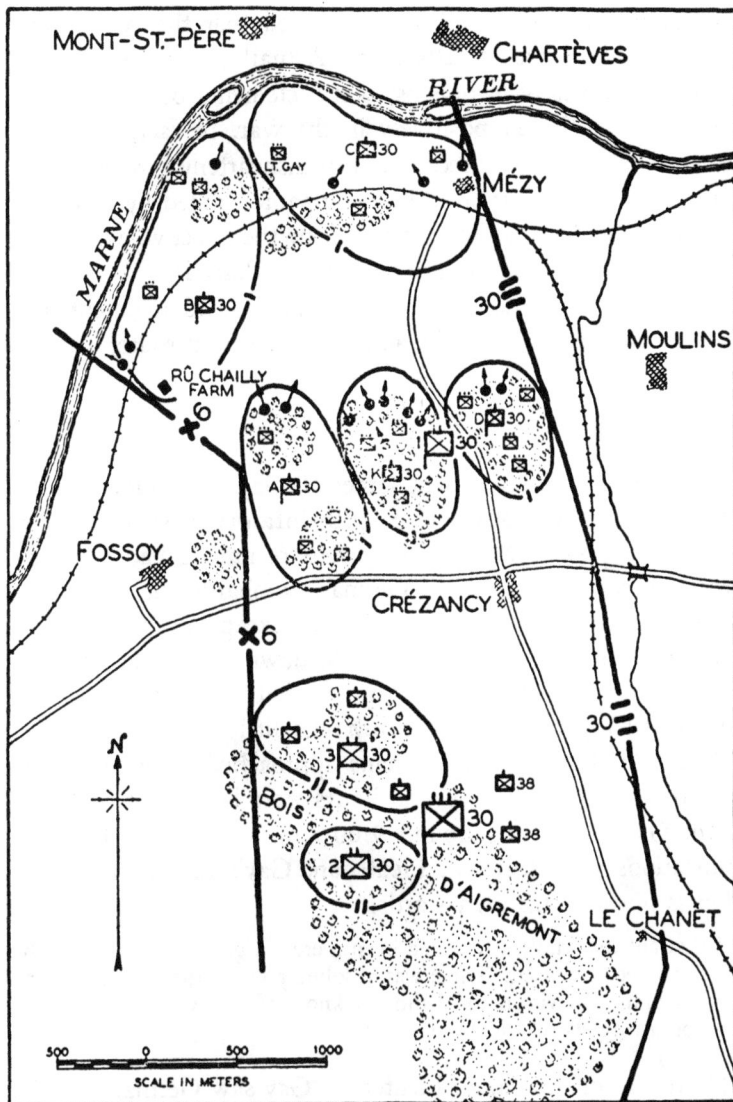

Example 2-B

the regimental commander was informed that the two front-
line companies were "totally lost." Actually, as we shall see,
this was completely erroneous. Some elements of these companies were still very positively in the war. In fact, at about
the time the colonel was receiving this disheartening report, two
platoons of one of his front-line companies, aided by machine
guns, were breaking a German attack by the effective expedient
of practically annihilating the battalion making it.

The incident of the message from brigade to regiment, received at the height of battle, and seven hours en route, is most
instructive.

✓   ✓   ✓

EXAMPLE 2-C. Lieutenant James H. Gay commanded a platoon of Company C of the U. S. 30th Infantry, posted near the
river bank opposite Mont-St.-Père. His command had not suffered a great deal from the German bombardment, but communication had been out with all units except one platoon located about 300 yards to his rear. "At dawn," states Lieutenant
Gay, "I knew absolutely nothing of what it was all about or
what was happening except in my own little sector."

About 4:30 a.m. some Germans approached from the front
and after a fight lasting several hours were beaten off by Lieutenant Gay's platoon. Around 9:00 a.m. a lull ensued. Communications were still out. Lieutenant Gay's idea of the situation is given in his own words:

> I thought the whole action had been merely a good-sized raid which
> had been repulsed. There was absolutely no further movement in
> our range of vision and I did not know of the events which were
> occurring elsewhere at the time.

Shortly after 9:00 a.m., Lieutenant Gay saw Germans to his
right-rear and to his left-rear. At this point American artillery
fire came down on his unit. He decided to move back and join
the platoon in his rear. When this was accomplished the two

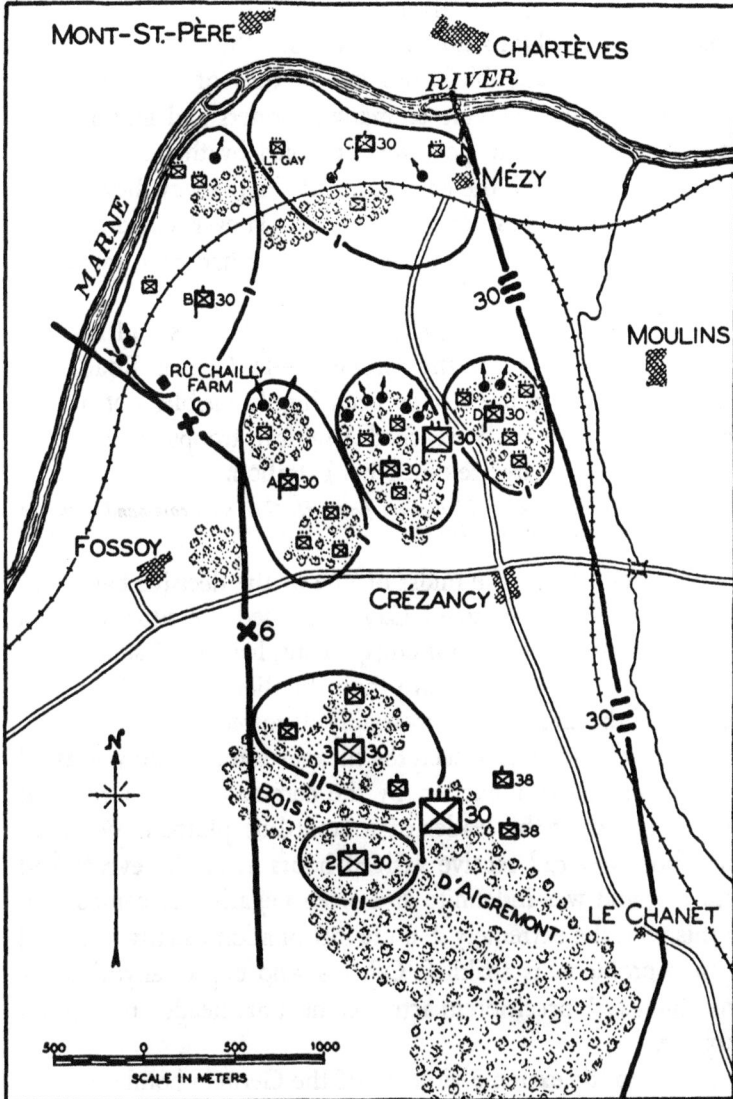

Example 2-C

platoon leaders met and, after discussing the situation, agreed to move their combined units back toward the company C.P.

En route they stumbled into two parties of Germans and took 150 prisoners. Having so many prisoners and finding that the company command post was occupied by the enemy, they decided to move on to the battalion C.P. On the way they passed another command post. It was deserted. They reached the old location of the battalion C.P. only to find it had been moved—no one knew where.

Lieutenant Gay then marched the two platoons and his 150 prisoners directly down the Crézancy—le Chanet Road. Although the column must have been highly visible, not a shot was fired at it. He finally reached American troops, turned over his prisoners and later rejoined his battalion.

Taken from a statement of Lieutenant James H. Gay, who commanded the 2d Platoon of Company C, 30th Infantry.

DISCUSSION. In the midst of one of the decisive battles of the World War, Lieutenant Gay diagnosed the situation as a good-sized raid. In a general engagement, leaders of small units will seldom know much more than this lieutenant. Their conception of the situation is invariably distorted.

In this action we have seen the meager information possessed by a regimental commander, by the commander of a forward battalion, and by the leader of a front-line platoon. What information they did receive arrived hours after the events had occurred, and was indefinite and often negative. A comparison of this with the extremely definite information usually provided in map problems is striking. Officers who expect anything approaching such precision in actual combat are headed for a bitter surprise.

Owing to the extreme violence of the German bombardment, communication in this battle was undoubtedly more difficult than usual. But on the other hand, this was a defensive action for the Americans; they were operating over familiar terrain, and their communication agencies were installed at the start of the fight.

✓   ✓   ✓

EXAMPLE 3. On July 17, 1918, the 2d Battalion of the U. S. 104th Infantry, which was then holding a position in Belleau Wood, received word that it would be relieved that night. Later, a message came in directing the battalion scout officer to report to regimental headquarters. Following this, another message arrived ordering the captain of Company E to report to the brigade. Neither of these officers returned. Preparations for the relief went on, but as hour after hour passed and no reconnaissance parties arrived, the battalion commander became concerned. At midnight he called the regimental command post but could locate no one except the supply officer, of whom he inquired:

"What about this Field Order No. so-and-so [the order for the relief]? There haven't been any friendly visitors up here."

The reply killed any idea of an early relief.

"Well, there isn't anybody around here, but I can safely tell you that it is all off."

At 3:30 a.m. the missing scout officer returned with word that the 3d Battalion would pass through the 2d and attack at 4:35 a.m.

Time passed. No one appeared. At 4:15 a.m. the 3d Battalion commander arrived alone with his hands full of charts and orders. He was visibly agitated. After complaining about "a horrible tie-up on the part of the higher-ups" he briefly explained the contemplated plan. This attack, which was to be launched from the north edge of the wood and drive toward the little town of Belleau, was believed to be merely a local operation for the purpose of rectifying the lines.

In due course the American barrage came down and at 4:35 a.m. began to roll forward. Not until then did elements of the

3d Battalion's assault companies begin to arrive. A heavy enemy artillery concentration began to fall on Belleau Wood.

The 3d Battalion commander, seeing that his troops had arrived late and were somewhat disorganized by hostile artillery fire, now declared his attack off, and directed his officers to have the men take what cover they could find in the woods. He then sent the following message by pigeon to brigade headquarters⸴

PIGEON MESSAGE: Time 6:05 o'clock.

LOCATION: At woods where 3d Battalion was to start from.

Did not reach starting-off place until attack had started. Machine-Gun Company did not arrive until 5:10. Their ammunition did not arrive. Infantry companies all late on account of lateness of arrival of ammunition and other supplies. When they arrived it was broad daylight and fully exposed and companies being shelled by the enemy. Battalion now scattered about woods, taking whatever cover they can find, as woods are being heavily shelled by high explosive. Can get in touch with me through P.C. 2d Battalion.

Meanwhile, the 2d Battalion commander had started for his C.P. En route he saw scattered men of the 3d Battalion frantically digging. When he reached his C.P. he was told that the regimental commander wished to speak to him. He heard the colonel's voice:

"The 3d Battalion has not attacked."

"I know it."

"Well, you take command of it and attack at once."

"It can't be done," the stupefied major replied. "They are scattered all over the world."

"Well, it has to be done. This order comes from higher authority. However, I'll give you a little time. What time is it by your watch?"

"7:05 a.m."

"All right, I'll give you until 7:30 and a rolling barrage. Go to it!"

Then the wire went out and ended the conversation.

The commander of the 2d Battalion took charge. At 8:20 a.m. he managed to launch the attack that should have started at

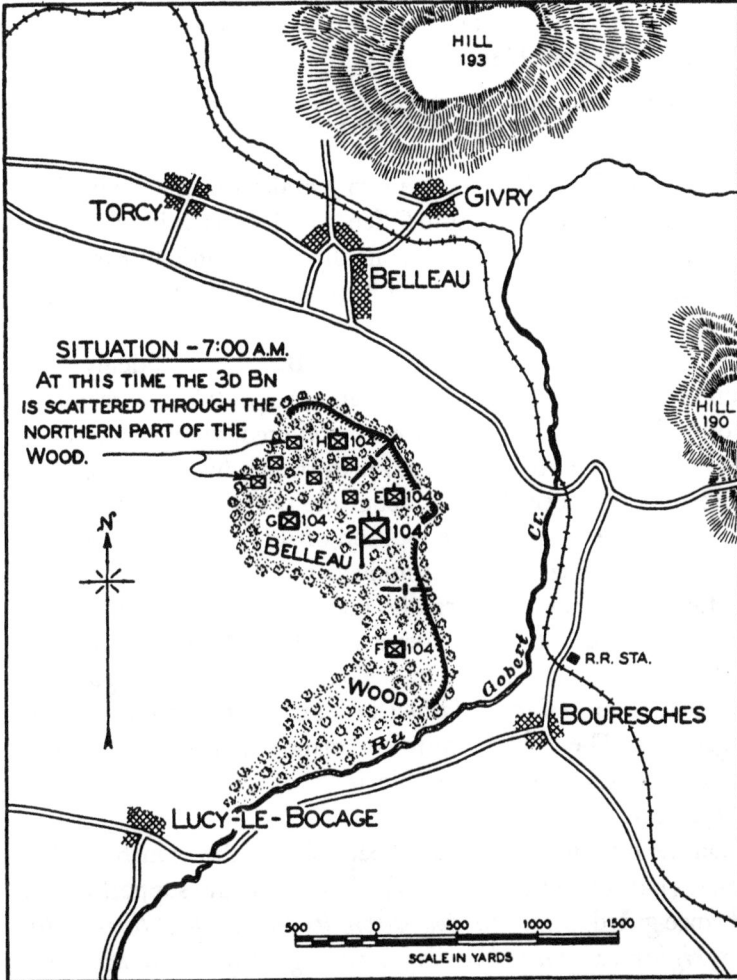

Example 3

4:35 a.m. Although the 7:30 barrage had passed, the attack at 8:20 a.m., in which he employed some elements of his own battalion, was reasonably successful.

From the personal experience monograph of Major Evan E. Lewis, who commanded the 2d Battalion of the 104th Infantry.

DISCUSSION. Here we see two battalion commanders participating in the Aisne-Marne Offensive, the attack in which the initiative on the Western Front finally and definitely passed to the Allies. Both officers believed it to be a local action to rectify the line!

We see the commander of the 2d Battalion suddenly confronted with a surprise situation—an order to take command of another battalion, whose men were scattered, whose units were disorganized, and to attack with it in twenty-five minutes. This officer had not been thinking about the problem of the 3d Battalion. He knew neither the location of its units nor the whereabouts of its officers, and yet immediate action was mandatory.

Hundreds of examples can be given; those cited are not isolated cases. Consider the experiences of the French Third and Fourth Armies and the German Fourth Army. On August 22, 1914, these huge forces clashed in a series of true meeting engagements. The French army commanders, in particular, did not believe that any appreciable force of the enemy was anywhere near.

On the morning of the 22d a battalion of the French 8th Division (part of the Third Army), detailed as the support of the advance guard, *was destroyed within its own outpost lines, without higher authority knowing anything about it at the time.* Even today it is difficult to say what actually happened. Apparently it was surprised in route column by Germans who had penetrated the French outpost in the early morning fog.

On the same day, a few miles to the west, the French 5th Colonial Brigade, marching north, stumbled into the flank of the German XVIII Reserve Corps, which was marching west. The battle started with the French advance guard striking the German column at right angles and shooting up the combat trains of part of one division.

Near St. Vincent, on this same eventful day, the commander of the French II Colonial Corps informed one of his division commanders, "There is nothing in front of you. You can push right on. It's just a march today." Soon afterward he and his staff became the private and personal target of German light artillery and scrambled to cover. When asked for information he replied, "I haven't the faintest idea of the situation."

In the Battle of Guise, on August 29, 1914, initial contact on the front of the German Guard Corps seems to have been made by the corps signal battalion which, through error, marched into the enemy lines.

Indeed, there appears to be no limit, save the imagination, to the astounding situations that evolve in the darkness and confusion of war. Consider the Turkish pursuit of the British in 1915, after the Battle of Ctesiphon. The Turkish cavalry was sending in reports of the location and movements of the retiring British. The Turkish infantry was pressing forward to gain contact with the British. According to the British official history the Turkish cavalry was actually in rear of the Turkish infantry without the infantry, cavalry, or high commanders being aware of the fact. The movements attributed to the British were presumably the Turkish cavalry's observation of its own infantry.

✓   ✓   ✓

CONCLUSION. Again it is stressed that these examples afford a striking contrast to the detailed and precise information that is given in map problems. In actual combat practically nothing is known. The situation, particularly in open warfare, is almost invariably shrouded in obscurity. Advanced units, at best, will have but little accurate knowledge of the enemy and frequently none of their own troops. Moreover, even the meager information they do possess will often be false or misleading.

But this does not mean that leaders must meekly submit to the proposition that war is likely to be a game of Blind Man's Buff and that nothing they can do will alter this condition. On the contrary, this realization of the dearth of reliable information in war should serve a dual purpose. First, it should stimulate leaders to adopt those positive and energetic measures that are necessary if vital information is to be gained. Secondly, it should so prepare the leader mentally that, instead of letting himself sink into the bog of apathy when no information is forthcoming, he will recognize the condition as normal and rise to prompt and decisive action.

We carry out in war what we learn in peace. In consonance with this principle the military student, after becoming familiar with the basic tactical concepts, should be given but little positive information of the enemy in his various terrain exercises, map problems and map maneuvers. Thus will he become conversant in peace with one of the most trying and difficult problems in war.

Chapter III: *Simplicity*

*Simple and direct plans and methods make
for foolproof performance.*

WHETHER we like it or not, combat means confusion,
intermingled units, loss of direction, late orders, misleading information, unforeseen contingencies of all sorts.
Troops must often carry out their orders under conditions of extreme fatigue and hunger, in unfavorable weather and almost
always under the devastating psychological and physical effect
of the fire of modern weapons. Not to take into account these
grim realities in formulating a plan of action is fatal.

But even when they are taken into account the leader often
faces a cruel dilemma. For instance, the situation may call for
an involved maneuver, and an involved maneuver increases the
chance of disastrous error. On the other hand, a simple maneuver, though decreasing the likelihood of serious error, may
fail to meet the situation. Therefore, it is fallacy to preach simplicity as a battle cure-all. But it is not fallacy to say that simplicity in plans, methods, and orders should always be striven
for and that elaborate and complicated maneuvers should not
be adopted except for the gravest reasons.

✓   ✓   ✓

EXAMPLE 1. On the morning of October 10, 1918, the U.
S. 30th Infantry was ordered to attack to the north toward the
little town of Cunel. Following an artillery preparation, the 1st
Battalion was to attack from the north edge of the Bois de Cunel.
Of the two remaining battalions of the 30th, the 2d was in sup-
port and the 3d in brigade reserve.

The attack jumped off at 7:00 a.m. The 1st Battalion reached
a point about 500 yards north of the wood where it was stopped
by heavy fire from the front and both flanks. The men sought

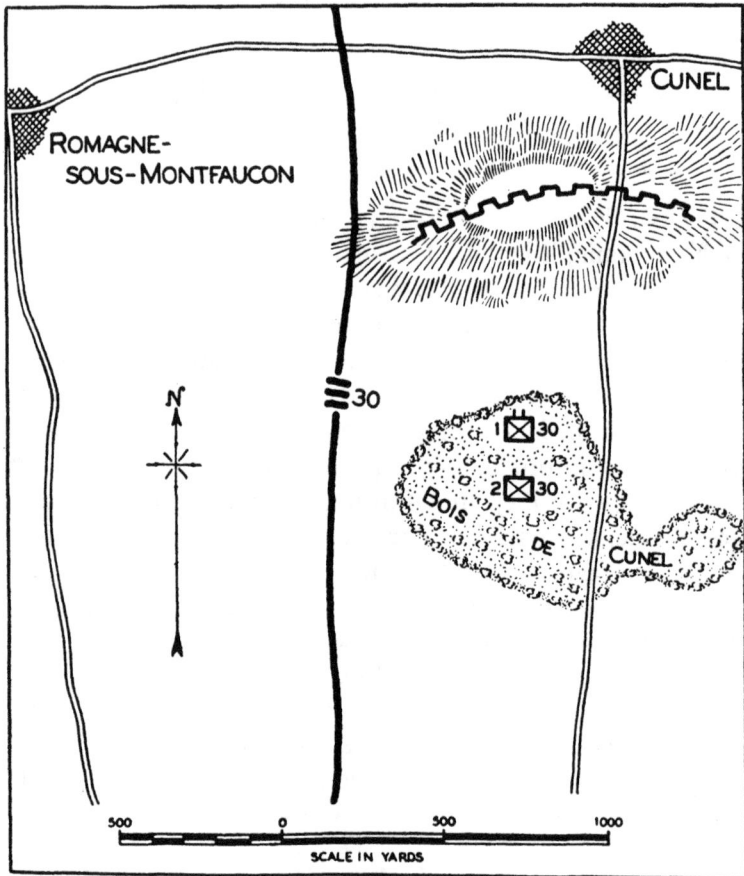

Example 1

holes in the ground for cover. The hostile fire was so heavy and
covered the area so thoroughly that movement in any direction
appeared suicidal. Therefore, this battalion remained where it
was until dark. The 2d Battalion had not left the wood.

Meanwhile, an order came in from the division commander
directing that the trenches in the 30th Infantry zone, north of

the Bois de Cunel, be taken at once. To carry out this mission the following plan was adopted:

The 1st Battalion would withdraw under cover of darkness to the Bois de Cunel, where it would reorganize. At 7:30 p.m., after an artillery preparation had been fired on the trench, the battalion would again attack, closely following a barrage. The 2d Battalion would follow in support.

At dark the 1st Battalion fell back to the wood and began to reorganize for the new attack. This proved extremely difficult. In the darkness the withdrawing units lost direction and became intermingled. No vestige of control remained. To crown the battalion's difficulties, German artillery lashed the little wood with violent and tireless energy.

H-hour approached, and the American preliminary bombardment began, while the battalion commander still struggled to gather the remnants of his command and to bring some semblance of order out of the confusion that existed.

H-hour arrived and passed, but the battalion was still so disorganized that no troops moved forward at the designated time.

At 10:00 p.m. the 2d Battalion, which had not been committed during the day and which was completely in hand, made a surprise attack and captured the German position.

From the personal experience monograph of Major Turner M. Chambliss, who commanded the 2d Battalion of the 30th Infantry.

DISCUSSION. The plan of attack for the 7:30 p.m. operation can be explained simply and briefly. But although the words are few, simple, and readily understood, the operation that they dictated was far removed from simplicity.

A battalion that had been pinned down under hostile fire all day was required to withdraw under fire, reorganize in a wood in the darkness, and then resume the attack.

The withdrawal was difficult and had to be made by individual movement. Movement in the dark for 500 yards, across a shell-pitted, fire-swept zone, is not a simple operation for a battalion, which at the start is deployed in lines of skirmishers; neither is a night reorganization in a wood that is being shelled by the enemy.

The simple and effective solution would have been to attack with the 2d Battalion at 7:30 p.m.

✓   ✓   ✓

EXAMPLE 2. On October 3, 1918, the U. S. 5th Brigade, with the 4th Infantry on the right and the 7th Infantry on the left, occupied the zone of the 3d Division. Each regiment was disposed in column of battalions. In the 4th Infantry the 1st Battalion held the front line with Company B on Hill 274 and Company A along the Cierges—Nantillois Road, with patrols in Wood 268. The remaining companies of the battalion were located in rear of Companies A and B.

In the 7th Infantry, the 2d Battalion occupied the northern part of the Bois de Beuge with two companies in the front line and two in support. These companies were all partially deployed. The 1st Battalion of the 7th Infantry, with an attached company of the 8th Machine-Gun Battalion, was located south of the Bois de Beuge near a stream and a narrow-gauge railroad. This unit was well in hand and more compactly grouped than the 2d Battalion. The brigade had occupied approximately these same positions since the afternoon of September 30. It had been expecting to attack to the north.

Orders were finally received directing that the attack be launched at 5:25 a.m., October 4. By this order the boundaries of the 3d Division were moved a few hundred yards to the west and the direction in which they ran was slightly altered. The new right boundary of the division and of the 4th Infantry was the Nantillois—Cunel Road while the new left boundary for the division and the 7th Infantry was to the west of the Cierges—Romagne Road. The boundary between regiments approximately halved the zone. Therefore, in order that the troops

Example 2

might face their objectives at the start of the attack, both the 4th and 7th Infantry had to move to the west.

At 6:00 p.m., October 3, the regimental commander of the 7th Infantry issued an oral attack order at his C.P. located south of the Bois de Beuge near the narrow-gauge railroad. It was nearly dark at the time. This order directed the 2d Battalion, which was then in the front line in the Bois de Beuge, to side-slip to the left and be prepared to lead the attack the following morning. The 1st Battalion of the 7th Infantry was also directed to move to the left and, in the morning attack, to follow the 2d Battalion in support at 500 yards.

Although the 1st Battalion commander suggested that it would be simpler for his unit to be employed in assault, since its movement into the new zone would be easier, the order was not changed. This battalion completed its movement success-fully. A road, a stream, and a narrow-gauge railroad all pro-vided guiding features leading from the vicinity of its former position to the new location.

Arriving at its new position, the 1st Battalion was unable to locate the 2d. When the hour for the attack came the 1st Battalion moved forward with two companies leading and two following. Near Cierges a portion of the 8th Machine-Gun Bat-talion was encountered. Its commander requested information as to the location of the 2d Battalion. About this time Company G of the missing battalion was seen moving forward. The com-pany commander, however, had not been in touch with the re-mainder of the battalion for a long time and had no idea where it was. He attached himself to the 1st Battalion.

The 1st Battalion commander now reported to the regiment that he was unable to locate the 2d Battalion; that in pushing forward in the regimental zone his unit had come under fire and that, therefore, he was advancing it to the attack as assault bat-talion. This attack moved forward from the line of departure later than had been intended and, as a result, met with little success.

The 2d Battalion, in attempting to sideslip to the left during the night, had become so badly scattered that, as a unit, it was rendered ineffective on October 4.

*　*　*

Let us now turn to the 4th Infantry. In this regiment the assault battalion, the 1st, was similarly ordered to sideslip to the left in the dark. It successfully accomplished this movement.

Part of the battalion order, issued at 11:00 p.m., October 3, which referred to the movement of Company B, then on Hill 274, was in substance as follows:

> Company B will be relieved by units of the 80th Division. It will not wait for them but will withdraw at once and move into Company A's present position.

The company commander returned to his unit and issued his order about 1:00 a.m. The 1st and 2d Platoons were in the front line and the 3d and 4th were in support. The company commander ordered the two front-line platoons to withdraw due south until they reached the southern slope of Hill 274 and there assemble in columns of twos. He ordered the 4th Platoon (on the left) to move to the Nantillois—Cunel Road (near its location at the time), form in column of twos and then move south until it reached the Nantillois—Cierges Road; there it would wait for the company commander. He ordered the 3d Platoon to move to the left and follow the 4th in column of twos. The 2d and 1st Platoons, in order, were directed to follow the 3d. All platoon leaders were cautioned to have their men observe the utmost secrecy.

After all platoons had started, the company commander went to the head of the column. When the road junction was reached he directed the 4th and 3d Platoons to march to the west along the Nantillois—Cierges Road. When the last man had cleared the road junction these two platoons were halted, deployed in squad columns and marched to the south for 300 yards. Here they were again halted and faced to the front. The assault platoons, the 1st and 2d, similarly marched along the road, halted, and deployed in rear of it. Thus, by utilization of distinct terrain features and by care in making the movement, this company was enabled to deploy in the dark, in its proper zone, after a flank movement along the line of departure.

About 4:00 a.m. it reported that it was in position. Company A, the other assault company of the battalion, also made the sideslip successfully.

However, after Company B left Hill 274 the Germans moved forward and occupied it, thereby enfilading the attack with machine-gun fire. Little success was obtained.

From the personal experience monograph of Captain Fred During, who commanded Company B of the 4th Infantry; and from a statement by Captain George S. Beatty, who was adjutant of the 1st Battalion of the 7th Infantry.

DISCUSSION. It is not a simple movement for battalions to sideslip in the dark into positions with which they are not familiar and then attack at daylight. The failure of the 3d Division's attack on October 4 can be largely attributed to this attempt to sideslip the two assault battalions.

In the 7th Infantry, the 2d Battalion became scattered and lost, and the support battalion suddenly found itself in the front line. It would have been far simpler to move the 1st Battalion to the left-front and use it in assault. It was better grouped initially; it did not have to make such an extreme movement to the flank; and finally, there were distinct, unmistakable terrain features that could be easily followed, even in darkness, to the new location.

In the 4th Infantry the assault battalion successfully completed its difficult movement by painstaking attention to detail; but even so, the evil features inherent in that move made themselves evident. Obviously the execution of such a complicated maneuver required a considerable amount of time and therefore it could not be postponed too long. This was undoubtedly the reason Company B was directed to move at once, without waiting for the arrival of the troops who were to relieve them. As a result, the Germans occupied Hill 274; and enfilade fire from the commanding ground played a major part in breaking the attack on the morning of October 4.

Attempts to execute complicated maneuvers in combat have both direct and indirect evils. They almost never succeed.

✓ ✓ ✓

EXAMPLE 3. On June 29, 1918, Company D, U. S. 26th Infantry, carried out a raid on German positions near Cantigny. The hour set for the action was 3:15 a.m., at which time there was just enough light to see. Part of the order for this raid follows:

HEADQUARTERS 1ST BATTALION,
26TH INFANTRY

France, June 24, 1918.

FIELD ORDERS
No. 10

INFORMATION

The enemy is occupying the woods to our front with one battalion, something in the manner indicated in the attached sketch.

INTENTION

On J Day at H Hour, we will raid the Wood, entering the woods at the angle 22.8—30.4 (point Y on sketch), and kill or capture the occupants of the trenches running north and northeast as far as the northern edge of the woods, returning from there by the northern edge of the BOIS DE FONTAINE.

ALLOTMENT OF UNITS

The raiding party will be composed of personnel of Company D, 1st Lieutenant Wesley Freml, Jr., officer commanding raid.

(1) Lieut. Dillon   —1 Sgt. —2 Cpls.—12 Pvts.—A Party
(2) Lieut. Dabney   —1 Sgt. —2 Cpls.—12 Pvts.—B Party
(3) Lieut. Ridgley   —1 Sgt. —2 Cpls.—12 Pvts.—C Party
(4) Lieut. Tillman   —1 Sgt. —2 Cpls.—12 Pvts.—D Party
(5) Lieut. Freml (O.C.) —2 Sgts.—3 Cpls.—18 Pvts.—E Party

(2 stretchers and 4 stretcher-bearers.)

FORMATION

A, B, and C Parties will form left to right on taped ground at point marked X (see sketch) at H minus 30 minutes. They will each be in column of files. E Party will follow in rear in same formation. D Party will, at the same time, be disposed in observation on the extreme eastern tip of the BOIS DE CANTIGNY.

*   *   *

SPECIAL SIGNALS

When he has assured himself that the party has withdrawn to within our own lines, the officer commanding the raid will fire three (3) star RED rockets—this will signify to all concerned that the raid is completed.

TASK

On commencing artillery bombardment, A, B, C and E Parties, preserving their general alignment, will advance as close as possible to the woods.

A, B and C Parties, in the order named from left to right, will advance directly into the woods. If opposition is encountered, B Party will hold with covering fire from the front, and A and C Parties will advance by the flanks, outflanking the resistance.

On entering the woods, A Party will split off to the left branch of the trench to the north edge of the wood, capturing or killing all occupants and from that point it will return.

B and C Parties will continue down trench running to the northeast, outflanking tactics being employed when necessary. On reaching north edge of the woods, they will function the same as A Party.

E Party will follow in rear. It shall be its particular function to guard the right flank and reinforce the assaulting parties when necessary.

D Party will remain in observation in its original position, ready to engage with fire any machine guns that may open from the slope of the ridge or northeast of the woods. It will retire on completion of the raid.

*   *   *

THEODORE ROOSEVELT, JR.
Major (USR), 26th Infantry
Commanding

Information and instructions as to fire support, dress and equipment, and many other details were included. The assault parties were directed to move forward during a ten-minute preparation by artillery and Stokes mortars. A box barrage

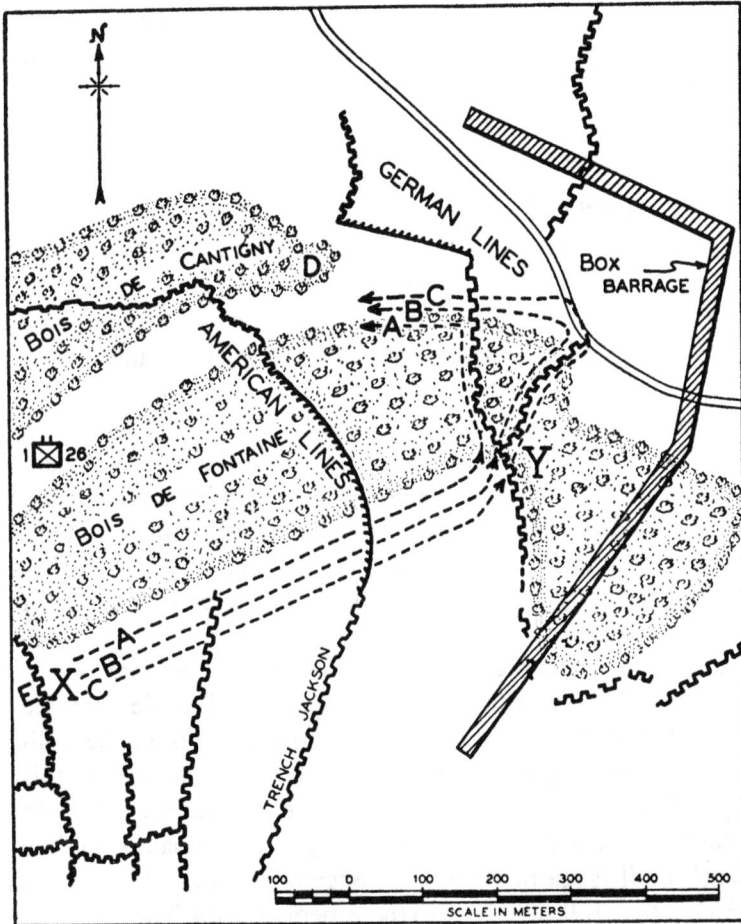

Example 3

would then be formed, while the infantry rushed the position. The plan called only for those supporting fires normally available in the sector. The position and routes followed by the assault parties are indicated on the sketch.

The raid was carried out as planned. Thirty-three prisoners were taken, including one officer, five noncommissioned officers, two artillery observers and two or three machine gunners. Several sacks of papers and other intelligence data were secured. The American casualties were one officer and one soldier killed and four soldiers wounded.

From records of the U. S. 1st Division.

DISCUSSION. We have previously examined a plan that was briefly and simply stated but that nevertheless was the antithesis of simplicity when it came to execution. Here we have a plan that appears complicated. It requires some time and thought to understand, and yet simplicity is its underlying feature. It is obvious, then, that simplicity in tactics is not necessarily equivalent to simplicity in words.

Let us examine this plan. In the first place, the order was published several days before the raid, thereby giving all concerned ample time to digest it and to make the necessary preparations.

The work planned for the artillery, machine guns, and Stokes mortars was simple. They were directed to do some shooting on a time schedule. That was all.

It is with the assault parties, however, that we are chiefly concerned. Note that the southern edge of the Bois de Fontaine parallels the route of advance of these parties. To maintain direction to their objective, each group had only to follow this edge of the wood. Arriving at the hostile position the left party turned to the left (north) following the German front-line trench until it reached the north edge of the Bois de Fontaine which it then followed back to the American lines. The two right groups moved along the trench that runs to the northeast until they, too, reached the north edge of this wood which they followed back to their own position. All three parties had clear-cut features to guide them and each route formed a circuit.

Thus we see that the tasks for the individual groups were not difficult to carry out on the ground. The chances for possible mishaps were greatly reduced by the care taken in selecting these guiding features for the parties to follow. Their mission was clear and simple. The action of Party A did not hinge on that of Party B. The plan did not depend on any delicate calculation of time and space. It was simple and it proved effective.

✓ ✓ ✓

EXAMPLE 4. On October 17, 1918, the French 123d Division attacked northeastward toward Grougis and Marchavenne. The scheme of maneuver follows:

Three battalions were employed initially in assault. On the left, a provisional battalion of the 12th Infantry (2d and 3d Battalions combined because of losses) had the mission of maintaining contact with the 66th Division to the north. This was considered particularly important. The 2d and 3d Battalions of the 411th Infantry, with a company of tanks attached, were on the right of this provisional battalion. These two battalions were ordered to move forward and establish themselves facing Grougis.

The 1st Battalion of the 411th, in second line, was directed to follow behind the interval between the 12th Infantry unit and the 2d Battalion of the 411th Infantry, and then, after the two right assault battalions had established themselves facing Grougis, push ahead and take Marchavenne. The 1st Battalion of the 6th Infantry was ordered to follow the 1st Battalion of the 411th Infantry initially and protect its right flank, finally taking position on the left of the 2d Battalion of the 411th Infantry, facing the northwest portion of Grougis.

The 2d and 3d Battalions of the 411th Infantry and the 1st Battalion of the 6th Infantry, having established themselves as a flank guard to the south, were to push forward to Marchavenne when successively liberated by the advance of the 15th Division on the south. Thereafter they would assist the attack of the 66th Division on the north.

The remainder of the 123d Division's infantry, which was holding the line of departure, was ordered to reform and become the division reserve. Artillery fires were to lift on a carefully arranged time schedule. Marchavenne was to be taken in one hour and thirty minutes after the jump-off by a battalion which, at the start of the attack, was some 4,500 yards away.

Marchavenne was captured practically on time, by an attack from the *south and southeast—carried out by the provisional battalion of the 12th Infantry which was to guard the north flank of the division.* This battalion lost contact with the 66th Division and got ahead of the troops on the right. Its two assault companies crossed each other's path and the bulk of the battalion, advancing rapidly, crossed the entire divisional zone diagonally. It found cover just north of Grougis (which was still held by the enemy) and took Marchavenne by an envelopment from the south and east about 7:45 a.m.

The battalion that had been ordered to take the town was still more than a mile to the rear, slowly advancing. It arrived at Marchavenne long after the town had fallen, but in time to help hold it against a counter-attack. These two battalions in Marchavenne held an isolated position for several hours.

The assault battalions of the 411th Infantry and the 1st Battalion of the 6th Infantry met with some success, but after reaching Grougis they were unable to go farther. At 5:00 p.m. they were still there, facing southeast. On this day, after the initial capture of Marchavenne, which could not be exploited, the division had no success. During the early part of the attack the provisional battalion of the 12th Infantry captured ten cannon and 300 prisoners.

From an article by Major P. Janet, French Army, in "La Revue d'Infanterie," December, 1926.

DISCUSSION. Here is a complex plan of attack devised by officers of long experience in the war, which was to be carried out by veterans. The original assault battalions were to fan out and form flank protection while a second-line battalion, advancing through the interval, was to take the objective. The flank battalions would then disengage successively, move on to the objective, and take part in a renewal of the advance beyond Marchavenne. Furthermore, the artillery support was arranged according to a carefully worked out time schedule; it would be

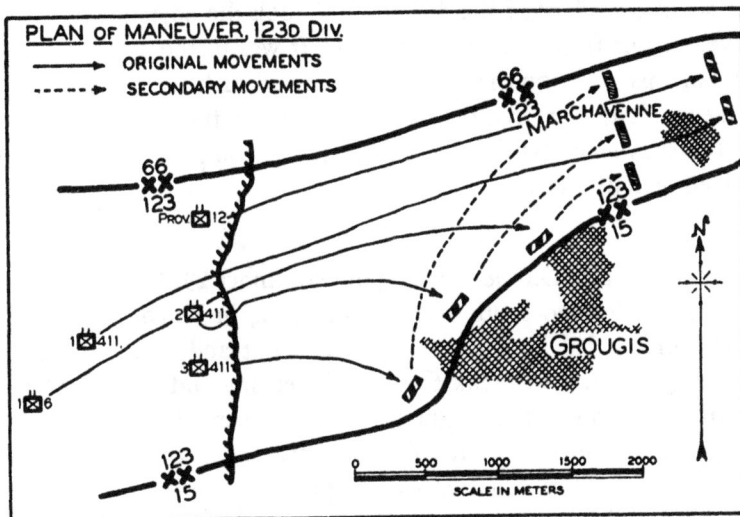

Example 4

upset unless this delicate time-table worked with mathematical precision.

True, the 123d Division achieved a modicum of success in this attack, but it certainly cannot be attributed to the plan. Nothing happened as expected. The assault battalions of the 411th Infantry managed to make some advance, as did the 1st Battalion of the 6th Infantry, but all three became involved near Grougis and were there the entire day. These were the troops that, according to the plan, were to carry the attack beyond Marchavenne.

The complicated maneuver of attacking to the front, then facing to the right, then disengaging, then pushing forward again, was too much even for these veteran troops. It could not be carried out at all, let alone according to the carefully prepared time-table.

It is interesting to note that the battalion which had been directed merely to maintain contact on the north flank, crossed to the south boundary of the division and took the objective by an envelopment from the south and east. It was to the aggressiveness of this battalion that the division owed such success as was achieved. It appears that the inability to exploit the rapid capture of Marchavenne was due principally to the complicated and involved plan of attack.

✓   ✓   ✓

EXAMPLE 5. On the morning of November 23, 1914, a German force, located south and east of Lodz, in Poland, finding itself surrounded by Russians, turned about and struck to the north in an effort to break through the enemy and escape. The Germans, who had been fighting for days, were at the point of exhaustion. Fresh Russian columns were converging on them from all sides. The situation was desperate.

The 3d Guard Division, part of the beleaguered German force, spent the 23d attacking northward toward the little town of Brzeziny, which it had passed through shortly before in its advance to the south. All day the Guards drove forward through a dense wood, against strong opposition. Russians appeared to be everywhere—on both flanks and in rear.

At 4:00 p.m. the Guards reached the railroad that runs through the wood south of Galkow, and here they were halted and reorganized while their sixty-five-year-old commander, General von Litzmann, took stock of the situation.

Along the railroad stood some 1,500 men, all that was left of seven battalions of infantry. The division artillery, under the protection of a handful of infantrymen, was still south of the wood. Information of other German units and of the enemy was virtually non-existent. Earlier in the day firing had been heard to the east, but this had gradually died away. Late in the afternoon the Russian resistance to the German advance had perceptibly weakened. But the Guards were in a deplorable state. All units were terribly depleted and hopelessly intermingled. The men

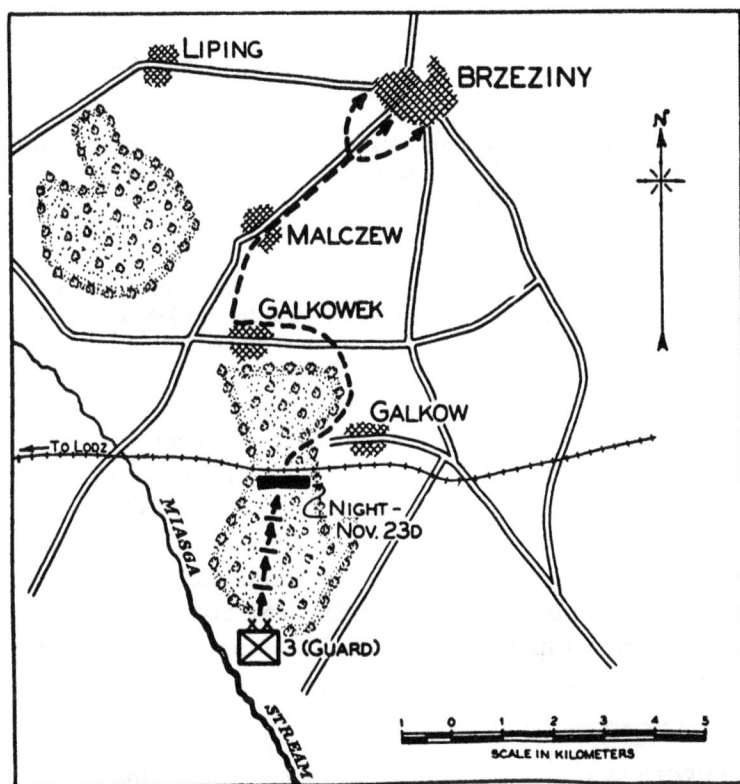

Example 5

were so exhausted that they could scarcely be kept awake. Such was the situation that confronted this remnant of a division as darkness and the bitter cold of a Polish winter night closed in on November 23.

Soon after dark a corps order arrived. In a stable filled with Russian wounded the division commander pulled a small candle out of his pocket, lighted it, and examined the order. It had been delayed in reaching the Guards. The instructions it bore pertained only to operations for November 23, but it did make clear the fact that the corps commander wanted them to reach Brzeziny on that day.

Therefore, at 7:25 p.m. the division commander rapidly outlined the following plan:

> This division captures Brzeziny tonight. It will advance in column, with advance guard via Galkowek and Malczew, in silence, and gain the road running from the southwest toward Brzeziny. It will develop when one kilometer in front of the town and press into it by a surprise attack.
>
> After the storming of Brzeziny, baggage will be brought forward. Messengers will report to receive orders at the marketplace in the building where division headquarters was located before.

The advance guard and the order of march were designated, and a supplementary order was sent to the artillery.

The division commander marched with the advance guard. The maneuver was successful. Brzeziny was stormed and the staff of the VI Siberian Corps captured. The success of this action materially aided the remainder of the German forces in smashing through the hostile lines. The Russians, becoming discouraged, withdrew while the German units, taking along thousands of prisoners and much matériel, rejoined their main army.

From the Reichsarchiv account.

DISCUSSION. The Guards were in a situation as difficult and desperate as can be imagined. They had no information of the location of other German troops and no knowledge of the hostile dispositions, except that the enemy seemed to be everywhere in superior numbers. Their men were exhausted and their units depleted and intermingled. They were in a dense forest; it was bitter cold, and night was falling.

Under such conditions a master effort could be made only by superior troops, commanded by determined leaders, working under a simple plan. The division commander took these considerations into account. His plan was based on the three essentials for a night operation—direction, control, surprise.

Troops become easily lost in a night march, particularly exhausted troops who are staggering forward in a daze. Things must be made as simple as possible for them. The route prescribed facilitated the maintenance of direction. First, movement along the eastern edge of the wood to the north edge. From here Galkowek could be reached with little danger of the column getting lost. From Galkowek the march could continue straight to the north and be certain of intercepting the road that led directly to Brzeziny.

To insure the utmost control the division commander ordered that the advance be made in route column. It was no time for half-measures. The men were completely exhausted, so much so that unless they were directly under the eyes of their leaders, they would lie down and go to sleep. An attempt to move in several columns or in any extended formation would have meant disintegration and certain failure.

To achieve the third essential, surprise, the order directed that the advance be made in secrecy and silence.

Finally, as a crowning bit of psychological bravado, came the order for establishing the command post in the marketplace of Brzeziny. A large dose of optimism was required by officers and men, and their commander, with the deft touch of the true leader, gave it to them. German accounts describe the thrill that ran through the assembled German officers on hearing the resolute words of their leader.

Here, one of the most complex, difficult, and desperate situations which troops have ever been called upon to face was met and solved by a simple order. In such a dilemma only the utmost simplicity of plan and execution stood any chances of success.

*   *   *

CONCLUSION. In war the simplest way is usually the best way. Direct, simple plans, clear, concise orders, formations that facilitate control, and routes that are unmistakably defined will smooth the way for subordinate elements, minimize the confusion of combat and ordinarily increase the chances of success.

In brief, simplicity is the sword with which the capable leader may cut the Gordian knot of many a baffling situation.

Chapter IV: *Scheme of Maneuver and Main Effort*

Every attack should have a scheme of maneuver. The main effort should strike the enemy's weakness.

ALL MEANS—reserves, fire support, ammunition—are concentrated for the decisive stroke. Economy of force at nondecisive points and greater mobility permit the concentration of superior forces at the decisive point. To make the main effort a real knockout blow, economy of force elsewhere may have to be extreme.

To determine the location for his principal effort, the leader seeks to discover the enemy's weakness. The flanks and rear of an enemy being weak points, he will strike at these when they can be reached. Often the ground itself will be the deciding factor. By a careful study the leader will be able to determine those parts of the terrain where the enemy cannot employ his weapons to advantage. At the same time he should not lose sight of the fact that the terrain should permit his own attack to be supported by artillery, machine guns, and tanks. Thus, strength will strike weakness.

Having made his choice, the leader's dispositions must correspond to his scheme of maneuver. The density of deployment is greater where the main effort is to be made. Troops must be available to assure continuity of the effort and to permit the leader freedom of action to deal with the incidents of battle. All available fire support is concentrated to assist the main effort.

The scheme of maneuver of small infantry units is simple and does not look too far in the future. It is concerned with the enemy resistance which is close; new decisions, based on the new situation, must be made later. For example, when confronted with a vague situation, or unsuitable terrain, it is possible that no definite idea will stand out. In such a case, there will be no true main effort at the start; it will be withheld. The scheme of maneuver will simply be an advance in order to determine what is in front, with the unit commander retaining control and freedom of action. His dispositions will be such that he will be able to reserve his main effort until the situation warrants the commitment of the bulk of his force.

ⅰ   ⅰ   ⅰ

EXAMPLE 1. On September 26, 1918, the U. S. 33d Division attacked north in the opening phase of the Meuse-Argonne offensive with the 66th Brigade in assault and the 65th Brigade in reserve. In front of the division lay the dense Bois de Forges which covered one side of a formidable height. Along the right of the division sector ran the Meuse River, but since there was to be no attack on the east side of the river the right flank would be wide open to fire from that direction. With these facts in mind the division planned its attack.

"The whole theory of the attack," said the division order, "is by echelon with the left in advance." The 131st Infantry, the left regiment of the 66th Brigade, would advance rapidly to open ground east and north of Gercourt and Drillancourt in order to assist the 132d Infantry in the capture of the Bois de Forges. Accordingly, the barrage in front of the 131st would move forward faster than that in front of the 132d. The 132d Infantry would strike the Bois de Forges from the southwest. As the advance progressed the attack of the 132d would gradually swing until it was headed almost due east. The Bois de Forges *would not* be attacked from the south or the southeast.

The 131st Infantry and 132d Infantry would, at first, attack side by side, each with two battalions in assault. The 132d, however, would make a sharper turn to the right than the 131st; the interval thus formed would be taken care of by reserves.

The zone of the 131st would be 2,000 meters wide, but it would actually follow a rolling barrage about 800 yards wide.

Following an intense preparation, the attack jumped off

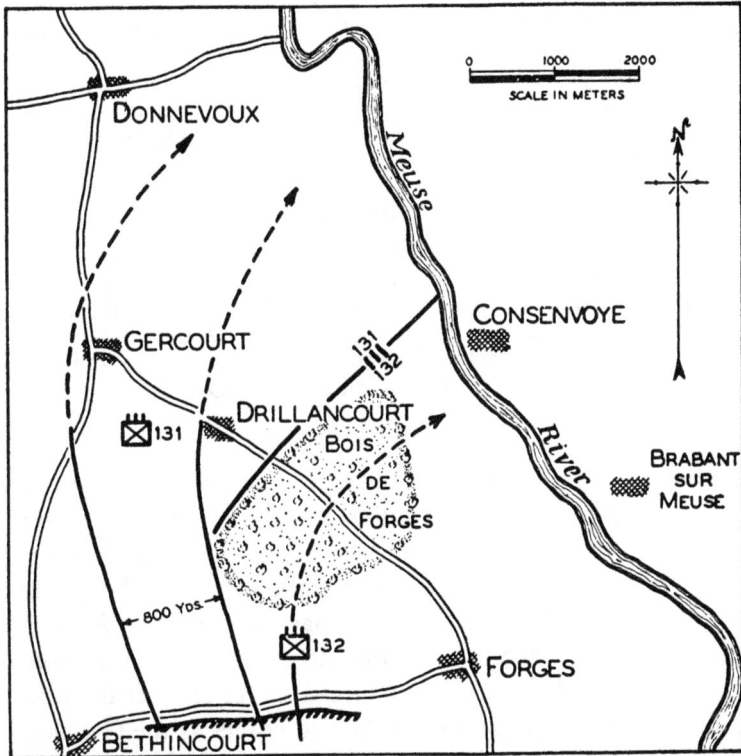

Example 1

and drove forward with the support of an artillery and machine-gun barrage. The machine-gun barrage, which was directed against the southern edge of the Bois de Forges, was particularly helpful in that it fostered the idea of a non-existent attack from the south.

By 10:00 a.m. the two attacking regiments had carried their objectives and captured 1,400 prisoners, at the cost of only 250 casualties.

In his report of the operation the brigade commander stated:

> The 132d Infantry, on a front of about two kilometers, attacked the enemy positions in front of and in the Bois de Forges from the southwest, and making a turning movement to the east while in the woods, using the roads in the center of the woods as a guide and a dividing line between battalions, came out at the objective exactly as planned in the orders of the brigade at 10:00 a.m.
>
> This maneuver struck the enemy's works in the flank and rear, took them entirely by surprise and also was responsible for the few casualties inflicted upon the troops.

The history of the division has this to say:

> This entire engagement was particularly interesting because of the fact that it was an action planned and executed by a brigade as a unit. It was entirely successful owing, first, to the courage and dash of our splendid troops, and, second, because the plans had been carefully worked out and studied by all concerned, and during the action these plans were followed with marvelous exactness.

From "History of the 33d Division."

DISCUSSION. On this day the 66th Brigade took about five prisoners for each casualty it suffered. Its two regiments swept through the enemy and were on their objective in a few hours.

The brigade was an interior unit making an attack against enemy positions to its front. But that did not keep it from striking in an unexpected direction at enemy weakness—from having a main effort. It did not spread troops all over its zone. It did not smash up against the Bois de Forges as the Germans expected. In parts of the zone no troops attacked at all. Any Germans between Forges and the Bois de Forges were in a trap if the main attack went through, and that attack did go through.

The 33d Division was not making the main effort of the American attack; its mission was rather one of flank protection. Here, then, we see a main effort within an attack which itself is not a main effort.

The main effort is usually characterized by the assignment of comparatively narrow zones of action, and by massing many reserves behind and much fire in front of the attacking troops.

In this case we see a regiment with two assault battalions make a main effort on a front of approximately 800 yards.

*   *   *

EXAMPLE 2. On October 11, 1918, the 1st Battalion of the French 412th Infantry reached the Oise River. The Germans held the east bank in strength, but owing to the general situation, it was thought that they would probably withdraw. Therefore, in spite of the fact that the French battalion occupied a front of three kilometers, it was ordered to seize the crossings of the Oise and be prepared to pursue the Germans.

All efforts to seize the crossings on the 11th and 12th having failed, a stronger attack was organized on the 13th. For this attack the three rifle companies and 12 machine guns of the battalion were disposed to cover the four groups of crossings. Five additional machine guns had been picked up during the previous advance and these, too, were emplaced to fire on the disputed passages. A Stokes mortar and a 37-mm. gun completed the picture.

The battalion had a very good idea of what it was up against. It knew that the enemy had posted advanced groups along the river to cover the crossings and that these groups were tied in by patrols. It also knew that there was a continuous line of resistance on the east bank of the canal, and that there were reserves and supporting artillery at Senercy Farm, Sucrérie, and along the west edge of Séry-les-Mézières.

The terrain in front of the battalion, though flat, was covered with a rather lush vegetation which afforded a certain amount of cover. The river, fifteen to twenty yards wide and seven or eight feet deep, constituted an appreciable obstacle, but the canal was fordable. Reconnaissance revealed that the enemy had demolished all the bridges and had emplaced machine guns to cover the ruins. Heavy undergrowth on the far bank of the Oise provided excellent cover for the Germans along the river.

The French attack was fruitless. The slightest movement near the river bank provoked a storm of fire from the well-concealed enemy. Nevertheless, the battalion struggled throughout the afternoon to gain a foothold on the east bank. By nightfall the casualties had mounted to alarming proportions and this unit, which had battered at the river line for three successive days, knew that it had again failed.

In spite of this stubborn enemy resistance, the higher command still believed that it had nothing but a German rear guard to deal with and continued to call on the infantry to hammer its way through. Thus, at nightfall this battalion received still another attack order. The entire division would renew the attack at 8:00 a.m. the next morning and the 1st Battalion of the 412th Infantry would again be in assault.

Shortly after dusk a patrol which had been reconnoitering the river line made an important discovery. At X (see sketch) it found an undamaged foot bridge so well hidden by overhanging branches that until now it had gone undetected. The patrol leader, followed by his men, quickly and quietly crawled across. At the far end they surprised but failed to capture two German sentinels and in a few minutes the bridge was blown up.

The patrol now moved to the destroyed railroad bridge to the northeast and struck the enemy post there by surprise. After a short fight the Germans withdrew. The patrol leader then posted his men so as to form a small bridge-head near X, swam back across the Oise, and reported the situation to his battalion commander.

The battalion commander at once decided to throw troops across the Oise near X, form a larger bridge-head, and attack in the direction: canal bend—Sucrérie. He then sent a message to the regiment stating that the battalion intended to handle the whole affair by its own means, and asking that all friendly artillery fire cease in front of the battalion, except as requested by the battalion commander himself.

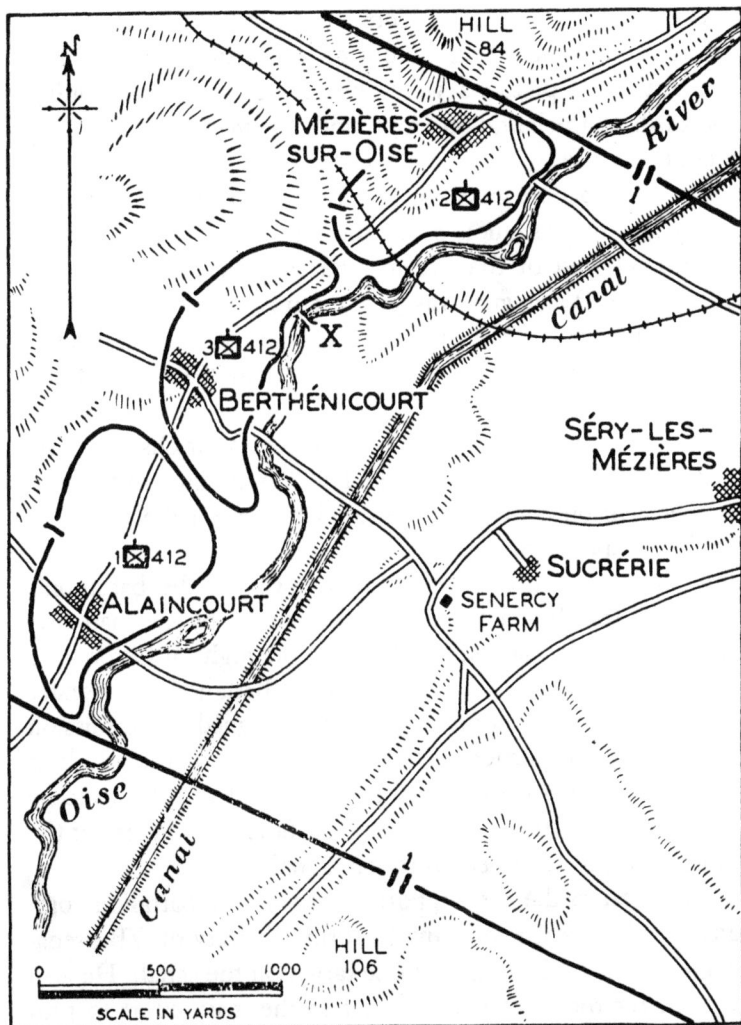

Example 2

By 2:00 a.m. the bulk of the battalion had crossed the river. At dawn it attacked to the southeast. Let us examine that attack. The entire 3d Company, three platoons of the 2d Company and two platoons of the 1st Company, constituted the attacking force and advanced on a front of less than 500 yards. The other three rifle platoons were spread out on the remaining 2,500 yards of the battalion front, with the mission of assisting the attack by fire.

Seventeen machine guns plus one captured from the Germans —every gun the battalion could muster—were located on the high ground west of the stream, and supported the attack by overhead fire. Each gun was given a mission of neutralizing a definite portion of the zone between the river and the canal and between the Berthénicourt—Senercy Farm Road and the railroad.

The Stokes mortar emplaced near Mézières-sur-Oise fired on the railroad bridge over the canal. The 37-mm. gun, in position near Berthénicourt, fired on the canal bridge on the Berthénicourt Road and on Senercy Farm.

A 75-mm. gun previously located north of the battalion's zone, had been driven from its emplacement by German fire, and its commander had reported late on the night of October 13 to the 1st Battalion. That same night the battalion commander ordered it to a position on Hill 84 and assigned it the mission of enfilading that portion of the canal in front of the attack as soon as it was light enough to see. The fire of the 75 was to be the signal for all other fires to open. A short time thereafter the assault would be launched on rocket signal.

In addition to the fire support described, the battalion commander ordered each company to form a battery of VB grenadiers, each battery having a precise target on the canal. He also arranged for the three platoons not in the main effort to protect the flanks and assist the attack by fire.

The attack was launched at about 7:15 a.m. and was a complete success. The battalion, advancing on a narrow front, captured the hills east of the Oise. Other troops were pushed across the river behind the successful battalion.

From Infantry Conferences at l'École Supérieure de Guerre, by Lieutenant Colonel Touchon, French Army.

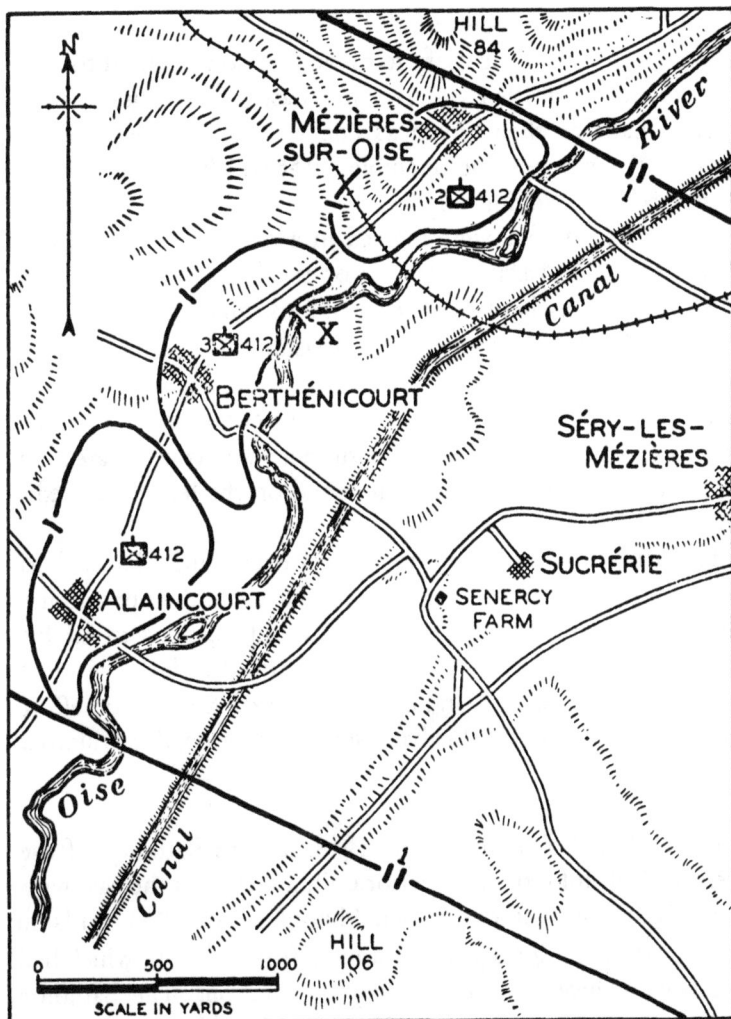

Example 2

DISCUSSION. The actors state that in all this there was not the reasoned method that we are pleased to find there today.

"Because of the urgencies of the situation," said the battalion commander, "it was necessary to move fast, to muddle through. There were no written orders, only hasty, fragmentary, oral orders—many of them given as one went from one place to another. The whole scene resembled that which probably exists on the deck of a sinking ship."

Nine rifle platoons were massed in a main effort on a front of less than 500 yards. The rest of the battalion zone—over 2,500 yards—was held by three platoons which were charged with flank protection and with fire assistance to the main effort.

The main effort was supported by every available weapon— 18 machine guns, a 37-mm. gun, a Stokes mortar and a 75. And every weapon *fired!* All the fire support was concentrated on the area in front of the main effort and on the terrain immediately to its flanks.

The action of the leader dominated everything. He had so familiarized himself with the terrain that when the opportunity came, he was able to assign positions and missions to all his machine guns and to a 75-mm. gun in the dark. And it worked! Because of this and because he knew that a main effort should be a main effort, his battalion scored a notable triumph.

✓   ✓   ✓

EXAMPLE 3. On August 20, 1918, the 4th Battalion of the French 365th Infantry, an interior unit, attacked to the east with the mission of taking Cuisy-en-Almont. About 900 yards in front of the battalion's position stood a fortified work which had not been reduced by the artillery preparation. The battalion commander believed that machine-gun fire from here might smash his attack before the battalion even got under way. He therefore adopted the following plan:

The 15th Company, with one platoon of machine guns, would be the only unit of the battalion to move out at H-hour. This company would move into the zone of the unit on the north and, taking advantage of the cover in that locality, would swing wide past the field work, then turn south and storm it from the rear.

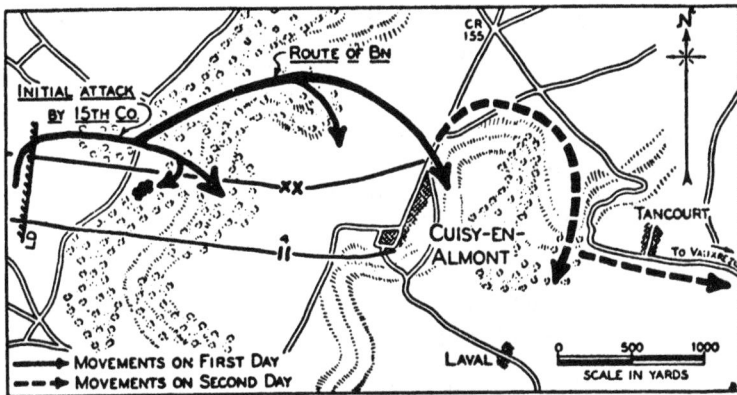

Example 3

As soon as the fortification fell, the rest of the battalion would attack. The 14th Company, following the 15th, would advance via the wooded slopes that border the northwestern portion of the Cuisy-en-Almont plateau, and attack the town from the north.

The 13th Company would maintain contact with the unit on the right and outflank Cuisy-en-Almont on the south.

The battalion commander with the machine-gun company would move straight toward the town (between the 13th and 14th Companies).

The attack, carried out according to plan, was highly successful: 530 prisoners and 24 machine guns were captured. In this connection it is interesting to learn that at the start of the attack the companies of this battalion averaged some 60 effectives.

The next morning the battalion was just east of Cuisy-en-Almont. The battalion commander and his command group were making a reconnaissance near the east edge of the town.

While engaged in this work they heard a sudden roar and saw the bare plateau to their left-front (which was held by the enemy) erupt under a heavy bombardment. The battalion commander at once concluded that the French units on his left were launching a powerful attack. Although he had not been notified of any such attack, he immediately issued the following order:

> Our left has just attacked; we must keep touch with it.
>
> The 15th Company will cling to the flank of the 127th Infantry (unit on the left). The 13th Company will follow the 15th. The 14th will hold Cuisy-en-Almont temporarily. Two platoons of machine guns will support the movement.
>
> All our movement will be made without going down into the ravine. [Reconnaissance had revealed that the ravine was thoroughly covered by enemy machine guns.]
>
> Our objective is Laval, but Laval will fall of itself if we turn the Cuisy-en-Almont ravine by the north and then swing south. We will thus gain the spur east of the town. From there we will take Tancourt and Vauxrezis.
>
> We will advance by individual movement, by infiltration, avoiding the ravines and outflanking them on the north. According to latest information, the Germans still hold the crossroads (155).
>
> The 15th Company will send a patrol, commanded by a very energetic leader, to determine if the 127th Infantry has really advanced. Our attack will start on my order.

The patrol found that the 127th was attacking and, upon receipt of this information, the 4th Battalion began its advance. Without loss it captured an entire German machine-gun company which occupied the spur east of Cuisy-en-Almont. These machine guns were sited west and southwest to cover the ravine of Cuisy and Laval.

The battalion continued its advance.

The division commander, who had gone forward, met a runner coming back with a message. He glanced at it.

12:30 p.m.

Lieutenant Gilbert (13th Company) to the Battalion Commander: I am at Tancourt. We have gone 300 meters beyond the village.

From the sound of the firing the 5th Battalion must be still at Laval. No liaison with the 14th and 15th Companies. I push on toward Vauxrezis. I have met some resistance which has been reduced. Prisoners were sent back in three groups, altogether 70 to 80 men. The German machine guns were left on the ground.

Having no resistance in front of me, I am advancing until I get contact.

The division commander took a pencil and scribbled on the message:

My congratulations to Gilbert. That's the way to make war.

From an article by Major St. Julien, French Army, in "La Revue d'Infanterie,"
November, 1927.

DISCUSSION. On two successive days this battalion scored striking successes. This was a real feat for an interior assault unit in the usual Western Front push. We do not have to look far for the reason: the commander of the 4th Battalion was not a copy-book soldier. He did not traffic in schematic solutions and neatly-turned maxims. Instead, he determined the enemy's vulnerable point and then devised a scheme of maneuver in which his main effort would strike that point.

On the first day he moved his battalion through wooded ravines; the second day he avoided ravines and moved over a bare plateau. In the first instance he moved through the wooded ravine because this route offered cover and enabled him to fall on the flank and rear of a dangerous field work. On the second day the situation was different. The ravine east of Cuisy-en-Almont was thoroughly covered by enemy fire. Therefore, he elected to move his battalion, man by man, over the open plateau. But again his scheme of maneuver was marked by a main effort that struck the enemy at a vulnerable point and from an unexpected direction. The success of this leader's shrewd reasoning is attested not only by the ease with which his command took its objectives, but by the fact that the number of prisoners taken exceeded the battalion's effective strength by some 300%.

Of course it will not always be possible to maneuver in the

zone of a neighboring unit as this battalion did. Frequently it will not be advisable and still more frequently it will not be permitted. In this case it so happened that movement in the neighboring zone was both desirable and permissible, and the battalion commander was quick to avail himself of the opportunity.

↑   ↑   ↑

CONCLUSION. In each case examined, the scheme of maneuver of the commander played a major part in the success achieved.

Generalship consists of being stronger at the decisive point— of having three men there to attack one. If we attempt to spread out so as to be uniformly strong everywhere, we shall end by being weak everywhere. To have a *real* main effort—and every attack and every attacking unit should have one—we must be prepared to risk extreme weakness elsewhere.

Chapter V: *Terrain*

In the absence of definite information small infantry units must be guided by their mission and by the terrain.

MANEUVERS that are possible and dispositions that are essential are indelibly written on the ground. Badly off, indeed, is the leader who is unable to read this writing. His lot must inevitably be one of blunder, defeat, and disaster.

The intelligent leader knows that the terrain is his staunchest ally, and that it virtually determines his formation and scheme of maneuver. Therefore he constantly studies it for indicated lines of action. For instance, there may be no evidence of the enemy, yet the terrain may say clearly and unmistakably, "If you come this way, beware! You may be enfiladed from the right." Or it may say, "Right-o! This way to the hostile position." Or again, "Close your formation here or a platoon or two will be lost."

Although small infantry units cannot choose the terrain over which they will attack or on which they will defend, they can make the best use of it. For example, a small infantry unit may find portions of its assigned zone devoid of cover. It will seldom be desirable to attack over such exposed ground. It is usually better to fix the enemy by fire in such a locality and utilize more favorable portions of the allotted area for the advance. On the defense a unit may find that part of the terrain to its front is open and presents a splendid field of fire while another part affords good cover by means of which the enemy may be able to work up close to the position unobserved. This covered approach fairly shouts, "Hold me strongly! This is the danger point."

The ground is an open book. The commander who reads and heeds what it has to say is laying a sound foundation for tactical success.

[69]

EXAMPLE 1. On July 15, 1918, the 1st Battalion of the German 47th Infantry took part in an attack against the U. S. 3d Division south of the Marne. This battalion crossed the Marne at a bridge near Mont-St.-Père. Other units, utilizing crossings at

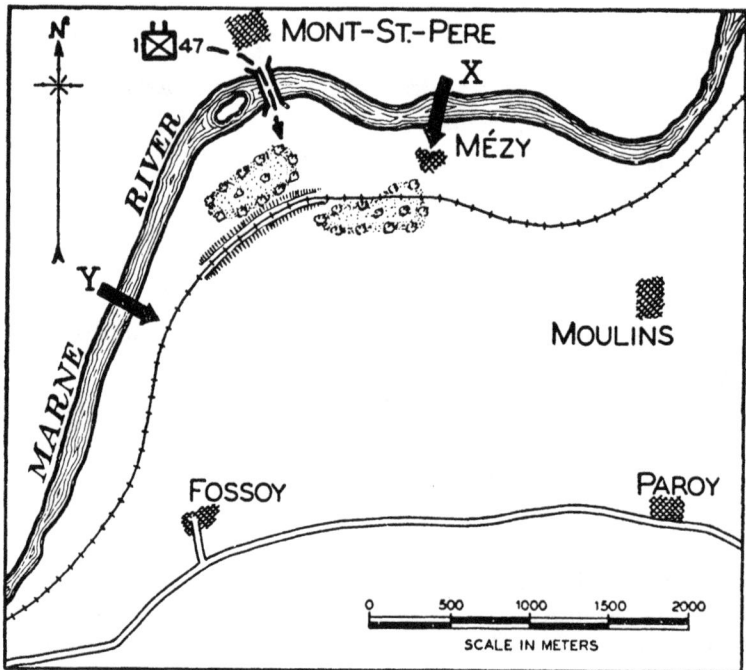

Example 1

X and Y, had gone before with orders to clear the ground in front of the 47th.

The battalion commander had no information whether or not this had been done. The situation was vague and his battalion was the first unit to cross the bridge. A few hundred yards beyond the bridge stood a small wood and beyond that a railway embankment. Between the river bank and the woods the ground was open.

The battalion, in route column, continued its advance toward the railway embankment. It was suddenly surprised by heavy, close-range, rifle and machine-gun fire and virtually destroyed as a combat unit for the day.

From the battle report of the German 47th Infantry.

✓ ✓

EXAMPLE 2. On August 4, 1918, the advance guard of the U. S. 7th Brigade, consisting of elements of the 39th Infantry, approached the Vesle River. German artillery had been firing from the north bank earlier in the day. The last 1,000 or 1,500 yards to the Vesle offered little or no cover and was dominated by the high ground north of the river. The situation was vague.

The advance guard moved forward on the road. The advance party, in column of twos, followed by the support in column of squads, had almost reached the river bank when the German artillery suddenly opened with deadly accuracy and inflicted heavy losses.

From the personal experience monograph of Major Manton S. Eddy, who commanded the Machine-Gun Company of the 39th Infantry. (This action is described more fully in Example 1 of Chapter I: Rules.)

DISCUSSION. In both the preceding examples the situation was obscure, but the terrain clearly decried the maneuver that was actually carried out. In each case, failure to take the possibilities of the terrain into account was roundly and soundly punished.

✓ ✓

EXAMPLE 3. On November 4, 1918, the French 6th Infantry, with the 152d Division on its right and the 411th Infantry on its left, attacked across the Sambre-Oise Canal with the 2d and 3d Battalions in assault, the 2d on the right.

By 7:30 a.m. the 3d Battalion had captured the north portion of Venerolles, had reorganized, and stood ready to renew the advance. The 2d Battalion was still mopping up the southern part of the town. On the north, the 411th Infantry had advanced rapidly, captured Étreux and pushed on. Right elements of the

411th were approaching the long rectangular wood between Étreux and Caucreaumont. Other units of the 411th were still farther advanced. The attack gave every indication of a brilliant success.

East of Venerolles, in the central portion of the 3d Battalion's zone, lay a flying field—flat and bare. Some slight cover existed south of the field. East of the Valenciennes Road an interlacing network of thick hedges divided the ground into many inclosures.

Without effective artillery support, the bulk of the 3d Battalion attempted to advance straight across the bare aviation field. It encountered a deadly machine-gun fire. With tremendous losses and in the utmost confusion, it fled back to Venerolles. So great was this battalion's demoralization that it was unable to resume the attack for many hours.

The repulse of the 3d Battalion had its effect on the 2d, constraining that unit to advance at a snail's pace. It was 1:00 p.m. before the 6th Infantry succeeded in crossing the Valenciennes Road.

Shortly after 9:00 a.m. leading elements of the 411th Infantry reached the eastern edge of Caucreaumont, but the slow progress of the 6th Infantry permitted the Germans to concentrate their reserves against the 411th, with the result that at midnight this regiment was 400 yards in rear of the point it had reached at 9:00 a.m.

Although the attack succeeded, the French were unable to exploit it.

From the account by Major P. Janet, in "La Revue d'Infanterie," January, 1928.

DISCUSSION. The dislocation of the 6th Infantry's attack, which in turn compromised that of the entire division, appears to have been caused by the brash attempt of the 3d Battalion to cross terrain that was utterly devoid of cover without proper artillery support.

Although the French were not aware of the German dispositions to their front, one glance at the terrain should have shown them the danger ahead. If the battalion moved out across the flying field and the Germans did happen to be on the other side, that battalion would be in a bad way.

The rapid advance of the 411th Infantry indicates that a maneuver either to the north or south, combined with fire action across the flying field, would have been effective. The 3d Battalion, however, in utter disregard of the terrain, took a chance

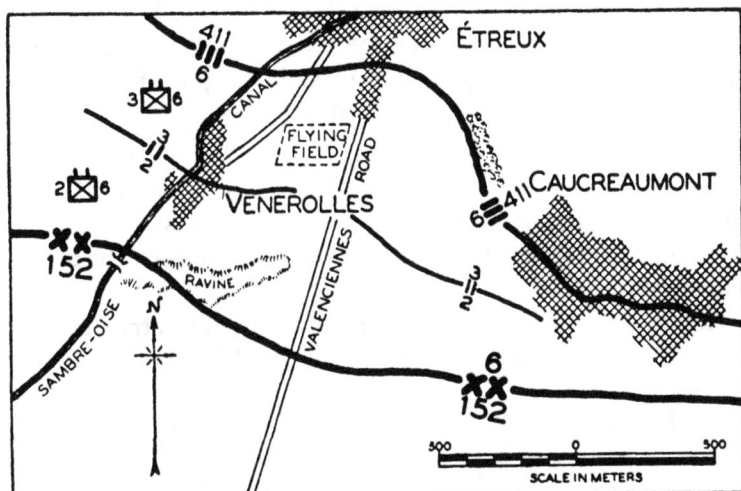

Example 3

and advanced in the open with the result described. The bulk of the casualties in the 6th Infantry on November 4 were sustained by this one battalion in its few disastrous minutes on the flying field.

Infantry unsupported by artillery or tanks has practically no chance of success in a daylight advance over bare, open terrain against machine guns.

✶   ✶   ✶

EXAMPLE 4. On October 10, 1918, the U. S. 29th Division crossed the Meuse, fought its way northward, and captured

Molleville Ridge, where the attack came to a halt. The division's front line on Molleville Ridge ran northwest and southeast, roughly parallel to Etrayes Ridge which lay beyond the deep Molleville Ravine. The 26th Division prolonged the 29th's line to the southeast.

When orders were received to take Etrayes Ridge, it was decided to strike to the east.

The 101st Infantry (26th Division) would attack to the northeast from the position shown on the sketch. The 1st Battalion of the 113th Infantry (29th Division) would jump off from a position 600 meters northwest of the 101st Infantry and attack due east. By referring to the sketch it will be seen that the lines of attack of these two units left a large triangular section of the front uncovered. The Germans in this sector would, of course, be cut off by the junction of the two American units on the common objective.

The lines of advance of the 115th and 116th Infantry and the positions of the 110th, 111th and 112th Machine-Gun Battalions are shown.

The late Brigadier General L. S. Upton, from whose article this account is taken, says:

> I saw the opportunity to employ a machine-gun barrage from Molleville Ridge and directed Major Tydings to work out the details of an interlocking barrage paralleling the line of advance.
> Major Tydings' task was to keep his parallel barrage 125 meters in advance of the attacking infantry. On the sketch are four black dots—A, B, C, and D. These represent four machine-gun batteries of four to six guns each. About 10 meters in front of each gun he placed a number of stakes in a semicircular row. By traversing the guns through the angles formed by these stakes, each gun gave a beaten zone 100 meters wide and 100 meters deep. Therefore, the beaten zone before the 113th and 116th Regiments consisted of four to six interlocking zones.
> The attacking troops dropped back from their line of departure before H-hour to allow the artillery barrage to fall on the German line which was close up. The machine guns took advantage of this movement and at 5 minutes before H-hour, Battery A put down its interlocking zone just in front of the line of departure.

At H-hour each gunner of Battery A swung his gun so that his line of sight was directly over Stake A. This placed his cone of fire 125 meters in advance of the line of the 113th Infantry. Batteries B, C, and D remained silent. The artillery and machine-gun barrages were synchronized to the rate of advance of the infantry, 100 meters in 10 minutes. The machine gunners traversed slowly and steadily. At the end of ten minutes they were firing over Stake C, and their beaten zone had moved 100 meters on the ground and was still 125 meters in advance of the infantry. Each gunner continued to traverse: from Stake C to D in ten minutes, then to Stake E in ten minutes more, reaching Stake F forty minutes from H-hour.

When Battery A had completed forty minutes it ceased firing and Battery B commenced. When Battery B completed its mission, Battery C opened up. As soon as a battery completed its firing, it withdrew.

At their intermediate objective the troops were halted and reorganized. There was no machine-gun firing during this halt. It was Battery D's mission to fire if it should be necessary. Six minutes before the jump-off from the intermediate objective, Battery D concentrated all its fire on Hill 361 where the German observation posts were located. At one minute before the jump-off it switched its fire back to the zone last fired on by Battery C and then resumed its mission of covering the advance of the infantry to the final objective.

The 111th Machine-Gun Battalion fired approximately 300,000 rounds of ammunition during this attack. None of its personnel was killed and but few wounded. Casualties were kept low by the successive withdrawal of each battery when through firing.

The 113th Infantry captured about 50 machine guns in its zone of advance. These guns were in brush piles and were sited down the Molleville Ravine. All were laid for short-range work.

The losses of the attacking infantry of the 29th Division were light. The effectiveness of the machine-gun barrage drove the German gunners from their pieces and enabled the infantry to advance with slight opposition. It was a good illustration of the importance of fire superiority and of the ease of winning a fight when this has been established. The flank barrage of machine guns, carefully laid and timed, was a major factor in the success of this attack.

From "The Capture of Etrayes Ridge," by Brigadier General L. S. Upton and Senator Millard E. Tydings, in "The Infantry Journal," August, 1927.

DISCUSSION. The results achieved in this attack were almost entirely due to an appreciation of the possibilities offered by the terrain. General Upton says, "The conditions of the attack gave a rare opportunity for a flank barrage of machine-gun fire generally paralleling the line of advance."

It was the ground and its relation to the front line that made this unusual and highly effective type of machine-gun support possible. As told, it all appears simple and obvious. The terrain was there and the relative positions of the opposing forces offered the opportunity. In this case it was recognized. Too often such opportunities pass unnoticed. After the disaster has occurred or the favorable chance has gone by, someone usually suggests what might have been done. It is too late then. Opportunities presented by the terrain must be seen and utilized before they are revoked by the chance and change of war.

Consider the experience of the French 3d Colonial Division. On August 22, 1914, this unit blithely advanced across the Semoy (a stream that was fordable in only one or two places) and plunged into the forest north of Rossignol. To its right-front the ground was open and completely dominated the bridge on which the division was crossing. The location of the enemy was unknown but some of his cavalry had been encountered.

The terrain fairly screamed that machine guns and artillery should be emplaced to cover the division and that every means of rapid reconnaissance should be utilized to search the ground commanding the defile. This mute warning was either ignored or not seen.

The divisional artillery, once across the Semoy and approaching the forest, found itself on a road flanked on both sides by swampy ground, hedges and ditches. If the enemy was encountered, the artillery could do practically nothing. The enemy *was* encountered, both to the front and the right-front. The artillery, unable to leave the road, was helpless. That part of the division which had crossed the Semoy was cut off and captured or destroyed.

The French had had ample time to occupy the keypoints beyond the river, but they failed to do so. They had been afforded

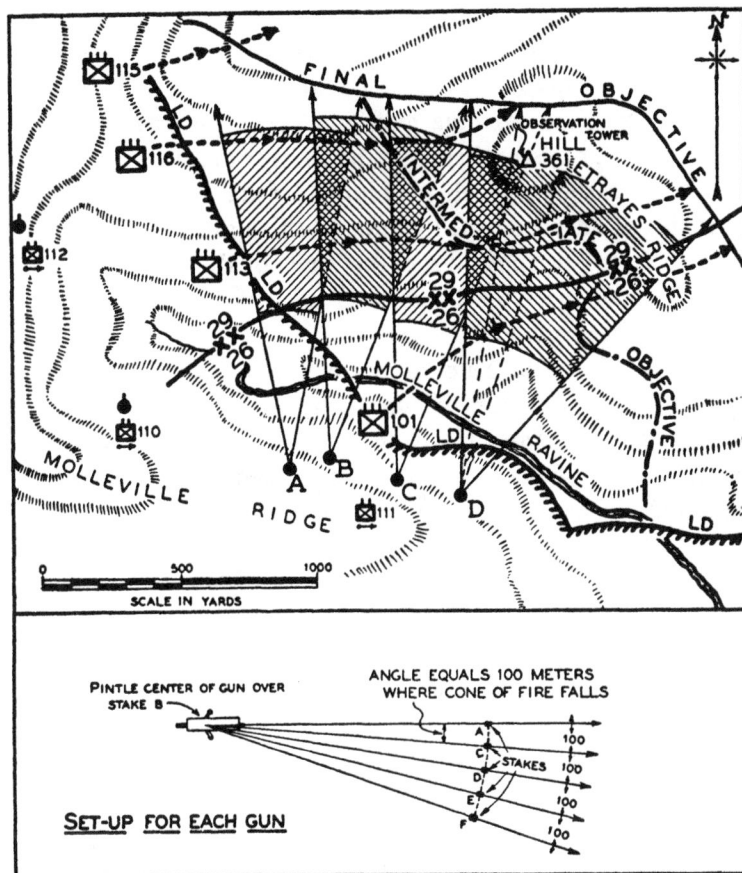

Example 4

an opportunity to select their battlefield but had let the opportunity slip by. They neglected the possibilities of the terrain, and for that neglect they paid dearly.

✓ ✓ ✓

CONCLUSION. The ability to read the writing of the ground is essential to the infantry leader. In open warfare he will never be able to arrive at a detailed idea of the hostile dispositions. He can, however, see the ground. He can see where enemy weapons are likely to be located. He can see critical points from which a few well-emplaced machine guns can knock his attack into a cocked hat. He can see what areas the enemy can cover effectively and what areas are difficult for him to defend. He can pick out the routes of advance which permit effective fire support by his own supporting weapons. From this study of the ground he can plan his attack, make his dispositions and send back requests for definite artillery missions.

So it goes. If we have a clear idea of the enemy's dispositions, which will be seldom indeed, we will attack him, taking the terrain into consideration. If his dispositions are obscure and the situation vague, we can still solve the problem; for by attacking the terrain, we can effectively attack the enemy.

Chapter VI: *Time and Space*

....

In war a large safety factor should be included in all time-and-space calculations.

....

INCORRECT ESTIMATES of the amount of time required for the distribution of orders, for the movement of units to new locations and for the necessary reconnaissances by subordinates, frequently lead to tactical failure. A strict application of the various rates of march set forth in neatly compiled tables of logistics, without consideration of the special conditions prevailing, may easily disrupt an operation. Obstacles will arise, mishaps will occur, hostile activities will intervene—and without ample allowance for these unforeseen inevitabilities, the most promising plans will, at the very outset, be sadly disjointed.

In war, time always presses; therefore leaders should be quick to seize upon any time-saving expedient. Where time is the essential factor, let orders go forward by staff officer or by wire rather than require front-line commanders to go to the rear. Let officers be assembled beforehand when it is known that orders are about to be received. Prescribe the necessary reconnaissance in advance when the course of action is reasonably obvious. When practicable, make use of operations maps, oral orders and fragmentary orders. In brief, utilize every time-saving device that ingenuity and forethought can devise.

✓   ✓   ✓

EXAMPLE 1. On August 6, 1918, the U. S. 47th Infantry (in brigade reserve) occupied a defensive position in the northern part of the Bois de Dôle.

The 39th Infantry, then in the front line, had been trying to cross the Vesle and establish a line along the Rouen—Reims road, but this regiment had suffered so heavily from artillery fire that its relief appeared imminent. The commander of the

2d Battalion of the 47th Infantry realized this. Furthermore, he believed that his battalion would take part in this relief and then drive forward as an assault element. Finally, he was convinced that orders for this operation would arrive that night.

Acting on this assumption, the battalion commander moved forward during the afternoon and made a detailed personal reconnaissance of the front line near St. Thibaut. There he learned a good deal from the officers of the 39th; among other things that the Vesle was "not very deep" and that, except for a few snipers along the river and in Bazoches, there would be little or no resistance between the river and the road. From this information it appeared that a night relief of the front line and a subsequent move to the river could be made with little difficulty.

After he had completed his reconnaissance, he returned to the Bois de Dôle, assembled his company commanders on a wooded hill that commanded a view of the front line, and acquainted them with the situation. Then, with the aid of a map, he issued an oral warning order, in substance as follows:

> The enemy, supported by considerable artillery, holds the heights north of the Vesle. A few machine guns and snipers occupy scattered positions north of the Rouen—Reims Road. The 39th Infantry reports one of their battalions across the river. Our engineers have been constructing foot bridges over the river. The river itself is twenty or thirty feet wide and not very deep. In the event we are directed to relieve the 39th Infantry, we will probably be ordered to cross the Vesle and take up a position on the Rouen—Reims Road. If our battalion is in the assault, the boundary lines of the present 39th Infantry sector will be maintained. They are shown on the map and include the town of Bazoches. The direction of advance will be due north. Companies G and H will be in the assault echelon and Companies E and F in support; Company H on the right supported by Company E. If the advance from St. Thibaut is to the Rouen—Reims Road, companies will form for the movement in the sunken road immediately east of St. Thibaut. As your companies arrive at this point you will take up whatever formation you believe best.

Throughout the night the rain came down in torrents. About midnight the regimental commander received a message to report to brigade headquarters, located at Chartreuve Farm. There he received an oral order directing the 47th Infantry to relieve the 39th by 5:00 a.m., cross the Vesle and establish a line on the Rouen—Reims road. Two companies of the 11th Machine-Gun Battalion were attached to the regiment. Boundaries were the same as those of the 39th Infantry. Bazoches would be pinched out by a combined French and American advance.

Returning at 1:00 a.m. to his command post in the Bois de Dôle, the regimental commander assembled his unit leaders and issued a brief oral order, which was similar to the warning order issued by the commander of the 2d Battalion during the afternoon. The 2d Battalion was designated as the assault unit; the 3d Battalion, with the regimental machine-gun company attached, was ordered in support; and the 1st Battalion was held in regimental reserve. Battalions were directed to move out at once in the order: 2d, 3d, 1st.

The regimental commander then proceeded to St. Thibaut.

Darkness and heavy rain made reconnaissance almost impossible.

The forethought of the commander of the 2d Battalion now served its purpose. He assembled his company commanders and explained the battalion's mission. He stated that no information, other than that already given, was available and that the orders he had issued during the afternoon would be carried out. He then directed his adjutant to bring up the battalion as soon as it could be assembled, and left for St. Thibaut.

At 2:00 a.m. on August 7 the regiment, covered by a small advance guard, marched on St. Thibaut. No guides were furnished. The road was a knee-deep quagmire. Dead men and animals added to natural obstructions of the narrow way. Slowly, and with great difficulty, the column struggled forward. The enemy continued to shell the road, but owing to the darkness this fire was largely ineffective. In reply, American artillery steadily shelled the heights north of the river.

About 3:30 a.m. the 2d Battalion reached St. Thibaut, where it was met by the battalion commander. He told his company commanders that he had been unable to obtain any additional information but that the situation looked worse than had been represented to him the previous day. In fact, the only protection against hostile machine guns and snipers lay in reaching the Rouen—Reims road before daylight.

The 2d Battalion moved quickly to the sunken road 200 yards east of the village, took up an approach-march formation and at 3:45 a.m. moved out. Enemy artillery fire increased. The 3d Battalion, followed by the 1st, moved slowly along the St. Thibaut road, in order to allow the 2d Battalion time to clear the sunken road.

The regimental commander was extremely anxious to have his assault battalion reach the Rouen—Reims road before daylight; therefore he personally directed the initial stage of the approach to the river.

The enemy evidently expected the relief, for an artillery barrage was laid on the sunken road, the roads leading into St. Thibaut, and on the village itself.

Dawn was breaking and a light mist hung over the ground as the 2d Battalion crossed the narrow-gauge railroad track north of the sunken road. Three hundred yards more brought the battalion to the river. Foot bridges reported to have been constructed by the engineers could not be located. The company commander of the right company moved forward and attempted to wade the river. In so doing he made two discoveries: first, that wire entanglements extended from the middle of the stream to the opposite bank; second, that the stream was too deep for wading. Nevertheless, a few officers and noncommissioned officers managed to struggle across. Once across they made another disheartening discovery: the north bank was wired with a line of double apron entanglements and beyond this with a line of spirals. The noncommissioned officers who had reached the far

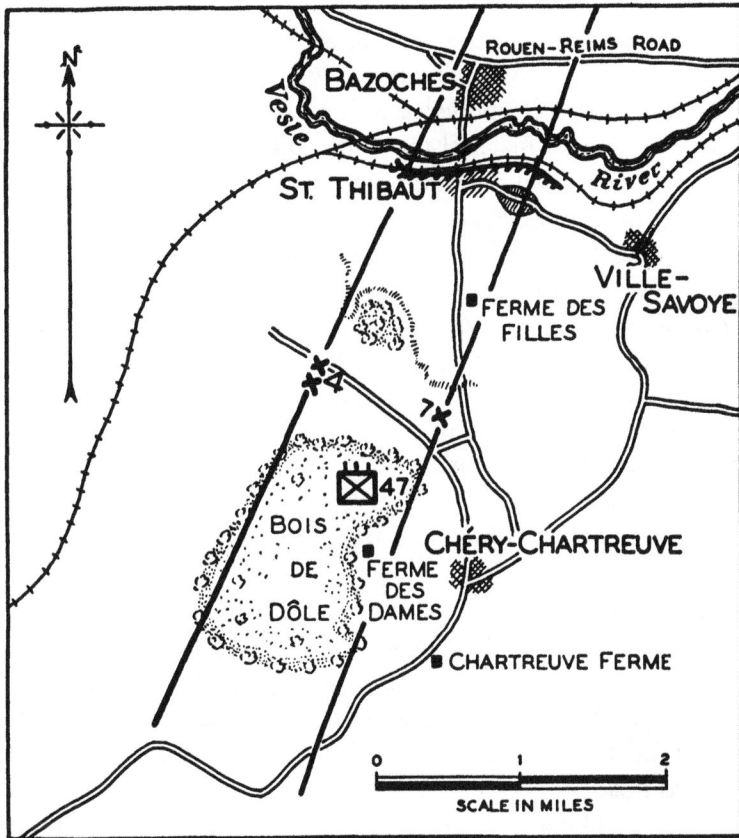

Example 1

bank at once began to cut gaps through the wire while the officers strove to get the troops across as quickly as possible.

Meanwhile, enemy artillery had opened up on the river line
with mustard gas. In order to expedite the crossing, heavy
articles of equipment such as grenades, bandoliers, and automatic-rifle clips, were thrown across. Many of these items fell in
the river and were lost. All men who could swim were then
ordered to sling their rifles and swim across. The water was soon

full of struggling soldiers. Leggins were lost, clothing slashed to ribbons, and many men badly cut about the arms and legs by the entanglements. Several soldiers were drowned. Men who could not swim were pulled across on crude rafts improvised out of any buoyant material that came to hand.

As the line moved forward through the wire the mist lifted and immediately the assault waves came under heavy enfilade machine-gun fire from the left flank. It was now broad daylight.

Although sustaining severe casualties, the two assault companies succeeded in pushing on to a line about 50 yards short of the Rouen—Reims Road. The remainder of the regiment, however, was cut off along the Vesle by hostile artillery fire. After several days of fruitless effort, all units were withdrawn to the south bank.

From the personal experience monograph of Captain William A. Collier, Infantry.

DISCUSSION. This example shows some of the reasons why time-and-space calculations taken from the book often go awry. It also shows how time can be wasted and how it can be saved.

First, consider the situation at midnight. Brigade headquarters wanted the 47th Infantry to move forward and reach the Rouen—Reims Road by daylight. This meant that the 47th would have to make a night march of at least three miles, partly across country, in a torrential rain, and with a stream crossing included.

The regimental commander was called back to the brigade command post to receive his orders. He did not get back to his own command post until 1:00 a.m. It appears that time might have been saved had the order been sent forward instead of calling the colonel back. On his return he assembled his officers and issued his order. Another hour went by before the regiment moved out. If the officers had been assembled prior to the return of the colonel, time again could have been saved and time, as usual, was vitally important.

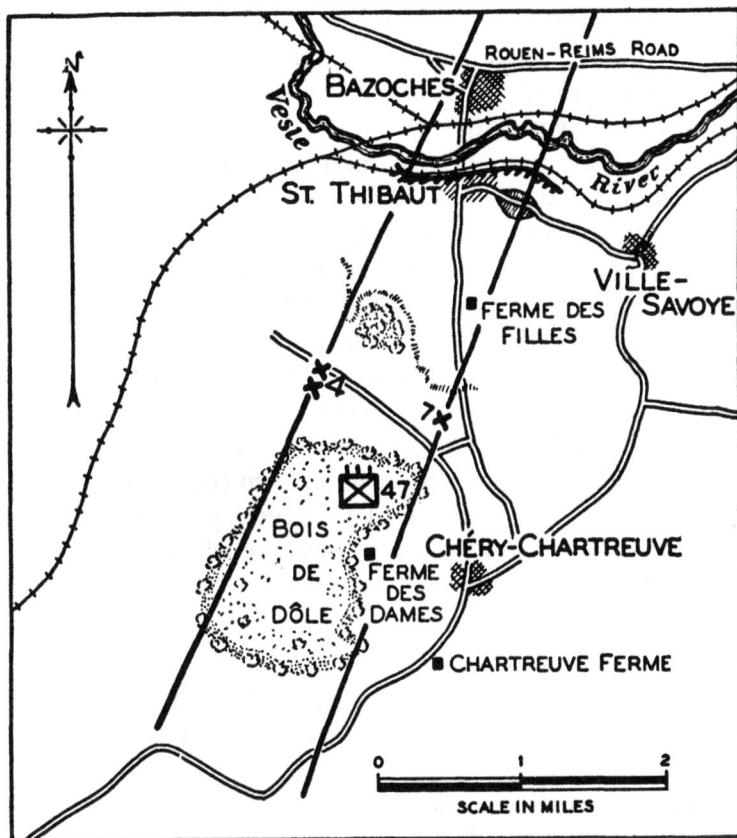

Example 1

Secondly, we see the valuable results of the preparation made
by the commander of the 2d Battalion. During the afternoon he
had made his reconnaissance. He had gone over the situation
with his subordinates. He had issued a tentative order based
on the probable course of action. When he found that the regimental order coincided with his surmise, all he had to say was,
"The orders I gave this afternoon will be carried out."

The 47th Infantry started on its three-mile march at 2:00 a.m. It appeared just possible for it to reach the Rouen—Reims Road by 5:00 a.m. provided the march was continuous and no obstacles were encountered.

Unfortunately, the 47th did meet obstacles—serious ones. Rain fell in torrents, the road was knee-deep in mud, dead animals and men blocked the way, the enemy shelled the road and no guides were furnished. The 2d Battalion, leading, did not reach St. Thibaut until 3:30 a.m., did not leave the sunken road, where it changed to combat formation, until 3:45 a.m., and did not reach the Vesle until dawn. The foot bridges could not be found and further advance was opposed by enemy fire.

Calculations of time and space were evidently based on rates of march without allowances for unforeseen contingencies. An hour, or even a half-hour, saved in launching the movement would have been invaluable in this instance where time was a paramount consideration.

✦   ✦   ✦

EXAMPLE 2. In November, 1918, the U. S. 91st Division, attached to the French Army of Belgium, took part in the Ypres-Lys offensive.

Throughout the day of November 2, the 364th Infantry (part of the 91st Division) had been held in division reserve at Spitaals-Bosschen. During the evening the commanding officer of the 364th Infantry received oral orders for an advance that night. Returning to his command post at 9:40 p.m., he met his unit commanders, who had been previously assembled, and immediately issued his order. Within twenty minutes the 364th Infantry was on the road moving toward Wortengem. The written order for this movement reached the regiment after midnight.

The 364th had been directed to proceed to temporary foot bridges which had been thrown across the Scheldt River between Eyne and Heurne (about a mile out of the 91st Division's zone).

After crossing the Scheldt it was to move south and attack Fort Kezel in conjunction with the remainder of the division which would be located along the west bank of the river.

To accomplish this mission two things were essential: first,

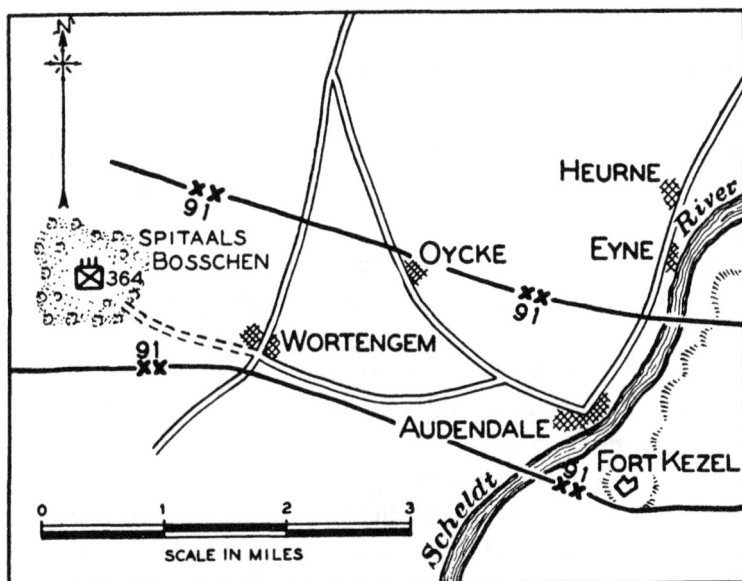

Example 2

the regiment would have to march nearly ten miles, cross the river, form for attack and advance about two and a half miles more, all under cover of darkness; second, if the enemy were to be surprised, the troops would have to reach a position close to Fort Kezel before daylight.

At 4:00 a.m. the 364th reached a point about three kilometers beyond Oycke where it was met by guides. Here the column was delayed by a message directing the colonel to proceed to the artillery command post for a conference with the brigade and artillery commanders relative to supporting fires.

At 4:45 a.m., a half hour before daylight, the head of the column was still three kilometers from the foot bridges. Enemy artillery had been interdicting the roads. Appreciating the situation, the regimental commander ordered the battalion to march to areas east of Oycke and dig in. The crossing was not attempted.

From the personal experience monograph of Captain Frederick W. Rose, Infantry.

DISCUSSION. This regiment received orders so late that its task was almost impossible. The distance to the point of crossing was a little less than ten miles. Two and a half miles more remained from the crossing to Fort Kezel. Using the usual rate of march by road at night (two miles per hour) it would take about five hours to reach the crossing. Following the crossing, the march would be across country at one mile per hour. This would require two and a half hours more. The whole movement would require seven and a half hours of steady marching—not including the time lost in crossing.

In this case, the colonel had his unit commanders assembled and waiting for him on his return. Due to this, the regiment was in motion in the exceptionally good time of twenty minutes, or at 10:00 p.m. Daylight came about 5:15 a.m., or seven and a half hours later. Theoretically, the movement was just about possible, but practically, it was not. No time was allowed for delays —not even for such obvious things as enemy artillery fire, crossing the river, issuing the attack order or taking up the attack formation.

The account does not explain the cause of the delays in the march of this unit, but that there were delays may be seen by the fact that at 4:45 a.m. the head of the column was still three kilometers from the crossing.

The calculation of time-and-space factors had been too optimistic.

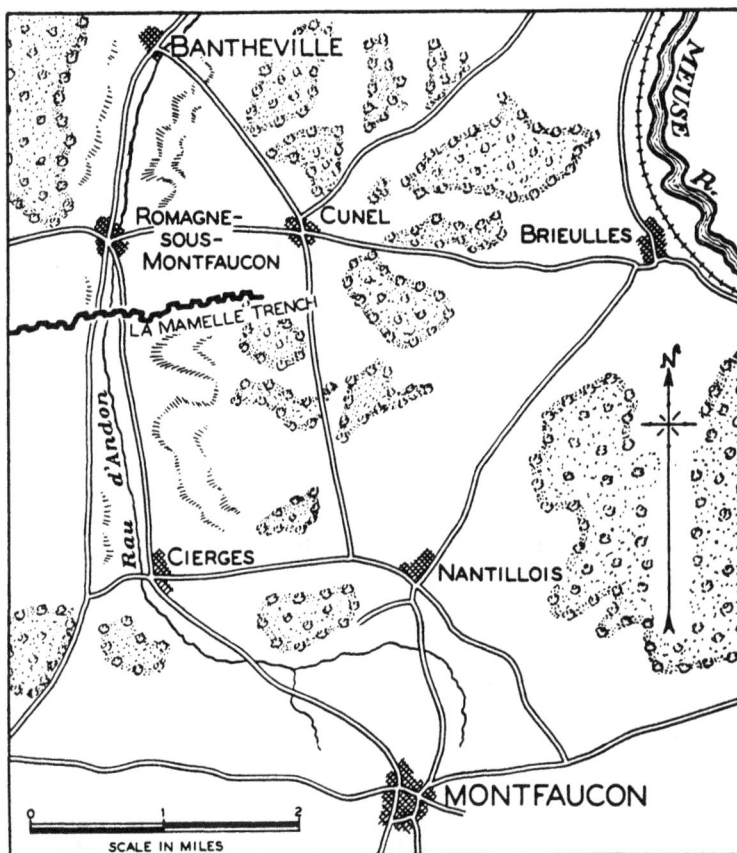

Example 3

EXAMPLE 3. At 4:30 p.m., October 9, 1918, the 2d Battalion of the U. S. 38th Infantry was ordered to move from its position at Cierges, leapfrog the 1st and 3d Battalions which were holding la Mamelle Trench near Romagne-sous-Montfaucon, and attack toward Bantheville. The ridge southwest of Bantheville, which was the battalion objective, was four miles away. Darkness would fall in an hour and a half.

The battalion, advancing over the ridges northeast of Cierges in approach-march formation, came under heavy artillery fire and had to break up into smaller sub-divisions. It did not arrive in time to attack that day.

From the personal experience monograph of Captain Francis M. Rich, Infantry, who commanded Company G of the 38th Infantry.

DISCUSSION. Here we have an attack ordered in which the objective could not possibly be reached before night, and yet a night attack was not intended.

The comment of Captain Rich on this phase of the operation follows:

> The objective was four miles off, there had been no preliminary reconnaissance, and darkness was only one and a half hours away. The briefest consideration of time and space would have shown that it was impossible to execute the order. A better plan would have been to make the approach march under cover of darkness, thus avoiding the bombardment to which the battalion was subjected, and attack at daylight.

✓   ✓   ✓

EXAMPLE 4. On June 6, 1918, the 23d Infantry (U. S. 2d Division) held a position northwest of Château-Thierry. At 3:15 p.m. that day division issued orders for the 23d Infantry and the units on its left to attack at 5:00 p.m. This order reached the commanding officer of the 23d Infantry at 4:00 p.m. He ordered the 1st and 3d Battalions, then in the front line, to attack in conjunction with troops on the left.

It was nearly 5:00 p.m. before the battalions got this order. Both battalion commanders assembled their company commanders at double-time and issued their orders. Captains literally gathered their companies on the run and started toward the enemy lines. The 3d Battalion attacked at 5:50 p.m. Its attack was repulsed with considerable losses.

✓   ✓   ✓

On July 18, 1918, the 23d Infantry was attacking eastward in the Aisne-Marne offensive. The advance had been rapid all morning, but in the afternoon it began to slow down.

Early in the afternoon the division commander met the commander of the 3d Brigade (9th and 23d Infantry Regiments) and ordered a resumption of the attack at 4:30 p.m. The brigade commander, however, did not even find his two regimental commanders until after that hour. When he finally located them he ordered them to resume the attack at 6:00 p.m.

Fifteen French light tanks were to support the attack. Most of the units of the 23d were badly intermingled. Both regimental commanders were of the opinion that the attack could not be launched by 6:00 p.m. The tank commander wanted even more time than the colonels. The colonel of the 23d Infantry conferred with the French captain commanding the tanks, and then, at 6:30 p.m., moved forward to organize the attack.

At 7:00 p.m. the 23d Infantry jumped off under the personal command of the regimental commander. The 9th Infantry, also led by its colonel, jumped off fifteen minutes later.

From the personal experience monograph of Captain Withers A. Burress, who was Operations Officer of the 23d Infantry.

DISCUSSION. Such experiences as that of the 23d Infantry on June 6 are avoidable, yet they occurred with monotonous frequency in the World War. There were undoubtedly many excellent reasons why the order for a 5:00 o'clock attack did not reach the regimental commander until 4:00 and the battalion commanders until nearly 5:00. But in spite of reasons good or bad, the fact remains that the order should have reached the troops at an earlier hour. The chances are that much time would have been saved all the way down the line, had each headquarters visualized the ultimate effect of cumulative delay.

On July 18 the same thing happened. Battalion and company commanders had almost no time in which to make arrangements.

The troops were good, the leadership was vigorous, but all time estimates were profoundly in error. It took more than five hours for the division commander to make his will felt. In this instance there was an excuse for the delay, for the 3d Brigade had been in full battle. The fault here is that due allowance for the disorganization incident to combat was not made in arranging for the resumption of the attack.

Within each of the attacking regiments the commanding officers obtained coördination by personally conducting the operation. The confusion of the battlefield, particularly in resuming an attack that has been stopped, makes coördination by time extremely difficult. For small units other methods should be considered. If the time method is used, the allowance must be generous.

✔   ✔   ✔

CONCLUSION. These illustrations are by no means extreme. Accounts of the World War bristle with tactical failures that are directly due to fallacious conceptions of time and space. Indeed, instances abound in which attack orders were received after the hour specified by the order for the jump-off. In many cases unpredictable circumstances intervened—circumstances that disjointed even the most generous time allowances. But it is equally true that many leaders based their calculations on parade-ground logistics, completely ignoring the inevitable obstacles that arise in war.

Commanders and their staffs must give the most careful thought to considerations of time and space. The time element should be computed from the specific conditions that will be encountered, or that are likely to be encountered, and not be taken merely from theoretical tables setting forth rates of march and time required for distribution of orders under average conditions.

Actual application of troop-leading methods, as taught at our service schools, will save many precious minutes. Forethought in making reconnaissance, shrewd anticipation of the probable course of action, tentative warning orders issued on this hypothesis, and arrangements for the instant transmission of orders, represent but a few of the time-saving devices the aggressive leader will adopt.

Chapter VII: *Mobility*

||||||||||||||||||||||||||||||||||||||||||||||||||||||||||||||||||||||||||||||||||||||||||||||||||||||||||||||||||||||||

*Open warfare demands elastic tactics, quick
decisions, and swift maneuvers.*

||||||||||||||||||||||||||||||||||||||||||||||||||||||||||||||||||||||||||||||||||||||||||||||||||||||||||||||||||||||||

MOBILITY includes far more than mere rapidity of movement. From the leader it demands prompt decisions, clear, concise orders, anticipation of the probable course of action and some sure means for the rapid transmission of orders. From the troops it demands promptness in getting started, the ability to make long marches under the most adverse conditions of terrain and weather, skill in effecting rapid deployments and abrupt changes of formation without delay or confusion, facility in passing from the defensive to the offensive, or the reserve, and finally, a high morale. In brief, then, mobility implies both rapidity and flexibility.

✝   ✝   ✝

EXAMPLE 1. In the early days of the World War the 35th Fusiliers, part of the German II Corps, made the following marches:

August 17: 13.1 miles
August 18: 25.0 miles
August 19: 06.2 miles (Battle of the Gette)
August 20: 21.9 miles
August 21: 06.2 miles
August 22: 07.5 miles
August 23: 28.1 miles
August 24: 10.0 miles (Battle of Mons)
August 25: 18.7 miles
August 26: 12:5 miles (Battle of le Cateau)
August 27: 21.9 miles
August 28: 23.8 miles
August 29: 05.0 miles (Fighting on the Somme)
August 30: 15.6 miles
August 31: 20.6 miles
September 1: 18.8 miles (Fight at Villers-Cotterêts)

September 2: 08.8 miles
September 3: 20.6 miles
September 4: 18.8 miles (Fight at Montmirail)
September 5: 15.6 miles
September 6:   none   (Battle of the Marne)
September 7: 23.1 miles (Battle of the Marne)
September 8: 20.6 miles (Battle of the Marne)
September 9:   none   (Battle of the Marne)
September 10: 20.0 miles
September 11: 18.1 miles
September 12: 07.5 miles (Battle of the Aisne)

DISCUSSION. In 27 consecutive days the 35th Fusiliers marched 408 miles, an average of 15.1 miles a day. This period included at least 11 battle days and no rest days. All marches were made under full pack.

On September 7 and 8, in the movement to attack the north flank of the French Sixth Army, this regiment marched 43.7 miles with only a three-hour halt. The entire march was made under the most difficult traffic conditions.

From the "Militär-Wochenblatt," February 25, 1932.

✝   ✝   ✝

EXAMPLE 2. On May 30, 1918, the 7th Machine-Gun Battalion of the U. S. 3d Division was training near la-Ferté-sur-Aube. This battalion was motorized, but its motors were of unsuitable design and its personnel had had comparatively little training in handling them.

At 10:00 a.m. an unexpected order directed the battalion to proceed at once to Condé-en-Brie, using its own transportation. This order was occasioned by the headlong drive of the Germans for the Marne, following their successful break-through along the Chemin des Dames.

A warning order was promptly issued. Troops were recalled from drill, extra trucks borrowed, and at 2:30 p.m. the column cleared la-Ferté-sur-Aube. Within the space of a few miles the trucks were found to be seriously overloaded. On steep hills the men had to detruck and, in some cases, push. Tires were old and punctures many. Delays were frequent. Motorcycles proved valuable in carrying spare parts to broken-down trucks.

About 9:00 p.m. a short halt was made near Sézanne in order to rest the men and refuel and overhaul the cars. Thereafter no lights were used. At daybreak the column encountered refugees who crowded the roads and made progress difficult. Nearer the front, infantry, artillery, and supply wagons appeared in the intervals between the refugees. At 12:30 p.m., May 31, the head of the battalion halted at Condé-en-Brie, having made 110 miles in 22 hours over congested roads. The battalion arrived at Château-Thierry, went into position in the afternoon, and at dawn engaged the Germans.

From the personal experience monograph of Major John R. Mendenhall, who commanded Company B of the 7th Machine-Gun Battalion.

DISCUSSION. In this case mobility was obtained through the use of motors. Although the equipment was deficient and traffic conditions difficult, this battalion moved 110 miles and deployed in position against the enemy within some twenty-seven hours after receipt of its orders.

⚞ ⚞ ⚞

EXAMPLE 3. On August 17, 1914, detachments of the German I Corps were disposed on the East Prussian frontier with the main German forces concentrated well in rear. A strong Russian advance was in progress from the east.

The I Corps had been given a covering mission, but its commander believed in an aggressive defense.

The 4th Infantry Brigade, a squadron of cavalry and a regiment of field artillery were located at Tollmongkelmen. To the north, elements of the 1st Division covered a wide front east of Stalluponen.

Early on the 17th the Tollmongkelmen detachment was confronted with the following situation: The elements of the 1st Division, to the north, were engaged against much stronger Rus-

sian forces, and their situation was serious. The south flank of
this fighting was some eleven miles from Tollmongkelmen.

According to reliable information, a Russian division advanc-

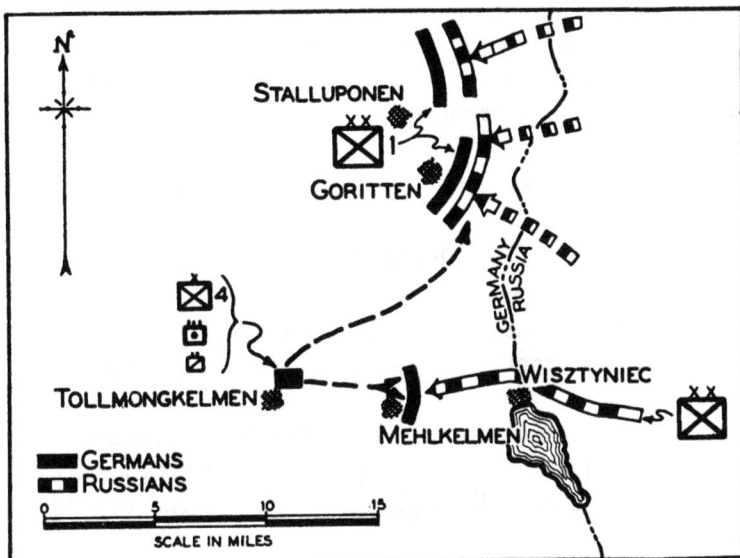

Example 3

ing west from Wisztyniec was now but a few miles from Mehlkelmen.

The German commander at Tollmongkelmen at once decided
to contain this Russian division with a small force and, with the
bulk of his command, move north and strike the southern flank
of the Russians who were attacking the 1st Division elements
near Goritten.

From his command, which had already been assembled, he
sent two battalions of the 45th Infantry, a squadron of cavalry,
and a battery of field artillery against the Russian advance from
Wisztyniec, with orders to stop the Russians at Mehlkelmen at
any cost.

With the 33d Infantry, one battalion of the 45th Infantry,

and five batteries of artillery, he marched to the northeast, arriving in the vicinity of the fighting about 11:30 a.m. This detachment promptly attacked toward Goritten directly against the rear of the enemy. The effect was immediate. The Russians withdrew in disorder with heavy losses, including some 3,000 captured. German losses were slight. The delaying detachment to the south carried out its mission, holding the Russians at Mehlkelmen the entire day.

From "Tannenberg," by General von François, German Army, and the Reichsarchiv account.

DISCUSSION. Although the Russians were vastly superior in numbers, they were overwhelmed by their faster-thinking, faster-moving opponents. A quick decision, a rapid march, and a sudden attack from an unexpected quarter completely routed them.

Had the German force at Tollmongkelmen not been moved north promptly, the result would probably have been a successful defense east of Tollmongkelmen, and a reverse near Stalluponen.

The German commander at Tollmongkelmen took a chance. He risked defeat on his own front in order to put weight into his effort to redress a critical situation on a more decisive front. His confidence in the superior mobility of his troops and in the ability of a weak detachment to effect the required delay near Mehlkelmen was justified.

ㅤㅤㅤㅤㅤ✶ㅤㅤㅤ✶ㅤㅤㅤ✶

EXAMPLE 4. On November 5, 1918, the 28th Infantry, part of the U. S. 1st Division, bivouacked about three miles east of Buzancy. The division was in corps reserve. The Germans were withdrawing.

About 2:30 p.m., the regiment received warning that the 1st Division would relieve the 80th Division that night and that orders for the movement would be issued later. The troops were given a hot meal, packs were rolled, and a tentative march order prepared. By 4:30 p.m. all arrangements were complete; the regiment was in readiness, waiting only for the order to move out.

About 5:00 p.m. a written message came in, directing the command to march at once to the vicinity of Beaumont, via Nouart and la Forge Farm. The regimental commander was instructed to report to the brigade commander at la Forge Farm for further orders. A few minutes after this message arrived the regiment was in motion.

The march was difficult. Nouart's narrow streets were congested with units of the 2d and 80th Divisions. Beyond Nouart the road meandered through thick woods and over marshy ground; shell holes and fallen trees blocked the way; in many places the mud reached halfway to the knee; fields and ditches, bordering the road, were filled with water. Often the men had to march in column of twos. Rest periods were few. But in spite of the difficulties a steady rate of march was maintained (about one and one-third miles an hour for the greater part of the distance).

At la Forge Farm orders were received directing the 1st Division to attack towards Mouzon on the morning of November 6. The 28th Infantry was ordered to occupy a position in the woods two miles west of Beaumont.

When the leading element reached Beaumont it found the bridge destroyed and the exits of the village under shell fire from positions east of the Meuse. After studying the map the regimental commander decided to move across country to the prescribed position.

Since it was too dark to pick up landmarks, battalion commanders were given compass bearings. Three unimproved roads that intersected the route of march furnished a check on the distance. When the third road was crossed, the regiment would be near its destination.

The going was heavy. Ditches and shell holes barred the way;

fields were wet and soggy; fences had to be cut. To add to these difficulties, the enemy steadily shelled the area through which the column was passing, making it necessary to extend the distance between units.

Dawn was breaking when the column reached the third road. The terrain did not check with the map! The regiment was halted and an officer was sent down the road toward Beaumont. He found that there were four roads instead of three; the Germans had built one for use in transporting supplies to the front. The command was marching in the right direction and had only a short distance to go. The regiment resumed its march and arrived at its designated position in good time.

Since the attack toward Mouzon met but little resistance, the 28th Infantry remained in brigade reserve. About 4:00 p.m. this same day, the regiment received a telephone message from the brigade commander, in substance as follows:

> The brigade is going on a long march. Move out at once on the Beaumont—Stonne road toward Stonne. The regimental commander will report to me in person at the crossroad at la Bagnelle for orders. The 26th Infantry will be withdrawn and follow you in column.

In a few minutes the regiment was again en route. Orders received at la Bagnelle directed the 1st Division to march on Sedan in five columns, seize the hills southwest of that city, and attack at daylight. The 28th Infantry and Company D of the 1st Engineers were ordered to march via Stonne—Chéhéry—Frenois.

Neither the location of the enemy front line nor that of friendly units, other than the division, was definitely known. Therefore the brigade commander decided to move forward in route column, preceded by an advance guard, and push through such resistance as might be encountered with as little extension as possible.

The regimental commander was ready with his orders when the 28th Infantry reached la Bagnelle. The regiment marched all night. About 7:00 a.m. the advance guard was fired on from a

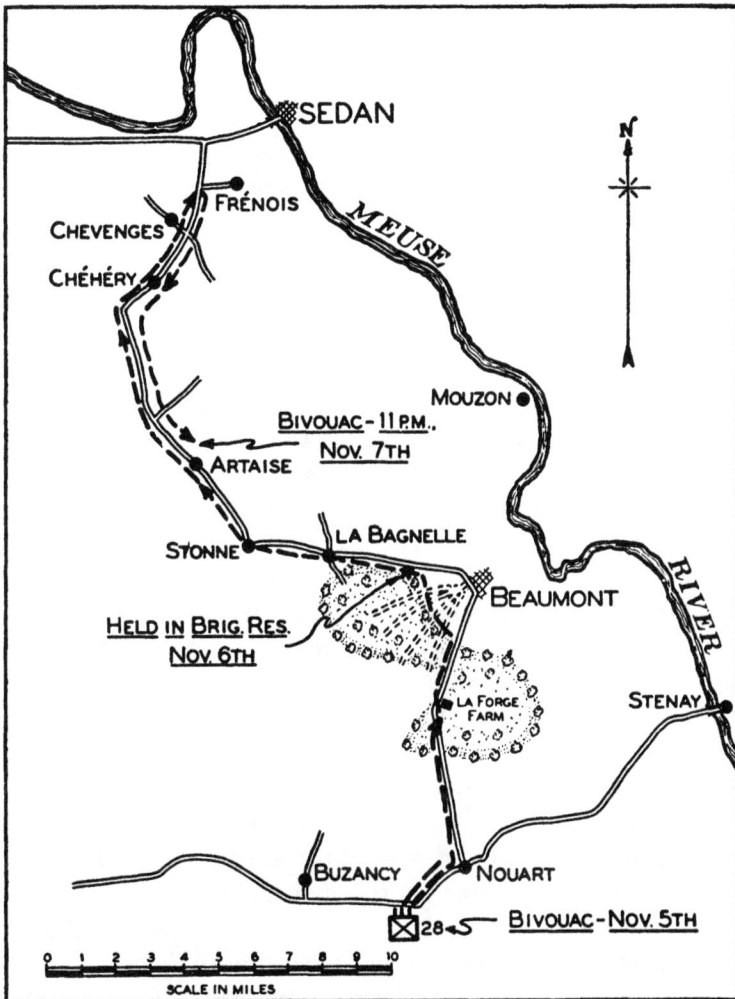

Example 4

position near Chevenges. The regimental commander, who was with the advance-guard commander, at once ordered an attack. The attack got away promptly and drove past Chevenges to within two or three miles of Sedan.

At 11:00 a.m. orders were received to halt the advance and organize the ground for defense. Five hours later the 28th was ordered to withdraw to the vicinity of Artaise, as it was not desired that the 1st Division enter Sedan. The last units of the regiment arrived in Artaise about 11:00 p.m.

From the personal experience monograph of Major William G. Livesay, who was Plans & Training Officer of the 28th Infantry.

DISCUSSION. Between 5:00 p.m. November 5 and 11:00 p.m. November 7, the 28th Infantry covered about thirty-five miles. During this period it made a difficult and exhausting night march to take up a battle position, a second all-night march in pursuit, an attack, a transition from the offensive to the defensive and, finally, a withdrawal. For fifty-four hours this regiment marched and fought without food and virtually without rest.

Although this outstanding performance would have been impossible without the physical efficiency and high morale that characterized the regiment, it would have been equally impossible without first-rate troop leading. Instructions were anticipated and warning orders issued. In each case, the regiment was able to move immediately on receipt of the order. The regimental commander was directed to put his troops in march toward a certain point, and then told where to report for further instructions. There was no time wasted in issuing elaborate march orders, nor was there any delay in taking prompt, positive action when the column encountered unforeseen difficulties.

Intelligent foresight, rapid decisions, prompt orders and high morale are factors that make for mobility.

✓   ✓   ✓

EXAMPLE 5. On August 19, 1914, the 30th Chasseur Battalion, with one battery of artillery attached, was ordered to

move east from Stosswihr along the north side of the Fecht, in
order to cover the debouchment of other troops. One battalion
of the 152d Infantry was assigned a similar advance and mission
south of the river. The 30th Chasseurs consisted of six companies
of well-trained, well-conditioned troops, ready for any eventuality.

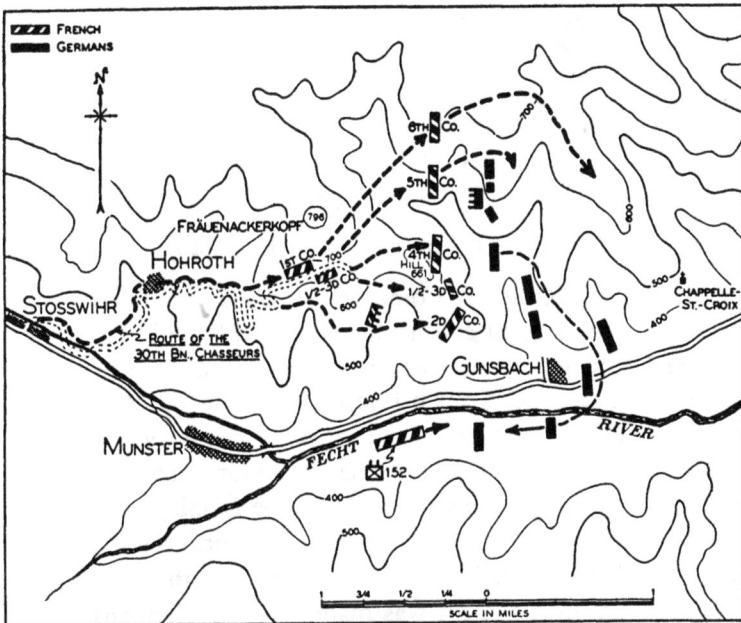

Example 5

The valley of the Fecht is about a mile wide. The valley itself
is relatively flat and open, but is dominated on both sides by
steep, wooded hills. The secondary valleys entering the Fecht
from the north are pronounced depressions. Progress through
the woods by deployed units would be slow.

The battalion commander, knowing that German covering
forces were near and combat imminent, decided to move the bulk
of his command along the slopes of the north bank to envelop

any resistance met. Crests were to be used as successive objectives. Few troops would be left in the valley. He explained his general idea before the march started and issued his order, extracts of which follow.

> The battalion will follow the road Stosswihr—Hohroth—Fräuenack-erkopf and then, without losing height, will move parallel to the valley. Order of March: 4th, 5th, 6th, 2d, 3d, 1st Companies.
> The 4th Company (advance guard), will deploy astride the route followed as soon as the enemy is met; the 5th, then the 6th, will deploy to the north.
> The 2d Company will deploy to the south, maintain contact with the 4th Company and cover the valley road.
> The 3d and 1st Companies will be in reserve.
> The battery will move behind the 2d Company, keeping generally near the south edge of the woods, abreast of the reserve. The machine-gun platoon will also follow the 2d Company.

About 8:00 a.m. the 4th Company, near 661, encountered an enemy force to its front and deployed, as did the 2d Company. The 5th Company at once moved to the north, deployed two platoons and advanced against resistance. The 6th Company farther north, met no enemy and continued its advance.

Along most of the front the French deployed more rapidly than their opponents, whom they could see fanning out under their fire. This was particularly true on the north flank, where the French definitely had the advantage of being the first to deploy. Here an envelopment was made and the Germans were taken under a converging fire. Meanwhile, the French battery and machine guns had promptly gone into action, directing their fire against German elements in the open valley.

In spite of the fact that the Germans had artillery support, the French envelopment made progress. About 3:30 p.m. the 6th Company arrived on the spur northwest of Chapelle-St.Croix and turned southward, surprising a command post and the German elements that were located there.

A strong German attack in the valley, near Gunsbach, failed. As a result of this repulse and the progress of the French envelopment, the Germans withdrew in confusion. The French pushed on and reached their assigned objective.

This battalion, assisted by fire from the battalion of the 152d south of the Fecht, had defeated the 121st Württemburg Reserve Regiment and some elements of the 123d and 124th.

From Infantry Conferences by Lieutenant Colonel Touchon, French Army, at the École Supérieure de Guerre.

DISCUSSION. Here is an instance where a battalion commander regulated his deployment in advance. His maneuver had been carefully planned in the event the enemy was encountered—fire in the open valley, maneuver in the covered area. He realized that the negotiation of such steep slopes as those along the Fecht would be a slow and fatiguing job, even for his hardy Alpine troops. Therefore he wisely began the climb before gaining contact with the enemy, but without deploying. Thereby he saved his men and increased his speed.

That the French were able to deploy faster than their opponents was largely due to the almost automatic nature of their maneuver. A few shots and the movement got under way. No time was lost in making decisions and issuing orders.

Those cases in which a prearranged deployment can be used will be few. Situations seldom develop in accordance with preconceived ideas. Nevertheless, this action graphically illustrates the tremendous advantage that may result from a previously planned course of action.

The defeat of this larger and stronger German force may be directly attributed to the superior mobility of the 30th Chasseurs. This superior mobility resulted from two things: First, the excellent performance of the troops, who were well-trained and in good physical condition; second, the foresight of the battalion commander.

✦   ✦   ✦

CONCLUSION. The physical marching ability of troops is an important factor in mobility, but it is only a part. Rapid decisions and clear, quick orders are vital. No less important are the requirements demanded of the troops—prompt execution of orders, rapid deployment, quick changes of formation and observance of march discipline.

Superior mobility must be achieved if we are to surprise our opponent, select the terrain on which we are to fight, and gain the initiative. There is no alternative. If we are slow in movement, awkward in maneuver, clumsy in deployment—in a word, not mobile—we can expect to be forestalled, enveloped, or constrained to launch costly frontal attacks against an enemy advantageously posted.

Chapter VIII: *Surprise*

Surprise is a master key to victory.

SURPRISE is usually decisive; therefore, much may be sacrificed to achieve it. It should be striven for by all units, regardless of size, and in all engagements, regardless of importance. When the squad opens fire it should do so suddenly and simultaneously. When an army attacks it should strike from an unexpected direction, at an unexpected time, with unexpected violence.

When the enemy confidently expects a certain course of action his dispositions are made with the view of meeting that action. If, however, an unexpected plan be adopted the hostile dispositions and arrangements must be hastily improvised, and are therefore less effective. Concealment of the point of attack permits the offense to mass superior forces against a critical point before its action can be countered by a hostile concentration. Similarly, concealment of the time of attack prevents the defense from initiating appropriate counter-measures and, at the same time, adds tremendously to that moral effect which is the soul of offensive action.

Surprises gained by large forces in the World War are well known. For example, on July 18, 1918, the French and Americans surprised the Germans. On May 27, 1918, the Germans won an easy victory by surprising the French on the Chemin des Dames. The British and French surprised the Germans on August 8, 1918—"the black day of the German Army."

In all these cases the precautions taken to insure secrecy were extreme and so were many of the chances. On the 8th of August, for instance, all the infantry of the French 42d Division formed for an attack in a block some 400 yards deep by 1,200 yards wide. If the Germans had suspected this, few of their shells would have missed. The formation was not discovered, however, and at the prescribed hour of attack the French infantry moved forward in mass. It completely escaped the enemy's counter-preparations and barrages, smashed through his lines, advanced miles into his territory, and captured 2,500 prisoners. True, this division took a chance, but it got away with it and made one of the most successful French attacks of the war.

The French spring offensive of 1917 failed chiefly because it lacked surprise. Many earlier Allied offensives failed for the same reason; they had been too well advertised by days of artillery preparation.

Surprise is by no means a monopoly of the larger units. It applies to the squad as well as the army, and for both it is almost invariably decisive. Indeed, it is not too much to say that without surprise of some kind an operation will fail, or at best achieve but a limited success.

✓   ✓   ✓

EXAMPLE 1. On November 7, 1918, the U. S. 356th Infantry reached the Meuse River, whose far bank was held in strength by the Germans. Colonel R. H. Allen, the regimental commander, had orders to prepare a plan for effecting the crossing.

Colonel Allen, in consultation with engineers, selected a point for crossing. His plan was based primarily on surprise. Six captured German pontoons (borrowed without leave from the 2d Division) were to be used. The crossing was to be made at night just west of the mouth of Wame Creek. A covering detachment of twenty-five men would go over first and fan out across the neck of the river bend to stop hostile patrols.

Immediately after this the 1st Battalion would cross and push forward in silence, with rifles unloaded. They would pass to the north of Pouilly, cut the wire lines leading to the town, and then seize the heights east of it. Later this battalion would continue to the high ground on the edge of the Bois de Soiry.

The 3d Battalion would follow the 1st, pass around Pouilly and move to the Bois de Hache. As it passed Pouilly it would drop off one company to overcome organized resistance in the town.

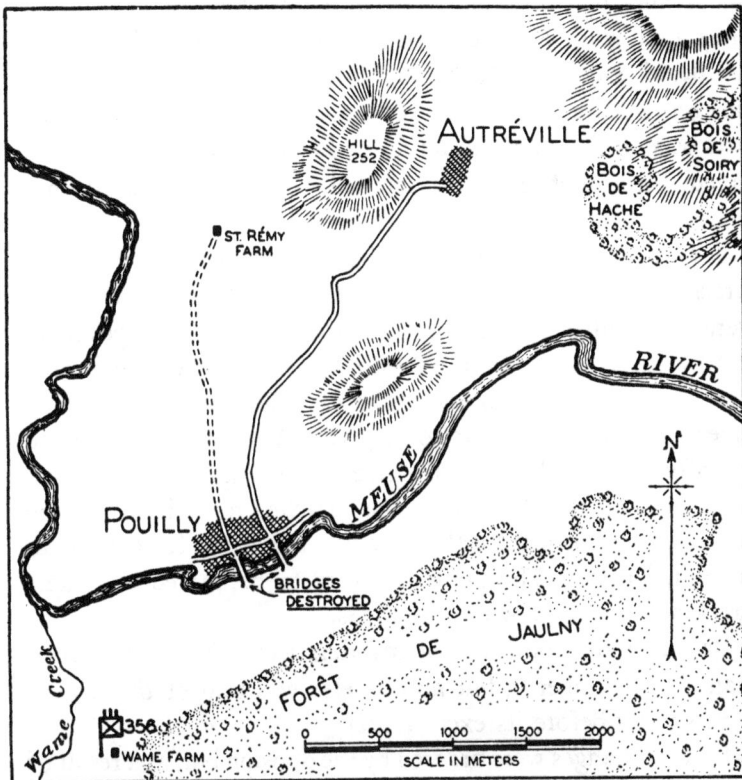

Example 1

The artillery prepared concentrations on a time schedule carefully calculated to keep ahead of the infantry. Fire would be opened only on receipt of orders or on rocket signal from the regimental C.P. at Wame Farm. If fire had not been opened by the time the 1st Battalion reached the Pouilly—St. Rémy Farm Road, the artillery would open up on signal from this battalion.

Similar arrangements were made for machine-gun support—the machine guns to remain silent until the artillery opened.

A demonstration was planned at Pouilly. The river was shallow here and the enemy obviously expected an attack, for a previous attempt had been made to build rafts near this town and effect a crossing. The Germans had noted the preparations and had heard pounding. At the slightest movement in this vicinity they opened fire. Full advantage was taken of this. Lumber for rafts was piled near the Forêt de Jaulny and imperfectly camouflaged. Each night men were detailed to hammer on boards in a quarry near Pouilly.

For the main crossing, boats were to be lashed together in threes thus making two rafts of the six pontoons. These rafts were to be pulled back and forth across the river by ropes manned by shore parties of the 314th Engineers. Hay and boards were placed in the metal boats to deaden the sound of hobnailed shoes. No commands were to be given. Absolute silence was to be enforced. Signals across the river were arranged by the engineers. A light telephone wire was attached to each end of the rafts. A vigorous jerk on the wire was the signal for the raft to be pulled across. The pontoons were to be hauled to Wame Creek and floated down to the Meuse.

Battalion and company commanders were given the detailed plan on November 9, but no one else was told of the scheme until shortly before its execution.

Certain changes were ordered by the division but, as a result of protest by Colonel Allen, these were reduced to a minimum. For instance, the division ordered an artillery preparation but the regimental commander felt that this would eliminate the element of surprise. He protested and the original plan for artillery support was allowed to stand.

The crossing was ordered to be carried out on the night of the 10th. The demonstration staged at Pouilly succeeded beyond expectation. Practically all of the hostile artillery in the vicinity

placed its fire on this area and kept it there during the entire
operation.

At the real crossing, the first troops were ferried over at about

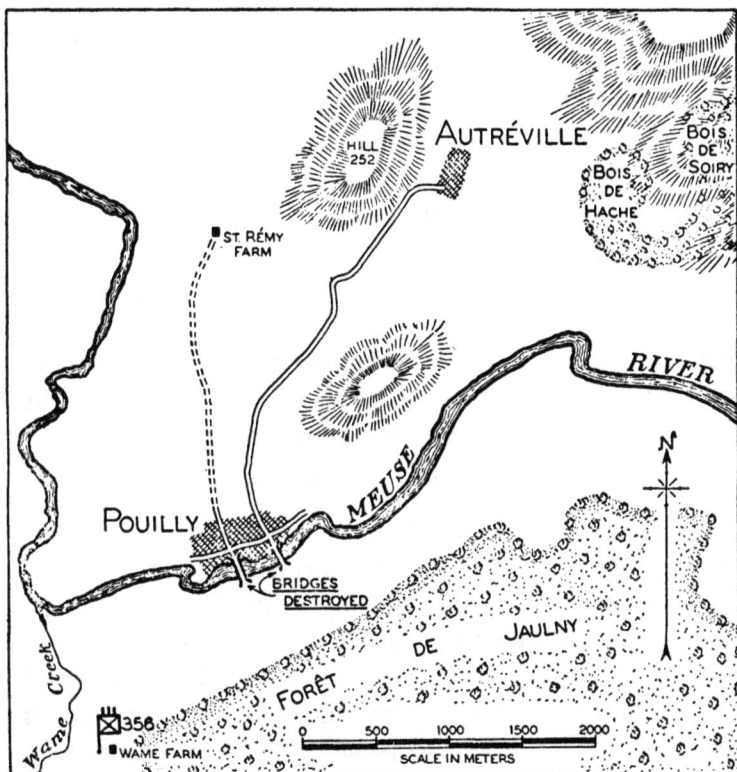

Example 1

8:20 p.m. Soon after this some German artillery came down
nearby, whereupon Colonel Allen ordered the signal rocket fired
and the American artillery and machine guns opened. In a few
minutes the enemy shifted his artillery fire to the Pouilly area
and from that time on not another shell fell near the ferry.

The crossing continued, generally according to plan, and was entirely successful. Many prisoners were taken in Pouilly and Autréville. At the last place an entire machine-gun company was captured as its was falling in to move on Pouilly.

The 1st Battalion, moving through darkness and fog, advanced to its objective by compass bearing. This battalion and the 3d, which followed it, suffered few casualties. The enemy was taken completely by surprise.

The experience of the 2d Battalion of this regiment was different. It had been ordered to move to a foot-bridge where the 2d Division was crossing. It reached the designated bridge at 9:00 p.m., but had to wait until 1:00 a.m. before it could cross. The enemy discovered the movement. His artillery came down with deadly accuracy on the crossing and on the 2d Battalion. Most of the officers of this battalion, including the battalion commander, were killed or wounded, and 232 men out of the 600 who began the operation shared the same fate.

From the personal experience monograph of Captain Arthur S. Champeny.

DISCUSSION. Colonel Allen's plan was based on surprise, and surprise succeeded as it almost always does.

The Germans expected a crossing at Pouilly and the regimental commander took great pains to encourage them in that belief. For several days he fostered this idea. The building of rafts nearby, the imperfect camouflage of lumber, the previous threat of a crossing, the nightly pounding on boards near Pouilly, all confirmed the Germans in their belief. Further, since secrecy was the basis of the operation, the colonel strongly opposed the division's desire for an artillery preparation prior to the crossing. His views prevailed.

The sum total of all these precautions resulted in the 1st and 3d Battalions attacking in an unexpected manner from an unexpected place. The Germans were not even sure that a crossing had been made. That the surprise was complete is clearly shown by the fact that practically no artillery fire fell at the point of the actual crossing, whereas the Pouilly area was pounded unmercifully during the entire operation.

The disastrous effect of the lack of surprise upon casualty lists is forcefully illustrated by the experience of the 2d Battalion, which lost nearly one-half its men in crossing the same stream.

✓ ✓ ✓

EXAMPLE 2. Late on July 17, 1918, the 1st Battalion of the U. S. 39th Infantry made a trying march to the front. By the time the battalion reached the front line, which ran along the Faverolles—Troësnes Road, the men were tired out.

Late that night an attack order came in. The regiment had been ordered to take the Boisson de Cresnes and the colonel had decided to do this by attacking with the 1st and 3d Battalions abreast, the 1st on the left. The 1st Battalion staff hastily examined maps. Diagonally across the battalion front flowed the Savières. Beyond the stream rose the densely wooded ridge of the Boisson de Cresnes, which was believed to be strongly held by the enemy.

The 1st Battalion did not make any reconnaissance of the ground to the front. On the map the Savières appeared too insignificant to occasion any difficulty in crossing. The battalion attack order was issued, therefore, without reconnaissance. Companies A and B were placed in assault, and C and D in support. Company C of the 11th Machine-Gun Battalion was directed to follow the right support company. The Faverolles—Troësnes Road was designated as the line of departure.

The American attack was scheduled to jump off at 5:30 a.m., while the French, in adjacent zones, were to attack at 4:30 a.m., an hour earlier. The idea was to pinch out the formidable Boisson de Cresnes by a simultaneous advance on each side of it. The Americans would then drive forward and mop up the wood.

At 4:30 a.m. the French attacked. Coincident with this, German artillery and trench mortars placed heavy concentrations on the American front line. At 5:15 a.m. the 1st Battalion was informed that the American hour of attack had been postponed to 8:00 a.m.

At this hour the battalion moved forward. The German bombardment had ceased. Not a sound was heard as the men moved across the long, wheat-covered field that sloped down toward the Savières. Finally, the assault companies broke through a fringe of trees and scrambled down a bluff to the river.

Then it was discovered that the Savières, which had appeared so insignificant on the map, was swollen by heavy rains to twice its normal width and depth. The banks on each side had become deep and difficult swamps.

Companies A and B, continuing the advance, became intermingled and forthwith fell into the greatest confusion, not 200 yards from the hostile position. The floundering, the splashing, and the shouting made enough noise to alarm every German in the Marne salient, but strangely enough drew no fire.

Finally, a few patrols, armed with automatic rifles, succeeded in crossing the swollen stream. One of these killed or drove off the crew of an enemy machine gun that was just about to go into action. The noise of this sudden burst of fire spurred the other men to greater effort and the crossing was at last completed.

Once over, the battalion promptly reformed and pushed on into the Boisson de Cresnes. It advanced rapidly, meeting surprisingly little resistance. A captured German sergeant explained the lack of opposition by saying that the Germans had not expected anyone to be daring enough or foolhardy enough to attempt an attack over the flooded and swampy Savières in broad daylight. Therefore the Germans had massed their machine guns and organized the terrain on the northern and southern approaches to the woods where the ground was firm and the cover suitable for an attack.

From the personal experience monograph of Captain Walter B. Smith, who was Scout Officer of the 1st Battalion of the 39th Infantry.

DISCUSSION. The Germans had made a painstaking, logical estimate of the situation. They had placed their strongest defense where an attack seemed most probable. Opposite the 1st

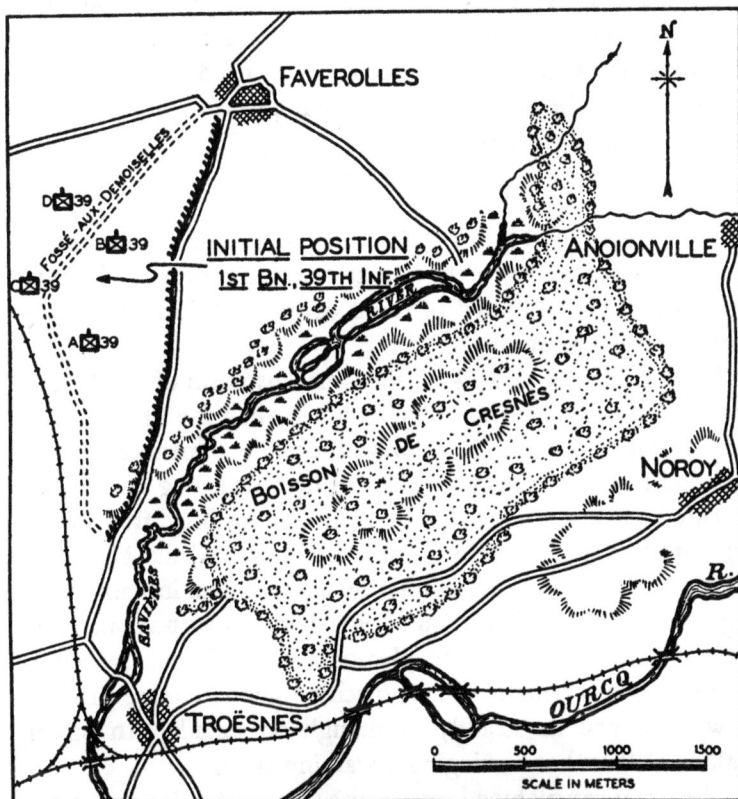

Example 2

Battalion of the 39th, where an attack appeared incredible, they had only a handful of troops.

Thus, when the Americans blundered into the illogical solution, the Germans were caught completely off guard. After floundering through a marsh where a few well-placed machine guns could have stopped a regiment, the battalion captured a strong position—a position so formidable that it was almost undefended.

This battalion was unquestionably lucky. The failure to reconnoiter and to ascertain the true condition of the Savières should, by all odds, have resulted in a bloody repulse. Instead, it resulted in a brilliant success. Why? Because the attacking troops, by stumbling into the unexpected and the improbable, achieved the decisive element of surprise.

*   *   *

EXAMPLE 3. On July 14, 1918, the 4th Platoon of Company A, U. S. 30th Infantry, held a small wood northeast of Fossoy. Farther forward, scattered platoons of the 30th formed an outpost along the Marne.

About midnight July 14-15, the Germans north of the Marne opened a terrific artillery bombardment, but the 4th Platoon escaped without casualties. At dawn the bombardment ceased but rifle and machine-gun fire could still be heard. Fog and smoke obscured the view of the river. Men coming back from other organizations said that the Germans had crossed the Marne.

Some time later the platoon leader saw German infantry moving toward his position in an approach-march formation. They were near the railroad. The platoon leader did not open fire. The German infantrymen and machine gunners came on at a slow walk and as steadily as though on parade. An officer walked at their head swinging a walking stick.

The American platoon leader waited "until the Germans came as close as the British did at Bunker Hill, perhaps 30 yards." He then gave the order to fire, and the men opened up all along the line at point-blank range. To use his own words, "The automatic-rifle squads made their Chauchats rattle like machine guns."

The Germans fired only a few shots. Two Germans, who were trying to get a light machine gun into action, were very conspicuous. They were literally riddled with bullets. Nearly every man

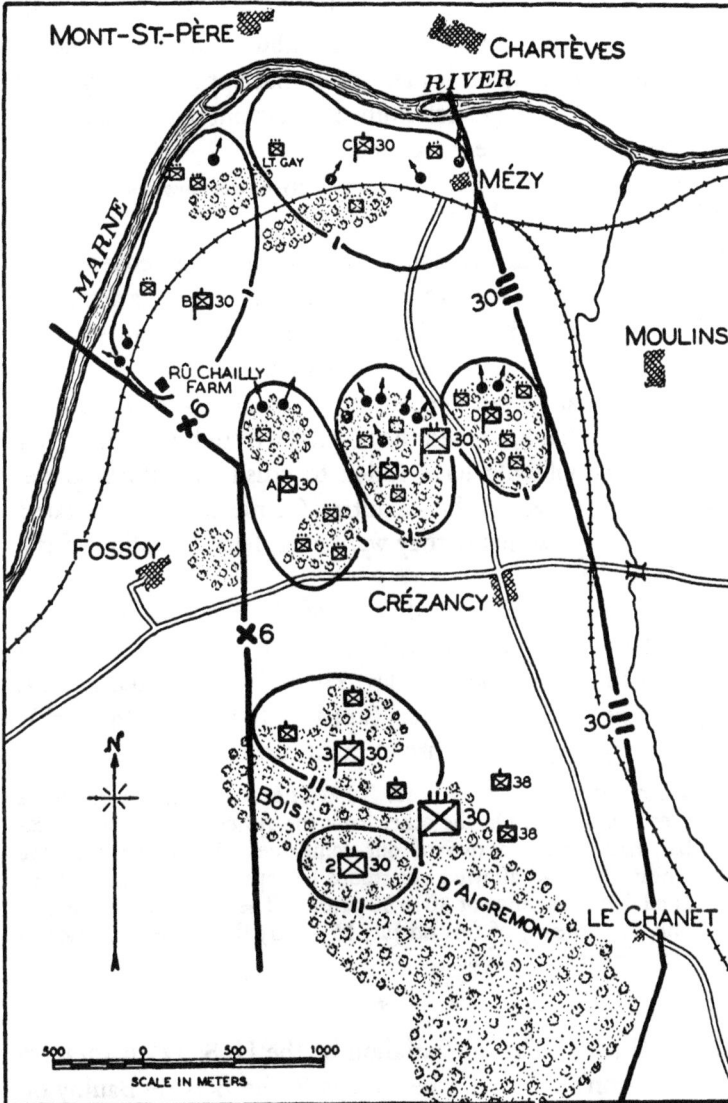

Example 3

in the platoon claimed to have killed them. The enemy took what cover they could find and later withdrew to the Marne.

The American platoon leader stated that approximately forty Germans were killed (as determined by a count made later) and an undetermined number wounded.

From a statement by Lieutenant William C. Ryan, who commanded the 4th Platoon of Company A, 30th Infantry.

DISCUSSION. Surprise can be obtained in the defense as well as in the attack. The surprise effect was gained in this action by withholding fire until the enemy was within thirty yards of the position, then opening suddenly and simultaneously.

Had Lieutenant Ryan opened fire when he first saw the Germans he might have stopped them farther from his position, but he would undoubtedly have failed to crush the attack so decisively. The strength of the assaulting Germans cannot be stated definitely, but presumably they were a depleted battalion of the 398th Infantry.

Lieutenant Kurt Hesse, adjutant of the German 5th Grenadiers, tells of a similar experience in his description of the fighting along the Marne on this day. His unit, committed against troops of the U. S. 3d Division (apparently the 38th Infantry), was similarly surprised by fire at point-blank range. He says:

> I have never seen so many dead. I have never seen such a frightful spectacle of war. On the other bank the Americans, in close combat, had destroyed two of our companies. Lying down in the wheat, they had allowed our troops to approach and then annihilated them at a range of 30 to 50 yards. "The Americans kill everyone," was the cry of fear on July 15—a cry that caused our men to tremble for a long time.

ˀ   ˀ   ˀ

EXAMPLE 4. The 2d Battalion of the U. S. 127th Infantry (32d Division) relieved other troops in the Bois de Baulny on the night of October 3-4, 1918. On the morning of the 4th it took part in a general attack as an assault battalion. Its first objective was the Bois de la Morine and the Bois du Chêne Sec.

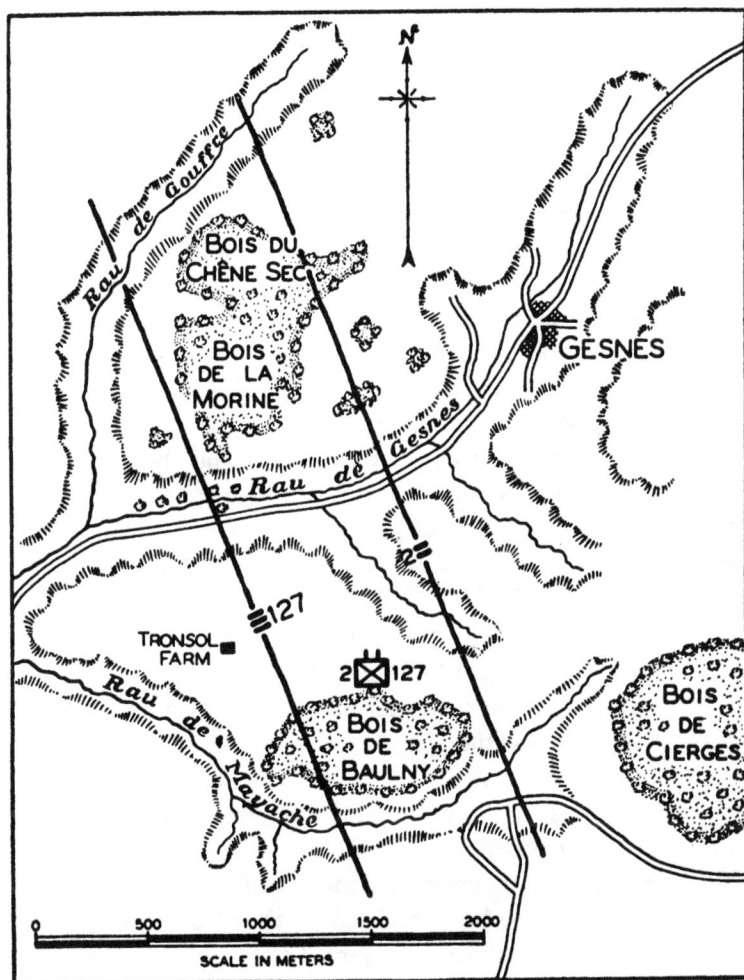

Example 4

Although supported by artillery and machine guns, the attack soon broke down under heavy and accurate German machine-gun fire. Several attempts to resume the attack with the aid of further artillery preparation, got nowhere. The battalion suffered fairly heavy losses.

During the night, orders were received to resume the attack at 6:00 a.m. A heavy fog covered the ground the next morning when the battalion jumped off. When the attack reached the Gesnes stream it encountered machine-gun fire, but this was high and ineffective. The battalion reached a point 100 yards from the Bois de la Morine with only a few casualties. From this point it launched a frontal attack in combination with a flanking attack by two platoons from the east. This attack carried the position along the forward edge of the wood and the battalion pushed on to the north edge of the Bois du Chêne Sec, where it halted and reorganized. About 100 prisoners were taken.

From the personal experience monograph of Major Ralph W. Dusenbury, who commanded the 2d Battalion, 127th Infantry.

DISCUSSION. Here we see a battalion carry out a successful attack against a position it had failed to take the previous day. On October 5 it was much weaker numerically than on the 4th, and yet it succeeded without great difficulty. The fog made the difference. The Germans could not tell where or when the attack was coming. Thus the movement on the second day contained the element of surprise.

When enemy fire renders terrain impassable by day, that same terrain may frequently be negotiated under cover of darkness, fog, or some artificial screening agent. Leaders must, therefore, be prepared to take prompt advantage of unusual weather conditions that offer sudden and golden opportunities. Thus, may they achieve surprise.

↗   ↗   ↗

CONCLUSION. Though all leaders recognize the decisive effect of surprise, it does not follow that all leaders are able to achieve it. Too often are routine methods adopted with the idea that surprise will result. Too often are schemes, that have gained surprise several times in the past, relied upon to gain that same surprise again. Frequently they end in failure. For instance, prior to July 15, 1918, the Germans made several successful attacks, gaining surprise each time. But on July 15 the same methods failed. This time the French adopted effective counter-measures against tactics that had become stereotyped. The German tactics were the same that had succeeded before, but they had now lost all the decisive qualities of the unexpected. Failure resulted.

The importance of varying methods cannot be overemphasized. Often the good, standard solution, particularly if it be the obvious one, will not be as effective as some other solution that has many apparent disadvantages, but has the transcending quality of the unexpected.

Tactical surprise is usually the reward of the daring, the imaginative, and the ingenious. It will rarely be gained by recourse to the obvious.

Chapter IX: *Decisions*

⎧⎧

A leader must meet battle situations with
timely and unequivocal decisions.

⎧⎧

DECISIONS IN WAR are difficult. More often than not they must be made in obscure and uncertain situations. Frequently the time at which a decision should be made presents a greater problem than the decision itself.

Solving map problems, particularly those which depict detailed and definite situations, is only slight preparation for the mental ordeals of war. The map problem has an important place in military instruction, but by itself it is inadequate. Academic knowledge and a stored-up accumulation of facts are not enough on the battlefield. The leader must know when to act as well as what to do in certain well-defined situations, but above all he must be willing to accept responsibility for positive action in blind situations. To develop these qualities to the full, map problems should be supplemented by exercises with troops in conditions more closely approximating those of actual combat.

⚐   ⚐   ⚐

EXAMPLE 1. On the morning of August 22, 1914, the French 5th Colonial Brigade, with a battalion of field artillery attached, marched north through the Ardennes Forest with the destination of Neufchâteau. Other French columns marched north on both flanks. Although these columns were only a few miles apart, the heavy woods virtually precluded intercommunication.

The advance guard of the 5th Brigade consisted of a regiment of infantry, less one battalion. Orders directed that the enemy be attacked if met. Although hostile cavalry patrols had been encountered, no strong enemy force was believed near.

Shortly before noon the brigade neared Neufchâteau. Billet-

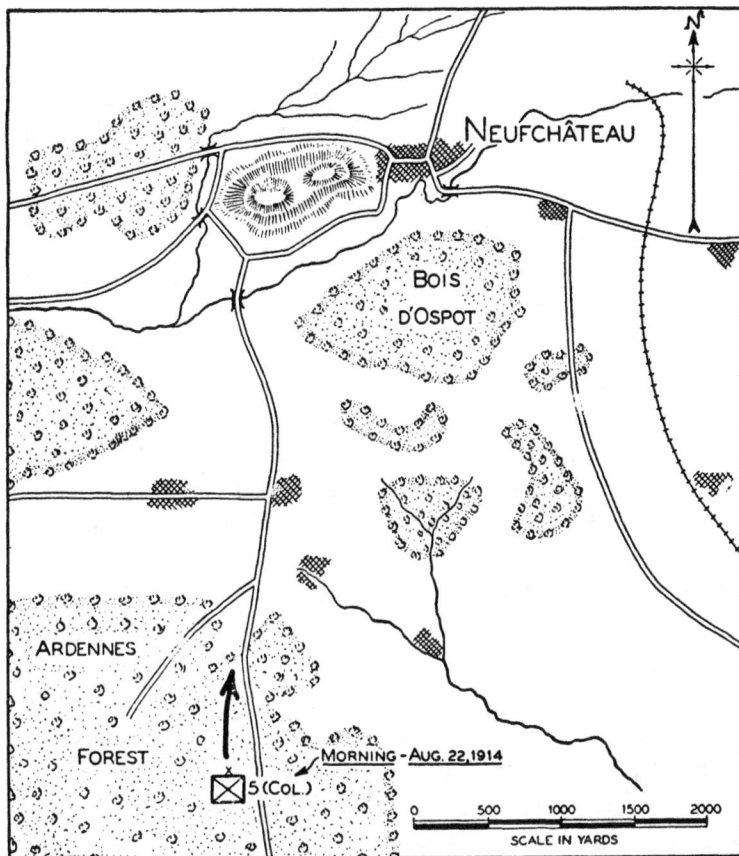

Example 1

ing parties moved ahead of the main body to enter the town.

Suddenly the advance party darted up the hill west of Neuf-château and began firing to the north and northwest. The point was heard firing near Neufchâteau. A company of the support, which was then nearing the bridge west of the Bois d'Ospot, turned to the right and moved rapidly into the wood. The rest of the support moved up the hill west of Neufchâteau. At this time the head of the main body was near the north edge of the forest marked Ardennes on the sketch.

It was now discovered that the first firing had been directed at a long train of vehicles moving west on the road from Neufchâteau and on a squadron of hostile cavalry halted in close formation near the tail of the train. An enemy force, strength undetermined, was now seen approaching Neufchâteau from the east. The reserve of the advance guard immediately attacked to the northeast into the Bois d'Ospot.

The brigade commander promptly directed his main body to assemble near the north edge of the forest and ordered his artillery into positions from which it could assist the advance guard, cover the deployment of the main body and support the attack. This decision was made a few minutes after contact had been gained and before any but the vaguest information had been received.

The support of the advance guard, on the hill west of Neufchâteau, was now attacked in force from the east, the northeast, the north and the west.

The German attack that came from the east struck the Bois d'Ospot and, after a brief but bloody fight, drove the reserve of the French advance guard to the southwest.

Even before all his main body cleared the forest, the brigade commander issued an attack order. He had four battalions. Three would attack the Bois d'Ospot from the south and southeast. Their attack would be supported by artillery. The fourth battalion would remain in brigade reserve.

Just as these units moved out it became evident that the situation on the left was desperate. The force on the hill west of Neufchâteau was fighting for its life. It was being enveloped from two sides. The brigade commander therefore diverted one battalion to meet this menace to his left and continued his planned attack with the other two.

The main attack encountered strong German forces moving

from the east and the French enveloping movement was itself enveloped. The attack stopped. The two assault battalions now found themselves in a serious situation. Much stronger forces were holding them in front and striking them in flank. The Germans were employing a great deal of artillery. To prevent the threatened envelopment of his right, the French brigade commander committed his reserve. At about 5:00 p.m. he established a position on the line of villages south and southwest of the Bois d'Ospot and passed to the defensive. The German attack was stopped.

From "Neufchâteau," by Colonel A. Grasset, French Army.

DISCUSSION. During the period considered, the decisions of the French advance-guard and brigade commanders met the actual situations. Indeed, they are much like approved solutions to a map problem in spite of the fact that they were based on little information.

What happened was this: The French brigade stumbled into the bulk of the German XVIII Reserve Corps which was marching across its front from east to west. Thereafter events moved rapidly.

The action taken by the advance guard was on the initiative of its commander. The brigade commander acted with equal celerity: although the situation was vague, he immediately assembled his main body and issued a hasty order prescribing a coordinated attack. He put in all his artillery. He gave weight to his main effort. Just as this attack moved out, it became evident that the advance gaurd would be routed or captured before the blow at the enemy right could take effect. The brigadier therefore took the necessary action to cover the left flank, even at the expense of weakening his main effort. When the main attack was enveloped, the brigade reserve—which the commander had hoped to employ for the decisive blow—was used to protect the right flank. The brigade then passed to the defensive and held.

The brigade commander did not wait for the ideal situation to develop. Instead, he met the recurring crises of the action as they arose. Even when the situation developed unfavorably and entirely at variance with what he had expected, his prompt and intelligent decisions were equal to the occasion. As a result his brigade fought the bulk of a corps to a standstill!

✱   ✱   ✱

EXAMPLE 2. On the morning of July 15, 1918, the 1st Battalion of the U. S. 30th Infantry held the forward area in the 30th Infantry sector south of the Marne. Companies B and C, as outpost, were disposed by platoons close to the river bank. The remainder of the battalion, with Company K and some machine guns attached, held positions in the woods north of the Fossoy—Crézancy Road.

A German bombardment began about midnight. Neither the battalion commander nor the regimental commander received any definite information for several hours. (A more detailed account of this action is given in Examples 2-A, 2-B, and 2-C of Chapter II.)

About 5:00 a.m. the battalion commander made the following report to the regimental commander:

The losses of the battalion have been very great.

Companies B and C (the outpost) are a total loss and survivors of these companies are stragglers.

Communication within the battalion is impossible.

Germans have crossed the river and are now on the south side of the Marne.

The enemy's rolling barrage has passed Companies A, K, and D, but the enemy does not appear to be following the barrage.

He then recommended that the artillery fire its SOS barrage (prepared concentrations within the American position to the south of the railroad line).

From the personal experience monograph of Major Fred L. Walker, who commanded the 1st Battalion of the 30th Infantry.

DISCUSSION. The regimental commander had to make a de-

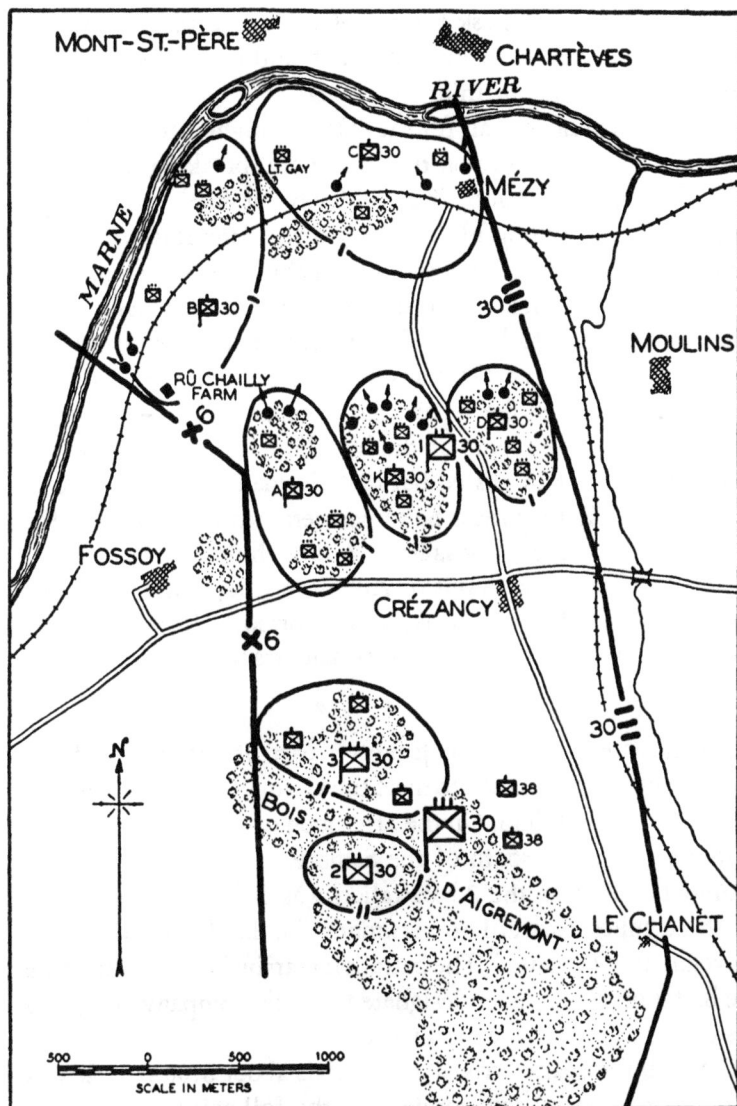

Example 2

cision here. Should he ask for this SOS barrage which could be put down in a matter of minutes, or should he wait just a little longer before doing anything?

If he decided not to call for the SOS, he might miss the chance of bringing effective fire on the enemy and breaking up the attack. On the other hand, if he did have it fired, the barrage might be in the wrong place; it might hit American troops, or it might waste ammunition by falling behind the Germans.

This was far from an ideal situation, but none-the-less it was a situation that had to be met. To the regimental commander it seemed clear that the Germans were somewhere south of the Marne. He accepted the report that Companies B and C were a loss. He noted the report of the battalion commander that the German barrage had passed but that Germans were not following. Presumably they must be somewhere near the railroad. He asked for the barrage. It was fired. Although it did inflict casualties on at least two platoons of American troops who were still holding out on the river bank, it is reported to have played an important part in stopping the German attack.

✦ ✦ ✦

EXAMPLE 3. The 70th Infantry, part of the French Fifth Army, had marched north to meet the German enveloping movement through Belgium. On the afternoon of August 20, 1914, it halted a few miles south of the Sambre.

About 5:00 p.m. the 2d Battalion was ordered to move two or three miles forward to Arsimont "to hold the bridges at Auvelais and Tamines." The battalion marched at once. En route the battalion commander designated the 5th Company "to guard the bridge at the village of Auvelais."

The 5th Company arrived at Auvelais about 8:00 p.m. It was dark. The company commander had the following surprises:

(1) Auvelais was not the village he expected, but a sprawling town of some 10,000 inhabitants. His company, figuratively speaking, was lost in it.

(2) There was not one bridge to guard, but eight, and these were scattered along some three miles in a bend of the Sambre.

(3) The town extended to the north bank of the Sambre in a populous suburb. The company had been formally forbidden to cross the river. All of Auvelais was extremely low and com-

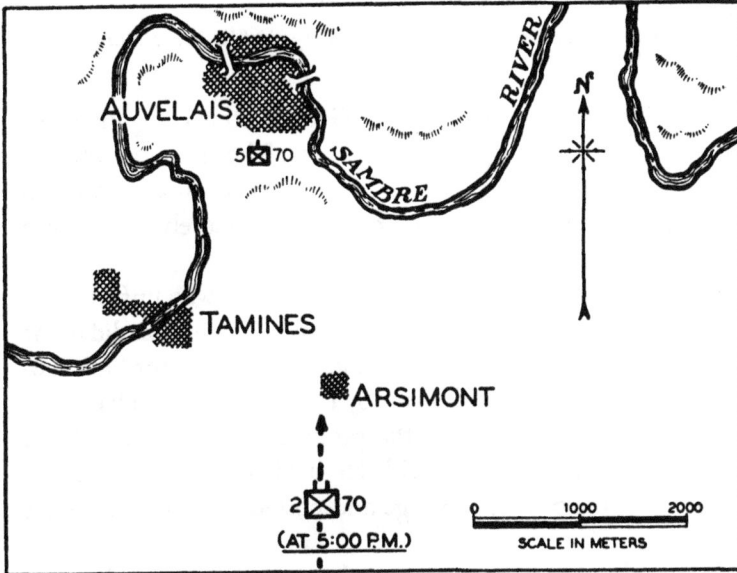

Example 3

pletely commanded by high ground on the north bank where good cover abounded.

At 10:00 p.m. the captain of the 5th Company received a curt message: "You can expect to be attacked early tomorrow morning."

He got his battalion commander on the telephone and explained the situation.

"The main bridge and the bend of the river at Auvelais are down in a hole. My company will be shot here like rats in a trap. I request authority to move to the north bank and organize the defense there."

"No, the order is strict not to go north of the Sambre."

"Well, then, I request authority to organize the defense on the higher ground just south of Auvelais."

"No, the order is to guard the bridges, not to abandon them."

The company commander was promised one more rifle company, and with that he had to be content.

From an article by Captain Pots, French Army, in "La Revue d'Infanterie," December, 1929.

DISCUSSION. Before seeing a German, this company commander had several unpleasant surprises. The situation differed completely from what he had expected. Never in all his training had he been placed in anything even remotely resembling this situation and told to solve it.

Everything appeared illogical. The terrain was unfavorable and his force was too small. Even the two solutions that did occur to him were rejected by the battalion commander, for both violated rigid injunctions laid down by the army commander.

There was no use fighting the problem; it had to be solved. Therefore he did what he could. He held the bulk of his force in reserve at the principal bridge and posted small guards at the other seven.

Skirmishing began at 8:00 a.m. the next morning and gradually developed into an attack. The French held the town until about 3:30 p.m.

✓   ✓   ✓

EXAMPLE 4. On the night of October 8-9, 1918, the U. S. 117th Infantry held a position near Prémont, with its three battalions disposed in depth and generally facing east. Late in the afternoon of the 8th it had been passed through by fresh troops who were reported to have advanced the line somewhat to the east.

Early on the morning of October 9 the regiment received an order directing it to attack in the direction of Busigny at 5:30

a.m. There had been no warning order and there was no time for the regiment to issue a written attack order. To launch the attack at the scheduled hour, the regiment decided to jump off in the formation in which it stood—the 2d Battalion in assault,

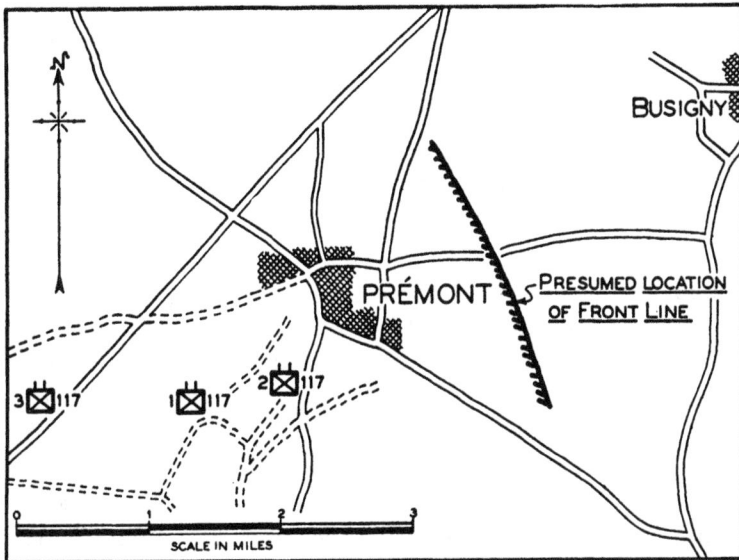

Example 4

the 1st in support, and the 3d in reserve. The order would have to be telephoned.

And then the trouble began. The line from the regiment to the 2d Battalion had gone out. However, the 2d Battalion was still connected with the 1st, so it was arranged that the 1st Battalion should relay the order to the 2d. But before the order to the 1st Battalion was completed that wire also failed. The hour of attack, the general plan, the general direction of attack, the objective and the boundaries (in part only) had been transmitted before the line went dead. This message was received at 3:40 a.m. —one hour and fifty minutes before H hour.

While checking map coördinates, the 1st Battalion found that an error had been made in defining boundaries. The line of departure was indefinite; it was believed to be some three miles away but its exact location was unknown. Information of the enemy was lacking and no information was at hand as to the proposed activities of reserves and adjacent troops. The hour was growing late. It was obvious that much time would be lost in relaying the order to the 2d Battalion. It narrowed down to the question of whether or not the 2d Battalion would arrive in time.

The following steps were taken in the 1st Battalion:

At the first word that an advance was to be made, company commanders were ordered to report in person at battalion headquarters. The sergeant-major attended to this while the message from regiment was still coming in.

At the same time the adjutant notified the 2d Battalion by telephone that it was instructed to attack and that details would be sent as soon as received. At this point wire connection with the regiment went out.

The battalion intelligence officer and his detachment were immediately sent out to locate the line of departure, obtain as much information as possible and send back guides along the route of approach. This officer, who had heard the telephone conversation, had his detachment ready and moved out at once.

It was apparent that the 2d Battalion, although closer to the front, might be late. Since the 1st Battalion had been able to start its preparations earlier, it was decided that it would also march to the front and, if it arrived before the 2d Battalion, take over the assault rôle. In other words, both battalions started forward, the one arriving first to be in assault, the other in support.

Both battalions arrived at the same time; each one had two companies available and two far to the rear. Consequently the attack was made with battalions abreast, each battalion initially employing one company in assault and one in support. The barrage which had started was overtaken. The rear companies finally got up and the attack drove forward successfully.

As the result of a lucky guess, the attack seems to have been made in the proper zone.

From the personal experience monograph of Major Charles W. Dyer, Infantry.

DISCUSSION. The situation confronting the 1st Battalion was abnormal and illogical. The troops should have been warned earlier. Orders should have been received sooner. At the very least the battalion should have been given the location of its line of departure and told what its boundaries were. The communications do not appear to have been well handled. Obviously there are many things to criticize.

By the terms of the order the 1st Battalion was in support. If the attack failed to jump off in time, it would not bear the onus. But this battalion does not appear to have spent any time dallying with the consoling thought that it was not responsible. The essential feature of the plan was that a battalion of the 117th Infantry attack at 5:30 a.m. from some ill-defined location. Since it looked as if the 2d Battalion might not be able to reach the jump-off line in time, the commander of the 1st Battalion decided to be prepared to pinch-hit for it if necessary. What matter if it were the 1st Battalion or the 2d? Either one was capable of launching an attack.

Therefore, acting in harmony with the general plan, the 1st Battalion disregarded the attack order, agreed on a solution with the 2d Battalion, and started on its way. A decision was taken that met the situation. Perhaps there are things in this decision that could be criticized. If events had gone seriously wrong the 1st Battalion commander might have been in a tough spot. If we sit down in the peace and quiet of a map-problem room and meditate for an hour or two, we may reach a better solution. This battalion commander had to make a decision quickly. He did, and as a result the 117th Infantry attacked with the right number of troops at approximately the right place and time.

EXAMPLE 5. On April 7, 1916, during the Verdun offensive, the 1st Battalion of the German 22d Infantry attacked a French strong point on a hill southeast of Haucourt.

The 1st Company was to attack straight toward 289. The 3d Company was to attack toward 288, then wheel to the west, taking the strong point in rear. The 156th Infantry was to attack on the left of the 3d Company and the 10th Reserve Infantry was to attack on the right of the 1st Company.

The 3d Company overcame resistance near 288 and faced generally west as shown on the sketch. One platoon, commanded by Ensign Bötticher, was sent to 287 with the mission of protecting the flank of the 3d Company.

Upon arrival at 287 the following situation confronted the platoon leader:

He heard heavy firing near 289 and concluded that the 1st Company was hotly engaged.

He saw that the 3d Company was confronted by a French force at A, and that this force seemed to be preparing for a counter-attack.

Near 292 the 10th Reserve Infantry was engaged in a fight with the French and seemed to be making no progress.

Near B he saw French troops marching toward the strong point, and near C another group resting in reserve.

The German platoon had not been seen by the French.

Bötticher decided to attack the French reserves at C. This he did, scoring a complete surprise and capturing a French colonel, two captains and 150 men. Reorganizing rapidly, the platoon then attacked the French opposing the 10th Reserve Infantry near 292. The attack was successful and several hundred additional prisoners were taken.

From an article in "Kriegskunst im Wort und Bild," 1931.

DISCUSSION. This is an example of a security detachment that accomplished its mission and more by means of an attack.

The leader reasoned that the French moving forward near B

could be dealt with by the 1st Company, since the French direction of advance was such that they would meet the 1st Company frontally.

He considered the advisability of aiding the 3d Company by

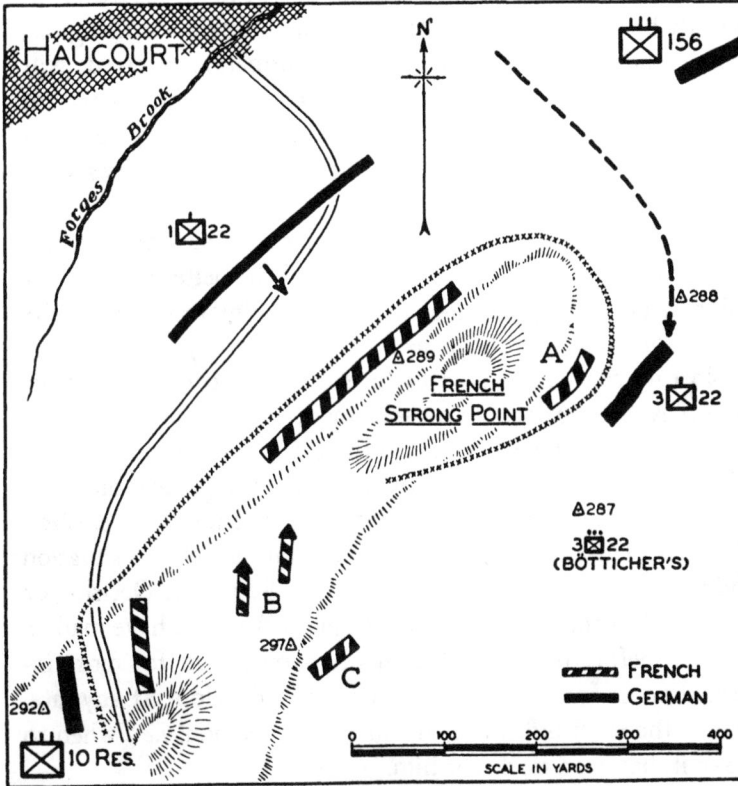

Example 5

firing on the enemy at A, but this would leave the company still exposed to the danger of being attacked in rear by the French reserves at C. These reserves constituted the chief threat. Once they were disposed of the whole problem would be solved.

Ensign Bötticher's estimate of the situation was correct, and his prompt action met with spectacular success.

✓   ✓   ✓

CONCLUSION. Decisions will have to be made regardless of the fact that the situation may be vague, abnormal or illogical. Each event that occurs, each bit of information received, will cause the leader to ask himself, "Shall I continue with my present plan and dispositions, or is it now necessary for me to give a new order?" Whatever the answer to this question, it involves a decision on the part of the commander.

Even if information be lacking, the leader must produce decisions. In most cases a poor decision will be better than no decision at all. Negligence and hesitation are more serious faults than errors in choice of means.

No rule can tell us how to time decisions correctly. All we can say is that the decision must be made early enough for action based upon it to be effective. On the other hand, it must not be taken prematurely, lest it fail to meet a changing situation.

How can we learn to make decisions that meet the existing situation? Uusally our map problems state a definite situation and then conclude, "It is now 10:00 a.m. Required: Decision of Captain A at this time." Possibly Captain A would have made a decision before this time. Perhaps he would wait for more information or for a more ideal situation to develop. At any rate, one of the most difficult elements of his decision, *i.e.,* when to make it, has been made for him.

Problems and exercises in which the principal element is the time at which decisions are made should be included in peacetime instruction. By such means the natural tendency to temporize in obscure situations may be counteracted and leaders trained to take timely action.

In war, situations will frequently arise which are not covered by express orders of superiors. Perhaps the situation will appear entirely different from that which higher authority seemed to have in mind when it issued orders. The subordinate may feel that literal compliance with orders received would be disastrous. In such cases he must act in accordance with the general plan. He must take the responsibility and make a decision.

Marshal Foch said:

> There is no studying on the battlefield. It is then simply a case of doing what is possible, to make use of what one knows and, in order to make a little possible, one must know much.

Chapter X: *The Plan*

*A unit must be engaged in accordance with
a definite plan. It must not be permitted to
drift aimlessly into battle.*

I T REQUIRES perfect performance by a leader to insure that
his unit is committed to action according to a clear, workable plan and under favorable conditions. Indeed, it may require
extreme energy and forethought to insure that his command is
engaged according to any plan at all.

We consider it axiomatic that in war there will always be
a plan. But history is replete with instances where organizations have drifted into battle for no particular reason and with
no particular plan. It is true that the leader's plan may, and
frequently will, change with changes in the situation, but the
motivating idea behind it must remain. "Battles of which one
cannot say why they were fought and with what purpose, are the
usual resource of ignorance," said Napoleon. And this indictment holds true for any pointless maneuver in the presence of
the enemy.

The effective coördination of the means at hand for the ac-
complishment of some desired end has been a major problem
since wars began. Too frequently the problem has not been
solved and splendid fighting units have been expended in pur-
poseless effort or have failed to accomplish anything at all by
reason of masterly inaction.

> Lord Chatham with his sword undrawn
> Was waiting for Sir Richard Strachan.
> Sir Richard, longing to be at 'em,
> Was waiting too. For whom? Lord Chatham.

Hundreds of similar situations are revealed in the World
War. Operations of the British at Suvla Bay in August, 1915,
are particularly reminiscent of the two fiery noblemen.

It has been well said that "in war all is simple, but it is the simple which is difficult." Misunderstandings, misleading information, late orders, the fact that troops are not actually where the higher commanders think they are, often result in units being engaged aimlessly. But, on the other hand, subordinate leaders as well as their superiors can do much to mitigate such evils by forethought, by careful planning, and by good troop leading.

In every operation there must run from the highest to the lowest unit the sturdy life-line of a guiding idea; from this will be spun the intricate web that binds an army into an invincible unit embodying a single thought and a single goal.

✶   ✶   ✶

EXAMPLE 1. On July 29, 1918, the 3d Battalion of the U. S. 47th Infantry (attached to the 168th Infantry) had advanced to a position in the valley of the Ourcq south and southwest of Sergy. The enemy had been steadily driven back. Now he occupied positions a short distance north of the Ourcq.

The 3d Battalion knew little of the situation except that it had suffered heavily from German artillery and machine-gun fire during the advance to the Ourcq. Some American troops seemed to be on the south slopes of Hill 212.

The battalion, with units intermingled, was extended in one long line under cover of the woods along the stream. Most of Company L had become separated from the battalion. This is how the situation appeared to a platoon leader of Company M:

> Runners were sent to locate battalion headquarters and ask for orders. Of three runners sent out only one returned. He brought back word that both of the majors [there were two with the battalion] had been wounded and that the captain of Company I was in command of the battalion. We were to organize our position and remain where we were until further orders.
>
> The company commander [of Company M] decided to go to battalion headquarters. He came back in an hour with the information that Sergy was still occupied by Germans, but that patrols were working into it; that we would make no attempt to sort out companies until

after daylight the next morning. The present position was organized for defense.

It was now getting dark. Fire was decreasing. It was easier to move about. Rations were collected and ammunition distributed. We were now advised that the new battalion commander had been killed and that the captain of Company M would take command of the battalion. The runner who brought this message was told to notify all officers that the new battalion commander would remain with Company M, and to inform them of the location of his command post.

There was a shell crater about fifty feet in front of our line. Since it gave much better observation to front and flanks, the battalion commander and I went out there and spent the night. Save for gas alarms, the night was uneventful. We received one report from a patrol to the effect that the troops on our left were the 1st Battalion of the 47th Infantry. This was our first inkling that the 1st Battalion was in action with us.

At 7:30 a.m. a runner from the 168th Infantry located us and directed the battalion commander to report with his officers to the commanding officer of the 168th Infantry. He stated that we could find the headquarters by following the creek to the other side of the village. The battalion commander took me with him. On the way we picked up four officers. We reported to a major of the 168th Infantry southwest of Hill 212, who gave us the following oral order:

"You will form your battalion and move through the village. When you come to the sunken road leading out of the village, move due north, keeping the road as your right guide. A barrage will be fired. Keep as close to it as possible. You will find a lot of artillery and machine-gun opposition, but do not let it stop you. Continue the advance to the next village, Nesles, and consolidate your line on the north side of the village. The barrage starts at 8:00 a.m. Move out promptly at 9:00 a.m."

It then being after 8:00 a.m. and no barrage being fired, the question was asked if the time to start the barrage had been changed. We were informed that there had been some delay in receipt of the firing data, but that the barrage should be working beyond the village at that time.

We then returned and organized three platoons from Companies I, K, and M. I say platoons because the strength averaged five squads. (There were some men of the battalion not included in these three platoons. They were on the left under officers of Company K. A runner was sent to this group with an order to advance on the left of the village and join the battalion at the northern exit.)

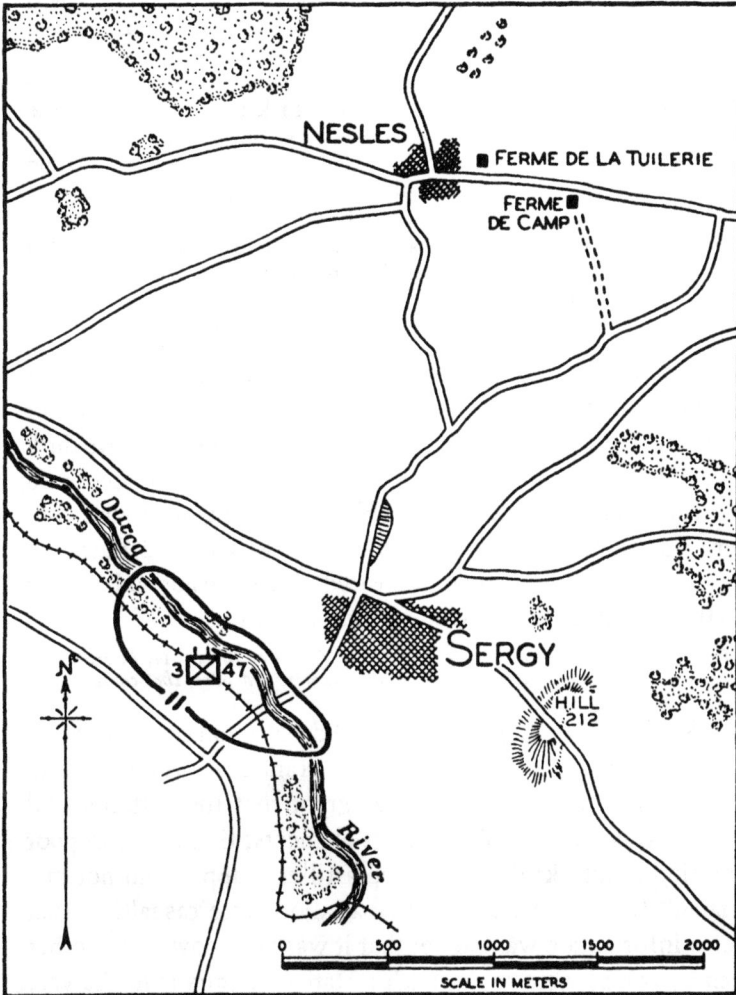

Example 1

The battalion then moved out in column of squads in the order I, K, and M. No battalion attack order had been issued. We moved through the village with no difficulty but came under machine-gun fire as we reached the northern exit. As the two leading companies moved up the sunken road, I could see that quite a few of the men were being knocked down, so I took my company into the field on the left. Here, too, we received considerable fire. I put the company into skirmish line. I could not locate the battalion commander or his adjutant although I had seen them get out of the road when the leading units began to get into trouble. The following day I learned that the battalion commander had been killed and that his adjutant died of wounds that night. I also learned that the leader of the first company was badly wounded and that the leader of the second company was dead.

Company M advanced some 500 yards in about two hours. At the end of this time the company commander, seeing no other troops near, stopped the attack and held his position. At dusk he received orders to withdraw Company M to the sunken road near the village, which he did. Here the survivors found that there was some conflict of opinion as to why the 3d Battalion had attacked. Indeed, there appeared to be considerable doubt whether it had been intended to attack at all.

From the personal experience monograph of Captain Howard N. Merrill, who commanded a platoon of Company M, 47th Infantry, and later, that company.

DISCUSSION. The attack of the 3d Battalion conveys an impression of utter aimlessness. Let us grant that orders came in late and were incomplete. Let us grant that the battalion did not have time to assemble all of its elements; that it was in poor condition to attack; that promised artillery support did not materialize; that the majors of the battalion were casualties; that enemy information was vague; that it was not known what other friendly troops were to do. Such a state of affairs is in the very nature of war. In this case it appears that some of the adverse factors could have been avoided, but let us forget that for the moment.

The attack order received by the battalion can be summed up as, "Attack at 9:00 a.m. toward Nesles with your right on the road." What the companies of the battalion now needed to know was "What part are we to play in this battalion attack? Where do we deploy? What company is on our right? Who furnishes flank protection? Who is in reserve?" In other words, a battalion attack order, no matter how brief, was desperately needed. Instead, the battalion commander issued what was, in effect, a march order.

The battalion moved to the north edge of Sergy in column of squads and there came under fire. At once everyone did what seemed best to him. There was no coördination of effort—no plan—and the battalion promptly ceased to function as a unit. It drifted blindly and aimlessly into battle. Company M, on its own, moved to the left and attacked, and for the rest of the day labored under the impression that it was fighting the war single-handed.

A brief order regulating the deployment before the battalion came under fire would unquestionably have made a great difference. That the time for this was short was no excuse. An attack should have been anticipated. The enemy was being driven back and the battalion was close to his position. What could be expected but an attack?

It is obvious that the battalion commander should have made a point of getting in touch with the 168th Infantry, to which he was attached, in order to learn the plans for the next day. Also, much could have been done during the night toward effecting a reorganization of the battalion. So, too, the most perfunctory reconnaissance would have disclosed the fact that the Germans were still close at hand; this would have averted the movement in the sunken road.

The battalion was in its first fight. It lost twenty-five officers and 462 men. Its courage was marked, but courage is not a substitute for experience and training.

✓   ✓   ✓

EXAMPLE 2. Late on the afternoon of July 25, 1918, the

U. S. 167th Infantry completed the relief of elements of the 26th Division northeast of Courpoil. The 1st and 3d Battalions, each with a machine-gun company attached, took over positions in the front line; the 2d Battalion was held in reserve near the north end of Etang de la Lagette.

Enemy artillery fire was heavy during the night and continued throughout the next day.

Early on the 26th, front-line battalion commanders sent patrols forward to gain contact and locate the enemy line. At 8:00 a.m. the patrols returned. They reported that the enemy line was only four to five hundred yards in front of the American position and that it bristled with machine guns. Patrols from both battalions had suffered casualties. Since the 26th Division had stated that the enemy was four or five kilometers away, this report was immediately forwarded.

The same morning, the regimental and battalion commanders inspected the front line. During this inspection the colonel oriented his battalion and company commanders on a proposed plan of attack. In fact, he issued what amounted to a tentative attack order. To be put into execution it required only confirmation and designation of H-hour.

The direction of advance, probable objective (which the regimental commander said would undoubtedly be la Croix Rouge Farm and the woods beyond) and the mission of each battalion were covered. Positions from which the 37-mm. guns and the Stokes mortars were to support the attack were specified. The aid station, the ammunition distributing point, and the regimental command post were located. Each company knew what it was to do.

Shortly after these arrangements had been completed, the regimental commander was directed to report to brigade headquarters. Expecting to receive an attack order, he ordered the battalion commanders to assemble at the regimental command post to await final instructions.

The brigade attack order was issued to assembled regimental commanders at Courpoil at 4:20 p.m. The order called for a two-hour artillery preparation. H-hour was designated at 4:50 p.m. The colonel of the 167th pointed out that the artillery could

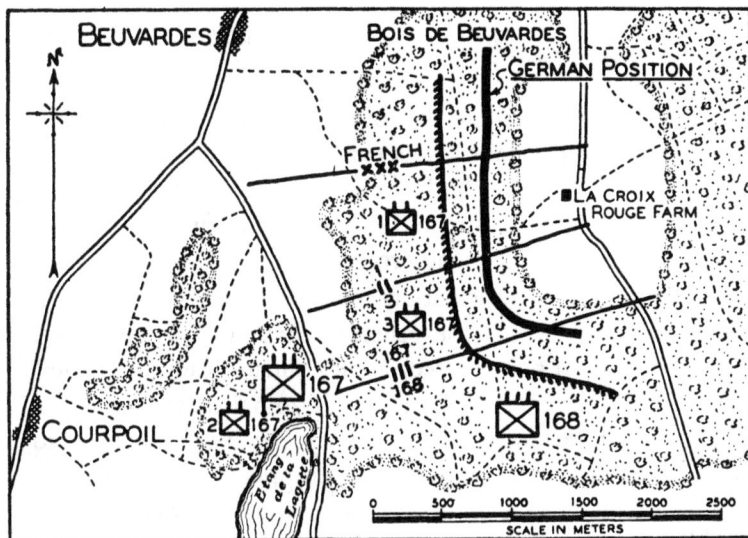

Example 2

not comply unless H-hour were changed. He further stated that the French commander on the left of the 167th said he had no orders to attack. The brigade commander replied, "We will attack as ordered, and be sure you jump off at 4:50 p.m."

The colonel of the 167th Infantry immediately issued an oral attack order to his executive who was waiting with a motorcycle and side-car to rush it to the assembled officers at the regimental command post.

The colonel's order was simply this:

> H-hour is 4:50 p.m. Tell battalion commanders to attack as we planned this morning. There will be no artillery preparation. Caution Major Carroll to place a platoon to protect his left, as I don't believe the French are going to attack.

The battalion commanders received the order at 4:42 p.m.

The regiment attacked on time, made a successful advance and captured 305 prisoners and seventy-two machine guns. The 168th Infantry on the right attacked somewhat later. The French did not attack.

From the personal experience monograph of Colonel William P. Screws, who commanded the 167th Infantry.

DISCUSSION. Owing to the foresight of its regimental commander, the 167th Infantry was enabled to attack on time. In anticipation of an attack he had carried his preparations to an extreme. Fortunately, his tentative plan was in full accord with the instructions he subsequently received.

In open warfare, anticipation to this extent is seldom advisable. Nevertheless, if the general situation clearly indicates the order that can be expected, a subordinate leader may well make many preliminary provisions. Reconnaissance, the establishment of contact with adjacent units, feeding a hot meal to the troops, issuing extra ammunition, dropping packs, providing for the instant transmission of orders, and the orientation of subordinates, are matters that need not await the receipt of an attack order. Indeed, such steps will frequently change many a laboriously logical explanation of failure to comply with orders to the succinct and satisfying phrase — "Attack launched on time."

✦ ✦ ✦

EXAMPLE 3. On October 9, 1918, the 1st Battalion, 16th Infantry, participated in an attack by the 1st Division in the Meuse-Argonne offensive. The first mission assigned the battalion was the capture of Hill 272. This hill was strongly held and several previous attacks against it had failed in the face of a well-prepared and highly-coördinated system of protective fires.

The attack was ordered to jump off at 8:30 a.m. behind a

rolling barrage. One company of the 1st Gas Regiment was directed to fire a thermite concentration on a German machine-gun nest located near Hill 176 to the left-front of the battalion.

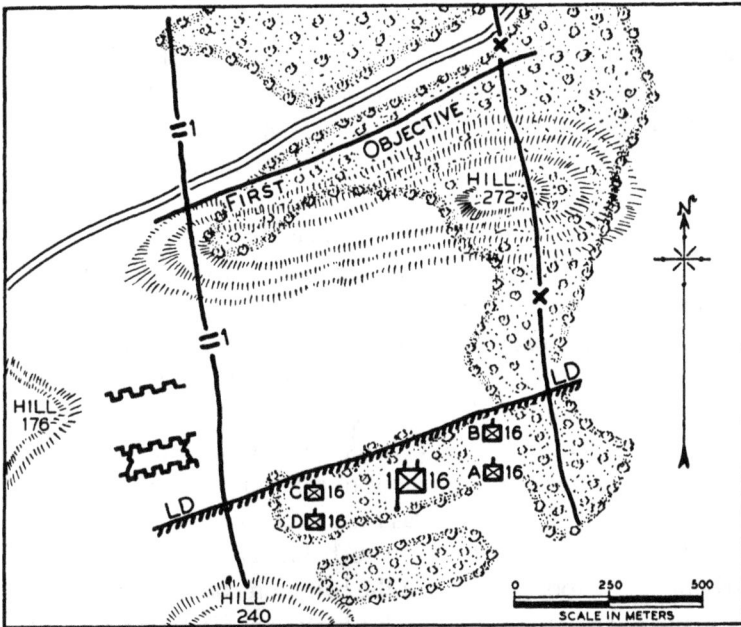

Example 3

The plan of the battalion commander was essentially as follows:

Companies B and C in assault (B on the right), each having one-half of the battalion zone.

Companies A and D in support (A on the right), to form just in rear of the line of departure. Both companies to be well-closed up to escape the German protective barrage known to be registered on the forward slope of Hill 240.

To charge Companies A and B with the protection of the right flank.

Company C to be particularly alert for activity near Hill 176 in the zone of the unit on the left.

Aid station in a shell hole to the right front of Hill 240.

Command post between Companies A and D. The battalion commander to advance initially with Company C.

Although the attack jumped off in a thick fog, the Germans realized that something was afoot and called for their defensive barrage. This came down in rear of the support companies, both of which held their position until the assault companies had gained distance.

Soon after the attack started, Company C came under heavy machine-gun fire from Hill 176. The left half of the company wheeled toward the hill and vanished in the fog; the other half continued to the north. The battalion commander immediately confirmed this action, directing the left assault and left support platoons to continue their efforts against Hill 176 and then to advance, protecting the left flank of the battalion. When Company D came up he ordered it to continue toward Hill 272, since the capture of that hill was the battalion's main mission.

In the fog companies lost contact, but all moved forward. Arriving at the foot of Hill 272 the battalion commander halted Company D and checked up on his battalion. He found that all companies had arrived at the foot of the steep slope. Company B, on the right, had advanced straight to its proper position and Company A had come up abreast of it on the left. Two platoons of Company C were to the left of Company A, and Company D was some distance to the left of these.

Having determined the disposition of his companies, the battalion commander issued oral orders for them to move forward and capture that part of the hill in their immediate front. Following this they were to spread out to the flanks until contact was complete within the battalion and all parts of the hill occupied. The companies were told to get to the top of the hill and stay there at all costs.

Each company gained a foothold on the hill by working small groups up the hillside between German machine-gun positions.

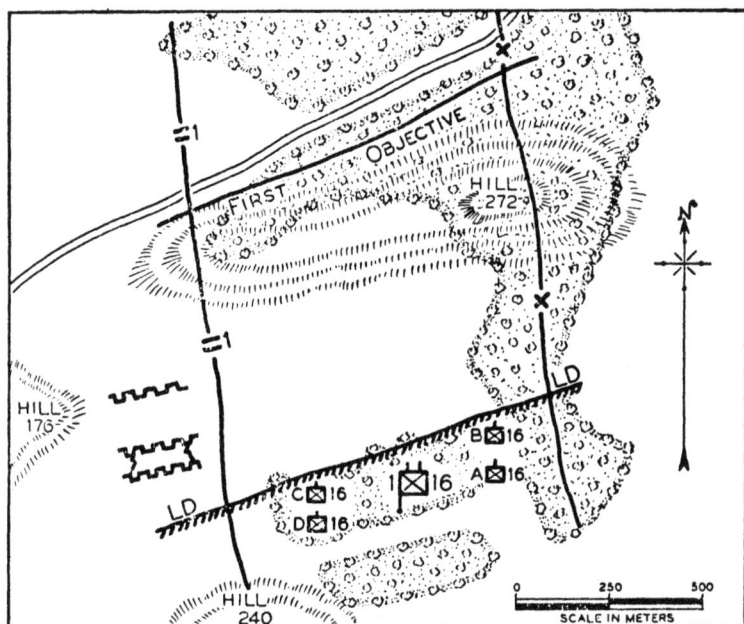

Example 3

The footholds thus gained were then enlarged by a continuation of this infiltration. At 11:00 a.m. the hill fell.

From the personal experience monograph of Major Charles W. Ryder, who commanded the 1st Battalion of the 16th Infantry.

DISCUSSION. The attack of this battalion appears to be just another frontal push. The artillery fired and the infantry moved forward to exploit the effect of the fire. The fog was a bit of luck. What is there noteworthy about the affair? There is this: the battalion was commanded. It acted according to a plan.

The plan was not merely a routine, stereotyped announcement of which two companies would be in assault and which two in support. It contained several ideas. First, it foresaw where the German protective fires would be dropped and arranged to mass the battalion well forward so that even the support companies would escape this fire. Nothing revolutionary, perhaps, but still not the usual thing.

Second, the battalion commander foresaw what was going to happen on his left. Accordingly, he took action to protect this flank by orders to Company C and by personal intervention there at the start of the fight.

Finally, at the foot of Hill 272 we see the battalion commander getting his units in hand. We hear him revise his plan, bringing it up to date, thereby insuring a battalion blow instead of a series of haphazard, disjointed efforts.

Thus, even in a frontal attack behind a rolling barrage, one of those cut-and-dried "once more, dear friends, into the breach" affairs, there is need for an infantry unit to have a plan and there is room for its commander to have an idea.

✦   ✦   ✦

CONCLUSION. We have examined a case or two where units have drifted into battle. We have seen what happened to them. Undoubtedly it would be going too far to say that every unit that becomes engaged without a definite plan is slated for defeat, for occasionally sheer valor is able to surmount passive leadership. In such cases, we have a "soldiers' battle." But even in those rare instances where such battles achieve a certain measure of success, they are seldom decisive since full exploitation is impossible. Regardless of the occasional exception, the fact remains that planless action is an open invitation to disaster.

We have examined other situations where the foresight of the leader enabled the unit to attack under conditions far more favorable than would otherwise have been the case. In these, success was achieved not by transcendent flashes of genius but merely by having an intelligent plan.

Insuring teamwork and coördinating the attack is the responsibility of the leader. Whatever the method adopted, he must guard against a disjointed, piecemeal effort. He can best accomplish this by keeping ahead of events instead of letting them drag him along in their wake.

It is always well to keep in mind that one fights to gain a definite end—not simply to fight.

Chapter XI: *Orders*

*An order must clearly express the will of
the leader and must fit the situation.*

IT IS FAR more important that orders be written clearly and
issued promptly than that they be correct in form. With well-
trained troops, little time, and poor maps, orders will tend to be
general. Especially should details be eliminated when time is
short and changes in the situation are probable before the order
can be executed.

With plenty of time, excellent maps, and troops lacking in
experience, more details may be advisable.

✔   ✔   ✔

EXAMPLE 1. Early in 1915 the 4th Company of the German
256th Reserve Infantry Regiment, part of the 77th Reserve Division, took part in an attack against the Russians.

Although the bulk of the troops had no war experience, there
were one or two men in every squad who had been in battle. The
officers were veterans.

The march to the front was long and difficult, but the fact that
General von Hindenburg was in command of the operation in-
stilled great confidence in all ranks. The Germans attacked at
dawn, surprised and defeated the Russians, and promptly took
up the pursuit. The battalion of which the 4th Company was a
part found virtually no enemy to its front. Occasionally it met
a few Russians who quickly took to their heels.

The battalion marched all day and all night, first toward the
east, later toward the south. The cold was intense and the snow
deep. The men who marched at the head of the column and broke
the path through the snow had to be relieved every half hour.

In spite of the exhausting march and its attendant hardships,
morale remained high. The entire command had estimated the

situation correctly: "This long march," they said, "is to enable us to encircle the Russians. This will be another Tannenberg."

Toward morning the weary column approached the town of Eydtkuhnen. The men were rejoicing over the fine billets they

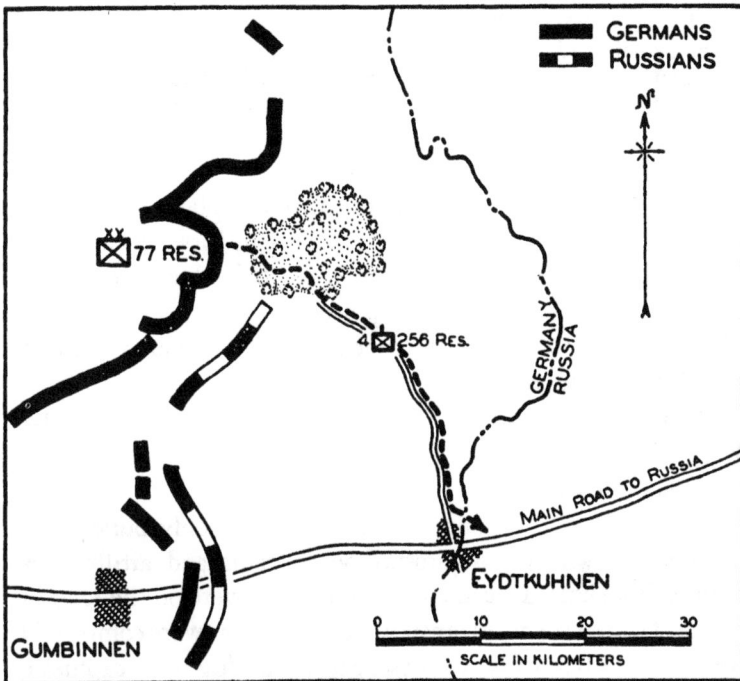

Example 1

would find there, when suddenly the column bent away from the main road and again moved east.

Some of the recruits began to growl. But the old soldiers said, "Shut up, you dumb recruits. Do you think you are cleverer than Hindenburg? If we old timers are satisfied, you ought to be. We were making marches when you were still at your mothers' apron strings."

Morning came but the troops marched on. Fog limited visibility to 100 yards or less. Suddenly the column halted. Company commanders were assembled and the battalion commander issued the following oral order:

> About two kilometers in front of us is the main road from Eydtkuhnen to Russia. It is possible that we will find the enemy on that road trying to escape to the east.
>
> The battalion advances deployed toward that road and gains possession of it. The 3d and 4th Companies lead the advance, moving on both sides of the road on which we are now marching. The 1st and 2d Companies follow at 500 meters.
>
> I will be at the head of the 1st Company.

The leading companies moved out with one platoon in assault and two in reserve. Each leading platoon sent forward two pairs of scouts. The advance had scarcely started when one of the scouts came running back and reported:

"The road is 300 meters in front of us. Russians are marching on it toward the east."

Upon receipt of this information the battalion commander merely ordered:

"Attack at once!"

The battalion, continuing its advance, suddenly burst upon the highway which was jammed with trains and artillery. A shout, a few shots, a rush, and the Germans were on the road in the midst of the enemy's transport. The Russians were completely surprised; all but a few who escaped in the fog were captured, with all their guns and vehicles.

From an address delivered at The Infantry School by Captain Adolf von Schell, German Army, who commanded the 4th Company in this action.

DISCUSSION. The battalion commander's order in this situation was brief, simple, and issued in time to permit subordinates to make their dispositions. The battalion commander did not refer to road junctions and points on the map; he spoke in terms of the ground which the troops could see. He did not go too far into the future, nor did he prescribe what would be done if various situations were encountered. He was satisfied to place his troops in such a formation that they could handle any situation that came up.

Of this order Captain von Schell says:

> Please notice that the order included no information of the enemy. We had no information of the enemy. Nevertheless as we approached the road, a decision had to be made; not because we had met the enemy, but because it was time to give an order. The situation demanded it.

✓ ✓ ✓

EXAMPLE 2. Near Cantigny on May 28, 1918, the U. S. 1st Division launched the first American attack of the World War. For obvious reasons it was highly important that their initial effort be a smashing success. To this end the operation had been planned far in advance and in the most minute detail.

The 1st Division had been holding this sector for several weeks and this, plus the excellent maps that were available, insured a high degree of familiarity with the terrain. Although seasoned in a defensive sector, the troops were still inexperienced in offensive combat.

The division order was an extremely lengthy affair that neglected no detail. Indeed, it left practically nothing to the initiative of subordinates. Finally, the attack itself was conscientiously rehearsed behind the lines on terrain that approximated the coming scene of battle. The attack succeeded.

From the personal experience monograph of Captain George E. Butler, Infantry.

DISCUSSION. The order for the Cantigny attack is an extreme example of the extent to which minute details may be prescribed in preliminary arrangements for combat. It illustrates the maximum authority a commander can exercise over a subordinate who leads a unit in combat. In war of movement, such an order would be wholly impracticable, but it was well suited to the special conditions at Cantigny. The troops were inexperienced; the objective was strictly limited; there were good maps;

there was plenty of time. Therefore the higher commander, having much at stake, exercised the maximum of authority.

✦   ✦   ✦

EXAMPLE 3. On November 22, 1914, a German corps, reinforced, had attacked westward and northwestward toward Lodz. In conjunction with other German troops it had wheeled down from the north as part of a wide envelopment. But the envelopment struck a snag: the attack was checked, communication with other German forces cut, and reports indicated superior Russian forces closing in on all sides.

The position of the German force is approximately given on the sketch. The 3d Guard Division (5th and 6th Guard Brigades) faced north and northwest. The 49th Reserve Division faced generally west and the 50th Reserve Division faced south and southwest. The troops were exhausted, and units were depleted and intermingled. The effective strength of the divisions was not over two or three thousand men each.

In this situation the commander of the German enveloping force decided to withdraw to the east of Miasga Stream, and then strike north. His written orders directed the 3d Guard Division to remain in position until midnight, and then move east of the Miasga between Bedon and Karpin. The order also directed the division to send "a flank detachment to the south of Bedon immediately." In addition to this order the Guard Division received various oral messages, and from these it understood that its mission was to secure the right flank of the corps.

Accordingly five battalions of the Guard were moved south to establish protection on that flank. The division interpreted "right flank" to mean "south flank," and the instructions to place a "flank security detachment south of Bedon" to mean that the Guard Division was responsible *for all flank security in the region south of Bedon*. Actually the corps intended that the Guard should furnish flank protection on the north.

The five battalions dispatched to the south repeatedly crossed columns of the 49th Reserve Division withdrawing to the east, and caused great confusion. The German force withdrew successfully and escaped, but this crossing of columns and the en-

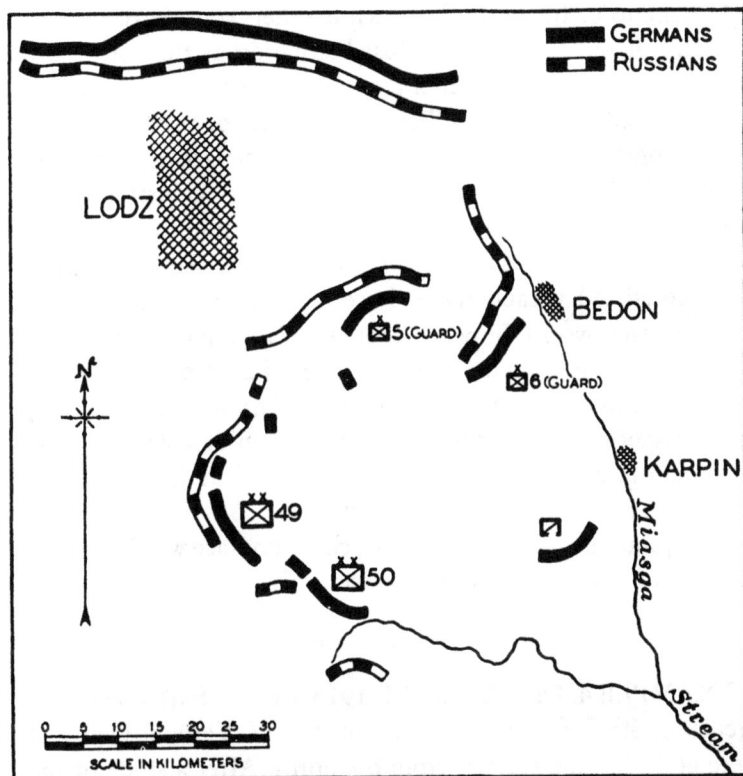

Example 3

suing confusion resulted in both the Guard and the 49th Reserve Division fighting on the following day in extremely unfavorable circumstances.

From the Reichsarchiv account and "Der Durchbruch bei Brzeziny," by Ernst Eilsberger.

DISCUSSION. A force which had been advancing west turned around and withdrew eastward. Everyone was tired and exhausted. Things were complex enough without having to puzzle over rules for writing orders. When the withdrawal began, it appears that some German headquarters considered the right flank to be the north flank, while others considered it to be the south flank. In such a confused situation as this, or in any situation where there is even a remote chance of misunderstanding, the words "right" and "left" should not be used.

The construction placed on the commonplace military expression "a flank security detachment south of" is instructive. It forcefully illustrates the dangers that may lurk in many a time-worn expression. If seasoned professionals can misinterpret their own specialized vocabulary, it is certain that nonprofessionals will fare even worse. In peace, then, special emphasis should be laid on the language employed in orders. Leaders of all grades should be trained to test every word, every phrase, every sentence, for ambiguity and obscurity. If, by even the wildest stretch of the imagination, a phrase can be tortured out of its true meaning, the chance is always present that it will be.

Short, simple sentences of simple, commonplace words, will go far toward making an order unmistakable.

*   *   *

EXAMPLE 4. On February 24, 1916, the 5th Battalion of the French 336th Infantry held a sector east of Verdun. Germans were attacking the fortress from the north. After a study of the situation the French high command decided that the troops in this sector should be withdrawn to a position closer to Verdun. Although this movement was planned for the night of February 24-25, the division order did not reach the 211th Brigade until after midnight, and orders for the front-line troops did not arrive until 4:00 a.m.

The division order went into great detail. In addition to pre-

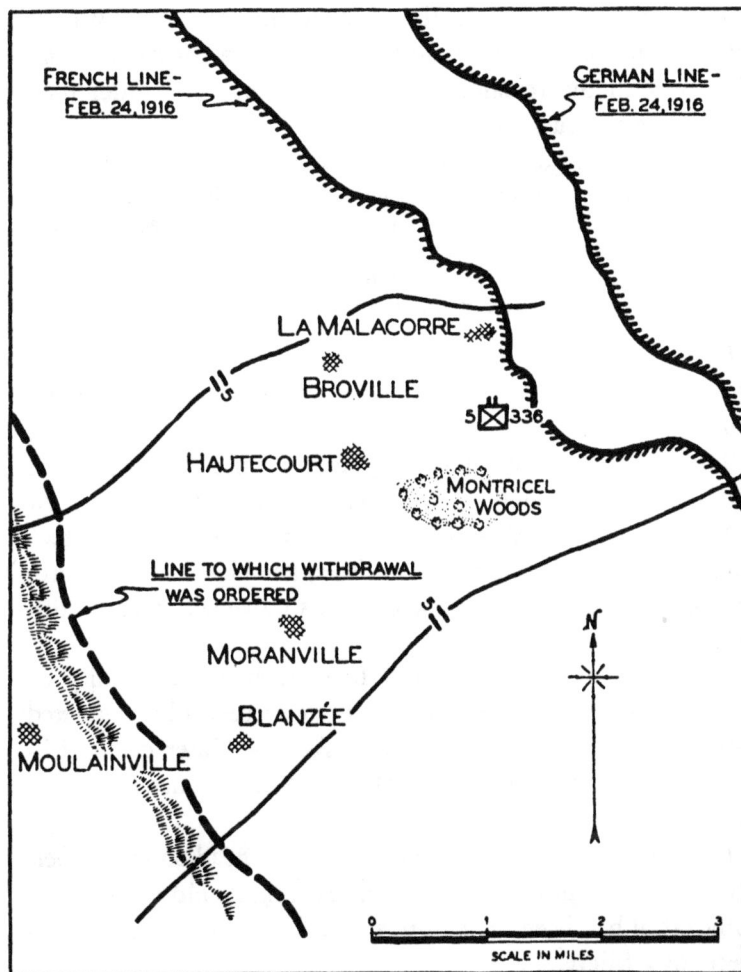

Example 4

scribing the line to which the division would withdraw and
boundaries between units, it directed two battalions of the 211th
Brigade to act as a covering force. Both battalions were
named in the order and their dispositions and duties minutely
covered. The 5th Battalion, for example, was ordered to hold

Hautecourt and Broville with one company, Montricel Woods and la Malacorre with another company, and Moranville and Blanzée with the remainder of the battalion. The order then summed up the mission in these words:

> The rôle of the covering detachments is to keep the enemy in igno-rance of our movement. To this end they will fight a delaying action, employing powerful fires. For this purpose each battalion will be assigned two platoons of machine guns. Weak outguards will be left in the front line with the mission of holding enemy patrols in check and covering the withdrawal.

In spite of the detail in which this order abounded, it was silent on one point—the hour when the covering detachment would withdraw.

The movement got under way and, from all accounts, the withdrawal of the bulk of the division was well executed. At 6:00 a.m., with the division safely out of the way, the 5th Battalion believed its mission accomplished and began its own withdrawal under cover of a snowstorm. Its movement went undiscovered.

By 10:00 a.m. the battalion had reached the vicinity of Moulainville. The movement had been successfully completed—or so the 5th Battalion thought. An hour later came disillusionment in the form of an order to return at once to the positions occupied that morning.

During the march back, the battalion ran head-on into a German attack and never succeeded in reaching its old position. Its withdrawal had been premature and had cost the French several pieces of artillery.

From Infantry Conferences by Lieutenant Colonel Touchon, French Army, at l'École Supérieure de Guerre.

DISCUSSION. Here is an order that violated two fundamentals: it was late in reaching subordinate units and it omitted one essential fact—when the covering force would withdraw. Though not stated in the order, the division commander intended this force to remain in position until *forced back* by the enemy.

The order may have seemed clear to the man who wrote it, but it was not clear to the man who had to execute it, and that is the all-important thing. One of the first things the commander of a covering force wants to know is "how long do we stay?" Upon the answer to that question depends the entire tactical course of the action.

In war, leaders of small units are usually no more than one or two jumps ahead of physical and mental exhaustion. In addition, they run a never-ending race against time. In such conditions long, highly involved orders multiply the ever-present chance of misunderstanding, misinterpretation, and plain oversight. Such orders also increase the chance of error on the part of higher commanders. In seeking to work out all details for subordinate units they may, like the division commander in this example, forget some essential. By looking too long through a microscope, they may lose sight of the big picture.

Perhaps in the above instance subordinates may be criticized for not correctly interpreting the order. But even if we concede this, the issuing authority must still shoulder the greater blame. The order should have left no room for misinterpretation. The elder Moltke's admonition, "Remember, gentlemen, an order that can be misunderstood will be misunderstood," still holds.

✓   ✓   ✓

EXAMPLE 5-A. On June 6, 1918, the 3d Battalion of the U. S. 5th Marines was due west of Belleau Wood. Late in the afternoon the captain of the 47th Company (part of the battalion) assembled his platoon leaders and issued an attack order. He briefly indicated the direction of attack, the company dispositions, and then directed:

"Get your men into position as fast as you can. We attack at 5:00 p.m."

He pulled out his watch, glanced at it and added, "It is 5:15 p.m. now."

From the personal experience monograph of Captain Raymond E. Knapp, U. S. Marine Corps.

ꚍ   ꚍ   ꚍ

EXAMPLE 5-B. The U. S. 35th Division attacked on September 26, 1918, and made a deep advance into the German lines. The division then issued an order prescribing a resumption of the attack at 8:30 a.m. on the 27th, after a three-hour artillery preparation. Among other things, the order provided that the 140th Infantry pass through the 138th Infantry. Shortly after the division order had been sent out, a corps order arrived directing the attack to be resumed all along the front at 5:30 a.m. The 35th Division attempted to change its first order. However, since some units had already been notified to attack at 8:30, it was considered impracticable to advance the time to 5:30. Therefore a compromise hour, 6:30 a.m., was decided upon.

In the midst of this confusion, the 140th Infantry received an order at 5:05 a.m. to attack at 5:30 a.m., after a five-minute barrage. The barrage failed to come down, but nevertheless the 140th moved out, passed through the 138th and attacked. The advance, unsupported by artillery, was quickly stopped with heavy casualties. The order directing the attack at 6:30 a.m. arrived too late.

From the personal experience monograph of Major Fred L. Lemmon, Infantry.

ꚍ   ꚍ   ꚍ

EXAMPLE 5-C. The 142d Infantry, part of the U. S. 36th Division, spent October 7, 1918, southeast of St. Etienne-à-Arnes, having relieved front-line troops in that vicinity. The 2d Battalion held the front line; the 1st Battalion was in support.

During the afternoon the commanding general of the 71st Brigade received an oral warning order of an attack that would jump off at 5:15 the next morning. Formal written orders, he was told, would follow. At about 8:00 p.m. he summoned his regimental commanders and passed on this meager information. Not until after midnight did the brigade receive its written orders and not until 3:00 a.m. did its written order go out to the regiments.

At about 3:30 a.m. the battalion commanders of the 142d Infantry were called to the regimental command post and given oral orders for the attack which was scheduled to jump off in one hour and forty-five minutes. There was little time left for the battalion commanders to formulate and issue orders to their companies.

Five-ten (5:10) a.m. found the four company commanders of the 1st Battalion crouched around a map spread on the ground near the entrance to the battalion command post. They had little idea what the attack was all about. They knew the 2d Battalion was ahead of them and would attack in the direction indicated by the big red arrow on the map. The names of some towns had been mentioned as possible objectives, but none of the company commanders had heard of them, or if they had they didn't remember them.

Companies A and B, A on the right, would follow the assault battalion at 1,000 meters and take advantage of whatever cover the terrain might afford. Companies C and D would follow A and B. No boundaries had been given nor was any other information forthcoming. Meanwhile, the American barrage had already started and the Germans were replying with their counter-preparation.

The attack jumped off a few minutes later and, after heavy casualties, scored a partial success. More time to acquaint the companies with the situation and tell them what was expected of them would undoubtedly have produced greater results at a smaller cost.

From the personal experience monograph of Major Ben-Hur Chastaine, who commanded Company A of the 142d Infantry; and from the monograph "Blanc Mont," prepared by the Historical Section of the War Department General Staff.

DISCUSSION. These examples are not rare exceptions. In

fact, almost every unit in the A.E.F. had the unpleasant experience of receiving orders too late. The cause was usually the same—too much time absorbed by higher echelons in preparing, issuing, and transmitting their orders.

It should always be remembered that no matter how perfect an order may be, it fails in its purpose if it does not arrive in time.

✓   ✓   ✓

EXAMPLE 6. In September, 1915, the German 256th Reserve Infantry Regiment was marching eastward into Russia. Although there had been fighting a few days before, the regiment was now meeting little resistance. This happy state of affairs was short-lived. At about 10:00 o'clock on the morning of September 20 the commander of the 3d Battalion, who had ridden forward, returned to his unit, assembled his officers and told them:

"The Russians have attacked our cavalry with strong forces and pressed it back. We are to assist it by defending a river which lies about two kilometers to our front."

The advance continued. When the battalion reached the river they found it wide and deep. On the far bank they saw a village. But they saw no Russians, no German cavalry, and heard no firing. The battalion commander then issued this order:

> Over there on the right about 500 yards away is a farm; a battalion of another German unit will be there. We defend generally along this edge of woods to the left. The 9th, 10th and 11th Companies, from right to left, will hold the front line, each with a sector 300 yards wide. The 12th Company will be in reserve behind the middle of the battalion. Our cavalry is to our left. Send patrols across the river. I will get in touch with the cavalry.

The 9th Company commander sent a patrol toward the farm and then, with a few subordinates, moved forward to the river to reconnoiter. Following his reconnaissance, he decided to place his 1st and 2d Platoons in the front line near the river, and hold

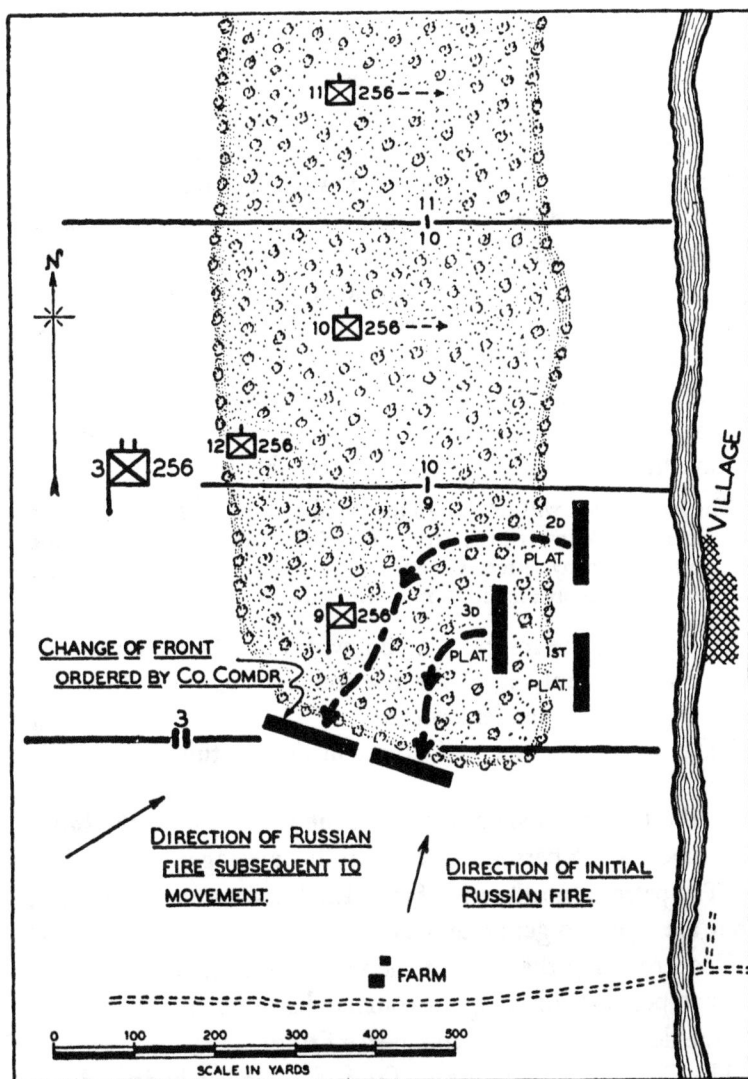

Within the figure:

11 ⊠ 256 →

11
10

10 ⊠ 256 →

3 ⊠ 256

12 ⊠ 256

10
9

2D
PLAT.

9 ⊠ 256

3D
PLAT.

1ST
PLAT.

VILLAGE

CHANGE OF FRONT
ORDERED BY CO. COMDR.

3

DIRECTION OF RUSSIAN
FIRE SUBSEQUENT TO
MOVEMENT.

DIRECTION OF INITIAL
RUSSIAN FIRE.

FARM

0   100   200   300   400   500

SCALE IN YARDS

N

Example 6

the 3d Platoon in reserve. He then issued a complete order and platoon leaders returned to their units.

The company commander remained near the river looking for a boat. Looking back he saw his platoons moving forward. Suddenly he heard a few shots off toward the right. At first he thought his men were shooting pigs, but as the firing increased he concluded that a Russian patrol had been discovered on the right. Then he heard another burst of fire, this time from his right-rear. Bullets whistled over his head. There was no mistaking the characteristic crack of the Russian rifle.

With a command to his runners to follow him, the company commander set off at a run for his reserve platoon. On the way he gave this message to a particularly reliable runner:

> The left platoon will retire into the wood and get ready to follow me in an attack toward the farm. The right platoon will defend the entire company sector. Give this order to the platoon commanders and then report this decision to the battalion.

On reaching the reserve platoon, which had faced toward the farm and was replying to the fire coming from that direction, the company commander ordered:

"The whole platoon will attack in double time toward the farm."

As the platoon advanced through the wood toward the farm, a member of the patrol arrived with this message:

"The patrol is north of the farm. The Russians are at the farm. They are trying to get around us."

Upon reaching the edge of the wood where he could see the Russian position the company commander ordered:

"Lie down; range 400; commence firing!"

The German platoon opened fire and immediately drew down a heavy Russian fire in return. A few moments later a runner reported:

"The 2d Platoon is 200 yards behind us."

The company commander called out:

"I am attacking with the 2d Platoon on the right. This platoon will keep up the fire and then join the attack."

The company commander ran back to the 2d Platoon and led it forward on the right. During the movement he pointed out the position of the platoon already engaged and gave the order:

"There are Russians on this side of the river near the farm. We are attacking."

As the platoon emerged from the wood, it received heavy fire on its right flank. The Russians were not only much stronger than expected, but were much farther across the river than anyone had thought. At this moment a runner from the battalion commander reported:

"The Russians have broken through the cavalry. The battalion commander is wounded."

Since there were no signs of the German battalion which was supposed to be at the farm, the company commander decided to retire. This was accomplished successfully.

From an address at the Infantry School by Captain Adolf von Schell, German Army, who commanded the 9th Company.

DISCUSSION. The more difficult the situation, the less time there will be to issue long orders. Furthermore, men will be excited, and only the simplest movement can be executed.

Usually the first order for the fight can be given without hurry. It should therefore be complete. Above all, the mission and the information at hand should be given. In this case both the battalion and company commanders issued orders for defense which oriented all concerned.

Once combat has started, new orders of any length are impracticable. New situations should be met as Captain von Schell met them—by fragmentary orders that are *brief* and *clear*. In the foregoing example the situation was critical; had time been taken to issue long, formal orders, the battalion would have been cut off. The troops being veterans, an indication of what was desired was enough.

CONCLUSION. A good order must meet three minimum requirements:

(1) It must cover the essentials.

(2) It must be unmistakably clear to the subordinates who are to carry it out.

(3) It must be issued early enough to reach subordinates in time for them to execute it.

Chapter XII: *Control*

The test of control is the ability of the leader to obtain the desired reaction from his command.

E VERY TRAINED SOLDIER knows that control is essential to success in battle, but combat records afford ample evidence that the measures necessary to insure it are frequently neglected in the early stages of a war. The reason is plain. Officers without combat experience—even those who have had considerable peace-time training—do not fully appreciate the difficulties of control under battle conditions. There is a tendency to take it for granted; to assume that it will be there when needed.

To maintain control in battle, the leader must keep constantly in mind the supreme importance and great difficulty of the problem. The control factor must be carefully weighed in every tactical decision. This requirement is absolute; for no plan can be carried through, no previously conceived maneuver executed, no fleeting opportunity grasped, unless a leader has control of his unit. If he has it, even indifferent troops may obtain decisive results. If he does not have it, the most highly trained organizations become partially or wholly ineffective.

During certain phases of an action, control may be temporarily sacrificed or attenuated for other advantages—such as a reduction of casualties. This, however, is justified only when the leader is sure that he can regain control of his command and makes positive arrangements to do so.

Some of the more important matters affecting control within the unit itself are its organization, its state of training, the capacity of its subordinate leaders, and its morale. Every commander should bear these things in mind in evaluating his control problem. In addition, he should remember those factors that tend to promote good control. Among these should be listed:

A simple plan, based on easily identified terrain features.
Convergent rather than divergent movements.
Clear, brief, definite orders.
A suitable formation.
Good communications.
Constant supervision.
Seizure of opportunities to reorganize.

✓   ✓   ✓

EXAMPLE 1. On August 19, 1914, the 7th Company of the French 153d Infantry made an approach march of some three miles in the preliminary phase of the Battle of Morhange. The 4th Platoon of this company numbered about fifty-five men—forty of them regulars and the rest reserves who had been called to the colors three weeks before. These reservists had forgotten much of their former training, and consequently lacked the dependability, confidence and aggressiveness of the other members of the platoon.

The platoon advanced some two miles under continuous artillery fire but, thanks to a combination of good leading and good luck, lost only two men. The remainder of the 7th Company was not so fortunate; it lost 33.

Late in the afternoon the platoon reached the reverse slope of a bare hill which had to be crossed. The crest, though out of small-arms range, was within easy range of the German artillery. A company to the left of the platoon attempted to cross in skirmish line and was shot to pieces. The platoon witnessed this.

The platoon leader studied the terrain carefully. He noted a ravine at the foot of the forward slope that offered fairly good protection. The only cover from the crest down to this ravine was a line of grain shocks spaced at intervals of four or five yards. The platoon leader decided to move his unit to the ravine a man at a time, taking advantage of the cover offered by the shocks.

He led the way and directed his platoon to follow. On reaching the ravine he took cover and waited for the platoon to rejoin him. One by one they filed in. The enemy had not fired a single

Example 1

shot. Nevertheless, a check revealed '12 men missing—all reservists. The platoon leader had not left anyone behind to see that all men made the forward movement.

From studies on the advance of infantry under artillery fire by Major André Laffargue, French Army. Major Laffargue commanded the 4th Platoon of the 7th Company.

DISCUSSION. The formation adopted for crossing the crest

was undoubtedly correct. It enabled the platoon to escape the enemy's notice, and thus avoid the disaster which had overtaken the company on its left. True enough, this formation temporarily sacrificed control, but in this case it was justified in order to save casualties. Furthermore, the leader made positive arrangements to regain control at the earliest possible moment. He prescribed the length and method of the advance and he led the way in order to be on hand to gather up his men as they came in. He probably had an additional motive in going first: his outfit was undoubtedly shaken by the fate of the company on the left; by leading the way he provided his men with a first-class sedative.

Indeed, this young officer can not be criticized for anything he did, but, as so often happens in war, he can be criticized for something he failed to do. In this instance he forgot half of his command problem—the rear half. He failed to charge any of his noncommissioned officers with the job of seeing that the entire platoon followed him as directed. We have seen the result: when the platoon reformed in the ravine 12 reservists—nearly one-fourth of the command—were missing.

So far as these twelve men were concerned, special precautions were necessary. These men were reservists; they had but recently joined the unit; the platoon leader knew practically nothing of their state of training or their dependability. In such circumstances the closest supervision is necessary if control is to be maintained. The figures speak eloquently—two men lost from physical causes, twelve from moral causes.

EXAMPLE 2. On September 26, 1918, the U. S. 131st Infantry attacked to the north with the mission of gaining the high ground beyond Gercourt. The 1st Battalion, in regimental reserve (Point X), was to follow the assault battalions at 500 yards.

The battalion commander prescribed a formation in line of

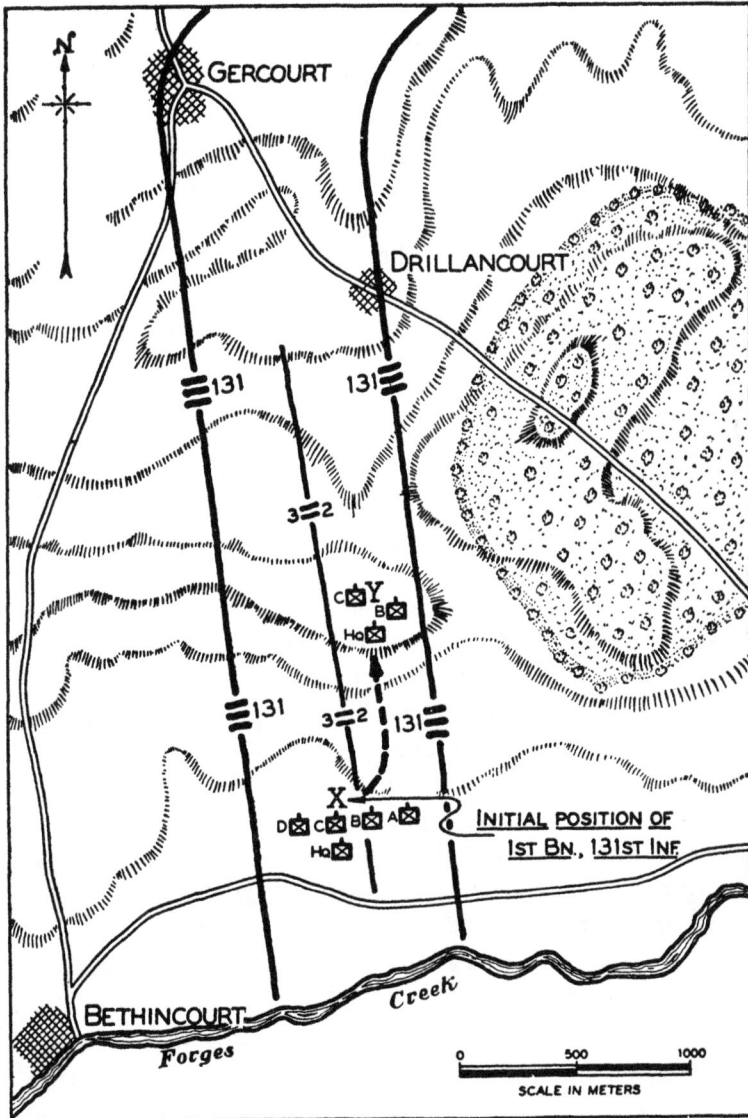

Example 2

companies in the order: A, B, C, D, from right to left. Battalion headquarters and attached units followed in rear.

At H-hour fog and smoke limited visibility to a few yards. After a short while contact patrols informed the battalion commander that the left assault battalion was held up by machine-gun fire and that they had been unable to locate the right assault battalion.

Realizing that both forward battalions were well behind the schedule of advance, the commander of the 1st Battalion decided, on his own initiative, to take advantage of the protection afforded by the rolling barrage, which was now some distance ahead, and advance in the zone of the right assault battalion.

He made no change in dispositions although his battalion was now moving forward as an assault unit. Much difficulty was experienced in maintaining direction owing to poor visibility and to the deep trenches that crisscrossed the areas. Frequent checks by compass were necessary.

About 20 minutes after the battalion moved out, it reached the top of the hill (Point Y) on which it had been advancing. At this moment the fog lifted from the hill and the sun broke through. Strange things had happened during the short advance. On the *right* the battalion commander saw Company B; on the *left*, Company C; just in rear, the battalion headquarters group. Companies A and D had disappeared. No other friendly troops were in sight. Visibility to the rear was still greatly limited by the fog and smoke which clung to the low ground over which the battalion had advanced.

From the personal experience monograph of Captain Carroll M. Gale, who commanded the 1st Battalion of the 131st Infantry.

DISCUSSION. The battalion entered the combat as regimental reserve. During this period it should have been held in as compact a formation as the covered approaches and the effectiveness of hostile long-range fire permitted.

The formation of four companies abreast spread the battalion over a wide area. This dispersion was particularly objectionable because of the poor visibility. In general, formations in column facilitate control; formations in line make it difficult. Premature development or deployment surrenders, before necessary, a portion of that full control which should be retained to the last possible minute. In this particular situation the formation adopted by the leader multiplied the chances for mistakes and for units getting lost.

When the battalion commander decided to take over an assault rôle, he might well have adopted the familiar "square" formation—two companies leading, two companies following. Certainly that disposition would have been far easier to control than four companies in line. Moreover, with visibility what it was, intervals and distances should have been reduced to the minimum.

The consequences of the faulty formation are instructive: at the moment the battalion required all of its fighting power, it found itself only fifty per cent effective.

✓   ✓   ✓

EXAMPLE 3. On July 18, 1918, the U. S. 16th Infantry attacked to the east in column of battalions. The 1st Battalion, in assault, reached the initial objective, quickly reorganized, and pushed on toward the second objective in the formation shown on the sketch.

Just as the battalion moved out, its leader was struck down and the captain of the left assault company (B) assumed command. This officer promptly delegated the responsibility of coördinating the movement of Companies C and D and the attached machine-gun company to the captain of Company C, while he undertook to do the same job for the assault companies (A and B). At the same time he continued actively in command of his own company.

After a short advance the assault companies met resistance

from the right front, veered in that direction, and eventually found themselves on the second objective, but out of the battalion zone of action. Meanwhile the rest of the battalion had disappeared.

After some delay, the battalion commander took steps to

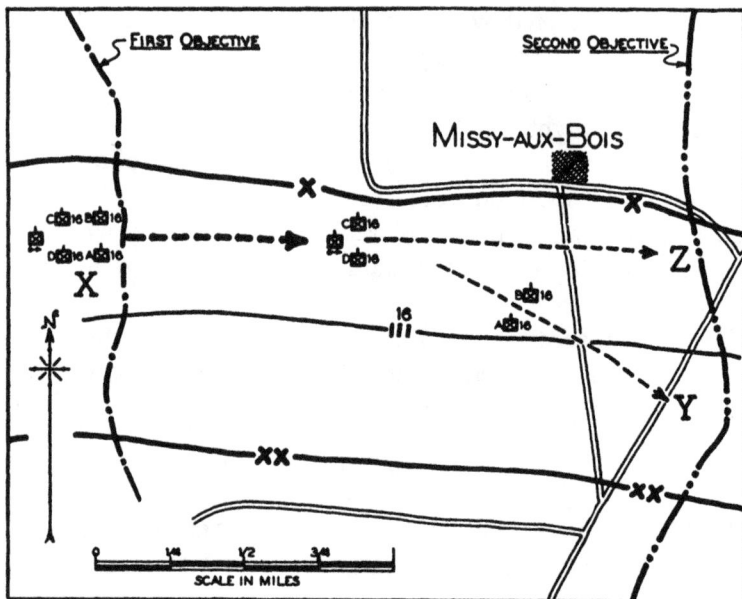

Example 3

rectify the error in direction and sent patrols to locate his other three companies. They were finally found at Point Z.

The time lost in locating the companies that got out of control gave the enemy an opportunity to restore order and strengthen his defensive dispositions, and compromise the battalion's chance of achieving a striking success.

From the personal experience monograph of Major Fred McI. Logan, who commanded Company L of the 16th Infantry.

DISCUSSION. The loss of control in this situation can be

attributed primarily to faulty organization of command. The new battalion commander assigned one officer to command the three reserve companies while he himself commanded the two assault companies. In so doing he failed to appreciate his new responsibility, which was the command of the battalion as a whole. In fact, it may be said that he inadvertently abdicated control.

When the reserve consists of more than one unit it may be desirable from a control viewpoint to have one officer responsible for its movements. This leaves the commander free to study the enemy situation and fight his assault units. He controls his command *through his subordinates.* In this particular case, the battalion commander was probably correct in designating an officer to command the three reserve companies but he erred in failing to restrict this officer to coördinating the advance of the reserve with the progress of the assault units. In effect, he set up two independent commands.

In retaining active command of his company, the new battalion commander committed his second error. He became so engrossed in the problems of Company B that he forgot his primary responsibility—control of the battalion. The result was all but inevitable: communication within the battalion broke down and the leader had no idea what had happened to the larger part of his command or even where it was.

Control presupposes that the leader know the location of all elements of his command at all times and can communicate with any element at any time.

*   *   *

CONCLUSION. The consequences in each of the three examples in this chapter were identical—a great reduction in the effective strength of the unit concerned. This reduction was caused by loss of control and not by casualties or pressure from the enemy. It is clear that a leader cannot strike with his full power unless the elements of his command are available when needed.

In maneuvers, with good visibility, no casualties, no confusion incident to battle, the most perfunctory effort is often enough to keep track of the location of subordinate units. It is far different in war; there, the control problem assumes giant proportions. Only those leaders who realize its difficulties and who take positive and constant action to solve it will find their units in hand and ready to strike at the critical moment.

Chapter XIII: *Command and Communication*

An infantry headquarters must be mobile and must keep close to the troops. From this forward position, communication must be rapid and reliable.

THE INFANTRY LEADER should have a good view of the terrain, personal observation of the enemy, and be in close touch with his own troops. Thus will he be able to deal promptly with rapid changes in the situation. He cannot be tied to a remote command post and take effective action in a sudden crisis. The mere fact that communications function well does not excuse him from intimate contact with his subordinates or from personal observation of the action. Even though technical means of communication fail, a commander must still be able to exercise his influence on events.

To quote Major General J. F. C. Fuller of the British Army:

> If intercommunication between events in front and ideas behind are not maintained, then two battles will be fought—a mythical headquarters battle and an actual front-line one, in which case the real enemy is to be found in our own headquarters. Whatever doubt exists as regards the lessons of the last war, this is one which cannot be controverted.

ʃ   ʃ   ʃ

EXAMPLE 1. On the night of July 18-19, 1918, the French 365th Infantry, which had been in reserve, made a march of eight kilometers to the front in order to effect a passage of lines and attack at dawn.

For this attack the 4th and 6th Battalions were to be in assault. The 4th Battalion, with its right resting on and following the Maubeuge road, was directed to attack toward Montagne de Paris while the 6th Battalion, on the left of the 4th, was ordered to move against Mont-sans-Pain. The line of departure was in the vicinity of the Carrières trench. H-hour was set at 4:45 a.m. Units were to move out when the first shells of the rolling barrage came down.

At 4:00 a.m. the 4th Battalion reached the locality indicated on the sketch. Here it found that the battalion zone of action was much wider than had been expected. Liaison had not yet been established on the right with the 1st Zouaves of the 153d Division nor on the left with the 6th Battalion.

The battalion commander made a rapid reconnaissance and issued his orders. Company commanders rejoined their units.

As the first shells of the barrage fell, the 6th Battalion suddenly appeared, moving directly across the front of the 4th. It disappeared in the dust and smoke, attacking along the right boundary of the regiment. The 14th Company of the 4th Battalion joined the movement and became intermingled with the 6th Battalion and the 1st Zouaves. The barrage began to move forward.

Observing this movement, the battalion commander at once assembled his company commanders and issued the following order:

> We were to attack on the right. Now we attack on the left of the regimental zone. Our objective was Montagne de Paris. Now it is Mont-sans-Pain. The 13th Company will cover the entire battalion front. Forward!

The attack of the battalion was fairly successful.

During the morning twenty-two messages dealing with tactical matters were sent or received by the battalion commander, who kept close behind the advance. All of these messages were *carried by runner;* not one was unduly delayed. This figure does not include messages sent to the regimental commander, or those dealing with anything but strictly tactical matters. The total number of all messages handled, including those dealing with losses and supply, is said to have been about seventy-five.

From an article by Major Pamponneau, French Army, in "La Revue d'Infanterie," October, 1930.

DISCUSSION. Here we see an instance of a battalion losing its direction in a night march and attacking in the zone of the

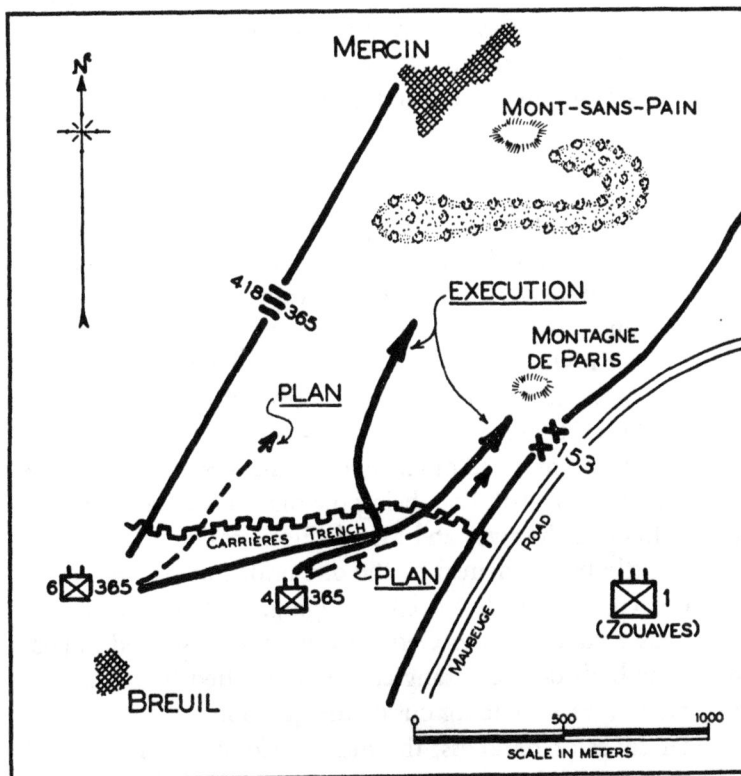

Example 1

unit on its right. This action, coming as a complete surprise and at the very moment of the jump-off, presented an unexpected and confused situation to the 4th Battalion. Fortunately, the commander of the 4th Battalion was well forward, in close contact with his units, and was thereby enabled to retrieve the situation. Had he been mulling over maps or orders in some sheltered command post, his entire battalion, instead of one company, would have become intermingled with the 6th Battalion and there would have been no assault in the left half of the regimental zone.

By means of personal contact with his unit commanders, supplemented by excellent communication within the battalion, this leader actually commanded.

In an attack, infantry commanders must be well forward.

◢   ◢   ◢

EXAMPLE 2. By desperate fighting from August 6 to 8, 1918, the U. S. 112th Infantry, supported by the 1st Battalion of the 111th Infantry, had succeeded in capturing the little town of Fismes and driving the Germans to the north bank of the Vesle. On the night of August 8 the 111th Infantry relieved the 112th, and the 1st Battalion of the 111th, which had been attached to the 112th, reverted to its proper unit.

The 111th Infantry had orders to cross the Vesle and continue the attack. The 1st Battalion, being the most available unit, was directed to cross the river and assault Fismettes.

What little had remained of the one bridge across the Vesle had been completely destroyed. Bridging, in the face of the murderous accuracy of the German fire, was considered impossible. The barbed-wire entanglements that filled the river rendered wading or swimming out of the question.

Under cover of darkness, the men of Company A gathered rocks and débris from nearby ruins and heaped them in the stream until the pile formed a species of footpath close enough to the opposite bank to be bridged by a stout plank.

Utilizing this slippery and treacherous causeway, the men of Company A, with other troops of the battalion, filtered across the river and took cover in the ruins along the southern edge of Fismettes. It was 4:15 a.m. when this move was completed.

It now developed that no one knew the plan. The company commander had been given an oral order. He did not know the line of departure, the time of attack or, for that matter, just where he was.

Suddenly heavy artillery fire fell to the front, all the American guns appearing to open simultaneously. At this moment a

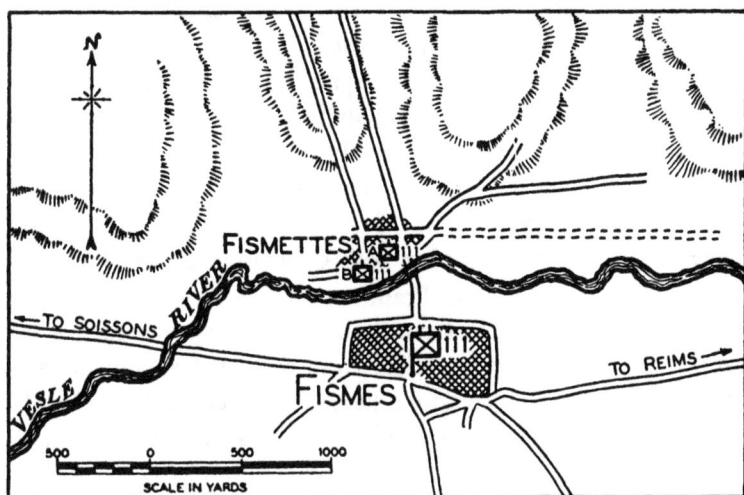

Example 2

runner appeared and thrust a package into the hands of a platoon leader. A hasty examination disclosed the fact that it contained the division's confirming order for the attack and was intended for the brigade. From this order it was learned that the artillery fire crashing to the front was a barrage in preparation for the attack and was due to raise to the objective at that very moment. The barrage was wasted as far as the 1st Battalion was concerned for this unit was supposed to be 500 yards farther to the front, 300 yards farther to the right, and ready to jump off at the next instant.

The battalion commander had remained in Fismes.

Daybreak found elements of the battalion huddled in Fismettes. The commander of Company B, being senior, took command and organized an attack to the north. The attack was broken up by heavy fire at close range.

The Germans now gradually filtered back into Fismettes and began firing on the battalion from the rear. Confused house-to-house fighting followed. After a desperate struggle the battalion, though seriously depleted, still held Fismettes.

Several messages were sent to the battalion commander advising him of the situation and requesting reinforcements, ammunition, rations, and help in evacuating the wounded. Runners went back, under fire, over the foot-bridge. No word came back. No help was received. The fighting continued.

On August 11, a vigorous German counter-attack was repulsed. Immediately thereafter both German and American artillery opened on the town. Frantic messages were sent back to battalion headquarters to have the American barrage raised or stopped. But there was no relief from the artillery and no response from battalion headquarters. All the Very cartridges and rockets in the battalion were fired, but to no avail. Heavy casualties piled up.

Finally an officer made his way back to the battalion command post south of the Vesle. He stated that there were nearly as many men around the C.P. as the battalion had in the front line—among them many of the runners who had carried messages back from Fismettes.

This officer asked why the messages to raise the American barrage had not been complied with. The reply was that the telephone was out and that the information could not be sent to the rear. Upon the insistence of this officer, the liaison officer started back in person to tell the artillery to stop its fire.

The battalion commander appears to have been equally out of touch with the regiment. Although many detailed messages had been sent back by the troops north of the Vesle and many got through to the battalion command post, a regimental report, dated August 20, stated that repeated requests sent to the C.P. of the 1st Battalion for information of the condition of the troops in Fismettes brought no definite information up to the afternoon of August 11.

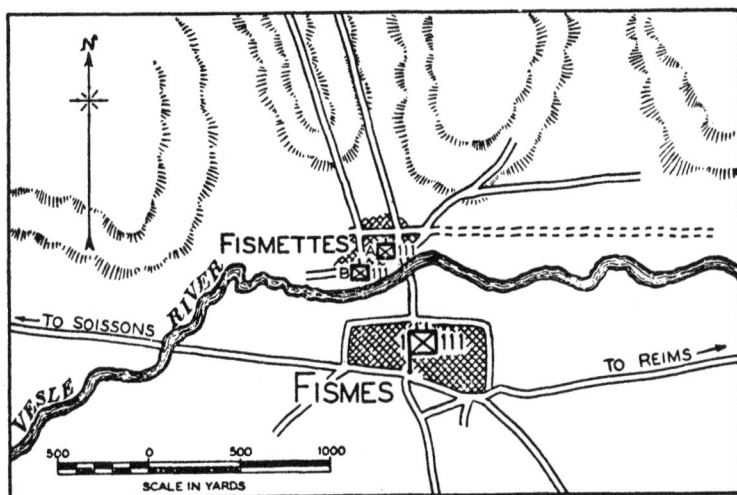

Example 2

On the morning of the 14th the battalion was relieved.

From the personal experience monograph of Captain Ottmann W. Freeborn, Infantry.

DISCUSSION. During the capture and occupation of Fismettes the battalion commander remained in his command post south of the Vesle. From such a position he was unable to deal with the many desperate situations which his battalion had to face—situations that demanded immediate action on the spot. In a word, he failed to command.

His only possible excuse for remaining south of the Vesle would be easier communication with the regiment and with the artillery. But even this must be invalidated since neither of these agencies was kept informed of the situation, although the units in Fismettes poured vital information into the battalion command post.

Because the wire system failed, the battalion commander assumed that he was unable to communicate with either the artillery or higher authority. This, of course, is no excuse. So long as anyone, including the commander, can walk, crawl, or roll, an infantry unit is not "out of communication."

⚹   ⚹   ⚹

EXAMPLE 3. After pushing forward all day August 19, 1914, in pursuit of a retiring enemy, the French 153d Infantry reached the heights of Signal de Marthil and Hill 321. During the day heavy artillery fire had been received from the direction of Baronville, but the region north of Signal de Marthil seemed free of the enemy.

Outposts were established on the north slopes of the heights between Hill 321 and Signal de Marthil. As the advance was to be resumed the following day, no elaborate communications were established between the observation elements of the outpost and the remainder of the regiment. There was no wire or radio, and the outposts had not been provided with pyrotechnics.

At dawn on the 20th, the battalions assembled on the south slopes of the hills, awaiting orders. Breakfast was being prepared. Suddenly a hail of shells fell on the French position. Men ran for the nearest cover. Since no message came from the outpost it was assumed that the Germans were laying down a counter-preparation to prevent a French advance. Fifteen to twenty minutes passed and then a rumor spread: "The enemy is attacking."

The battalions received orders to deploy on the crests to their front. Scarcely had the leading platoons climbed the slope when they encountered a strong hostile attack. The French left was enveloped. The Signal de Marthil fell. The undeployed battalions, still on the southern slope, were taken in flank by heavy

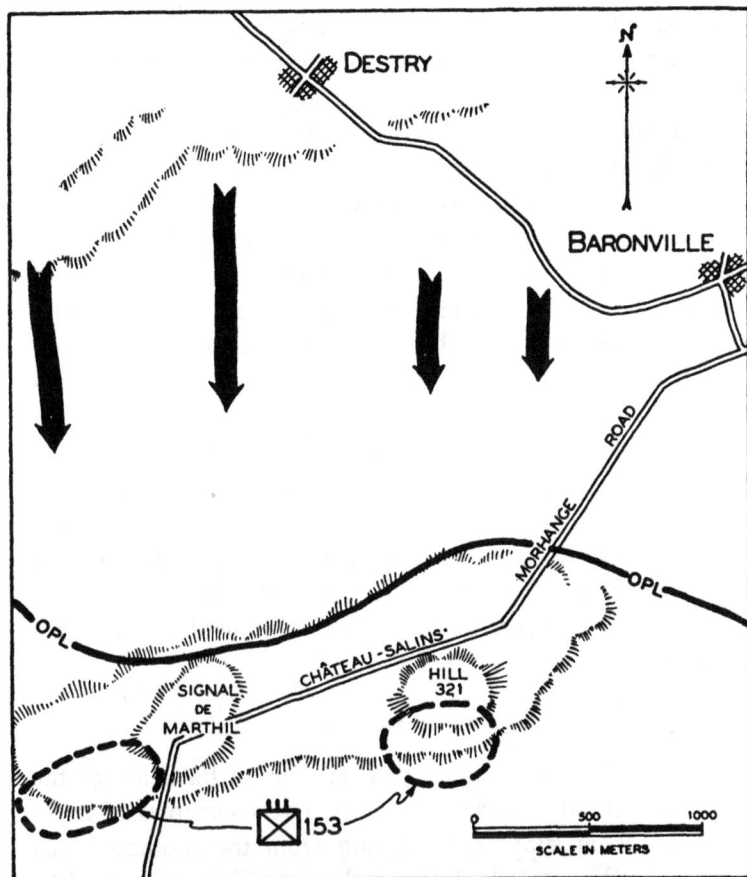

Example 3

fire. The French vainly strove to establish a firing line, but were
so confused that they did not even know in which direction to
deploy. They were driven back in disorder.

The French outguards had seen the Germans debouch from
the heights south and west of Destry, but messages sent to the
rear did not reach the French regimental and battalion commanders until the Germans were almost on them.

From an article by Major Laffargue, in "La Revue d'Infanterie," April, 1927.

DISCUSSION. The German attack progressed 1,500 to 2,000 yards in full view of the French outguards and reached the Château-Salins—Morhange Road before the French battalions received word of it. The Germans appear to have covered this distance in about twenty minutes.

The French battalions were only 400 yards or so from the crests. The commanders were among their troops. Their desire could be expressed simply: "Deploy on the hills to your front." Yet the Germans got there first. Regardless of the fact that the French appear to have been too confident to take warning from the artillery fire, the striking thing is that the German attack progressed 2,000 yards before messages from the outpost could travel a third of that distance and be acted upon.

In such a situation, the value of visual means of communication must be apparent. Pyrotechnics or projectors, using a prearranged code to express simple, important ideas such as "enemy attacking," would have met the situation.

The disaster to this regiment must be attributed, in large part to inadequate communications.

✓   ✓   ✓

EXAMPLE 4. On October 6, 1918, the 3d Battalion of the U. S. 26th Infantry attacked Hill 272. Two companies, K in assault and M in support, advancing from the southeast, had reached the slopes of the hill, which was still strongly held by the Germans. Company I, extending along the entire battalion front south of the hill, assisted the attack by fire. Farther to the left some guns of Company A of the 3d Machine-Gun Battalion and elements of a battalion of the 28th Infantry added their fire to the effort. Company L, with two machine guns, covered the right flank and rear of the attack from the ravine northeast of the Ariétal Farm. It was realized that this was a danger point since the 1st Division, to which the 26th Infantry belonged, appeared to be farther advanced than the troops on its right. Elements of the 7th Field Artillery supported the attack, and a system of rocket signals had been arranged with them in case telephone communication should break down. The support battalion of the 26th Infantry was located near Hill 212.

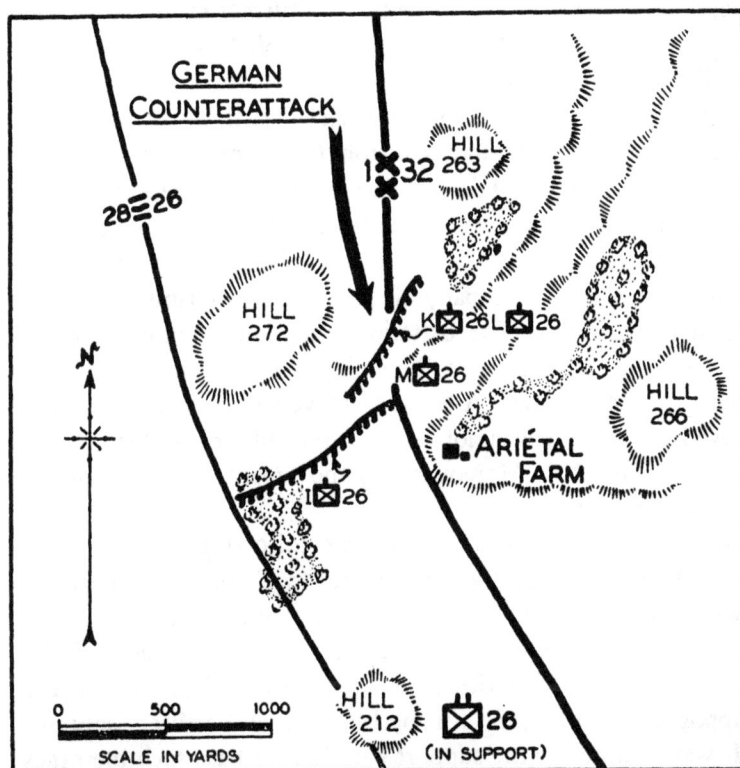

Example 4

About 3:00 p.m. the commander of the assault battalion was south of the left flank of the leading elements of Company M. He could see Hill 272 and Companies I and K. He also had a fair view to the northeast.

An extension of the telephone line from the battalion command post was within 400 yards of the battalion commander's position. Actually, he had expected to have a telephone with him, for it was well understood in the regiment that if the communications of any unit failed to function, that unit would soon have a new commander. But in this case casualties among the telephone detachments had prevented a further extension of the telephone, so an advanced C.P. was established at the end of the line.

About this time artillery fire and some scattered rifle fire were heard to the northeast, and men from Companies L and M came running past the battalion commander. They reported that hundreds of Germans were counter-attacking southwest down the valley east of Hill 272. This would take the American attack in flank and rear. Company K, the leading assault company, began to withdraw. The battalion commander could now see the Germans moving down the valley in close formation. They seemed to be in force. A forward movement of the widely deployed Company I was not believed possible in the face of the fire from Hill 272. Moreover, any movement by this company would take time.

The battalion commander took the following action:

He sent an oral message by runner to Company K directing that it hold its ground and continue to face Hill 272.

He sent two runners by different routes to the end of the telephone line with written messages to be telephoned to the support battalion asking for machine-gun and artillery support. (It was routine for the support battalion to pass such messages on.) The runners were then to find the artillery liaison officer, inform him of the situation and ask for Fire No. 9, data for which had been prepared. The liaison officer was known to be observing artillery fire from a tree in the woods south of Hill 272. He had a telephone line to the artillery.

Meanwhile, with the aid of three veteran noncommissioned officers of Company M, the battalion commander succeeded in halting and assembling some 40 of the retreating troops. Taking charge of these 40 men, he moved through the woods and counter-attacked the advancing Germans on their left flank.

The runners sent with the written message found that the officer left at the telephone extension had been killed, but they

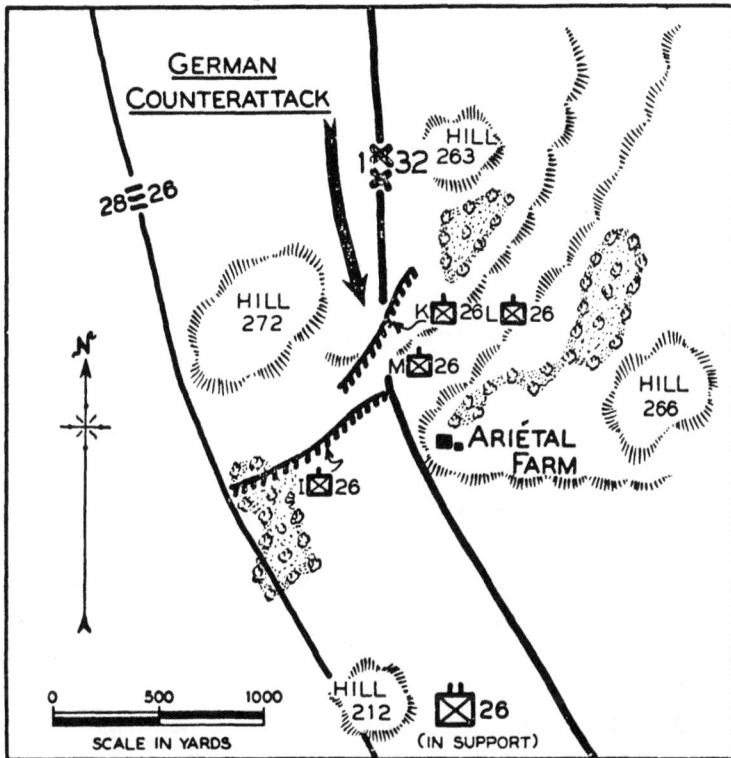

Example 4

telephoned the message properly and promptly. They then found the liaison officer and delivered their message to him.

The German movement had also been noted by the regimental command post. As a result of the prompt transmission of information, the machine guns of the support battalion on Hill 212 placed accurate, indirect fire on the valley. The artillery also brought down its fire promptly.

These fires, in conjunction with the efforts of Companies L and M, and the fire of the two machine guns that were covering the right flank, broke the hostile attack. The Germans suffered heavy losses and withdrew in confusion.

From the personal experience monograph and supplementary statements of Major Lyman S. Frasier, who commanded the 3d Battalion of the 26th Infantry.

DISCUSSION. This situation, which developed so suddenly, appeared extremely serious to the battalion commander. Men from two companies had started to run. A third company had started to withdraw. Intervention by the battalion commander was imperative.

Had he not been well forward where he could see the enemy, see his own troops, and exert his personal influence, he would have been helpless. Information would not have reached him in time.

Thanks to excellent communications, he was able to make his wants known to the regiment and to the artillery. The telephones were working and he was within 400 yards of one. Moreover, the artillery liaison officer, though not with the battalion commander, was not far distant, and he had a telephone connected with the artillery. The battalion commander knew just where this liaison officer was. So did the runners. They knew where they were to go, and in a crisis, they telephoned important messages promptly and properly.

This situation could not have been fully met if preparations had not been made for such an eventuality. The artillery and the machine guns were prepared to place fire in the valley. On receipt of a short, simple message, they did so and did so promptly.

The following passage from the monograph of Major Frasier indicates the methods used in the 1st Division (by that time a veteran organization) to insure communication in the Meuse-Argonne offensive:

Battalion commanders had been informed before the battle that their chief duty was to advance but that next to this their most important function would be to keep in touch with regimental headquarters. If these two things were done, the ground gained would undoubtedly be held.

It was understood that the assault battalion was responsible for the wire line as far back as the support battalion. The support battalion would maintain the line to the regimental C.P. The telephone section of the regimental signal detachment would assist in the supply and maintenance of the entire telephone system.

The wire scheme generally employed at that time was called a ladder line. The lines were laid about ten yards apart or at any other distance which would permit a lineman on patrol to observe both lines for breaks. At regular intervals these wires were bridged.

The linemen detailed to bridge the wires carried test sets. In order to keep the system working, men were detailed as line guards and patrols. At all times, both day and night, there would be one man patrolling every 500-yard section of wire. These guards would meet.

During the second phase of the Meuse-Argonne offensive it cost the 3d Battalion 74 men to maintain telephone communication, but had we not had communication at all times, the number of casualties that could have been charged to the lack of it might well have been 740 instead of 74.

Runners were depended upon entirely for communication between companies, and between companies and the battalion command post. Runners and mounted messengers were depended upon for communication (other than by telephone) with regimental headquarters.

An important message would be sent by at least two runners, one leaving some little time after the other. It was also found advisable to place some distinguishing mark upon runners. When no distinguishing marks were worn, it required that they carry their messages pinned on their blouses in a conspicuous place.

✦   ✦   ✦

CONCLUSION. In order to exercise control, battalion commanders should be well forward. In their field training, battalions should practice methods of maintaining communication between the commander's forward position and his command post. Frequently an extension of the telephone system will be the simplest solution.

As a rule, the battalion commander should move forward along the announced axis of signal communication. If, for any reason, he leaves this axis, a runner should be left behind who knows where he can be located. The command-post personnel should always be able to find the commander.

Runners must be relied upon for communication within the battalion. Unless this messenger service is carefully planned and its personnel is of high quality and well trained, it will not be able to survive the tests of the battlefield.

To fight his unit efficiently, a leader must be able to impart his decisions to his subordinates quickly and correctly. To insure prompt, intelligent assistance from the higher echelons, he must be able to keep them informed of the situation.

In brief, without effective communications the efforts of infantry in battle will be aimless and uncoördinated.

Chapter XIV: *Supervision*

Leaders must supervise the execution of their orders. The more untrained the troops, the more detailed this supervision must be.

A SUPERFICIAL READING of military textbooks is likely to convey the idea that the duties of a leader consist only of estimating the situation, reaching a decision, and issuing an order. It is evident, however, that unless the orders of the commander are executed, even a perfect plan will fail. On the other hand, a poor plan, if loyally and energetically carried out, will often succeed.

A commander, then, must not only issue his order but must also see to its execution. It is the omission of this final step that has caused many brilliant plans to go awry. Too often a leader assumes that once his plan is completed and his order issued, his responsibility for the action terminates. He seems to feel that he has discharged his obligation and that the execution remains entirely with his subordinates. Such an assumption is false even when dealing with veteran troops. Where poorly trained troops are involved, the necessity for vigilance and supervision becomes even more imperative. Initiative must not be destroyed, but the commander must nevertheless bear in mind that the responsibility for the result of the action rests squarely with him. Consequently, he is not only justified in carrying out the supervision necessary to insure proper execution, but is seriously delinquent if he fails to do so.

Of course, a leader cannot be everywhere, but he *can* and should weigh the capabilities and limitations of his subordinates, determine the critical point or time of the action, and lend the weight and authority of personal supervision where it is most needed:

EXAMPLE 1. On the foggy morning of August 29, 1914, the German 2d Guard Regiment, located just south of the Oise River, faced an obscure situation. French outguards were known to be a mile to the south, but the strength and intentions of their main force remained problematic. Although the French had been withdrawing for several days, this was no guarantee that the withdrawal would continue.

The 2d Guard Regiment was ordered to advance, making a first bound to the high ground near Hill 164. The regiment moved out with the 1st Battalion on the right as base unit, the 3d Battalion on the left, and the 2d Battalion in the second echelon behind the center.

Neither the regimental commander nor the 1st Battalion commander gave the direction of march by compass bearing. Routes of advance were not reconnoitered.

The 1st Battalion descended the slopes of the ridge east of Roméry, and reached a wooded valley which it took for the valley leading to Wiege. After marching for half an hour the battalion reached the edge of the wood, but found no Wiege. Thereupon the battalion commander ordered a halt. Maps were produced and officers became involved in a discussion as to the location of the battalion. The truth was soon apparent—the battalion was lost!

At this point the brigade commander, Major General von Schacht, arrived. He showed the battalion commander that he had followed the valley leading from Roméry to the southeast and that if the battalion continued on its present course it would march diagonally across the zone of the division on its left.

General von Schacht then reoriented the entire regiment, and with this information the correct position was soon reached. This proved of great importance, for the French had ceased retiring and were making a stand.

From the account by Lieutenant Colonel Koeltz, French Army, in "La Revue d'Infanterie," June, 1927.

DISCUSSION. Except for the fact that the brigade commander was well forward, supervising the execution of this movement, the attack of the brigade, and very possibly the at-

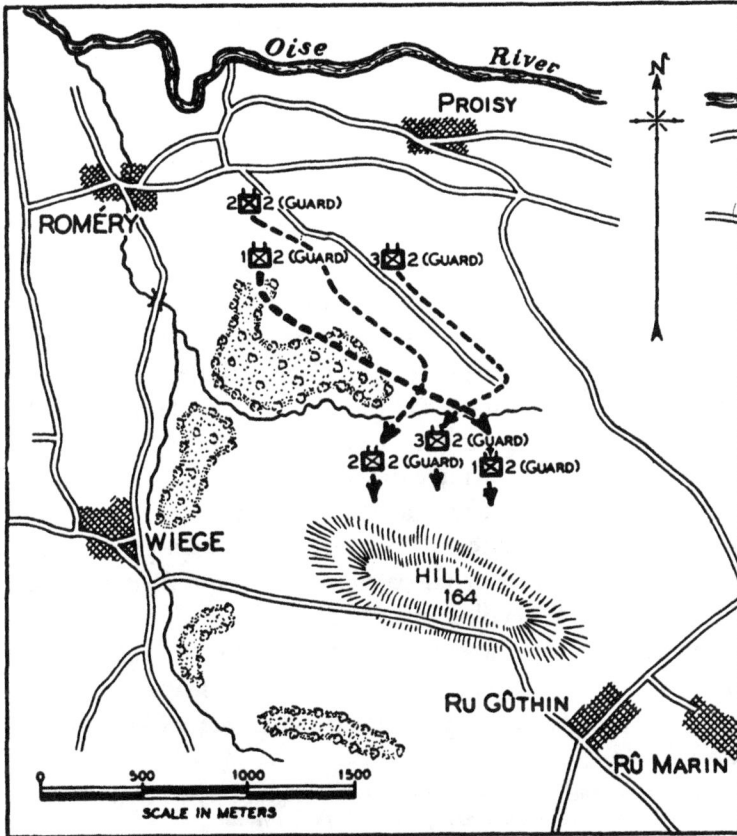

Example 1

tack of the entire division, would have been launched under most unfavorable circumstances. Had the brigade commander given orders and then remained at a command post in rear, one of his regiments would have gone wandering off into the zone of another division.

The brigade orders were correct; it was the execution by the regiment which was at fault. We may well put down for reference the fact that neither the regimental nor battalion commander had given the direction by compass.

Fortunately, the brigade commander knew that even with such excellent troops as the German Guards, mishaps and mistakes can occur; and that after an order has been given, it is necessary to see that it is properly executed.

*   *   *

EXAMPLE 2. On October 9, 1918, the U. S. 92d Division took over the Marbache sector. By November 1 it had been in line for three weeks. During this time patrols had been ordered out nightly, and at least two raids had been made. But in spite of this activity no prisoners had been brought in. This, coupled with the fact that reports sent in by patrols were highly conflicting, indicated that many patrols were not going far beyond their own wire. Consequently, a staff officer of the 183d Brigade (92d Division) was directed to keep a large-scale patrol map of the routes followed by all patrols as shown in their reports, together with any detailed information submitted, such as location of hostile wire, lanes through wire, trails, and enemy outposts. By checking patrol reports against recent maps and aerial photographs it was soon possible to determine which reports were reliable.

From the personal experience monograph of Captain Roy N. Hagerty, who was aide-de-camp to the Commanding General, 183d Brigade.

DISCUSSION. This example shows one form of supervision that a staff may take to assure itself that orders are being carried out. Junior officers—lieutenants and captains—had failed to see that orders were executed. It was not practicable for the brigade commander or his staff to go out personally with the patrols, but they could and did deduce from the means at hand which patrols were actually going out, and which were sending in misleading reports.

This incident illustrates the necessity for close supervision of a partly trained command whose discipline and morale are questionable. Here it would have been desirable to relieve all unreliable junior officers, but this was not practicable at the time.

✸   ✸   ✸

EXAMPLE 3. During the period September 26-October 6, 1918, the U. S. 305th Infantry, with Company D of the 305th Machine-Gun Battalion attached, took part in the Meuse-Argonne Offensive. Most of the officers of the 2d Battalion of the 305th Infantry had been recently promoted or had just joined and were new to their jobs. A few days previously the battalion had received replacements, many of whom had little training. These replacements constituted about 20% of the battalion's effective strength. There were several instances during the ensuing action when men asked officers how to place a clip of cartridges in a rifle.

Late on the afternoon of September 30 the 2d Battalion reached a position near the Naza Ridge where the Germans were making a determined stand. It was too late to organize and launch an attack, so the battalion was ordered to halt and dig in. The terrain was broken and shell-torn. The ridges all looked more or less alike. No two officers could agree from a study of the map as to what ridge they were on. The battalion commander therefore disregarded the map and, taking all company commanders with him, made a personal reconnaissance and assigned sectors. Company commanders then led their companies into position.

Early on the morning of October 1 the battalion commander inspected the dispositions. He found a wide gap between the 305th Infantry and the 28th Division on the right which had to be closed by the battalion reserve. He also found that the two machine guns attached to each company had been placed on the extreme flanks of the company lines without regard for fields of fire. In one case, the guns had been placed some 50 yards beyond the rifle company, without a single rifleman near enough to protect them. The machine-gun company commander had not been consulted in locating these guns.

Inspection of machine-gun emplacements showed that two had been dug with so much consideration for the protection of the gun crew that any firing would have to be done at an angle of 45 degrees!

From the personal experience monograph of Major Erskine S. Dollarhide, who commanded Company D of the 305th Machine-Gun Battalion.

DISCUSSION. The fact that soldiers were found in the front line who were unfamiliar with the simplest fundamentals of their weapons must appear incredible. Yet such conditions were not uncommon in our army during the World War and they may occur again in a future conflict of major proportions. They serve to emphasize the necessity for careful supervision.

We see a lack of training in map reading on the part of company officers, making it necessary for the battalion commander to conduct his unit commanders to their areas. Later, partly because of the character of the terrain and partly because the troops were unaccustomed to night movements, we see company commanders guiding their units into position by hand. The next morning's inspection of the dispositions disclosed that, in spite of all previous efforts, there was a dangerous gap on the right flank. Thanks to the battalion commander's vigilance this was discovered in time to take corrective measures.

Finally, the necessity for checking such details as the siting and construction of machine-gun emplacements, is clearly demonstrated. Personal safety is likely to be uppermost in the minds of partly-trained troops and only the most rigid supervision will insure that units and individuals are not sacrificing battle efficiency for an unwarranted amount of activity.

EXAMPLE 4. General Pétain, later commander-in-chief of the French Armies, commanded a corps in the French attack in Artois in the spring of 1915. After issuing his orders, the General repeatedly questioned subordinates in regard to their conception of the manner in which they would carry out those orders. He is said to have questioned every gunner about his part in the attack, and to have supervised the registration of every piece of artillery.

DISCUSSION. This is an extreme example of supervision and one that is rarely practicable. The results justified General Pétain. His corps achieved a remarkable success: it rapidly overran the German defenses in its front and effected a deep penetration. It was the only corps to achieve such a signal success in the general attack.

✓   ✓   ✓

EXAMPLE 5. On the evening of June 1, 1918, the U. S. 7th Machine-Gun Battalion (two companies) occupied positions on the south bank of the Marne at Château-Thierry. Company B was disposed with one platoon covering the right flank of the battalion, and two platoons generally covering a bridge across the Marne.

French troops who had been fighting north of the Marne began withdrawing south of the river, and a German attack developed against the American position on the south bank. Germans were reported to have crossed the Marne in the darkness. The battalion commander had exercised little supervision over his companies. The situation as it appeared to the captain of Company B is described in the personal experience monograph of Major John R. Mendenhall, who at the time commanded this company. He says:

> To the captain of Company B the situation appeared desperate. Runners sent to the battalion C.P. failed to return. His own reconnaissance and the report of a lieutenant from Company A, who had

been on the north bank, convinced him that, without rifle support, Company B could not avoid capture and was ineffective in the positions it then occupied. Moreover, failure to gain contact with the battalion C.P. implied that it had moved, probably to the rear, and orders had been to cover such a withdrawal.

The captain therefore sent oral messages by runners to his platoons, directing the 1st and 3d Platoons to withdraw to the second-line position, and the 2d, which he hoped was still commanding the bridge, to cover the withdrawal.

The company commander then went to the battalion command post which he found had not been moved. There he received orders to move his company back to its former positions. The captain, with his headquarters personnel and four reserve guns, moved back to the bridge. There he found the 2d Platoon had gone, as well as the others.

In his monograph Major Mendenhall then describes a fight in the dark between Germans, who could be recognized by their helmets, a few French, and the crews of his reserve guns which went into action.

The combined fire of these guns drove the remaining Germans across the bridge. The guns were then moved to positions from which they held the south bank until daylight when the remainder of the company was reëstablished in its former positions.

Investigation later showed that the runners had become confused and delivered the company commander's order to each of the three platoons as "Withdraw at once."

Let us now see what happened to the two platoons near the bridge. This is described by Lieutenant Luther W. Cobbey, who commanded one of these platoons.

About 9:30 p.m. a runner came to me with an order to retreat with all possible speed; that the Germans had crossed the river and were on our side. Supposing that the Germans had made a crossing without my knowing it, I followed the instructions given, which were nothing less than to "beat it."

On the way back we passed through an enemy barrage. We moved about four kilometers to the rear, taking up a position on a hill overlooking the river, where the French had prepared a line of resistance. On arriving there I found Paul (Lieutenant Paul T.

Funkhouser, commanding a platoon of Company B) with his platoon; he had received the same order.

After putting our guns into position, we waited for the German attack that we expected at any moment. At about 1:00 a.m. Paul said, "Don't you think we had better go back into Château-Thierry and find out whether the Germans are actually in the town?"

Paul and I took one runner and started back. We finally reached the place we started from and to our surprise found there were no Germans on our side of the river. We immediately went to battalion headquarters to find out why we had been ordered to retreat. The major denied any knowledge of our retreat, and showed no interest in the matter. He didn't seem to give a darn what we had done or might do.

Paul and I felt that the only thing to do was to go back, get our men and guns, and get into action again in our old positions, which we were finally able to do about daylight.

From the personal experience monograph of Major John R. Mendenhall, who commanded Company B of the 7th Machine-Gun Battalion.

DISCUSSION. The 7th Machine-Gun Battalion was lucky indeed that this mishap did not result in a serious reverse. Its predicament affords a triple illustration of the necessity for supervision.

First, partially because of lack of supervision and control by the battalion commander, one of his companies began an unauthorized withdrawal contrary to his desires. Since he had not kept in close contact with Company B and since he had failed to supervise its operations (either personally or through a staff officer), he must be credited with a share of the responsibility for its withdrawal. During the operations, he gave his subordinates the impression of inactivity and indifference.

Second, as the captain of Company B discovered, orders—particularly oral orders sent by runner—may be easily altered in the transmission or misconstrued. It will often be necessary to issue oral orders in the haste and confusion of battle, but the next step must invariably be a verification of the execution.

Finally, this example shows that when errors are promptly discovered they may be repaired. True, the captain of Company B discovered his error too late to keep his platoons from withdrawing, but he was able to prevent disastrous consequences by using)his four reserve guns.

In spite of all we can do, misunderstandings will occur in war. The leader's job, then, is to detect these errors early and correct them quickly; this can be done only through close supervision. If he fails to supervise he will usually learn of the blunder after the disaster has occurred.

*   *   *

CONCLUSION. Orders will be misunderstood by troops, regardless of their experience or degree of training. But even when orders *are* understood, fear, fatigue, or sheer inertia may result in a failure to carry them out unless leaders exercise a continuous and untiring supervision.

A simple, workable plan is important; a clear, understandable order is important; but supervision to see that the will of the commander is executed is all-important.

Chapter XV: *Direction*

The marching compass is the infantry
officer's most reliable guide.

|||||||||||||||||||||||||||||||||||||||||||||||||||||||||||||||||||||||||||||||||||||||||||||||||||||||||||||||||||||||

IN AN ATTACK, one of the leader's most important duties is maintenance of direction. *Infantry Drill Regulations (Provisional), 1919*, fresh from the experience of the World War, states: "More attacks fail from loss of direction than from any other cause." Whether or not this statement can be fully substantiated is not important. The important thing is that so many attacks *did* fail through loss of direction that this statement was written into post-war regulations.

Undoubtedly the best aids in maintaining direction are clearly visible terrain features that can be seen by all men and that cannot be mistaken. Distant direction points or such features as roads, streams, railroads, ridges or valleys that run in the desired direction are invaluable. It frequently happens, however, that these natural guides either do not exist in the desired locations or else lead only part way to the assigned objective. In such instances reliance must be placed on the marching compass.

Even when guides are furnished, the responsibility for getting a unit to the proper place at the proper time is still the commander's. It will therefore pay him to check on the guide.

✔ ✔ ✔

EXAMPLE 1. On the night of July 17, 1918, the 2d Battalion of the U. S. 28th Infantry moved forward with orders to attack at 4:35 the following morning. Leaving its position near Mortefontaine at 9:30 p.m., it marched via a trail and an unimproved road to the environs of le Chauffeur. A violent rainstorm set in shortly after the battalion got under way. A description of the march, as given by the battalion commander, follows:

The darkness became so intense that it was impossible for the men in ranks to see those in front of them. The trail, which was bad at best from recent shelling, now became a quagmire. It was necessary to close the units without distance and have the men hang on to the equipment of the men ahead. Great difficulty was experienced in keeping the column from being broken, as the men were constantly slipping and falling into shell holes.

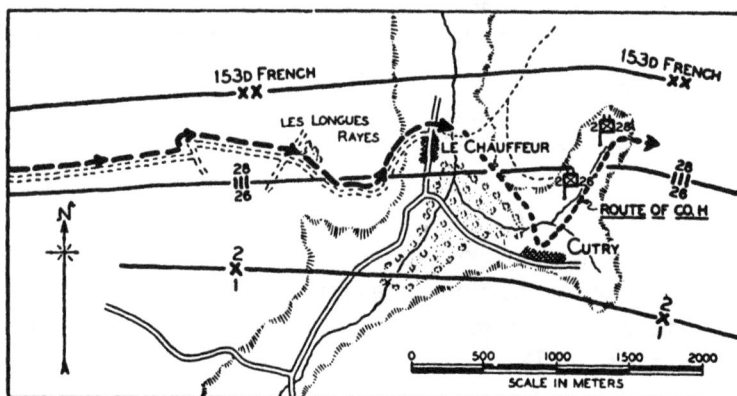

Example 1

As the column approached the front, the roads and trails became congested with horses, cannon, motor trucks, tanks and artillery, en route to their positions. This added to our difficulty and it was only through the almost superhuman efforts of the officers and the men that the battalion ever reached its destination.

The battalion commander joined the column as it passed the regimental command post. At this point the battalion was broken up and the individual companies, led by French guides, proceeded toward their respective positions.

The battalion commander had the only available map.

As Company H started to descend into the ravine near Cutry, the Germans began to scorch that area with artillery fire. The guide, becoming excited and confused, promptly led the company in the wrong direction. The company commander, having neither map nor compass, did not realize this until he arrived in a town. Here French soldiers told him that he was in Cutry and that there were some Americans to the east. Later he met the adjutant of the 26th Infantry, the unit on the right of the 28th, and this officer gave him general directions. The company then proceeded northeast.

At 4:15 a.m. it passed the command post of the 2d Battalion of the 26th Infantry, whose commander pointed out the position of Company H on the line of departure. Day was just beginning to break. The company dared not move out of the ravine to go into position lest it be seen by the enemy, and the benefit of surprise be lost. Therefore the company commander continued his march up the ravine until he reached the command post of the 2d Battalion of the 28th Infantry. Upon reporting to his battalion commander, he was directed to form his company near the top of the steep slopes of the ravine and be prepared to emerge at a run at H-hour and close on the barrage.

The company had failed to get into position for the attack on time. By a bit of good luck it did manage to get into a position from which it could join the advance at H-hour. This it did—quickly catching up with the barrage.

From the personal experience monograph of Major Clarence R. Huebner, who commanded the 2d Battalion of the 28th Infantry.

✓ ✓ ✓

DISCUSSION. That the troops got into position at all speaks highly for the energy and determination of both officers and men. It also speaks well for the capability of the guides that most of the companies were properly led to the line of departure.

However, the guide assigned to Company H lost direction and took the company south instead of east. The company commander had no compass, and did not realize the mistake. In fact, if he had not reached a town which he knew was not in his zone of action, where he could make some inquiries, his company would not only have been unable to attack with its battalion, but in all probability would have continued south into the zone of the other brigade of the 1st Division.

Guide or no guide, a leader should have a compass and use it.

✓   ✓   ✓

EXAMPLE 2. On October 7, 1918, the Germans in front of the U. S. 3d Division held a line that ran from Ferme de la Madeleine through the south edge of the Bois de Cunel and over the crest of Hill 253 to the Cierges—Romagne-sous-Mont-faucon Road. They seemed to be strengthening this position. Heavy fighting had been in progress for several days.

During this time the 6th Brigade was in reserve. On October 8, division orders directed that the attack be resumed at 8:30 a.m., October 9, with the 6th Brigade in assault and the 5th Brigade, which was then in the front line, in reserve.

The 30th Infantry, part of the 6th Brigade, was located near the north edge of the Bois de Beuge. On the afternoon of October 8, the regimental and battalion commanders made a personal reconnaissance of the front lines in Woods 250. During the course of this reconnaissance the regimental commander informed the battalion commanders of his general plan. At 10:00 p.m. at his command post he issued his formal orders which placed the 3d Battalion in assault and the 2d Battalion in support.

The 2d Battalion was ordered to be in position along the south edge of Woods 250 by daylight. Guides from the 3d Battalion were furnished for this movement. At 3:00 a.m. the battalion moved from the Bois de Beuge in column of twos and advanced across a shell-swept zone. Strict orders from higher authority prescribed that in all troop movements 50-yards distance would be maintained between platoons and 200-yards between companies. The battalion commander believed that this was impracticable for troops moving at night over a shelled area. Accordingly, he closed up the column.

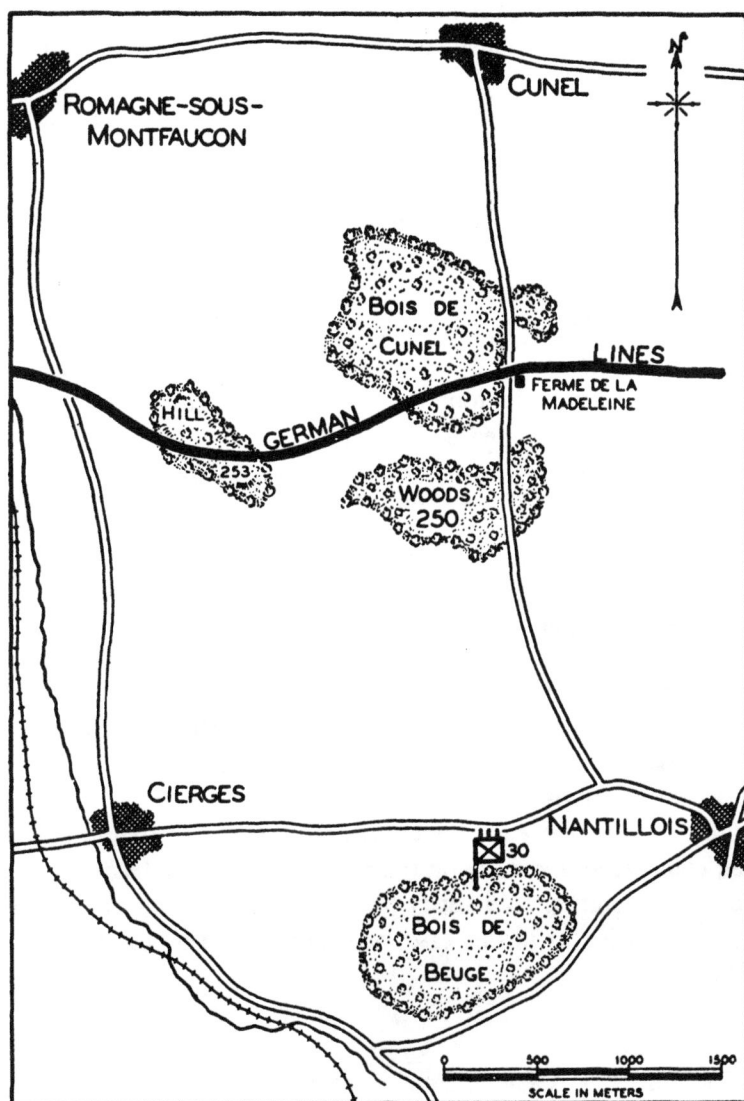

Example 2

The route taken by the guide was not the one the battalion commander had previously reconnoitered. About halfway to Woods 250, shells began to fall near the line of march. Then and there the guide lost the way and the column was compelled to halt.

At this point, the battalion commander took things in his own hands and conducted the march by compass bearing. He reached the designated location in good time, but here he discovered that the shelling had resulted in a break in the column and that he had with him only one and a half companies. Officer patrols were at once sent out to locate the missing units. These were eventually rounded up, and daybreak found the entire battalion assembled in the south edge of Woods 250.

From the personal experience monograph of Major Turner M. Chambliss, who commanded the 2d Battalion of the 30th Infantry.

DISCUSSION. Here we have the simple problem of moving a support battalion a short distance forward to a new position. True, the movement had to be made by night over a shelled area, but the occasion did not seem to call for special precautions to prevent loss of direction. It was natural to assume that the guide would conduct the battalion to its destination. However, as this battalion commander discovered, implicit reliance on guides is dangerous.

Officers responsible for the direction of the march should use their compasses as a check on their guides. Even the leaders of subordinate units should verify the direction of march by compass. Otherwise, as in this case, rear elements may become detached and lost.

EXAMPLE 3. General Pétain, later commander-in-chief of the French armies, commanded an infantry brigade at the Battle of Guise on August 29, 1914. His brigade attacked late in the afternoon. General Pétain had taken particular care to insure that his brigade would attack in the right direction, having given both compass bearing and distant direction points that could be easily seen.

However, as twilight closed in, the direction points became indistinguishable. Moreover, the brigade began to receive fire from several localities not directly to its front. This resulted in part of the command veering off from the proper direction. As night deepened, the situation became more and more confused. The brigade seemed to be disintegrating.

To the front a burning village was clearly visible. Although not in the exact direction of attack, it was not many degrees off. General Pétain sent orders to all units to converge on this village. By this device the bulk of his brigade was brought under control again.

✦   ✦   ✦

EXAMPLE 4. After repulsing the German attack on July 15, 1918, the Americans and French crossed the Marne and advanced north and northeast.

On July 22 the 3d Battalion of the U. S. 38th Infantry was advancing toward le Charmel in a diamond formation—Company I in the lead, Company K on the left, Company M on the right, and Company L following in rear. The 7th Infantry was on the left and the 1st Battalion of the 38th Infantry on the right, but contact had not been gained with either of these units.

The Germans seemed to be fighting a stubborn rear-guard action. Their light artillery hammered at the American advance; their airplanes struck at it with machine guns and bombs; and their snipers, concealed in trees, let the leading American elements pass and then fired into them from the rear.

Company K had two platoons leading and two in rear. The 1st Platoon, to the right front, was designated as the base unit of the company. A compass bearing—30° magnetic—was followed.

About 8:00 a.m. the leader of the 1st Platoon noted that

Company I appeared to be cutting across the front of his platoon. He reported this to his company commander. The latter, after personal reconnaissance, ordered a change of direction to 20° magnetic, the bearing on which Company I was then marching.

The company had marched about fifteen minutes on the 20° azimuth when a corporal from the 1st Platoon, in charge of a connecting group between Companies I and K, reported to his platoon leader that he had lost touch with Company I. The company commander, upon being informed of this, sent the corporal and his party out to the east to regain contact and continued the advance—going back, however, to the original 30° azimuth.

About thirty minutes later Company K became involved in a heavy fight near Crossroads 224, almost due north of les Franquets Farm. No friendly units were near and the company, after suffering heavy losses, finally withdrew.

At the same time the remainder of the battalion encountered serious resistance southwest of les Franquets Farm. They attacked but failed to dislodge the enemy.

On this day various American units lost contact. As a result little progress was made.

From the personal experience monograph of Captain John H. Hilldring, who commanded Company K of the 38th Infantry.

DISCUSSION. The loss of direction took Company K well into the zone of the 7th Infantry, where it became involved in a desperate fight to no purpose. In commenting on this incident Captain Hilldring stresses the necessity for visual contact in moving through dense woods. He says:

> Company I was responsible for direction. The other companies of the battalion should have linked themselves to Company I at close range and should have gone where Company I went. Such a formation has disadvantages, but in woods it is a far better scheme to close up and accept the disadvantages and losses arising from a

Example 4

too-compact formation. To make certain that the battalion went forward as a unit, the battalion order should have read:

Direction: For Company I, 30° magnetic azimuth; all other companies will conform to direction established by Company I.

It is true that the blame might be fixed upon the leader of the 1st Platoon, which was the base unit of Company K. However, in combat the platoon leader is a busy individual, and if he be made responsible for contact with some unit he cannot see, he must of necessity delegate that responsibility to another.

It will frequently be necessary for units to march on a compass bearing. The opportunity for error and confusion will be lessened by keeping the number of columns to a minimum as long as possible. For example, a company should move as a company as long as it can before breaking into platoons.

Visual contact will keep a unit together; the compass will take it in the right direction.

EXAMPLE 5. On August 8, 1915, the British and New Zealanders were attacking what was considered the key position on the Gallipoli Peninsula. A footing had been gained on the dominant ridge known as Chunuk Bair. Two battered New Zealand battalions were intrenched on the summit. Turks and British had both suffered heavy losses.

The British plan was to capture Hill Q (northeast of Chunuk Bair) by an attack at dawn on August 9. A heavy bombardment from 4:30 to 5:15 a.m. was planned, following which Hill Q was to be attacked by one force generally from the west and by another force from the general direction of Chunuk Bair. The latter force, commanded by General Baldwin, consisted of four battalions from three different brigades.

At 8:00 p.m. General Baldwin's force was within a mile or two of its attack objective. The intervening country, however, was extremely difficult, being traversed by high ridges and deep ravines. The slopes of the ridges were often so steep that they were impassable even for infantry, and the deceptive character of the terrain made it easy for units to lose their way.

General Baldwin's force was located in the Chailak Dere, a deep ravine. Casualties from Chunuk Bair were sent back to The Apex and thence down Chailak Dere. From The Apex a narrow saddle led forward to the advanced foothold of the New Zealanders on Chunuk Bair. Except for this, the approaches to the Chunuk Bair—Hill Q range consisted of steep ravines with corrugated, scrub-covered slopes on which no advancing line could retain its formation for half a minute.

"How on earth can we do it?" asked one of the reconnoitering officers. The Australian official history answers:

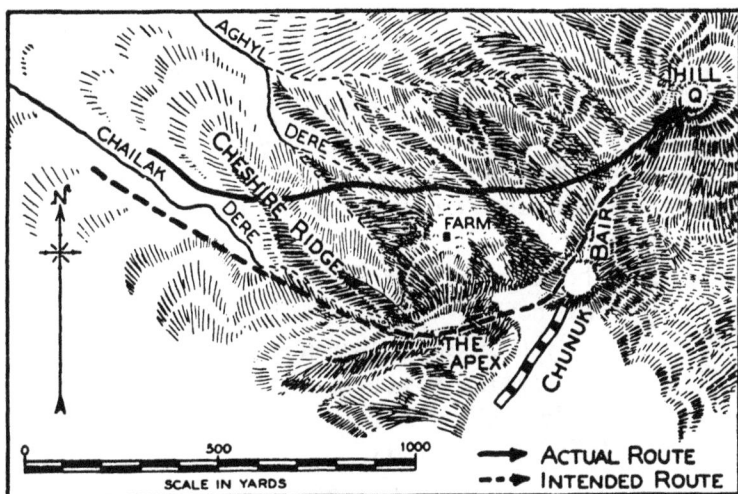

Example 5

> The one possible method was obvious to most of those on the spot. The assault could be made only if the battalions of the new force were marched up the Chailak Dere and right to the advanced New Zealand position, then at dawn turned to the north and straight up the crest of the ridge.
>
> This march would be possible, if, after a certain hour, the Chailak Dere were kept strictly free from all down-traffic—if no troops, even wounded, were allowed to descend it, and the new battalions were then led up it in single file. Some of the New Zealand brigade at The Apex explained this to Baldwin and his brigade-major and it was undoubtedly by this route that Godley (the division commander in charge of the attack) and his chief of staff intended the advance to be made.

The plan decided upon, however, was to move up the Chailak Dere, cross over Cheshire Ridge, drop down into the Aghyl Dere and then climb the far side to Chunuk Bair and Hill Q. This route had not been explored, but on the map it seemed to be the shortest and straightest. Baldwin considered the other route, which had been urged with considerable force by some officers, as unnecessarily circuitous.

Baldwin's battalions began their advance about 8:00 p.m. Movement was slow, and guides lost their way. Baldwin then turned the column back and guided it by an easier route into the Aghyl Dere. Exactly what happened is uncertain, since many of the leading participants in this famous night march are dead. The Australian official history states, "The available records at this point are very vague and defective, and the story cannot be told with certainty."

The results, however, are clear. Baldwin's force, after marching all night, was not in position to attack at the hour set. Indeed, it was nearly as far away as when it started.

"Hours later," says the Australian official history, "a brave, disjointed, pitiably ineffectual attack was made by Baldwin's force." It failed with heavy losses.

From "Official History of Australia in the War of 1914-18," Volume II, and "The Dardanelles Commission Report."

DISCUSSION. The shortest way in this case would have been the circuitous route urged by the New Zealanders. This route had the following advantages: it had been reconnoitered; it was practicable, as evidenced by the fact that the New Zealanders sent back their wounded that way; it followed clear-cut terrain features. The Chailak Dere led up to The Apex; from The Apex a narrow saddle led forward to Chunuk Bair; from Chunuk Bair the ridge toward Hill Q was clearly marked.

The movement recommended by the New Zealanders was not easy; it would take considerable time, and upon arrival near the New Zealanders the force would have to make a somewhat difficult deployment. However, the plan had one outstanding virtue: it practically insured that Baldwin's force would be within striking distance of its objective at dawn.

The shortest route proved to be the longest. The British commander-in-chief, General Sir Ian Hamilton, says in his report: "In plain English, Baldwin, owing to the darkness and the awful country, lost his way."

The Australian official history refers to Baldwin's decision as "a tragic mistake" and says: "The sum of its possible consequences is beyond calculation."

✓ ✓ ✓

EXAMPLE 6. On September 25, 1915, the British launched an attack in the vicinity of Loos. Although the similarity of such landmarks as mine-heads, buildings and oblong woods made the directional problem extremely difficult, no provision was made to keep direction by compass.

The British official history states that in England, where there are many hedges and other obstructions, some companies detailed a "navigating officer" who was responsible for maintaining the proper direction. This excellent peace-time arrangement seems to have been overlooked in the war training of the new divisions.

The 9th Black Watch, 8th Seaforth Highlanders, 10th Scottish Rifles, and 7th King's Own Scottish Borderers, were the assault battalions in the 15th Division which attacked east toward Loos. In this attack there were two towers in Loos which initially served as excellent points of direction.

During the early stages of the advance, direction was well maintained and the attack achieved considerable success. The German first position and Loos were quickly captured.

The towers, well known to all ranks, now lay behind.

The 47th Division on the right of the 15th, was supposed to halt and form a defensive flank after reaching the vicinity of Loos, but this does not appear to have been clearly understood in the 15th Division. Consequently the Black Watch, right battalion of the 15th Division, inclined to the right to maintain contact on that flank.

Resistance now seemed stronger to the right front. This, coupled with the fact that the battalions on the left flank crossed the two roads from Loos to Hulluch, which ran obliquely to their line of advance, caused these units to veer to the southeast. Hill 70 was captured and Germans were seen running to the south. Leading assault elements, badly intermingled with reserve battalions that had been pushed forward, now turned to the south. They were promptly fired on from the front and enfiladed from the east.

The entire division attack disintegrated. Losses were extremely heavy.

The British official history says:

> On reaching the top of the hill (Hill 70) a number of officers of the 44th Brigade, unaware of the change of direction, believed the houses they could see ahead of them to be those of Cité St. Auguste, and that they were still advancing eastward. Reports and sketches sent back to brigade and division headquarters during the morning showed that this erroneous view was fairly prevalent. As a matter of fact, the view east from Hill 70 and the view south are extraordinarily similar.

The history further says:

> In the meantime the change of direction which had destroyed the initial cohesion and weight of the attack, and exposed its left flank, made any continuation of the advance eastward more than ever out of the question.

Later in the day a German counter-attack retook Hill 70.

During the night the 63d Brigade of the 21st Division was moved up. Portions of this brigade attacked at 11:00 a.m., September 26, in conjunction with the 24th Division on its left. The men of the 63d Brigade moved over the same ground that had been covered by the left flank of the 15th Division the day before. Almost the identical thing happened.

The attack was to go east. After crossing the roads from Loos to Hulluch, fire was received from the right-front and units veered to the southeast, thereby exposing their left flank to enfilade fire of Germans from the Bois Hugo. In spite of this enfilade fire at close range, the attack moved southeastward up the slopes of Hill 70. Finally, flesh and blood could stand no

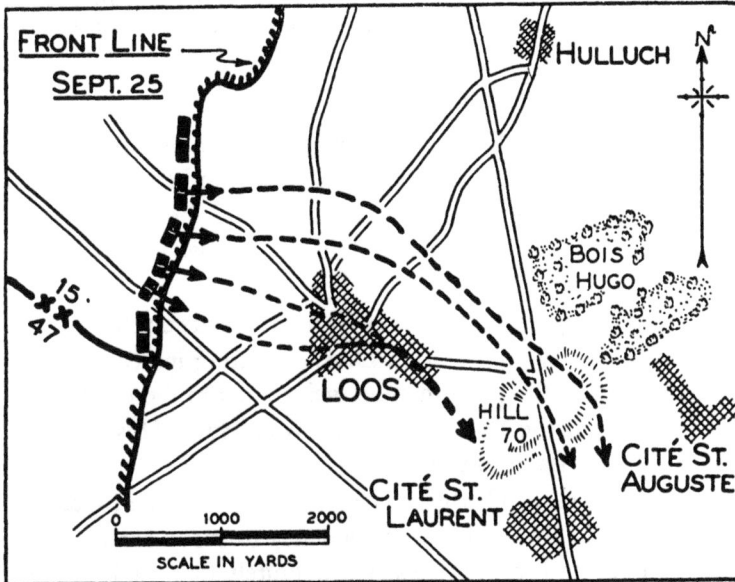

Example 6

more. The troops broke and retired in disorder.

The right flank of the 24th Division followed the example of the troops on their right. As a result, the attack of this division dwindled to the efforts of some two and a half battalions going in the proper direction. It failed with heavy losses.

The British official history suggests that the roads between Loos and Hulluch, running diagonally across the line of attack, were largely responsible for the loss of direction. It states: "The general movement was eventually at right angles to them (the roads) towards Hill 70."

From "British Official History of the Great War: Military Operations, France and Belgium," Volume IV.

DISCUSSION. Loss of direction was the principal thing that stopped the attacks of these three divisions. The British official history, in commenting on Loos, says:

> The number of occasions on which troops mistook their objectives is extraordinary. It was a difficulty that had been overcome by good staff work at maneuvers in England, even in blind country intersected with hedgerows.

Five points stand out at Loos:

(1) It is essential to use the compass to maintain direction.

(2) An unmistakable direction point that can be seen by all ranks is of great value. The Loos towers helped the assault battalions of the 15th Division maintain the proper direction as far as Loos.

(3) It is highly desirable to know what the units on the flanks are going to do. When the 47th Division, acting in accordance with its orders, halted to form a defensive flank to the right, the right battalion of the 15th Division followed suit. This helped draw the entire assault to the southeast.

(4) When a road, a hedge, or a stream intersects the route of advance there is always a strong tendency to move forward at right angles to it. It cannot be stated definitely that the location of the roads running from Loos to Hulluch was the only cause of the change of direction by two divisions on two successive days. Unquestionably there were other contributing causes. Nevertheless, it is extremely suggestive that, in each case, immediately after crossing these roads, the advance moved forward at right angles to them, and not in the direction desired. When such features are encountered, running neither parallel nor perpendicular to the desired direction of advance, the danger signal is being waved.

(5) Enemy fire attracts attacking troops. A unit fired on tends to face in the direction from which it thinks the fire is being received.

CONCLUSION. Maintenance of direction is a hard job and it cannot be solved without thought and effort. The casual manner in which we sometimes see this matter handled in prob-

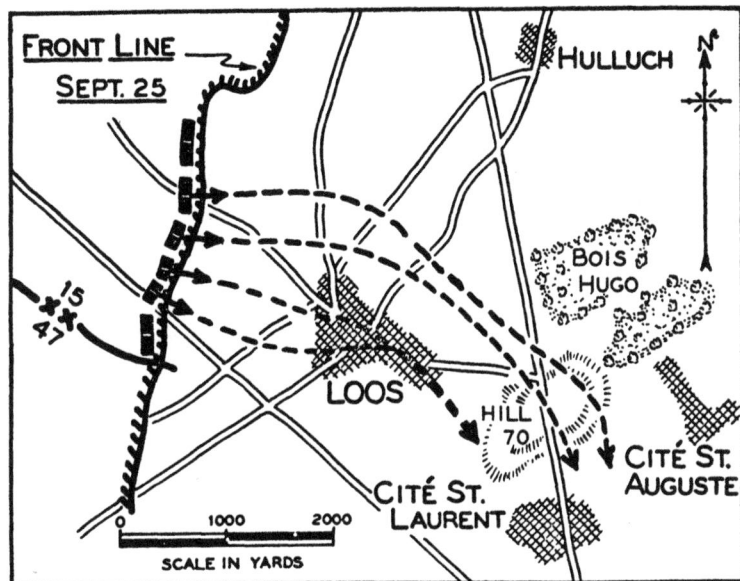

Example 6

lems, indicates that as the war recedes, many of its most vivid lessons grow dim.

We see boundaries of infantry units drawn with a ruler, bisecting woods and occasionally passing a house or a road junction. To be of real value a boundary should be visible on the ground. We see directions of attack that take troops diagonally over ridges, or that cut across main roads at an angle of 10° to 20°.

In planning attacks this matter of direction should be kept well to the fore. If it appear that a certain plan of attack will make maintenance of direction unusually difficult, the commander may well consider altering the plan.

Of course, attacks cannot be planned only from the viewpoint of ease in maintaining direction. Small units have to go where they are told. However, since so many attacks do fail from loss of direction, infantry commanders will be well repaid for time and thought expended on the question: "How can I make sure that my subordinates will go in the right direction?"

Maneuvers, over familiar terrain, in which a compass direction is given to subordinates may do some good, but not enough. Exercises in which the compass is actually needed will be far more valuable.

Chapter XVI: *Fire and Movement*

··

Fire without movement is indecisive. Exposed movement without fire is disastrous. There must be effective fire combined with skillful movement.

··

I F THE ENEMY is allowed full mastery of his fires, any advance toward him in daylight will be penalized by heavy losses. Therefore the attacker resorts to various expedients to circumvent or nullify the enemy's defensive fires. An attack screened by darkness, fog, or smoke, is one method that may accomplish this end. Surprise is another. A skillful utilization of covered approaches is a third. But often the situation or the terrain precludes any one of these methods. Then must the enemy's fire be beaten down by our fire if we are to advance. Even when one or more of the other methods are used, the time will inevitably come when we must resort to fire to neutralize the enemy's defensive fires. In short, fire must be fought with fire—with more effective fire.

In modern war mere numbers cannot be used as a substitute for fire. If the attack lacks surprise or superior fire power, an increase in men will merely mean an increase in casualties. Thus it becomes a vital duty of the leader to take all possible measures to provide adequate fire support for his attacking troops. Nor does this responsibility devolve only upon the high command— it applies to all leaders from the highest to the lowest.

The attacker's scheme of fire is built up on what is often termed a base of fire. For large units the base of fire consists of supporting artillery. For the infantry battalion it is made up of machine guns and infantry cannon. But even the rifle platoon and squad may have a base of fire. For instance, a platoon may use its first section to fire on the enemy while the second section maneuvers to strike him in flank; in that case the first section is used as a base of fire. In the squad the automatic rifle may be used as a base of fire to cover the advance of other members of the squad.

The composition of the fire support as well as the method of employing it will vary widely with conditions. Often it will be found advantageous for the riflemen to approach the enemy from one direction, while the fire support from the base of fire is delivered from another direction. In any event the base of fire should advance as the attack progresses.

Riflemen cannot be expected to reply effectively to hostile machine-gun fire at long and medium ranges, particularly if it comes from a flank. The exact location of the guns is difficult to determine and to pop away at the countryside in the hope of neutralizing their fire is futile. Therefore, riflemen in the attack work their way forward under the protection of the fire of supporting artillery, machine guns, and light mortars; seldom do they fire at ranges greater than 400 yards.

Experience in the World War indicates that riflemen meeting with machine-gun fire at the longer ranges will either seek the nearest shelter and wait for the fire to cease or push forward without replying—depending upon the effectiveness of the hostile fire. When, however, the advancing riflemen get close enough to determine the approximate location of the guns, their own fire becomes an important factor in furthering their advance. It becomes of vital importance when the supporting fire of artillery, howitzer weapons, and machine guns, is compelled to lift. At this stage, attacking troops must cover the final phase of their advance into the hostile position by their own fire—or pay the price. Enemy machine guns that are still in action—and there may be many of them—should be overcome by pushing forward a few men to get on their flanks or in their rear under cover of the fire of the other members of the attacking groups. To rush machine guns, even with fire support of other riflemen, is costly; to attempt to do so without it is suicidal.

EXAMPLE 1. On September 27, 1915, the French 254th
Brigade struck to the north with the mission of carrying that
part of the German position which lay between the Navarin
Farm and the clump of woods marked P15 (both inclusive).
The brigade sector was some 800 meters wide.

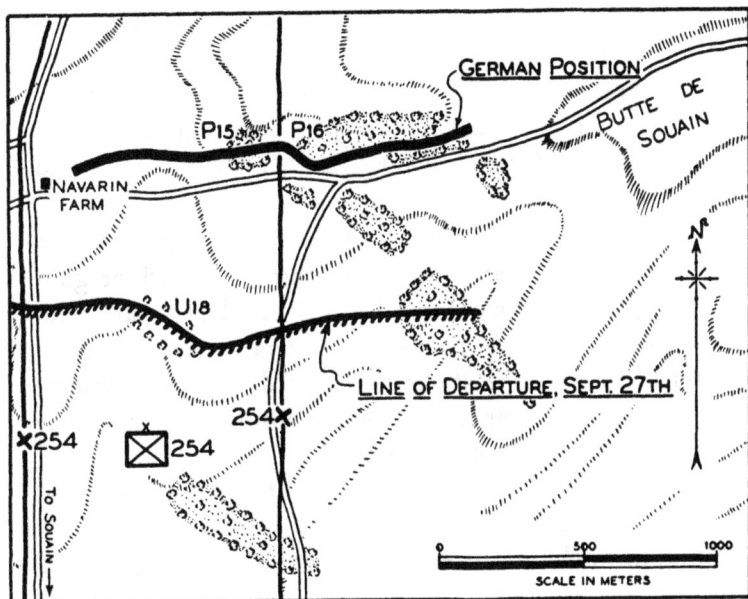

Example 1

The attack order called for a deep column of assault with
waves 300 meters apart. The 19th Battalion of Chasseurs, deployed in one dense skirmish line, would form the leading wave.
Behind it would march the 355th Infantry (two battalions only),
the 171st Infantry, and the 26th Battalion of Chasseurs.

The assault column would form prior to H-hour with each
wave completely deployed in line of skirmishers. At H-hour all
waves would move forward "and not allow themselves to be
stopped either by obstacles or by enemy fire."

Thus a mass of 6,000 bayonets was to assault a front of 800

meters. Enthusiasm ran high, for this was the third day of a great French offensive—an offensive that would bring Germany to her knees. The troops were confident that the hour of decisive victory was at hand.

And so, at the appointed hour, this brigade of 6,000 high-hearted and determined men stood up and at the word of command fixed their bayonets, shouldered their rifles, and marched forward in quick time and in step to assault an intrenched enemy armed with machine guns. One can only surmise the thought in the minds of those German gunners as they saw the dense and seried waves of skirmishers marching stolidly toward them.

As the leading wave approached the German position the French artillery lifted and the enemy's artillery, machine guns and rifles opened with a concerted roar. The leading wave went down, the others surging forward were literally blown apart. In a matter of minutes the attack had melted away. A few men reached the wire in front of the German position, but there they were forced to take cover in shell holes. The entire brigade, nailed to the ground by a merciless fire, could do nothing but wait for nightfall.

During the night units were reorganized and the higher command ordered a resumption of the attack the next day. The new brigade commander (the previous one had been wounded) issued his orders. Zone of action and formation were the same as for the 27th. The attack order included the following:

> The brigade commander insists particularly that it is with rifles on shoulders, bayonets fixed, and in good order, that the result will be achieved. Do not think of firing; just push on.

The attack was launched at 3:30 p.m., from a line only 200 meters from the German position. The massive column of assault rose, moved forward in step, and the events of the day before were repeated. Pinned to the ground, the débris of the brigade waited for night.

Under cover of darkness it managed to withdraw. Losses were more than fifty per cent and included nearly all the officers.

From an article by Lieutenant Colonel Ducornez, French Army, in "La Revue d'Infanterie," February, 1927.

DISCUSSION. The war had lasted more than a year when this attack was launched, yet we see the French still contemptuous of the effects of fire. No effort was made to utilize infantry fire power—in fact, firing was forbidden. The French sought to overwhelm the enemy by employing a massive column of assault —a formation of a bygone day which took no account of the annihilating power of modern weapons. The result is clear-cut. In attempting to win by movement alone, the 254th Brigade met with a costly reverse. Six thousand bayonets, massed on a narrow front, proved helpless against a far smaller number of defenders.

✔   ✔   ✔

EXAMPLE 2. At 3:15 p.m. June 6, 1918, the U. S. 23d Infantry received orders directing it to launch an attack to the east and northeast at 5:00 p.m. with two battalions in assault. It was planned to support the attack with a machine-gun company and the available one-pounders and Stokes mortars, but no arrangements were made for artillery support.

The time was inadequate for the necessary preliminary arrangements. The 3d Battalion attacked at 5:50 p.m. with companies K and M in assault—the company commanders literally gathering these companies together on the run and starting toward the enemy line.

The attack moved through a rolling wheat field toward its objective. Little, if any, supporting fire was placed on the German position as the riflemen advanced. When the battalion was deep in the wheat field, the enemy machine gunners opened fire from the front and flanks, inflicting heavy casualties and halting the attack. The battalion eventually withdrew to its original po-

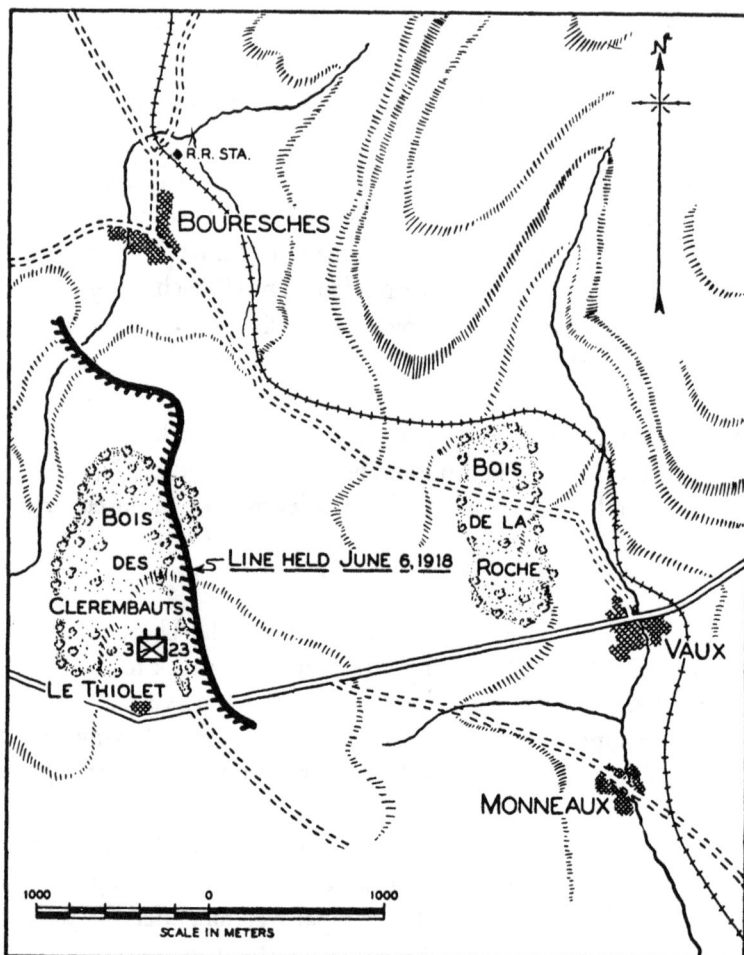

Example 2

sition. It had lost 8 officers and 165 men, virtually all from the assault companies, K and M.

❦   ❦   ❦

On July 1, 1918, the same battalion again attacked, this time from a line about 1,000 yards east of the position it occupied on

June 6. In the interim the regiment had received replacements and had been reorganized.

In this attack every type of fire support, including a rolling barrage, was utilized. One entire machine-gun company, one section of Stokes mortars and one section of 37-mm. guns, were attached to the battalion. Every detail for supporting fires had been completed.

The attack moved off promptly at 6:00 p.m. and advanced in perfect order. By 8:00 p.m. all units were on their objectives and consolidating their positions. More than a hundred prisoners and thirteen machine guns had been captured. After repulsing a strong counter-attack, supported by artillery, a check of casualties revealed the loss of four officers and 143 men.

From the personal experience monograph of Captain Withers A. Burress, Operations Officer of the 23d Infantry.

DISCUSSION. In this example we see the same unit attacking twice over practically the same terrain.

The first attack, notable for its lack of fire support, failed to attain its objective. Its only result was the temporary elimination of two companies from further combat usefulness.

The second attack clearly illustrates the effectiveness of adequate fire. Here, all available supporting weapons were brought to bear in order to further the advance of the attacking infantry. As a result, the same unit, but with less experienced personnel, overcame strong enemy opposition, and advanced to its objective in good order. Furthermore, it sustained fewer casualties than in its previous abortive effort.

The second attack was a limited-objective operation, prepared well in advance. In mobile warfare neither the time nor the matériel will be available for any such elaborate scheme of fire support, but by the same token the organization of the defense will usually be less complete. But be it trench warfare or open warfare, leaders must still bend every effort to provide their attacking troops with some form of effective fire support.

EXAMPLE 3. On July 30, 1918, the 1st Battalion of the U. S. 47th Infantry attacked to the north with companies B and D in assault, B on the right. No supporting fires had been provided.

Company D moved forward to the attack with the 1st and 3d Platoons in assault, the 1st Platoon on the right. After an advance of 250 yards the company came under fire. Thereafter, by dint of short dashes and crawling, the men succeeded in advancing the line some fifty yards farther, but here they were held up and here they remained for three hours with the enemy position only a little more than a hundred yards to their front.

The situation looked bad, particularly for the 3d Platoon, which had been caught in the open ground in the left half of the company zone, where it was being systematically cut to pieces by machine-gun fire from the front and both flanks. All efforts to advance this platoon had failed. The 1st Platoon, pinned to the ground in a partially-cut wheat field, was not much better off.

After three hours of this a message came in from Company B stating that machine guns in front of Company D were holding up their advance and asking Company D to clean them up. Spurred to renewed action by this message, the company commander directed the 1st Platoon to work two automatic rifles forward to a point just within the northwest corner of the wheat field. They were to open fire to their left-front whether they saw anything to fire at or not, since the machine guns which had been holding up the 3d Platoon seemed to be located in that general area. The 3d Platoon was ordered to be ready to rush when the automatic rifles opened fire.

The automatic riflemen reached their position, saw some Germans and opened fire to the left-front. At the sound of the Chauchats the 3d Platoon rushed the hostile position, covering the intervening distance of 125 yards at a run. The resistance was promptly overcome, about twenty-five prisoners being taken in the assault.

From the personal experience monograph of Captain John W. Bulger, who commanded Company D of the 47th Infantry.

DISCUSSION. In this action no fire support of any sort had been provided for the 1st Battalion which was separated from its regiment. The battalion pushed forward 300 yards and then

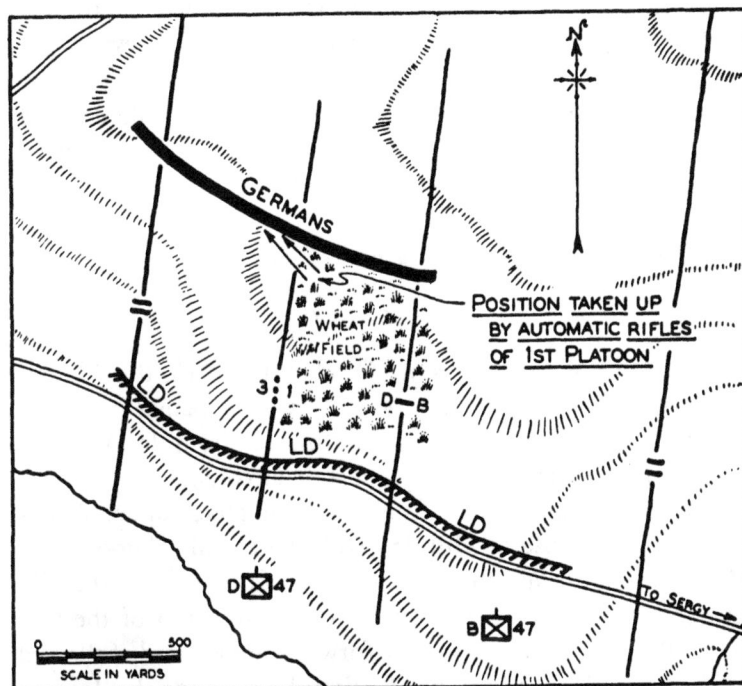

Example 3

was nailed to the ground. For three hours it stayed there while its casualties mounted. Then the captain of the left assault company ordered a very simple maneuver. He had two automatic riflemen work their way forward through the wheat and open fire to the left-front. Under cover of this fire the 3d Platoon rushed and carried the position. The effectiveness of this simple expedient probably lay in the surprise effect of fire coming from an unexpected direction which required a new distribution of

enemy fire. In any event, this reasoned use of fire and movement plus a seasoning of surprise resulted, as it so often does, in
success.

It is interesting to learn that Company B employed a similar
maneuver at about the same time. One automatic rifleman and
a lieutenant crawled forward on the extreme left flank until they
reached a position considerably in advance of the rest of the
company. The automatic then opened fire on the enemy to the
right-front. The fire of this well-posted automatic rifle enabled
Company B to resume its advance after it too had been held up
for several hours. The German position was then quickly over-
run.[1]

[1]*Statement of Captain Jared I. Wood, who commanded Company B of the 47th
Infantry.*

✓   ✓   ✓

EXAMPLE 4. At 7:30 a.m., October 10, 1918, the 2d Battalion of the U. S. 38th Infantry, with two companies in assault
and two in support, attacked northward from la Mamelle
Trench. Each assault company attacked in column of platoons.

Company G, on the left, formed for the attack under shelter
of the western nose of Hill 255 with the assault platoon in la
Mamelle Trench and the other platoons farther down the hill.
The scouts of the leading section were on the crest of the hill.
At 7:30 a.m. the scouts moved forward unmolested, followed
by the leading section in line of skirmishers. When this leading
line reached the crest of the hill, it was met by heavy machine-
gun fire and promptly disappeared from view. The sections in
rear continued to move forward and piled up on those in front.
Within fifteen minutes most of the company was pinned to the
ground on the crest and northern slopes of the hill. The enemy
artillery and machine-gun fire was so intense that the company
was virtually paralyzed. In twenty minutes it suffered fifty per
cent casualties.

The situation in the other companies was much the same.

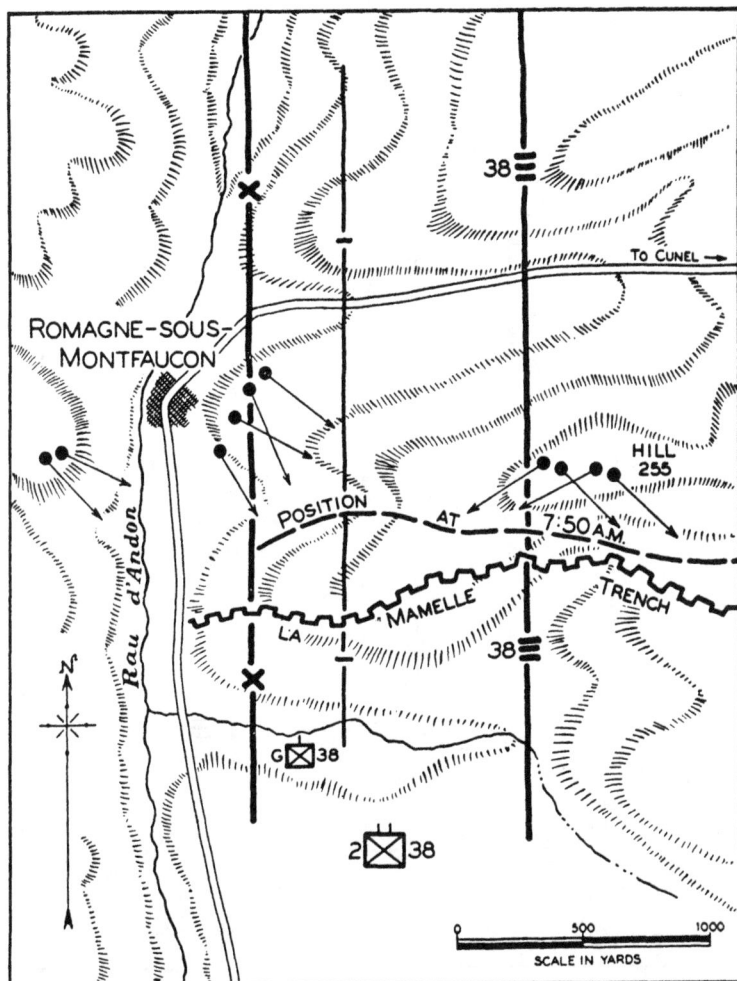

Example 4

Units became intermingled and the few remaining leaders lost control. The battalion, unsupported by fire, was unable to make effective reply to the deluge of German fire which converged upon it from the town of Romagne-sous-Montfaucon, from the ridge west of that town and, most disconcerting of all, from

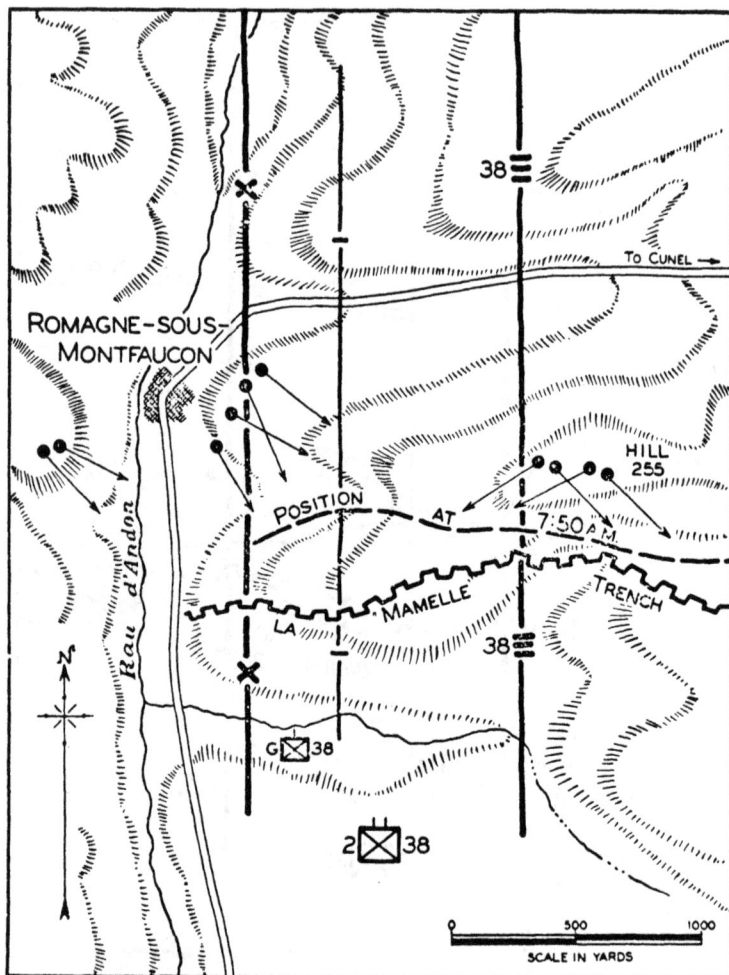

Example 4

the crest of Hill 255. By 7:50 a.m.—only thirty minutes after the jump-off—it was clear that the attack had failed. The battalion commander thereupon ordered a withdrawal to la Mamelle Trench. This was accomplished by individuals crawling back over the hill.

When the battalion withdrew, five or six riflemen remained on the forward slope of the hill. A lieutenant, commanding a machine-gun section, saw these men and ordered his guns to be set up near them. He then opened fire on the German position on the crest of Hill 255, from which the heaviest hostile fire was coming, and continued firing until his ammunition was exhausted. Then, led by the lieutenant, the riflemen and the gun crews rushed the position. Their charge was successful. Thirty-six prisoners and six machine guns were captured. The battalion was unaware of what had happened until the prisoners were marched into the American lines.

From the personal experience monograph of Captain Francis M. Rich, who commanded Company G of the 38th Infantry.

DISCUSSION. Here we see a battalion met by fire from three directions as it moved over the crest of a hill. The men were confused, control was lost, and the advance was definitely stopped. The reasons are clear. The battalion had no effective artillery support and it had not established a base of fire. In attempting to fight fire with movement alone, it merely offered itself as a target for the enemy. A few minutes of this was enough. It withdrew. The attack had failed.

Two machine guns and a few riflemen thereupon proceeded to accomplish more than the entire battalion. This small group began by placing heavy fire on the enemy on Hill 255. Here we see effective reply being made to the German fire; the Americans no longer had the exclusive rôle of targets. Then came the rush which carried the position. Movement combined with fire had again succeeded where movement alone had failed.

❦   ❦   ❦

EXAMPLE 5. At dawn on July 18, 1918, the 1st Battalion of the U. S. 16th Infantry attacked eastward with two companies in assault and two in support. On the first objective, Company D leap-frogged the assault company in its front and became the left assault company.

At 5:50 a.m. the advance was resumed. Smoke and the early morning mists limited visibility to a few yards. Shortly after

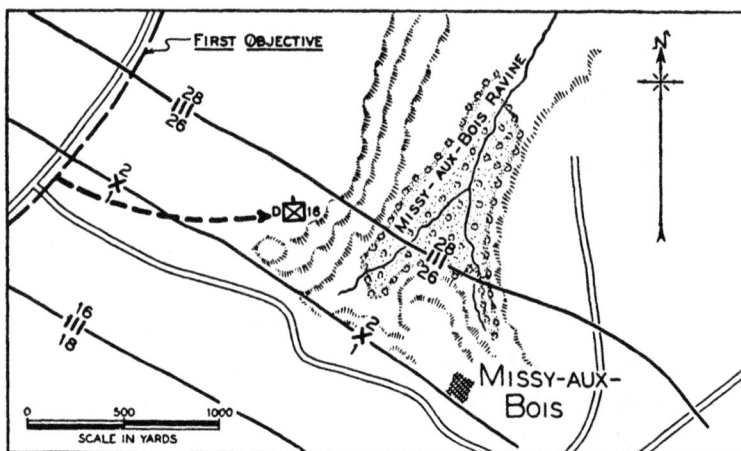

Example 5

this second advance began Company D lost contact with units to its left, right and rear. The advance, however, was continued. Suddenly the mist lifted and the company emerged on a small knoll on the western edge of the Missy-aux-Bois Ravine. Here it was stopped by concentrated enemy machine-gun fire from the front and both flanks. No friendly troops were in sight. The entire company was withdrawn in rear of the knoll. Patrols were sent out on each flank but the enemy fire was so heavy that any advance beyond the crest of the knoll was impossible. Enemy machine guns had been placed to rake the ravine.

Shortly thereafter, and much to the surprise of the company commander, four French tanks appeared from the rear and moved into the position of Company D. These brought down still more fire. The captain of Company D immediately took charge of the tanks and pointed out to the French lieutenant in command those targets which had been located. The tanks moved straight across the ravine under a hail of enemy fire and then turned south down the ravine toward Missy-aux-Bois, wreaking havoc among the enemy machine-gun nests.

When the tanks left the ravine, the company moved forward. Only one enemy machine-gun opened fire as the line crossed the crest of the knoll and advanced into the ravine.

From the personal experience monograph of Major Leonard R. Boyd, who commanded Company D of the 16th Infantry.

DISCUSSION. As so often happens in war, this company suddenly found itself in an unusual and unexpected situation. The lifting fog revealed that the company had gone astray. Contact had been lost with all friendly troops and with all weapons that had been supporting the advance. Such were the conditions in which this isolated unit stumbled against the strongly held Missy-aux-Bois position and there it was stopped in its tracks by a storm of machine-gun fire from the front and both flanks. Further advance was impossible.

Then came the tanks—literally a *deus ex machina.* Here were supporting weapons indeed; here was a base of fire—a *moving* base of fire—that could and did silence the murderous machine guns. Thus did Company D gain the fire superiority that enabled it to resume its advance.

ᛉ   ᛉ   ᛉ

CONCLUSION. From the time infantry becomes exposed to the fire of hostile infantry, fire and movement become inseparable. At the longer ranges, supporting weapons will furnish the fire and the riflemen will furnish the movement. This fire must be adequate and it must be effective if the infantry is to close to assaulting distance and still have strength enough to storm the position.

As the infantry nears the hostile position the supporting fires are forced to lift. Then must the riflemen themselves furnish both the fire and the movement. At this stage, fire without movement is useless and movement without fire is suicidal. Even with both, the last hundred yards is a touch-and-go proposition demanding a high order of leadership, sound morale, and the will to win.

Chapter XVII: *Fire of Machine Guns*

Machine guns affect the outcome of battle by fire power alone. Guns that have not fired have not attacked, no matter how many times they have been placed in position.

THE MACHINE GUN acts by fire alone; movement of this weapon has no other purpose than to secure positions from which more effective fire can be delivered. Maximum usefulness is obtained only when every gun within range of the enemy is firing effectively against him.

Studies of the use of machine guns on the Western Front disclose the fact that while some machine-gun companies performed many and varied fire missions, others performed few fire missions, and had no effect upon the outcome. Some commanders made great use of their machine guns; others merely had them tag along.

Leaders must know what the guns can do before the attack starts, what they can do while the attack is in progress, and what they can do during reorganization and consolidation. They must learn to seek and to recognize opportunities for employing machine guns in every phase of the action. Finally, they must have the aggressiveness to keep everlastingly at the task of getting the guns forward, so that when opportunity does present, they will be able to seize it.

✓   ✓   ✓

EXAMPLE 1. In the opening phase of the Meuse-Argonne offensive the well-seasoned U. S. 28th Division was given the mission of outflanking the Argonne Forest on the east.

Of the division's fourteen machine-gun companies, eight were ordered to support the assault battalions. The division machine-gun officer was directed to draw up a plan for the effective employment of the other six. These six companies were used in the following manner:

The 108th Machine-Gun Battalion was assigned tasks in the left half of the division zone and the 109th Machine-Gun Bat-

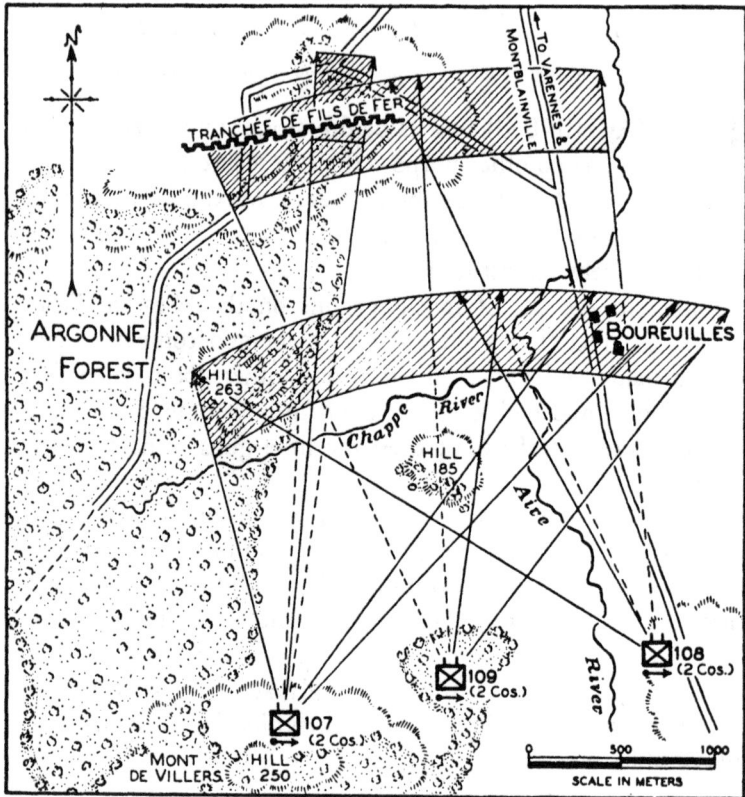

Example 1

talion in the right half. The four companies of these two battalions were to fire initially upon the enemy front line from Boureuilles to Hill 263, inclusive, then to lift to the Fils de Fer. One company of the 107th Machine-Gun Battalion was directed to fire initially on Boureuilles and the other upon Hill

263, after which both were to place an enfilade barrage along the edge of the forest.

It was all long-range fire, and much of it had to be delivered by indirect laying. Reconnaissance for positions was necessary and data had to be prepared, checked and rechecked. T-bases were put in and the guns placed in position. Each company was required to have 60,000 additional rounds of ammunition. Fire was to be delivered at the rate of 100 rounds per gun per minute. D-day and H-hour were announced as 5:30 a.m., September 26, 1918.

The actual occupation of positions began late in the afternoon of September 25. Despite difficulties and the great amount of preparation, checking and coördinating, everything was in readiness well in advance of the hour set for the jump-off.

At 2:30 a.m. the artillery preparation started. Shortly before H-hour, the machine-gun barrage commenced on schedule and as planned. Fire from guns of all calibers poured into the German position.

The advance began. During the day the left brigade carried Hill 263 and pushed on into the edge of the forest. The right brigade took Varennes, and then pushed up the Aire valley as far as Montblainville. Strong resistance was met but at the end of the day this alleged "impregnable position" had been successfully penetrated.

From the personal experience monograph of Major Stuart C. MacDonald, who was Machine-Gun Officer of the 28th Division.

DISCUSSION. This example shows that even when in reserve, machine guns may be used to good purpose during the initial stages of an attack.

Commanders of regiments and larger units must seize opportunities to use all the supporting fires their organization can furnish. Guns of reserve battalions are available for these missions and should be so employed. If they remain silent, they exert no influence upon the outcome of battle.

Of course, preparatory and supporting fires cannot eliminate the enemy, but they can reduce his defensive power by inflicting casualties, by making his fire less effective, by lowering his morale, and by interfering with his movement and reinforcement. The defense may thus be weakened to such an extent that the attackers can assault the position with a reasonable chance of success and without prohibitive losses.

✔ ✔ ✔

EXAMPLE 2. This example is a continuation of the operations of the 28th Division in the Meuse-Argonne. The next day, September 27, an unsupported rifle battalion attempted to advance to le Chêne Tondu but was driven back after suffering heavy casualties from machine-gun fire. It was reforming for a

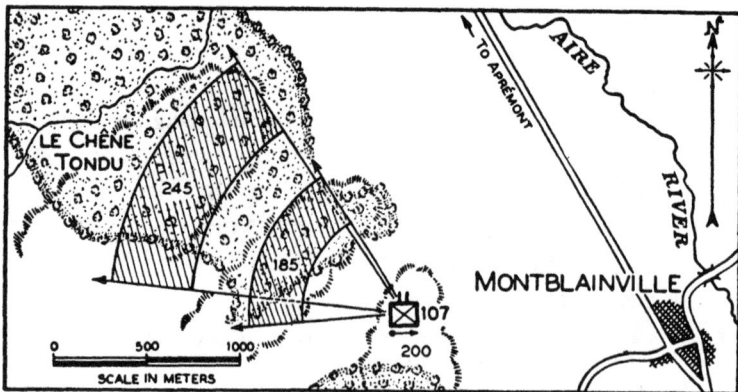

Example 2

second attempt when the division machine-gun officer arrived. This officer promptly arranged with the commander of the rifle battalion to support the attack by machine-gun fire. He brought up the 24 guns of the division machine-gun battalion (the 107th) and secured other guns from the 109th Machine-Gun Battalion, which was nearby. These guns were placed in position on the forward slopes of a commanding ridge from which the attack could be supported by direct overhead fire.

All was now ready, but there were no targets. There were no enemy columns, no enemy groups, no visible enemy trenches or other works. Nevertheless, the enemy was there and the American machine gunners knew a way to get at him.

Each pair of guns was given an initial mission of firing upon the first wooded ridge. This fire was to start two minutes before the battalion jumped off, and was to continue until masked by the advance. When this occurred, all guns would lift to le Chêne Tondu. In neither case were there any definite targets; therefore area fire was to be used and this was to sweep again and again through the suspected German positions. This plan, although worked out rapidly, was carefully coördinated.

When the American machine guns opened, the Germans attempted to silence them by fire. This failed, for the guns were well concealed and the German fire, directed at the summit, passed harmlessly overhead.

The attack succeeded. The assault units met no resistance whatever.

From the personal experience monograph of Major Stuart C. MacDonald, who was Machine-Gun Officer of the 28th Division.

DISCUSSION. This operation illustrates how machine guns may be used to aid assault units when they get into difficulties after having left the initial line of departure.

Whether this success was brought about because the machine guns found their targets and drove the Germans out, or because the Germans recognized this as a properly supported attack and withdrew to a new position in accordance with a prearranged plan, is not definitely known. But whatever the cause of the German retirement, the facts are that the unsupported attack failed with heavy losses, while the supported attack succeeded with no known casualties.

Two factors contributed to the success of the second attack:

the first, and most important, was the willingness of the rifle battalion to try again; the second was the presence of a machine-gun commander who saw something his guns could do and did not hesitate to offer them for the mission. Apparently no one had ordered this machine-gun commander to find this particular assault battalion and help it. He didn't wait to notify anyone or to get authority for this use of his guns. Instead he went to another battalion and borrowed more. He saw an opportunity to affect the outcome of battle by the use of his guns and seized it.

The ideal target seldom occurs in battle. Rarely will even small groups of the enemy be seen. But the absence of definitely located targets is not a bar to firing. If the enemy is thought to occupy an area, that area may be swept with fire to seek him out. Generally, the area in which he is located will be determined by the resistance encountered in the advance and this knowledge will afford the machine guns their opportunity. The machine gun is a suitable weapon to employ against areas. It has the necessary volume of fire and delivers it on a long and narrow beaten zone. It can be traversed uniformly to cover wide areas, and raised or lowered to cover deep ones. By searching critical areas, valuable results may be obtained from guns that might otherwise serve no useful purpose.

✓　　✓　　✓

EXAMPLE 3. On November 21, 1914, the German 49th Reserve Division had been roughly handled by the Russians. A powerful Russian attack had carried the three small hills north of Gospodarz, captured the 9th Battery, and driven back the 225th, 228th, and 231st Infantry Regiments, which had been defending the hills.

Shortly before dawn of November 22 these three German regiments attacked to the northwest in an effort to retake the three hills and the lost battery. The 228th Infantry, in the center of the line, was charged with the recapture of Hill No. 2 and the

9th Battery. The 225th Infantry, attacking on the right, struck at Hill No. 1 and the 231st Infantry, on the left, at Hill No. 3. The gruelling campaign had reduced all three regiments to skeleton strength; not one could muster more than a few hundred effectives.

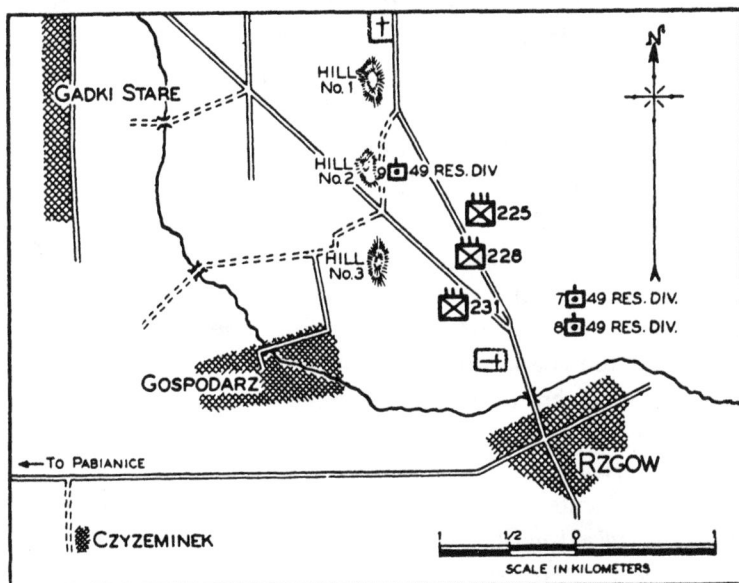

Example 3

It was still dark when the attack jumped off. The 228th Infantry, with its left following the left branch of the road from Rzgow, drove forward rapidly and soon recaptured the lost battery. At this point it became apparent that the 228th had outdistanced both the 225th and the 231st, for in addition to the heavy frontal fire from Hill No. 2, this hard-driving regiment was now taken under a murderous cross-fire from Hill No. 1 and Hill No. 3.

In an effort to escape this fire the 228th pushed forward to the shelter afforded by the slopes of Hill No. 2. Here it found comparative security from the Russian machine guns but it also found something else: it found that the German artillery was shelling Hill No. 2 and that much of this fire was falling squarely in the ranks of the 228th. The situation was critical: the regiment could not advance; it could not stay where it was; and if it withdrew it would again come under machine-gun fire from three directions. The regimental commander decided that a withdrawal was the best of three very bad choices and accordingly ordered his command to fall back to the battery position.

So back the regiment went while the Russian guns swept it from flank to flank. Back in the battery position they sheltered themselves as best they could and waited. The enemy's machine guns continued to rake the position. No man dared lift his head.

And, then, the men of the 228th suddenly heard German machine guns firing to their left and right. The sound and the tempo were too characteristic and too familiar to be mistaken. As this German fire increased in volume and intensity, the fire on the 228th steadily dwindled. Men began to lift their heads and look about.

Suddenly Lieutenant Kuhlow, the only unwounded officer of the 228th, seized a rifle with bayonet fixed, leapt to his feet, and shouted, *"Vorwärts! Kameraden, folgt mir! Auf, marsch, marsch!"* and started for Hill No. 2. "That cry," says the German account, "held magic." The remnant of the 228th—"there may have been a hundred men in all"—surged after their leader. This little German group swept up the disputed hill. "The Russians fired to the last minute," says the account, "and then surrendered."

From "*The Experiences of the 49th Reserve Division in the Campaign of Lodz, November 22, 1914.*"

DISCUSSION. Here are two perfect examples of machine guns used to assist adjacent units—one by the Russians in defense, one by the Germans in attack.

Opportunities to assist adjacent units by fire constantly occur in battle. In the attack some units advance faster than others; these will have enemy positions on their flanks. Often these positions may be subjected to enfilade or reverse fires from machine-gun units that have gone forward with the riflemen. By taking advantage of such opportunities, adjacent units are helped forward and, at the same time, serious threats are removed from the flanks of the more advanced units.

On the defensive, similar opportunities to assist adjacent units by fire will be frequent. The first penetrations of a defensive line will be made on a limited front. By cross fires from adjacent positions as well as by prompt counter-attack, the penetration may be stopped and the enemy ejected.

✓   ✓   ✓

CONCLUSION. The foregoing examples illustrate the use of machine guns in the attack. Good illustrations of this use of heavy machine guns by American troops in the early stages of the World War are none too frequent. In view of the innumerable examples that are available to show the decisive influence of this powerful weapon in defensive operations, the shortage of good attack illustrations is significant. It strongly indicates that the possibilities of machine guns as an adjunct to the attack were not fully appreciated until the war had nearly run its course. In the earlier American attacks, machine guns were seldom assigned specific fire-supporting missions. The idea seems to have prevailed that machine guns were fulfilling their mission as long as they maintained their place in the formation.

The following quotation from Colonel Walter C. Short's book, *The Employment of Machine Guns*, bears on this point:

> In the 1st Division at Soissons on July 18, 1918, the machine-gun companies were broken up and three machine guns were assigned to each infantry company. These guns were practically all placed in the first wave of the company to which attached. Almost the

only order given to the machine gunners was for them to take their places in certain waves. I talked with practically all infantry battalion commanders and machine-gun officers of the 1st Division after this fight, and I found no case where an order had been given for the machine guns to support the advance of the infantry with fire. The order had been invariably to take a certain place in the formation. The machine gunners had generally interpreted the order literally. They took this position in the formation and kept it. They were not interested in finding opportunities for shooting their guns nearly so much as they were in maintaining their position. The results were most serious. The machine-gun companies suffered very heavy casualties and accomplished practically nothing except during the consolidation. One company lost 57 men without firing a shot. Another company lost 61 men and fired only 96 rounds. This is typical of what happened to a greater or lesser extent throughout the whole division.

Later on the Americans began to realize some of the possibilities of the machine gun. Again quoting Colonel Short:

At St. Mihiel the 90th Division made practically no use of its machine guns. On the contrary, on November 1 it fired over 1,000,000 rounds with the machine guns, and practically all day the infantry advanced under the protection of machine-gun fire. The 2d Division at St. Mihiel used only 8 out of 14 companies at the beginning of the fight. On November 1 this division not only used all of its own guns but used 10 companies of the 42d Division. The 5th Division at St. Mihiel used only 8 out of 14 companies at the beginning of the fight. In the early part of November this same division was using overhead machine-gun fire to cover the advance of its exploiting patrols. These three divisions are typical examples of the great strides that were made in the use of machine guns during the last few months before the Armistice.

Although machine guns lend themselves more readily to the defense than to the attack, this is no excuse for a failure to exact the utmost from them in support of advancing troops. The handicaps to their effective employment in the attack can and must be overcome. An intelligent appreciation by battalion and regimental commanders of their power and limitations is essential and this must be supplemented by the determination to get the guns forward and use them. For their part the machine-gun units must be on the alert to seize and exploit every opportunity to assist the forward movement of the rifle units, without waiting for specific orders to engage a particular target or locality.

Chapter XVIII: *Infantry-Artillery Team*

*The effective functioning of the infantry-
artillery team depends upon the intelligent
and unremitting efforts of both members to
solve the difficult problem of liaison.*

WHEN INFANTRY has room to maneuver, or is not
faced by strong continuous resistance, it may be able to
advance with little or no assistance from tanks and artillery. This
situation may arise when the enemy is not determined to hold,
or after the rupture of his position. On the other hand, when
confronted by determined resistance from a strong enemy who
is well equipped with machine guns, infantry requires all possible assistance from the auxiliary arms, particularly the powerful help of the artillery, in order to have any chance of success.

In our problems and exercises we have adopted a liaison tech-
nique which permits infantry-artillery teamwork, but does not
insure it. Mere physical and intellectual liaison between these
two arms is not enough; there must be moral liaison as well.
The infantry must know and trust the artillery; the artillery must
know and trust the infantry.

Let us examine some of the many difficulties the infantry-
artillery team meets in the attack. Let us assume that a battalion has an artillery liaison officer with it, that communications
are working, and that in the initial stages of the attack the
artillery can fire its concentrations either on a time schedule or
by direct observation of the infantry's advance.

So far so good, or at any rate, not so bad. But now what
happens if the infantry goes too fast, or not fast enough, for a
time schedule of concentrations? What happens if it goes
through terrain where it and the enemy are both lost to view of
artillery observers?

Usually it will not be long before our battalion strikes a snag. The problem of infantry-artillery liaison then becomes acute. Pinned to the ground, platoon leaders have only a vague impression of the sources of hostile fire, and that impression may be in error.

Although it will seldom be true, let us assume that all officers are provided with adequate maps. Let us further assume that some of the enemy can actually be seen. Subordinate leaders must now transmit this information to the rear, together with the locations of their own units. Just how accurately will these platoon leaders be able to locate this hostile resistance on the map? How precisely will they indicate the positions of their own troops? Remember, this will not be done in the academic quiet of the map-problem room, but in the confusion and stress of battle; not on new, unfolded maps, but on maps that are muddy, wet, and wrinkled from a hundred folds. Under such conditions, just how legible will this information be?

The message goes back by runner and eventually reaches the battalion commander. This officer still has to formulate his request and, through his liaison officer, transmit it to the artillery. Even if we assume that this message is clear and accurate and contains all that the artilleryman must know, there are still other factors to be considered. The message may be long and involved. The artillery has to receive it, may have to compute data, and then has to get on the target. Even if everything is accomplished with 100% efficiency and good luck, how long will it all take? In exercises we do these things in a few minutes; in war they often take hours. The artillery may lack ground observation. The infantry's request may be incomplete or inaccurate. Communications may break down. These and a thousand and one similar obstacles may arise that must be overcome before the artillery can come to the aid of its partner.

Here are the things that artillerymen must know: accurate location of the target; nature of the target, whether it is an enemy machine gun, a line of foxholes, or a counter-attack; the location of the front line of friendly troops; when the fire is to start; and, finally, when it is to stop. Unless it has this information, the artillery can not respond effectively to the calls made upon it by the infantry it supports. But how often and how fast can the infantry furnish this? Artillery observers seldom know all of it unless they are told. They can see something, but not everything.

As a result of the lessons of the World War, we shall probably avoid some of the more common errors we made then. For instance, the artillery liaison officer will certainly not be chosen for his uselessness to the artillery, as seems to have been done in some cases.

We have a good mechanism, we prepare and number the concentrations that are likely to be needed, and we are well-schooled in theory. But how many infantry units frequently participate in exercises in which artillery is represented, and infantry-artillery liaison emphasized, when there is anything beyond the transmission of a routine message or so? Has the infantry been practiced under battle conditions, in transmitting requests to the artillery quickly—requests that the artillery finds adequate for fire on unexpected targets?

Unless infantry considers the artillery in all its actions, it is headed straight for trouble!

In many instances in the World War, artillery gave extremely effective support to the infantry. If we expect this to be normal we must make it normal. We must be prepared to deal with the difficult situation as well as the situation that solves itself. The infantry-artillery team is not a fair-weather partnership. For this reason the historical examples that follow deal largely with situations in which infantry-artillery teamwork was not attained or was difficult to attain.

✦   ✦   ✦

EXAMPLE 1. On August 22, 1914, the French Fourth Army

advanced northward in several columns. One of these columns, composed of elements of the XVII Corps, moved on Anloy via Jehonville. Although the situation was vague, the enemy was believed to have strong forces in the area Maissin—Anloy—Villance.

The advance guard of the French column, a battalion of the 14th Infantry, pushed through the woods north of Jehonville. At the north edge it ran into a violent and well-adjusted system of enemy fires and was unable to debouch. The other battalions of the 14th quickly entered the line and attacked. Although the regiment attacked again and again, it was uniformly unsuccessful. Each effort was repulsed with heavy losses. Another regiment, the 83d, moved to the west through the woods and attacked from that direction, but with no better result.

Meanwhile, what was the artillery doing? There were three battalions of artillery in the column. One battalion passed positions from which it could act to the north of the forest, and assembled in close formation in a dip northwest of Jehonville; the other two waited in rout column at Jehonville for orders that never arrived.

Of all this artillery only one battery went into position. This was located on the northwest slopes of Hill 435 behind a clump of trees. Although there was no observation post at hand that afforded a view north of the wood, the battery was nevertheless firing. (At this time French wire equipment was so limited that observation had to be close to the guns.)

A staff officer of the XVII Corps rode up to the battery commander and asked, "What are you firing on?"

The indignant artilleryman replied, "I am firing on the order of the general and on nothing else."

He had no target, and he was being very careful to fire "long."

From "The Combat of Infantry," by Colonel Allèhaut, French Army.

DISCUSSION. In this example the French infantry acted as

if the artillery did not exist. The artillery for its part, failed to solve a difficult problem but one that will be soon encountered in any war. There are lots of wooded areas in this world.

There was not the remotest indication of any infantry-artillery liaison here, and yet Colonel Allèhaut thinks that perhaps the artillery did some good. He says:

> Let us not forget that on this part of the battlefield infantry was succumbing to the combined fires of German machine guns and artillery. The voices of the cannons of this one battery were all that bolstered this infantry's impression that it had not been abandoned to its tragic fate. . . . The morale of the infantry of this column was rated among the best on this day. . . . [Perhaps] it was due to the illusion of support created by this one battery firing "into the blue."

Illusion may be better than nothing, but when it comes to artillery support of infantry what is actually needed is *reality*.

✓   ✓   ✓

EXAMPLE 2. On July 18, 1918, Battery A of the U. S. 7th Field Artillery formed part of the artillery supporting the 28th Infantry (1st Division). The initial artillery support was to take the form of a rolling barrage. Telephone wires had been installed, liaison detachments had gone to their respective headquarters, and H-hour (4:35 a.m.) found the battery in position, prepared to take its proper part in the attack.

In this operation the artillery battalion commander had been ordered to accompany the infantry commander whom he was supporting; this in addition to the usual liaison officer furnished the infantry. Since there was no executive officer provided at that time in the artillery organization, the senior battery commander was detailed to act in this capacity in the absence of the battalion commander. The commander of Battery A took over this duty. The procedure had certain disadvantages. To quote Captain Solomon F. Clark:

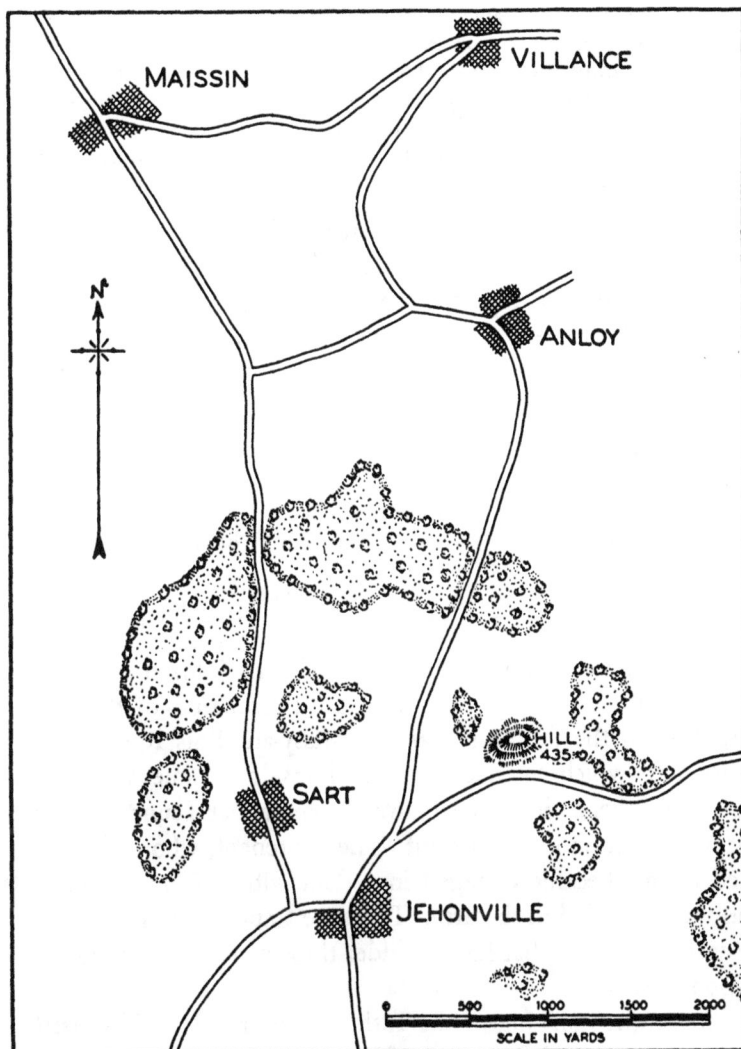

Example 1

Messages from the infantry came through the battalion commander. Messages, orders, fire charts, etc., from the artillery brigade, invariably came direct to the battalion C.P. near the batteries. This procedure practically deprived the artillery battalion commander of the ability to control his unit, and resulted, in those cases where it was followed to the letter, in command being assumed by junior officers for considerable periods of time.

At 4:35 a.m. the batteries opened. No caterpillar rockets were seen, so the artillery concluded that it was not firing short. Liaison officers soon reported that the barrage was satisfactory.

The attack progressed and Battery A displaced forward. On the way, a runner from the artillery liaison detachment met the battery. He delivered the following message:

From: Liaison Officer
To: B.C. Battery A.
The liaison detachment has captured a Boche 77 battery at (coördinates). They are marked "Battery A, 7th Field Artillery." Please have the limbers take them out.

2D LIEUT. ——————
Liaison Officer.

The liaison officer with his detail of a half-dozen men had gone over the top with one of the assault companies of the 28th Infantry. In the fighting near the Missy-aux-Bois Ravine, the platoon to which he had attached himself became separated from the others. Soon the platoon commander found himself out of contact on left and right. The lieutenant, who had never fired a rifle, became engaged in a duel with a German sniper and was wounded in the arm. To quote Captain Clark, "It may be easily imagined that liaison under these conditions practically ceased to exist."

Late on the morning of the 18th the commander of the artillery brigade visited Battery A. He stated that the infantry had far outrun the artillery fire, that they were at that time near Berzy-le-Sec, and that their front line was beyond the artillery's maximum range. Reconnaissance parties were sent out and, after some time, determined the location of the front line. It was by no means as far advanced as Berzy-le-Sec. In fact, the infantry did not take that town until several days later.

From the personal experience monograph of Captain Solomon F. Clark, Field Artillery.

DISCUSSION. The 1st Division had been in training in France for more than a year and had had six month's experience in the front line. It had participated in a limited objective attack

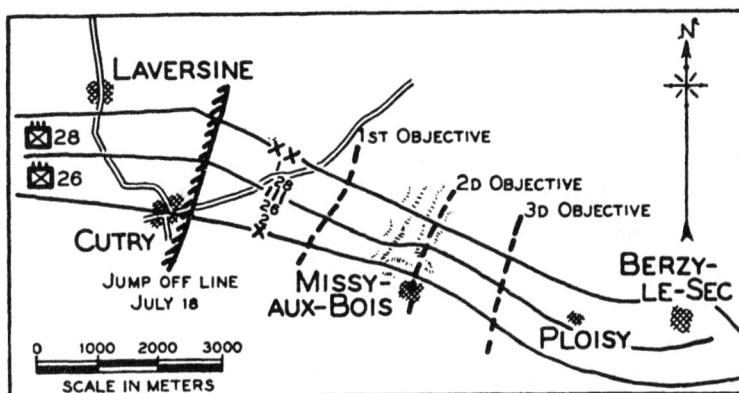

Example 2

at Cantigny. It was accustomed to the idea of liaison officers and was determined to solve the problem of tying in its artillery with the infantry. Is it reasonable to expect that the average division will be better prepared?

At the start of the attack liaison was perfect. The form of support—a rolling barrage—facilitated this at first. The rolling barrage, which lifts on a time schedule and moves forward, starts with the infantry but thereafter it may be either too slow or too fast. In one case it retards the infantry; in the other it outruns them, failing to give support where and when support is needed. However, "lifts" on a time schedule can solve the early part of the problem if the infantry and artillery have been coördinated beforehand.

The real trouble develops later. For instance, in the foregoing example, the artillery brigade commander was completely in error as to the location of the front-line infantry. It is obvious that unless the artillery knows the infantry's location it is going to hesitate to fire. Yet, despite this natural reluctance, it is only necessary to read the personal experiences of front-line infantry leaders to realize that all too frequently artillery does fire on its own troops. In fact, General Percin, of the French Army, estimates that 75,000 French casualties were caused by French artillery during the last war. American artillery frequently faced the same indictment.

It is infantry-artillery liaison that seeks to remedy such conditions and that strives to promote a more smoothly functioning partnership. This should be borne in mind when the artillery liaison officer reports to the infantry commander; an immediate conference should follow, and not a perfunctory one either. The infantry commander should thoroughly acquaint the liaison officer with the situation, and in turn be thoroughly acquainted with the artillery plan, the location of the artillery's OP's, the plan for displacement of observation, and the terrain the artillery commands with its observation and fires. Infantry should also have a clear understanding of the work of the liaison detail itself. During the World War an infantry commander often told his liaison officer, "You stay here," and then promptly forgot all about him.

The artillery believes today that a liaison officer, unless definitely needed at the front to check or observe fire, should stay with the infantry battalion commander. The artillery liaison sergeant remains at the command post in the absence of the battalion commander and the liaison officer. He keeps abreast of the situation and is authorized to transmit requests for fire. If the liaison officer is at the command post, the sergeant goes to the observation post.

In the example we have just examined, the artillery liaison

detail displayed great gallantry. They rivalled their infantry comrades in pushing forward against the Germans, but they did not do the job they were sent forward to do.

The infantry-artillery liaison mechanism existed then in much the same form it does today. The troops were better than the average that can be expected in the opening stages of any future war, and yet late in the morning of this attack "liaison practically ceased to exist."

Prearranged fires, assignment of specific artillery units to support specific infantry units, and the dispatch of liaison officers from artillery to infantry will not by themselves insure infantry-artillery teamwork.

◢   ◢   ◢

EXAMPLE 3. On August 20, 1914, the French 59th Division held a position near Nancy with outposts generally along the Seille. One battalion of the 47th Field Artillery, facing north and northeast, was located near Mt. Toulon and Mt. St. Jean. The 28th Battery was at B-1 with its observation at O-1, 300 meters in advance. The 27th had its observation on Mt. Toulon, and the 29th, farther east, had its observation on the spur to its front. The terrain permitted observation far to the front and to the east.

On the morning of August 20 the officers of the 28th and 29th Batteries were at the observation post of the 29th Battery with their battalion commander. To the east they heard an uninterrupted cannonade. It was known that the French Second Army had advanced in that direction. The 59th Division remained facing toward Metz. Beyond this the battery officers knew nothing of the situation.

About 10:00 a.m. a single shrapnel and a little later a salvo burst over Nomeny, where a French infantry company was on outpost. The captain of the 28th Battery rushed back to his O.P. The cannonade on Nomeny became more intense, then a sharp fusillade was heard. The artillery saw nothing to shoot at. Where were the French infantry of the 277th which was to the front? Some movement was noticed near Manoncourt. Men moved singly from the Seille toward the high ground to the south, then thin lines moved in the same direction, halted, and were hidden by the wheat.

Actually one battalion of the 277th Infantry had been strongly attacked and had fallen back and abandoned Nomeny, which had caught fire. At 11:00 a.m. this battalion was reinforced by another and a violent combat ensued on the front Nomeny—Manoncourt. But of all this the artillery was ignorant.

About noon the commander of the 28th Battery received an order through a liaison agent to open fire "to support the infantry toward Nomeny and Manoncourt." The order failed to state where that infantry was located. The liaison agent went back to the battalion O.P. at Mt. Toulon with the report that the O.P. of the 28th could not see Nomeny, and a request that the battery be permitted to change position. (The battery had only 500 meters of wire.)

In the meantime the battery commander had opened fire, because it seemed to him that the French had fallen back beyond the Manoncourt-Nomeny road; therefore in firing beyond that road (range more than 5,000 meters) there could be little danger to his own infantry. He chose a green field which stood out amid the yellow wheat and by progressive fires searched a wide area from the road to the stream. Enemy artillery fired on Mt. St. Jean and Mt. Toulon.

The rifle fire to the front died away. Soon after a battalion of the French 325th Infantry, which had been in reserve, moved forward on the road east of the 28th Battery. The battery commander found some personal friends in this battalion and, from them, learned that the 325th was to relieve the 277th and attack toward Nomeny. By this accidental conversation, he learned what had happened and what the infantry planned to do.

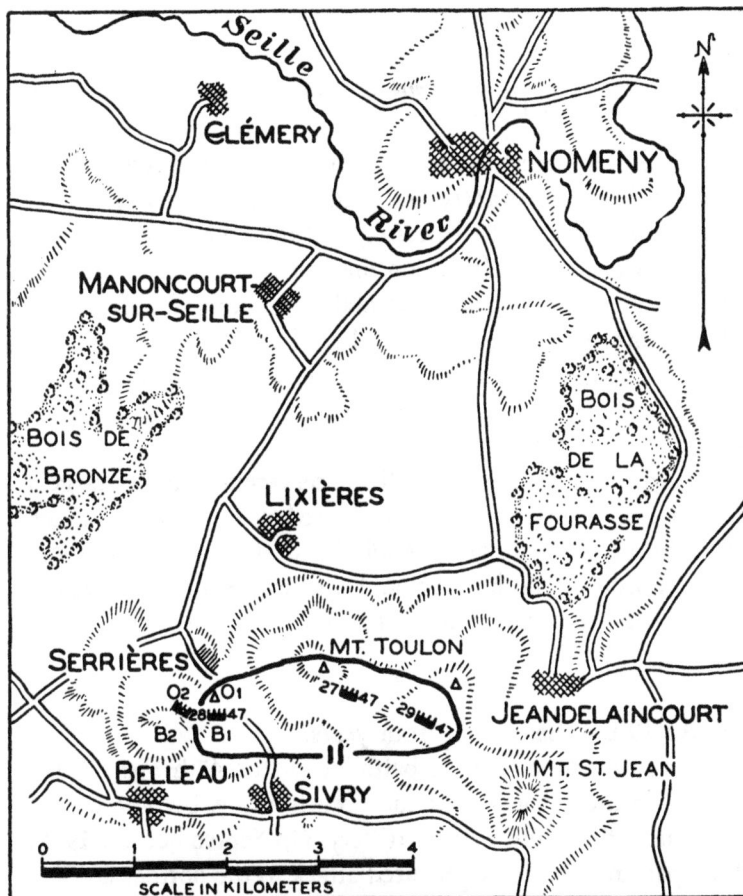

Example 3

Shortly after this the 28th Battery was ordered to accelerate its fire "to support the infantry toward Nomeny." The battery moved to B-2. From here the captain could see Nomeny and its environs.

About 4:00 p.m. he saw the 325th deploy one battalion on each side of the road and advance. The artillery placed fire in front of the 325th on the plateau which fell toward the Seille.

The infantry was enabled to advance. By dark it had nearly reached the Seille.

From an article by Major de la Porte du Theil, French Army, in "La Revue d'Infanterie," August, 1925.

DISCUSSION. Here the striking things are the absence of co-ordination between infantry and artillery, the lack of any precise missions given to the batteries, and the ignorance in which the artillerymen were left during the battle.

It was only through an accidental encounter of old friends that any information reached the batteries. There was no detachment charged with maintaining liaison. How much time would it have taken the infantry near Manoncourt to get a request for fire back to Mt. Toulon?

The artillery here had splendid observation; still its targets were far from conspicuous. It was forced to search areas where it thought the enemy might possibly be located. To a certain extent the action of the infantry and artillery was coördinated—but only because personal friends had accidentally met.

✦   ✦   ✦

EXAMPLE 4. Let us skip four years.

In 1918 this same artillery battalion of the 47th Field Artillery had, in the expansion of the French Army, become the 3d Battalion of the 220th Field Artillery. On September 14, 1918, it took part in a carefully prepared attack to the northeast.

Artillery support of the infantry was to be in the form of a rolling barrage; artillery units were assigned in direct support of infantry units; batteries were given precise missions; the artillery's command posts were located near the command posts of the infantry they supported; liaison detachments were furnished the infantry; displacements were planned in advance; and everything was worked out on an elaborate time schedule. Let us see what happened.

The French 165th Infantry and a battalion of marines were

the attacking elements of the division. They advanced at 5:50 a.m. The initial stages of the attack were successful. The artillery fired its barrage on schedule. At 8:20 a.m. the barrage reached the second objective. In accordance with orders, the 3d

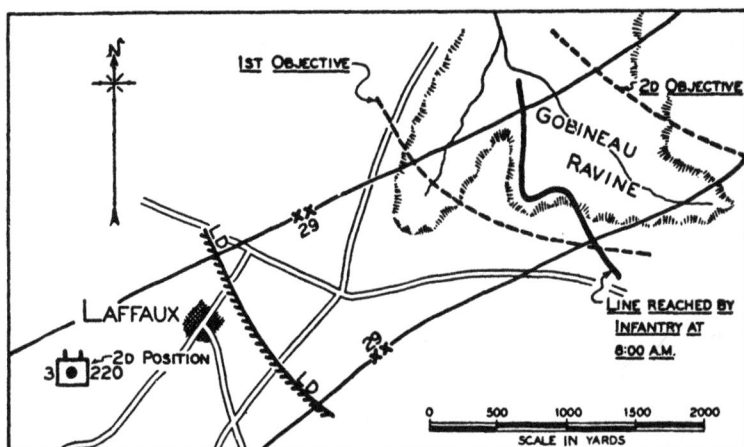

Example 4

Battalion of the 220th Field Artillery displaced forward. It was not expected to shoot again until 10:50, but was in its new position a kilometer west of Laffaux by 10:00 a.m. There it received orders to fire—not on targets beyond the second objective but on the Gobineau Ravine, much closer than that objective.

The infantry had not reached the second objective. It had been held up since 8:00 a.m. between the first and second objectives. The barrage had rolled on. The liaison details took more than an hour to acquaint the artillery with this situation. Artillery fires then had to be moved back toward the rear. The location of the French infantry still remained uncertain.

All morning, efforts were made to renew the advance. The artillery supported these attempts by firing on areas on the east slopes of the Gobineau Ravine. It was useless. At 6:00 p.m. the infantry was still in the immediate vicinity of the position it held at 8:00 a.m. Several days elapsed before the French were able to resume their advance.

From an article by Major de la Porte du Theil, French Army, in "La Revue d'Infanterie," August, 1925.

DISCUSSION. This operation was minutely prepared, but it was not possible to know in advance exactly what would happen. All details had been worked out on a time schedule, according to the concepts of the French command. When the rhythm was destroyed, it was difficult to tie in the artillery with the infantry. The infantry lacked support when it needed it most.

Despite signals, pyrotechnics, and all the other means of communication at its disposal, the liaison detachment took more than an hour to get word to its artillery of the existing situation. Even then the information was incomplete. Let us quote Major du Theil:

Only one thing was lacking: a knowledge of exactly where to fire.

The Gobineau Wood and Ravine are large. Tons of steel could be poured into them without reaching the few machine guns that stopped the 29th Division's infantry.

Who knew exactly where those machine guns were? Who could say? Maybe a few infantrymen of the 165th saw them. But no one could locate them exactly, much less direct the fire of a battery on them effectively, or send the necessary information to the captain, two or three kilometers to the rear.

The liaison detachments managed to transmit the approximate location of the lines. That was something. In an hour it was possible to bring back the barrages. Efforts were made to move out again—blind efforts. At no moment did we have precise fires, fires that kill the adversary aimed at, and which open the breach at the appointed place, as at the start of the attack.

Between 1914 and 1918 we had gone far. Nevertheless the experience of the war shows that the solution to this problem is not always effective in its present form.

Perhaps we may never be able to turn out a perfect solution to the problem—perfection of execution is seldom encountered in war—but we can overcome many difficulties that handicap infantry-artillery teamwork.

EXAMPLE 5. Following its defeat in the Battle of the Frontiers, the French Fourth Army withdrew slowly, and in the closing days of August, 1914, made a stand on the Meuse.

On August 27 the 87th Infantry Brigade, which had been in reserve near Beaufort and Beauclair, moved forward to take over a sector generally extending between Cesse and the Forêt de Jaulnay. Its mission was to prevent the enemy from debouching west of the Meuse. Limits of the sector were not precisely defined. It was understood that French outposts held the line of the Meuse.

Fourteen batteries of field artillery under an artillery regimental commander were attached to the 87th Brigade for the operation.

The brigade itself consisted of the 120th Infantry and the 9th and 18th Chasseur Battalions. The 18th Chasseurs were directed to occupy the woods just south of the Forêt de Jaulnay; the 9th Chasseurs were ordered into a position south of the Maison Blanche Inn; and the 120th Infantry was held in reserve.

The forward movement to these locations was made in a dense fog. The question of positions for the artillery was difficult. The woods were very thick, and from their edge the ground descended to the Meuse. It was finally decided to place all the artillery in a clearing about 800 yards wide in the Forêt de Dieulet. This position afforded excellent observation to the front.

As the result of previous successes in which artillery had played a large part, the 87th Brigade commander was strongly impressed with the necessity for artillery support of the infantry.

About 8:00 a.m. the fog lifted. German heavy artillery near Cervisy shelled the French position, blew up a caisson, and caused some losses. Because of the long range, the French artillery did not reply.

Through his field glasses the brigade commander noted some dark uniforms to the left front and, accompanied by the artillery colonel and a signal detail, went in that direction on a per-

sonal reconnaissance. He thought the troops seen were his own
18th Chasseurs. Instead he found troops of the II Colonial
Corps, the unit on his left.

He met a lieutenant whom he asked to explain the situation.

"General, we are at the place where the Beaumont-Stenay
road enters the Forêt de Jaulnay. The Maison Blanche Inn is
500 yards from here. Two kilometers farther in the same direction you can see some houses. That is the village of Cesse. The
Forêt de Dieulet is behind us, and to our left front is the Forêt
de Jaulnay. We have a post of Colonial infantry at Maison
Blanche. A battalion of the regiment of Colonel M, which occupies those trenches to your right toward that hill, 190, furnishes
the post at Maison Blanche.

"I belong to the regiment of Colonel L. We have one battalion in the Forêt de Jaulnay which is to advance in the woods
as far as the Inor bend, while the other two battalions under the
colonel attack in the direction of Luzy, with their left flank on
the edge of the Forêt de Jaulnay. Luzy is just behind that crest
you see on the horizon."

"What information have you of the enemy?"

"Cesse, Luzy, the Inor bend of the Meuse, and Pouilly are occupied by the enemy. Our outposts have been driven from that
crest this side of Luzy and the colonel is moving out to attack the
crest which he wants to hold. The Germans are on the military
crest now."

"Tell your colonel to hold up his attack until my artillery can
get in liaison with him and support his attack," directed the brigade commander.

The artillery colonel who had accompanied the brigade commander had a telephone wire connecting him with his batteries
in the clearing. He installed a telephone at an O.P. and began
to describe the situation to his commanders.

The lieutenant reached the Colonial colonel in time to stop
the attack. The colonel rushed to join the 87th Brigade com-

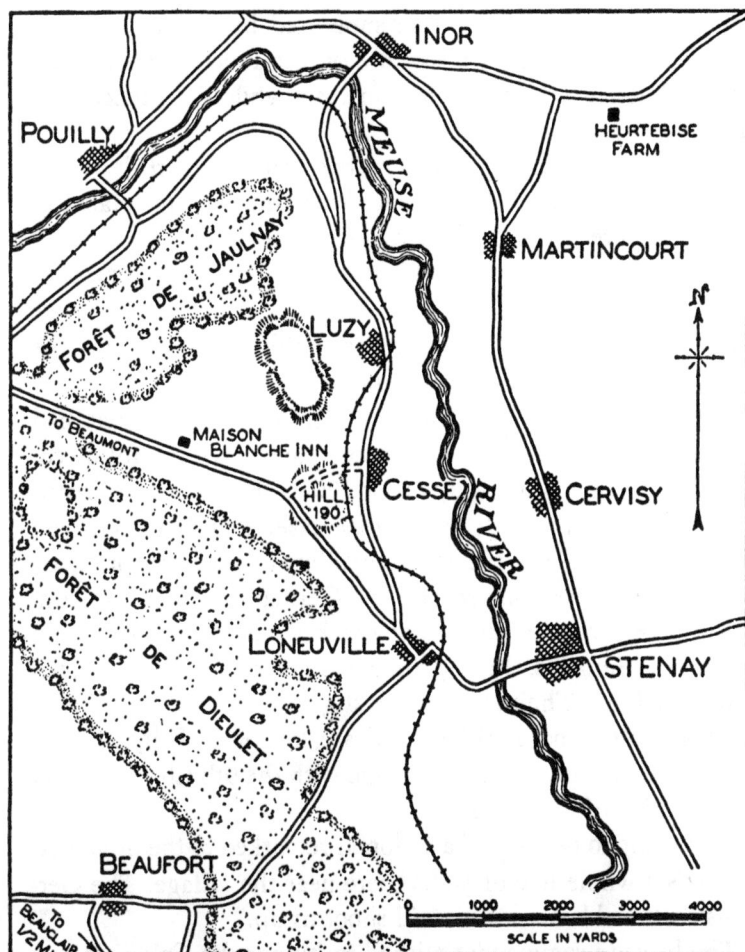

Example 5

mander, and a new plan was arranged. Two artillery battalions were to shell the Luzy crest while a third shelled the edge of the Forêt de Jaulnay.

The patrols of the Colonial infantry had moved forward in a thin line. The military crest of the ridge west of Luzy was held

by a strong German firing line supported by several machin
guns. This line opened a heavy fire on the French patrols. The
French Colonial infantry waited in rear, while the French batteries registered on the crest.

After a few minutes word came back from the artillery that
everything was ready. The artillery knew the infantry plan and
could open fire for effect at a moment's notice.

"You can go now, Colonel," the 87th Brigade commander
told the Colonial.

But before the French movement could get under way, the
Germans attacked. Their firing line executed rapid fire for two
minutes and then rushed forward. Behind the crest that had
sheltered them the German supports and reserves followed.
The three German lines were about 300 yards apart. The French
artillery was silent until the German reserves had gotten well
beyond the crest. Then the French artillery opened fire for effect.
Heavy losses were inflicted and the Germans thrown into confusion. The French infantry now attacked, completely scattering
the dazed Germans. In less than twenty minutes the French
were near Luzy. Their losses were slight.

Since the Germans still held Cesse, the 87th Brigade commander decided to attack this village with the 9th Chasseurs and
one battalion of Colonials.

"It's going to be tough," a Colonial remarked to the brigadier.
"There's a whole line of walls there near the village. The Germans sheltered behind them will shoot us up."

The brigade commander wished to humor the Colonials and
restore their confidence. They had met with a disaster a few days
before.

"Not at all," he replied. "You will go into Cesse with your
hands in your pockets, and I will go with you, my hands in
mine."

The two attacking battalions formed; the artillery was informed of the plan. The entire fourteen batteries supported the

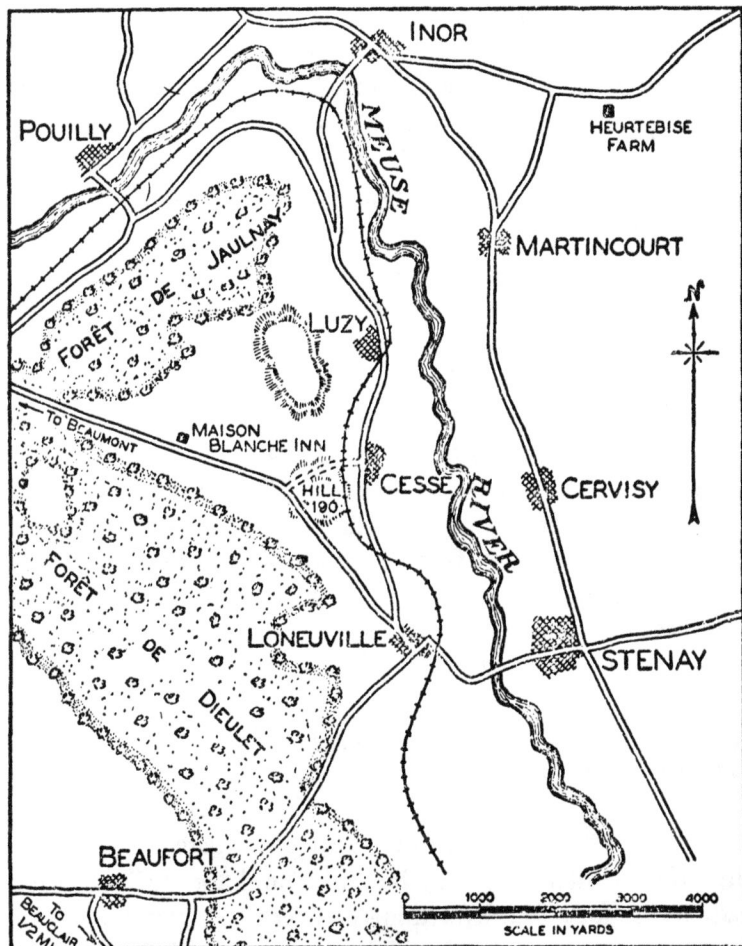

Example 5

attack by fire on Cesse and its environs. The Germans in Cesse were taken under a powerful concentration and sustained severe losses. To quote the French brigade commander: "We reached Cesse with our hands in our pockets."

From "Une Brigade au Feu," by General Cordonnier, French Army.

DISCUSSION. The Germans had crossed the Meuse on the morning of the 27th. Therefore, the French, in accordance with their mission, attacked. The Colonial Infantry was about to go it alone. The intervention of the 87th Brigade commander, who belonged to another army corps, resulted in excellent infantry-artillery teamwork. The infantry brigade commander his artillery colonel rapidly coördinated their artillery with the Colonial infantry. The brigade commander ordered the coördination. The artilleryman acted both as an artillery commander and as his own liaison officer.

The essential points are:

(1) The commander on the spot was deeply impressed with the necessity for infantry-artillery teamwork.

(2) The infantry knew the location of the Germans.

(3) A representative of the artillery was with the infantry and got this information from them. He was also informed of the infantry plan.

(4) He had instantaneous communication with the artillery, and was thereby enabled to transmit this information promptly.

(5) Artillery observers had an excellent view of the terrain and could identify the targets and objectives from the description given over the phone.

(6) As a result of the intervention of the 87th Brigade commander, the infantry and artillery were coördinated as to time. The infantry attack was not launched until the artillery was ready to fire for effect. Everything had been hastily improvised, but that is often necessary. In this case it was effective.

In commenting on the combats of the 87th Brigade in August, 1914, General Cordonnier says:

The artillery with this brigade had been loaned by the division or the army corps. Sometimes the brigade had one artillery unit, sometimes another. Each time it was necessary to arrive at an understanding in advance. It was only with the Stenay battalion (which had trained with the 87th Brigade in peace) that one could go into action without feeling one's way and without fear of being misunderstood. The best results are obtained only if infantrymen and cannoneers are accustomed to working with each other.

✦ ✦ ✦

EXAMPLE 6. On October 4, 1918, the U. S. 1st Division launched its attack in the great Meuse-Argonne Offensive. By noon the following day the 1st Battalion of the 26th Infantry had captured Hill 212 and the woods east of that hill. At this time the 3d Battalion, which had been in reserve, was ordered to advance, pass through the 1st Battalion, and continue the attack. At 1:15 p.m. the relieving battalion reached the forward lines of the assault units.

Here the battalion commander was informed that a barrage would be laid on the southwestern part of the Bois de Moncy, which dominated the valley from Hill 212 to Hill 272. This valley had to be crossed in the advance. The barrage was scheduled to come down at 1:45 p.m., stand for fifteen minutes, and then roll forward. To quote the battalion commander:

> This necessitated a nerve-racking wait of forty-five minutes under heavy artillery and machine-gun fire delivered at short range from across the valley, and enfilade fire of all arms from the Bois de Moncy. But it was too late to do anything about it.

The battalion advanced behind the barrage and, against strong opposition, fought its way forward to a point south of Hill 272. To quote the battalion commander again:

> During all this time the artillery liaison officer, who had accompanied the 3d Battalion commander, did excellent work. He controlled the fire of two guns that were located southeast of la-Neuville-le-Comte Farm. He had direct telephonic communication with these pieces. Instead of giving targets to his guns, this unusually competent officer issued fire orders from wherever he happened to be. He thus destroyed many machine guns and two pieces of artillery. His fire could not only be directed on all targets to the front, but on targets located along the Bois de Moncy as well.

Later, while the battalion was attacking Hill 272 from the east, the Germans counter-attacked toward its flank and rear.

The battalion commander, through the liaison officer, asked the artillery to fire a numbered concentration which had been previously prepared to cover the area over which the Germans were advancing. The fire came down promptly and was effective.

From the personal experience monograph of Major Lyman S. Frasier, who commanded the 3d Battalion of the 26th Infantry.

DISCUSSION. We see here an example of good infantry-artillery liaison. The bulk of the supporting artillery was used to fire a rolling barrage in accordance with the general artillery plan. In the future we shall probably make little use of the rolling barrage. The form of support will be different. Nevertheless, at the start of an attack artillery will fire according to some general plan.

By October, 1918, the 1st Division was a veteran organization. It had learned much about infantry-artillery liaison. The effectiveness of the artillery support is all the more notable when we learn that the 1st Division in this operation did not have as much artillery supporting it as was usual in 1918 Western Front attacks. The remarks of the battalion commander speak for themselves.

Some enemy machine guns, as well as two field pieces located well forward, were not neutralized by the barrage. Prearranged fires will never put out all hostile machine guns. Sometimes machine guns will remain silent until the infantry has gotten close. In this example the artillery liaison officer was with the infantry battalion commander and in direct communication with the artillery. He personally conducted the fire on these machine guns. His method was a short cut which will probably be resorted to frequently.

✓   ✓   ✓

CONCLUSION. A study of the early Franco-German engagements in 1914 reveals the striking fact that virtually no unit that effectively tied in its infantry and artillery suffered a severe

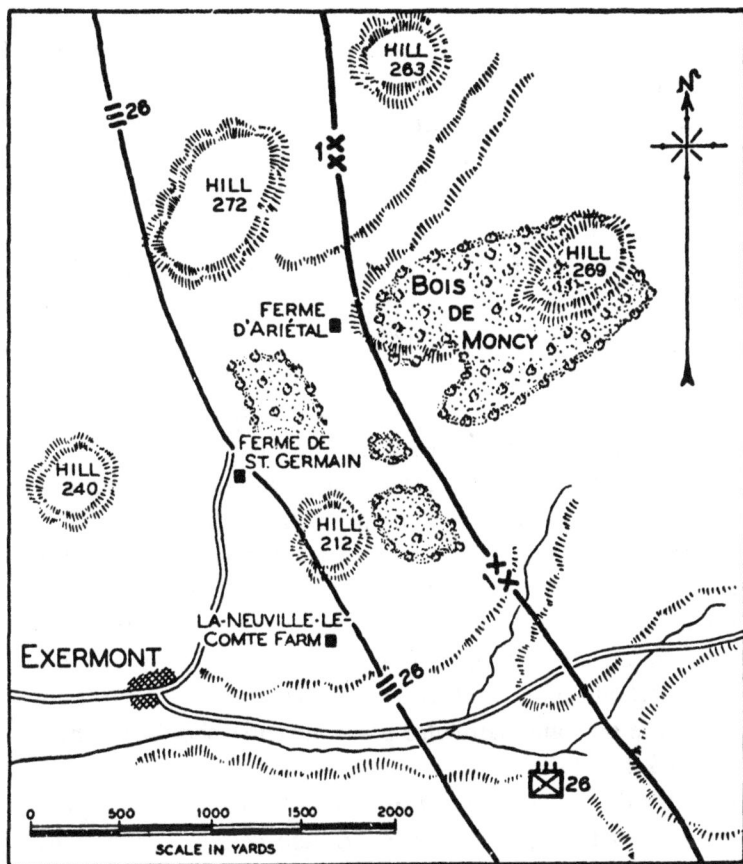

Example 6

reverse. On the other hand, where severe reverses were suffered the loser had invariably failed to coördinate his artillery with his infantry. It would be an exaggeration to say that, in the early days of 1914, all a commander had to do to win was to achieve infantry-artillery teamwork, but nevertheless such a statement would not be very far from the truth.

The phrase "The artillery conquers; the infantry occupies"

was coined when trench warfare began. It was not true, as the officer who originated it undoubtedly realized. But it did represent the reaction to numerous reverses that were attributed to the artillery's failure to support their attacking infantry properly. It focused attention on what might be called ARTILLERY-infantry teamwork. When this was changed to the infantry-artillery team, decisive results began to be achieved.

The importance of infantry-artillery liaison is undeniable; the real question is: "How can the action of these two arms be tied together on the battlefield?"

Any intervention of direct-support artillery, which has not been foreseen and prepared for, usually requires much time. And once infantry has asked for this fire, it must wait until it materializes, or run the risk of being fired on by its own artillery. Although artillery will try to comply with all requests for fire, the supply of ammunition is by no means unlimited; it is important to remember this. For these reasons, infantry should try to settle local incidents with its own weapons, leaving the artillery to fire on larger targets in accordance with the previously arranged scheme. On the other hand, when a real need exists for artillery fire on some particular place, infantry should not hesitate to ask for it.

Infantry that is accustomed to working with a definite artillery unit has the opportunity to arrange certain conventions. Conventional signals might be arranged to insure the immediate execution or renewal of certain fires. The duration of any particular fire asked for by the infantry might habitually last for a definite period of time—three minutes, for example—unless otherwise requested. The artillery might signal the fact to the infantry that it is about to cease certain fires by some peculiarity in its fire at the end—greater rapidity the last minute, a long salvo, a smoke salvo, or a high-bursting salvo Individual infantrymen, lying down, need some such warning—something they can see or hear. These are but a few conventions that might be used; the number is limited only by the ingenuity and familiarity of the units involved.

Infantry requests for fire might include a statement limiting the *duration of the request.* If at the end of a request for fire made, say, at 9:00 a.m., the message added "Request good until 10:00 a.m.," that would mean that the artillery would not comply with the request at all if it had not been able to do so by 10:00 a.m. Then at 10:00 a.m. the infantry would be free to go ahead, if the situation had changed, without being exposed to the fire of its artillery, or it could make a new request.

If the physical distance, and sometimes greater mental distance, that separates the infantry and the artillery on the battlefield is to be spanned, the following considerations should be observed:

Habitual designation of definite artillery units to support definite infantry units.

Intellectual liaison and mutual familiarity between the arms, so that infantry will not call on artillery to do the impossible, the unnecessary, or the unsuitable; while the artillery, for its part, will be capable of appreciating the infantry's problems.

Determination by the artillery to support the infantry when support is needed, even at some cost, and to seek OP's that will enable artillery observers to follow the combat by direct observation.

Use by the infantry of its own weapons against small targets that are difficult to describe to the artillery, thereby freeing the artillery to fire on larger targets.

Recognition by the infantry that prompt advantage must be taken of opportunities afforded by artillery fire.

Proximity of infantry and artillery leaders in combat, with command posts as close together as practicable.

Particular attention to communications.

A moral liaison, reciprocal esteem, confidence and friendship, preferably personal friendship between the two elements of the particular infantry-artillery team.

Previous joint training of the two specific units of the team.

Careful selection and actual training with infantry units of artillery liaison officer.

Maximum use of prearranged fires.

Chapter XIX: *Nearing the Enemy*

In a meeting engagement a great advantage accrues to that side which first succeeds in making effective preparation for battle.

AS THE INFANTRY nears the enemy, it deploys and advances, protected by part of the artillery. The German regulations state: "At the outset the first endeavor should be to lay down the law to the enemy, thereby securing one's own freedom of action. This is best accomplished by the early development of the main body in the direction in which the decision is sought, with a view to timely deployment."

Early and effective entry of the artillery is of the greatest importance. To quote the German regulations further,

The artillery of the main body first gives the necessary stability to the front which is being formed.

The alert commander does not await the clash of leading elements before taking action. When contact is imminent he deploys his artillery and his infantry supporting weapons in order to protect the forward movement of infantry elements in rear. Ordinarily he will see that his infantry (except those elements well in rear) leaves the road and advances by bounds.

During this advance, active reconnaissance is pushed to locate the most advanced detachments of the enemy. As the infantry nears these it assumes a formation preparatory to combat. The nearer it gets, the more closely this formation resembles a complete deployment. From such a formation a coördinated attack can be launched with great rapidity.

Clinging to the road, when contact is imminent, invites punishment by hostile artillery, and is almost certain to rob a command of any chance to surprise the enemy. Furthermore, it may easily lead to a piecemeal engagement.

EXAMPLE 1. On September 5, 1914, the German IV Reserve Corps (7th and 22d Reserve Divisions) echeloned to the right rear of the German First Army, had the mission of protecting the flank and rear of this army from the west—the dangerous

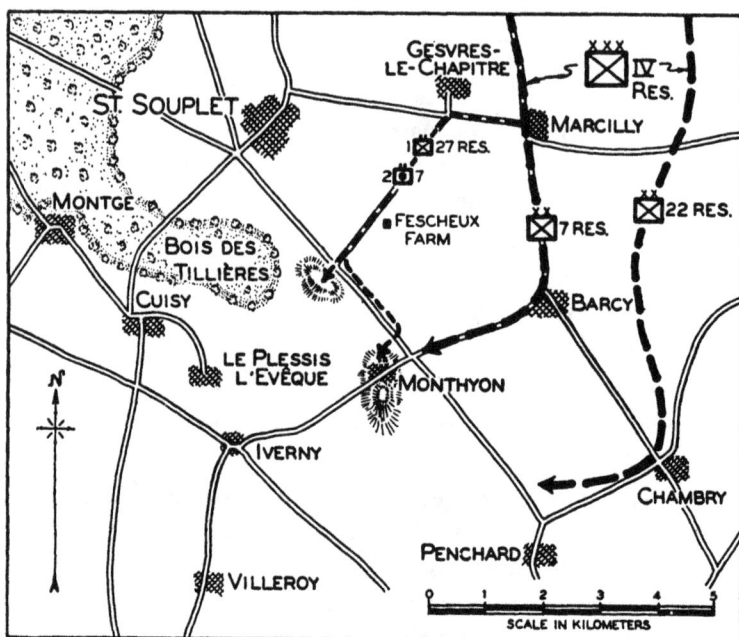

Example 1

direction of Paris. The IV Reserve Corps marched south in two columns with cavalry on its west flank.

Early on September 5, the 1st Battalion of the 27th Reserve Regiment and the 2d Battalion of the 7th Artillery were detached from the 7th Reserve Division and ordered to march west to support the cavalry. Suspicious French activity from the direction of Paris had been reported.

About noon this small force was overtaken near Gesvres-le-Chapitre by a messenger who brought the following order:

> The French are coming from the west. The IV Reserve Corps changes
> direction to the west. The 7th Reserve Division moves on Mon-
> thyon. Turn southwest and rejoin it at Monthyon.

The artillery battalion (with the exception of one platoon which remained with the 1st Battalion of the 27th Reserve Regiment) immediately set off for Monthyon at an increased gait. The infantry followed. Near Fescheux Farm the infantry battalion commander received a second order.

> Move to Cuisy by roads through the Bois des Tillières. The cavalry
> reports the French are within a few miles.

Since the terrain near Fescheux Farm afforded no observation to the west, the infantry battalion commander and his staff galloped forward to the hill a mile northwest of Monthyon. From there observation was excellent—and startling! Near le-Plessis-l'Evêque the little German group saw a French force that they estimated as a brigade. To the northwest they saw a line of French skirmishers moving east between the Bois des Tillières and the village of St. Souplet.

The battalion commander at once galloped back to his command and ordered his platoon of artillery to trot ahead and occupy the hill he had just left. He then deployed his three-company battalion. One company faced the skirmish line north of the wood; one faced the wood itself; and the third remained in reserve. The artillery platoon moved out at a trot and after climbing the steep hill went into position at the gallop. A moment later the guns of this platoon roared the opening octaves of the Battle of the Ourcq and the Battle of the Marne.

Meanwhile, the artillery battalion continued its rapid march on Monthyon. As it neared the town it was met by a German cavalry officer who quickly explained the situation. "The French," he said, "are just over there a short distance." In a matter of minutes the battalion wheeled off the road, raced up the northern slopes of Monthyon Hill, went into battery and opened with a burst of surprise fire.

Although the French in this locality were partially deployed, the German artillery's early entry into action effectively covered the advance of the 7th Reserve Division, whose units were thrown into battle as fast as they arrived. Despite the numerical

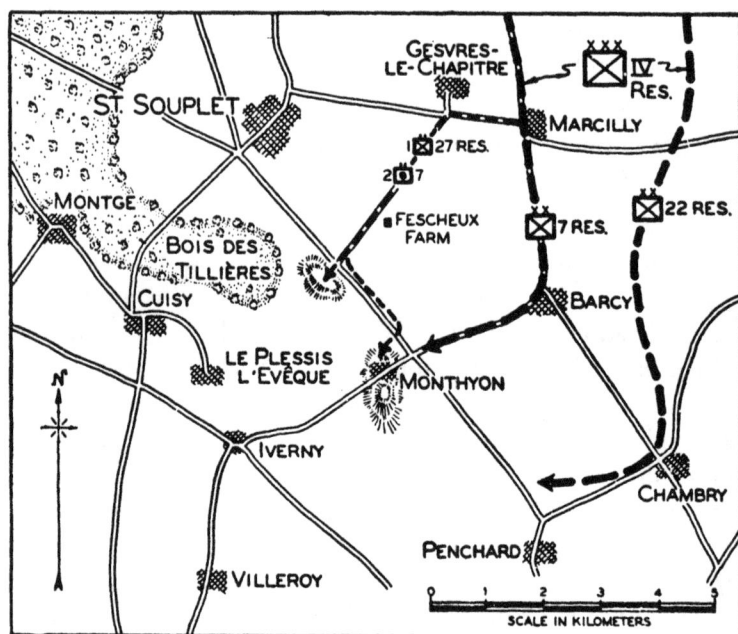

Example 1

superiority of the French, the tactical laurels of this day seem to go to the Germans. Even the threatened envelopment from the French near St. Souplet was stopped in its tracks.

From an article by Lieutenant Colonel Koeltz, French Army, in "La Revue d'Infanterie," October, 1930.

DISCUSSION. A successful French attack driving southeast from St. Souplet would have taken the IV Reserve Corps in flank and might well have had far-reaching results. Had this corps been broken on September 5, the Battle of the Marne might have been as decisive tactically as it was strategically.

The check of the French movement near St. Souplet may be partially attributed to the early engagement of the German artillery. This effectively covered the deployment of the larger German elements on the north flank.

The action of the one platoon that trotted ahead of the German infantry, and went into position on the hill a mile north-west of Monthyon, was the result of a definite order. It was a bold movement and provides an extreme case. The action of the rest of the artillery battalion was accidental. Nevertheless, it clearly indicates the importance of the early deployment and early commitment of artillery in a meeting engagement.

With the wire equipment of today, the battery positions would not be so advanced. The observers—not the guns—would occupy the hills.

Finally, the action of the infantry battalion commander adds one more bit of testimony to the value of personal reconnaissance.

✗   ✗   ✗

EXAMPLE 2. On September 5, 1914, the German IV Reserve Corps encountered the French Sixth Army, which was moving eastward from Paris to strike the flank and rear of the German First Army. The IV Reserve Corps was charged with the protection of this threatened flank. However, after a heavy engagement it withdrew a short distance under cover of darkness The next day the German II Corps, located south of the Marne, was rushed north to the assistance of the IV Reserve Corps, which was threatened with a double envelopment.

The German 3d Division, part of the II Corps, marched north in one column. It had been alerted about 1:00 a.m. At the head of the division rode the 3d Dragoons, followed immediately by the corps commander in his automobile and the commander of the 3d Artillery Brigade and his staff.

At 5:00 a.m., from a height near Trilport, these officers saw five strong French columns moving eastward, north of the

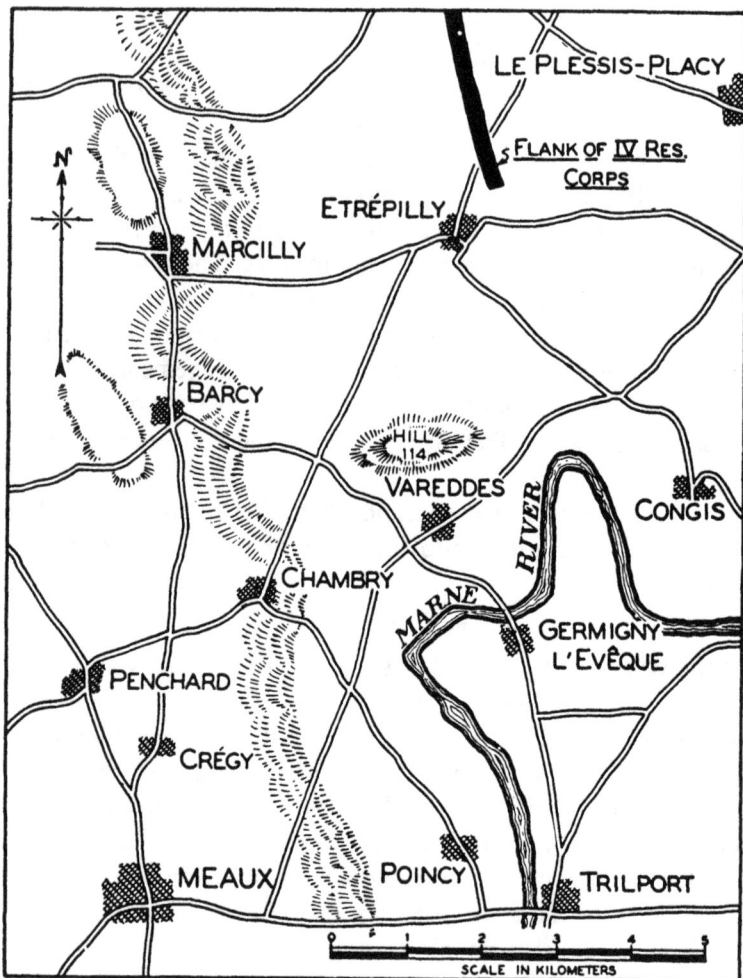

Example 2

Marne. Evidently the IV Reserve Corps would soon be attacked by very superior forces.

The corps commander forthwith ordered the artillery of the
3d Division to pass the infantry and get into action quickly in

order to assist the IV Corps and cover the crossing and debouchment of the 3d Division beyond the Marne. The dragoons were directed to cover the batteries.

The artillery (three battalions of light artillery and one battalion of howitzers from the corps artillery) received this order about 6:00 a.m. and moved forward at a trot, passing the infantry's leading elements.

The commander of the artillery brigade preceded the column to reconnoiter. About 8:30 a.m., from Hill 114, he saw French infantry crossing the high ground at Marcilly, Barcy, and Chambry. He saw no friendly infantry anywhere on the plateau east of Barcy. (Actually there were a few German companies near Vareddes.) This artilleryman immediately ordered his guns into position. Two battalions of light artillery and the battalion of howitzers went into position near Hill 114 and the third battalion of 77's near Germigny-l'Evêque. By 9:00 a.m. three battalions had opened fire; the remaining battalion was in action fifty minutes later.

At about 9.30 a.m. the fire of the German artillery stopped the advance guard of a French brigade near Barcy and delayed the advance of two other brigades. Thereafter it intervened with particular effectiveness near Chambry.

About 10:00 a.m. the German 5th Infantry Brigade crossed the Marne and went into position on the plateau just north of Vareddes. The 6th Brigade reached the crest west of Vareddes about noon.

The French attacks, starting about 12:45 p.m. and continuing throughout the afternoon, were repulsed. The south flank of the IV Reserve Corps was secured.

From the article by Lieutenant Colonel Koeltz, French Army, in "La Revue d'Infanterie," October, 1930; and from the articles on Monthyon by Captain Michel, French Army, in "Revue Militaire Française," 1930.

DISCUSSION. Although a few German troops were at Vareddes on the morning of September 6, the operations of the 3d Division had all the earmarks of a meeting engagement. The

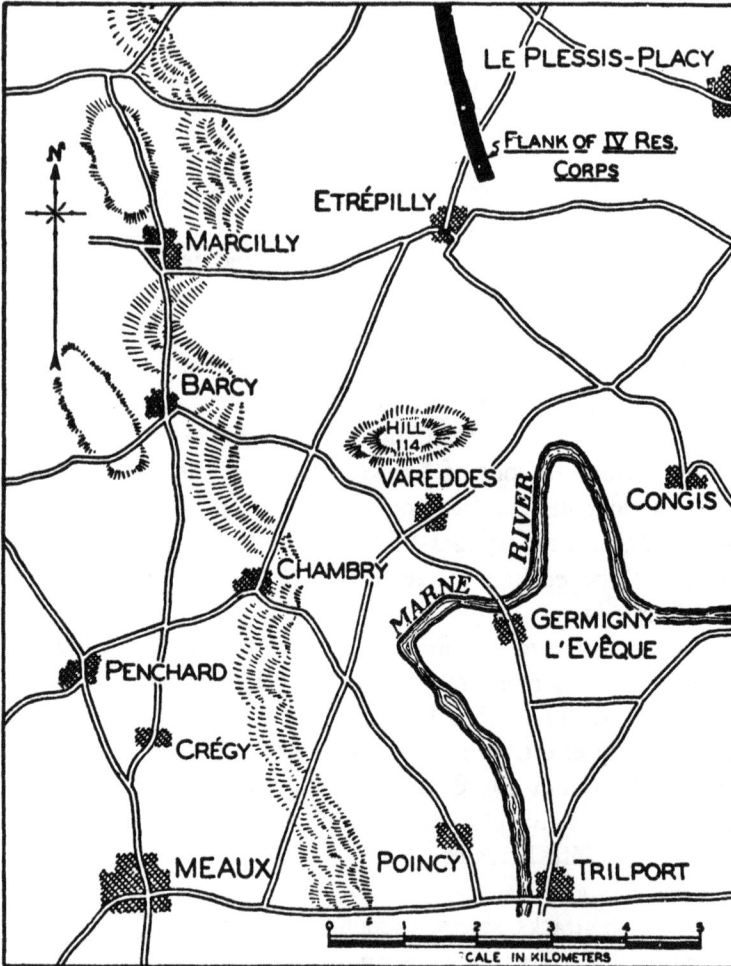

Example 2

French were advancing in several columns from the west, the Germans in a single column were moving north. Possession of the crests north and west of Vareddes was highly important to both sides.

All the German artillery was in position and firing effectively before their infantry had crossed the Marne. This artillery not only delayed the French advance, but covered the approach and deployment of the German infantry. When the French attacked in force, they were repulsed again and again.

The decision to advance the artillery was taken early. The movement was covered by mobile troops, the 3d Dragoons. The failure of the French on the south flank on this day may be attributed in large part to the early deployment of all the German artillery.

✓   ✓   ✓

EXAMPLE 3. On August 27, 1914, the French, who had been withdrawing to the south and west, made a stand on the line of the Meuse River. The French 87th Brigade occupied the woods west of Cesse, with small outposts near the river bank. Fourteen batteries of artillery supported the brigade from a position in a clearing in the woods.

During the morning it was discovered that some Germans had effected a crossing. The French promptly attacked near Cesse and Luzy and drove them back. The fighting then died down.

In the afternoon a German column of infantry was seen descending the long slope from Heurtebise Farm toward Martincourt. It was estimated that there were some 3,000 men in the column. French artillery had previously registered on points on this road. The fourteen batteries divided the target, each taking a part of the column.

As the head of the column neared Martincourt the French batteries simultaneously opened fire. The German column suffered heavy losses and was completely scattered.

Fifteen minutes later German artillery appeared on the same road, following the infantry. It, too, was in route column. The leading batteries attempted to go into action but were prevented by the massed fire of the French artillery. The German artillery withdrew.

From "Une Brigade au Feu," by General Cordonnier, French Army.

DISCUSSION. It appears that the commander of the German force failed to make provision for a vigorous and searching reconnaissance. In any event, the highly vulnerable formation he adopted definitely indicates that he was unaware of the situation to his front. The artillery, which should have been in position to protect the forward movement of the infantry, actually followed fifteen minutes behind it. The infantry had been dispersed before the artillery even attempted to go into position.

The infantry first, and then the artillery, made separate and successive efforts which led to disaster. For the German infantry to have reached the Meuse, it would have been necessary for it to get off the road, abandon such a vulnerable formation as column of squads, and advance under the protecting fire of its own artillery.

There are many similar examples in the mobile operations of the World War where troops approached the enemy in route column, on roads, and paid heavily for their temerity.

The advance guard of the U. S. 7th Brigade approached the Vesle in this manner: its support was caught by a devastating artillery fire while in route column. (See Example 1, Chapter I.)

At Ethe, the artillery of the advance guard of the French 7th Division was caught in route column on a forward slope and on a narrow road from which it could not escape; it was virtually destroyed by German artillery. On the same day a large part of the French 3d Colonial Division, marching in route column on the road near Rossignol, was surprised by German artillery fire. Half of it was destroyed or captured.

✓   ✓   ✓

EXAMPLE 4. On August 22, 1914, the French 40th Division, echeloned to the right-rear of other French forces, marched northeastward in two columns. This division was charged with the protection of the right flank of the French movement north.

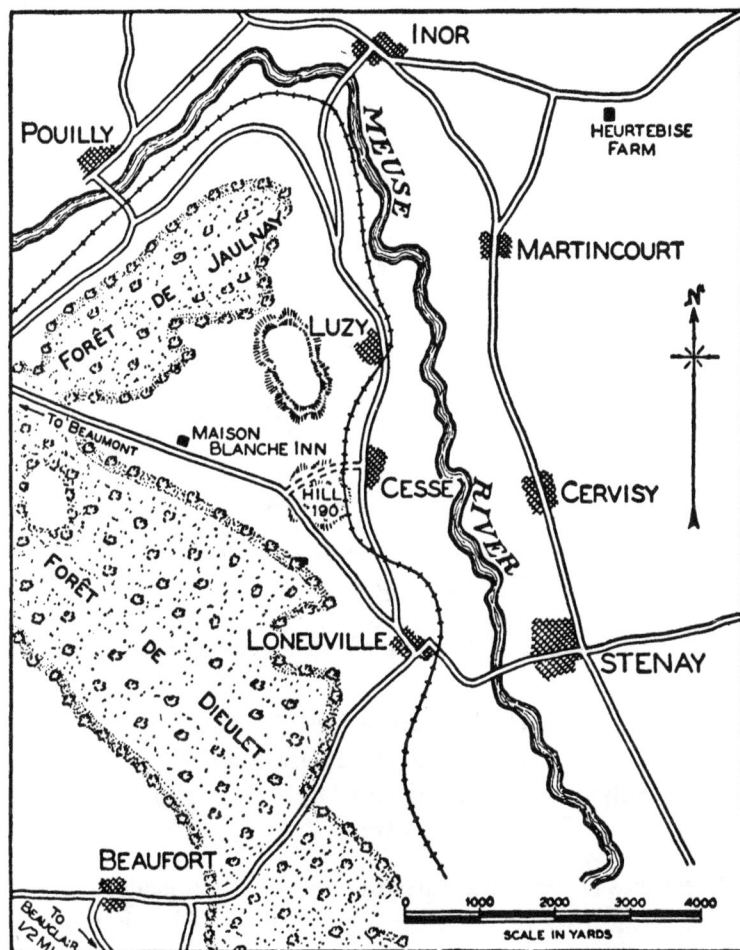

Example 3

Farther to the right a cavalry division reconnoitered to the north and east.

The situation was obscure. Small German forces were known to be near, but nothing was known of the larger elements.

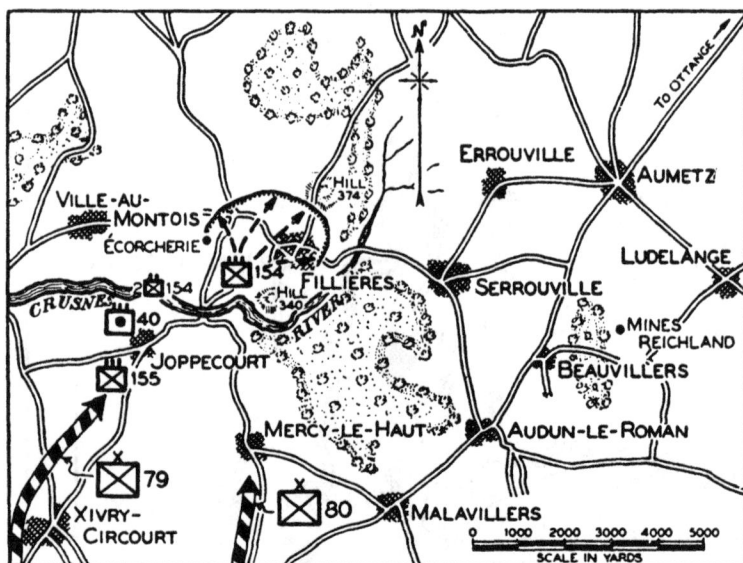

Example 4

The 79th Brigade (left column) marched in the following order:

Advance Guard: 154th Infantry (less 2d Battalion)
                2d Battalion of 154th Infantry
Main Body: 40th Field Artillery (3 Battalions)
                155th Infantry

There was no French cavalry in front of the brigade.

The point passed Xivry-Circourt and entered Joppecourt. Here it saw and fired on hostile cavalry. About 8:30 a.m. the 11th Company of the 154th Infantry (the leading element) was fired on from Hill 340 near Fillières. The leading battalion, assisted by the remainder of the advance guard, attacked and drove some Germans to the north and west.

With its units somewhat intermingled, the advance guard reached the line: Ecorcherie—Hill 374—southeastern edge of Fillières. The 2d Battalion of the 154th Infantry, leading ele- of the main body, was crossing the Crusnes. Suddenly, a Ger- man attack, effectively supported by artillery, debouched from the woods east of Fillières.

The 2d Battalion of the 154th attacked toward Fillières but as it neared the southern edge of the town it was driven back by Germans attacking from the wooded ravine in that vicinity. The French artillery, in position near Joppecourt, attempted to sup- port the infantry, but its fire was ineffective.

The 154th Infantry, opposed by a strong enemy who was well supported by artillery, lost heavily. It reported that it could not hold. It was then ordered to withdraw south of the Crusnes toward Joppecourt. The 3d Battalion of the 155th covered the withdrawal.

The remainder of the 155th now moved north of the Crusnes toward Ville-au-Montois. Here it encountered advancing Ger- mans who drove it westward in disorder.

The remainder of the 40th Division was equally unsuccessful. That night it was ordered to retreat some twenty miles south- west of Joppecourt.

Let us now examine the movements of the Germans opposed to this brigade.

That morning the German 34th Division, an interior unit, had been ordered to move so as to be disposed at 7:00 a.m. as follows:

Advance guard (furnished by 86th Brigade): On the line Errouville—Mines-Reichland.

Remainder of the 86th Brigade (which was composed of the 30th and 173d Infantry Regiments) and the 69th Field Artillery, in assembly positions in rear of this line. The ar- tillery prepared to support leading elements.

The 68th Infantry in two columns just southeast of the Ottange—Aumetz road, with its head near Aumetz.

The 70th Field Artillery on this road abreast of the 68th Infantry.

The 14th Uhlans (cavalry) reconnoitering to the front.

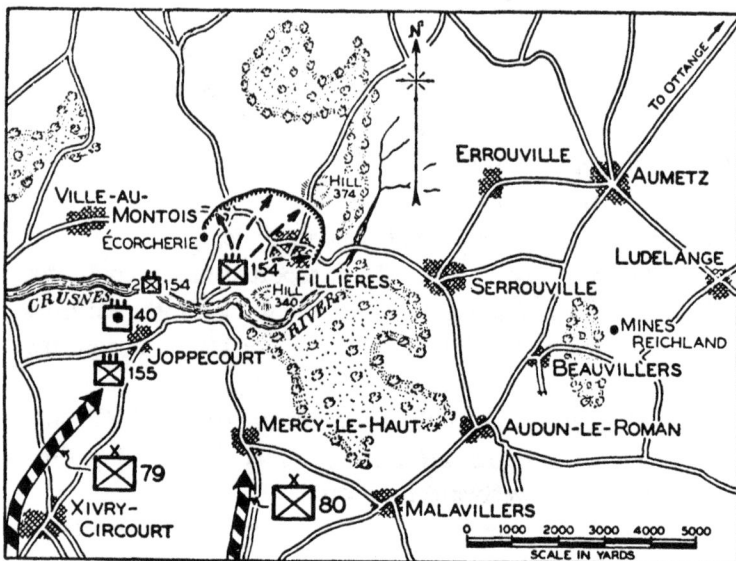

Example 4

By 7:00 a.m. these dispositions had been carried out. Meanwhile, a vigorous cavalry reconnaissance had brought in positive information of the French movement and, based on this, the division made a new bound forward at 7:30 a.m.

The 14th Uhlans were directed to march on Fillières, continuing reconnaissance.

The 86th Brigade was ordered to move to the line Serrouville —Beauvillers.

During this movement the 69th Field Artillery was told that it would support the 173d Infantry, and the 70th Field Artillery that it would support the 30th Infantry. Thus, all the artillery was prepared to cover the movement of the leading brigade.

The 68th Brigade (67th and 145th Infantry Regiments) followed the leading brigade toward Serrouville moving across country in approach formation.

By the time this bound was completed enough definite information was at hand for the division to issue its attack order.

The 86th Brigade, supported by the bulk of the artillery, attacked toward the line Malavillers—Mercy-le-Haut. The 68th Brigade (less two battalions in division reserve) moved north of the 86th Brigade and, supported by one battalion of artillery, drove hard for Fillières. Both attacks succeeded and the French were driven to the west.

Further to the south, the German 33d Division employed similar measures and was equally successful.

From an article by Colonel Étienne, French Army, in "La Revue d'Infanterie," March, 1926.

DISCUSSION. The French 79th Brigade, marching in column behind a conventional advance guard, was caught flat-footed by an alert, aggressive, well-prepared enemy. The Germans did not fumble their way forward in a clumsy, inelastic and vulnerable formation. Realizing that battle was in the offing, they made a partial deployment long prior to contact and then advanced by bounds until the situation became clearer. As a result they were able to launch a coördinated attack with great rapidity.

The French fought a piecemeal action, battalion by battalion. Their artillery was late and ineffective. Contrast this with the smashing German attack, effectively supported by artillery from the very inception of the action.

The French 154th Infantry was crushed. Its casualties were appalling. Every officer in its 2d Battalion was killed or wounded. The two battalions of the 155th sent north of the Crusnes met a similar fate.

The German attack came as a complete surprise. The French 79th Brigade was unable to get its full power under way at one time. Its advance guard, in attempting to explore the situation, was decisively defeated before it could be effectively supported, and two battalions of the main body became involved in the débâcle. Further south, the remainder of the French 40th Division was similarly surprised. Night found it in full retreat.

Colonel Étienne contrasts the French forward movement "made too fast and without prudence" with the method by which the Germans gained contact and became engaged.

He says:

> An examination of the orders issued in this action makes the advance of the German 34th Division stand out. This division advanced by successive bounds, in a formation preparatory to combat, and with an artillery unit prepared to support each infantry unit.
>
> Before an adversary in movement, even more than before an adversary in position, contact should be effected by successive bounds—the advance being covered by elements seeking to discover the hostile front and direction of march.
>
> Advance guards should be sufficiently early in making dispositions that approximate combat formations. Unless one wishes to be caught deploying, dispositions must be taken at least 10 or 12 kilometers from the enemy. If both sides continue to advance it isn't at kilometer 12 that contact will be made, but at kilometer 6.
>
> Moreover, it is essential that such dispositions be made as will enable the artillery to intervene in the minimum time in support of the advance elements.

�**✦** ✦ ✦

CONCLUSION. In his book *Development of Tactics—World War*, Lieutenant General Balck, German Army, says:

> Without considering long-range batteries, troops in march column approaching the effective zone of hostile fire can expect to be fired on when within 10 kilometers of the front. This requires that the column formation be broken into separate elements. In this day of long-range guns, it may easily happen that the enemy's projectiles will arrive sooner than the first reports of the reconnoitering units; thus the infantry will have to feel its way after it reaches the fighting zone.
>
> In no case must troops enter the hostile zone of fire in close order. . . . The development of the attacker must be made under the assumption that artillery fire may start at any minute, and that the

larger his force, the sooner will the enemy open fire. The utilization of cover, the adoption of formations calculated to lessen the effect of fire, the timely removal of all vehicles from the column and their movement from cover to cover, are the best means of avoiding hostile artillery fire.

We have seen that German regulations emphasize early development of the main body. French regulations go even further. They prescribe deployment or partial deployment *prior to contact.*

It must be noted, however, that for small units acting alone, partial deployment before contact makes it extremely difficult to change direction. In such cases the distance from the enemy at which partial deployment may profitably begin will be greatly reduced. It should be remembered that the figures mentioned by General Balck and Colonel Étienne assumed the proximity of large forces, adequately provided with artillery.

The desirability of the early deployment of at least a portion of the artillery was clearly brought out by many meeting engagements in the World War. Artillery and machine guns must go into position early if a decisive effort in the critical early phases of a battle is to be strongly supported. Finally, repeated disasters should teach infantry that a daylight movement in route column on roads in the neighborhood of an alert enemy is a short cut into action that will usually be paid for in heavy casualties.

Chapter XX: *The Advance to the Attack*

*The approach march should bring the troops
into their assigned zone, opposite and close
to their attack objective, in good physical
condition and with high morale.*

FORMATIONS taken up in the approach march should be
flexible and should be adapted to the terrain and the situation. A skirmish line, for instance, is not flexible; it cannot
maneuver to take advantage of cover nor can it be readily controlled. Therefore it is an undesirable formation for an approach march. Since column formations facilitate maneuver,
control, and maintenance of direction, they are generally preferable.

At all times the greatest care should be taken to move along
reconnoitered routes, to cover the advance with patrols, and to
avoid premature deployment.

✸ ✸ ✸

EXAMPLE 1. Late on July 28, 1918, the 1st Battalion of the
U. S. 47th Infantry was ordered to march to a certain farm in
the Forêt de Fère, where it would receive further orders from
the 42d Division, to which it had been temporarily attached.
After an all-night march the battalion reached the designated
farm where it received an order attaching it to the 167th Infantry and directing it to report to the command post of that
regiment.

Since the heavy foliage of the Forêt de Fère afforded perfect
concealment from the air, the battalion marched north on the
main road through this wood in a column of squads. It was
known that the Germans had recently been driven out of this
area, but beyond that there was no information. The woods

were alive with American artillery and troops, apparently in some confusion.

Early on the morning of July 29 the battalion reached the north edge of the forest. Previous to this a halt had been called and the troops given a breakfast which consisted of a fraction of their reserve ration. Being detached from their regiment and unaccompanied by their kitchen section, the battalion commander had authorized the use of a portion of the reserve ration on his own responsibility.

The battalion, in column of twos, then moved along the edge of the forest to the Taverne Brook where the stream and the wooded ravine provided intermittent cover. Distances between platoons were increased. Taking full advantage of all cover, the battalion made its way to the grove of trees which harbored the command post of the 167th Infantry. There the troops were placed under cover. Although machine-gun fire had been encountered, no casualties were incurred.

After a short delay, instructions were received to move forward and make a daylight relief of a front-line battalion of the 167th.

Reconnoitering parties were immediately sent out. Two captains, accompanied by their own runners and runners from the 167th Infantry, moved down the Taverne Brook, acquainting themselves with the situation to the front and reconnoitering routes of approach. They learned that assault elements of the 167th were a short distance beyond the Ourcq, that the enemy occupied the crest of the hill just beyond that stream, and that he had machine guns well sited and well concealed in the waist-high wheat on the hilltop.

The reconnoitering party also noted that after it crossed the road south of and generally parallel to the railroad, it was shielded from hostile observation to the north by trees along the Ourcq and scattered cover near the railroad.

The 1st Battalion moved out that afternoon. Company B,

whose captain had been forward on reconnaissance, led the way. The battalion, in column of twos and with increased distances between companies, moved along the Taverne Brook where it could not be seen.

Arriving at the point where the trees along the Ourcq hid it from enemy observation on the north bank, the column bore to the right, moved through the woods, and forded the river. At this point the battalion ceased to move as a single column. Companies now moved separately to their assigned locations, in different formations. For instance, Company B advanced with two platoons in the lead and the other two following at 200 yards. Each platoon was in line of squad columns.

The forward movement of the battalion continued to the un-improved road just north of the Ourcq which generally marked the front line. Here the approach march ended and the ordered relief was made.

This battalion had moved by day into a position close to the Germans without drawing any unusual amount of fire. It was in position facing its objective, in good condition. Only one or two casualties had been incurred. These resulted from artillery fire during the halt near the command post of the 167th.

Let us now examine the experiences of the 3d Battalion of the 47th Infantry, which made a similar movement at the same time and on almost the same terrain. This battalion was also detached from its regiment and ordered forward. En route the battalion commander received word that the 168th Infantry had captured Sergy and that the battalion would advance and mop up that town. He was further informed that hostile artillery fire could now be expected.

The battalion continued down the road in column of squads. As the head of the column reached the road fork about one mile south of Sergy, the enemy's artillery opened with a sudden fury; shells plastered the fields near the plodding column. The battalion commander met this situation by ordering "Column right"

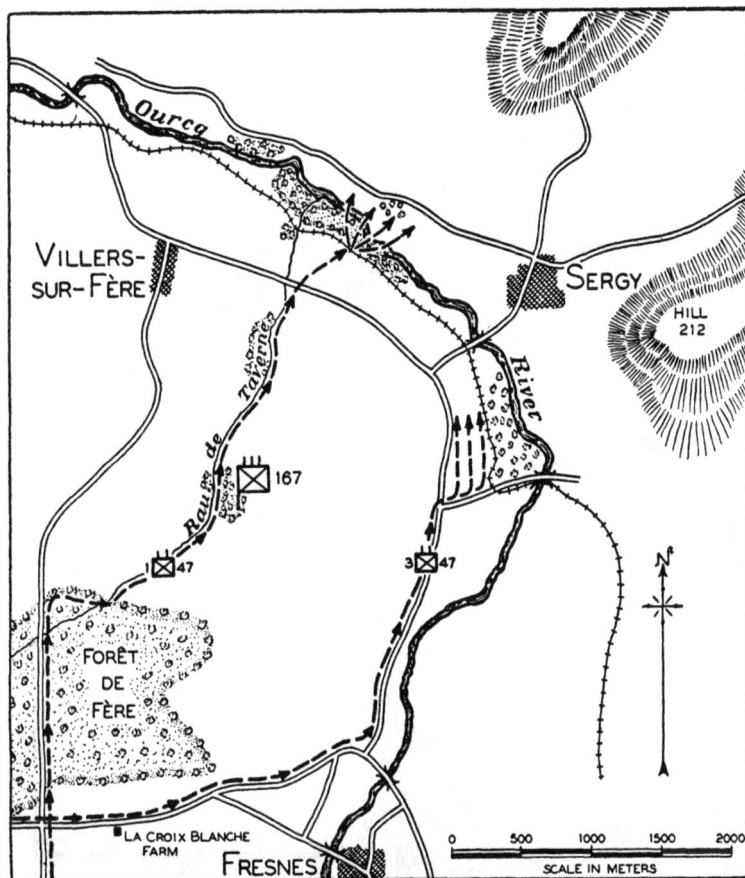

Example 1

and, when the tail of the column had completed the turn, "Squads left." He then ordered each company to form line of platoon columns and continue the advance with Companies I and L leading and K and M following. Each platoon marched in column of twos; in some cases half-platoons were staggered. The forward movement, in general, paralleled the Ourcq.

Thus the battalion deployed suddenly and continued its ad-

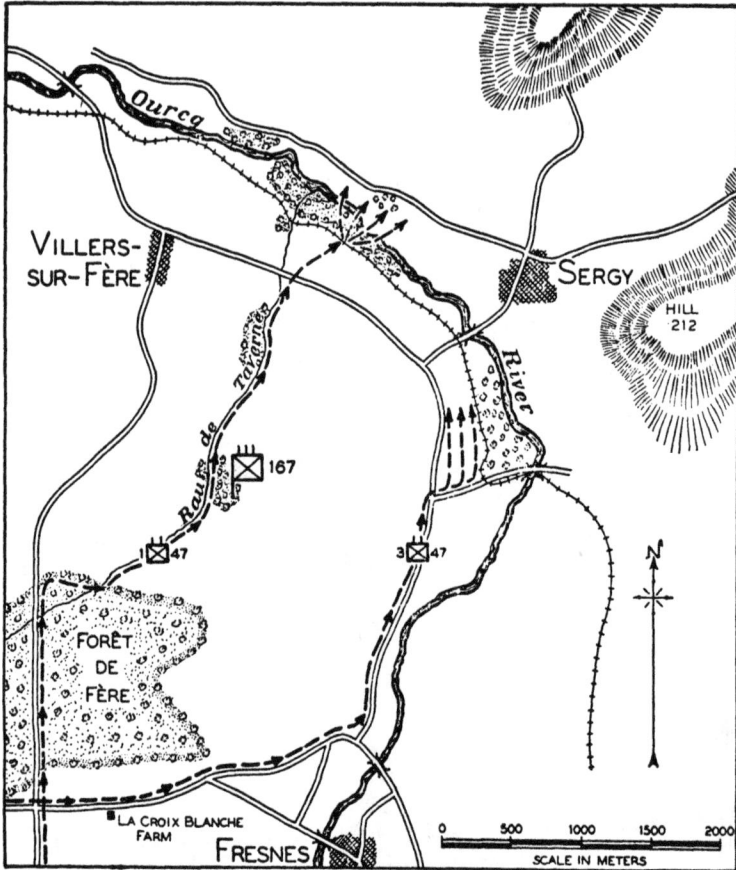

Example 1

vance across country. No reconnaissance had been made. To the right, American troops could be seen moving to the crest of Hill 212 but they appeared unable to get beyond the crest.

The hostile shelling became heavier and heavier. Casualties mounted. Platoon and company commanders did not know where they were supposed to go or what they were supposed to do.

A little later a village was seen through the trees to the right-front, and machine-gun fire from this direction was added to the shell fire. The right assault company inclined to the right toward the firing while the left assault company continued in its original direction. By this time the battalion had become so intermingled and had so lost direction that concerted action was impossible.

Companies broke up. Small groups of men milled around, not knowing what to do. There were two majors with the battalion, but both had been wounded. Losses were heavy. Intermingled units straggled into the trees along the Ourcq and there the battalion remained all night.

From the personal experience monographs of Captains Jared I. Wood and Howard N. Merrill, who commanded Companies B and M, respectively, of the 47th Infantry.

DISCUSSION. The problem of these two battalions was very similar—to get to the Ourcq in good condition and with minimum loss. Both organizations were ordered to make their advance by day. Friendly troops covered their movement.

The approach march of the 1st Battalion brought it close to and opposite its objective. The troops, sustaining practically no casualties, reached this position in excellent physical condition and high morale. That is certainly the aim of an approach march.

The 1st Battalion's movement was characterized by a thorough utilization of the terrain. It was not seen; hence it was not shot up. It took advantage of the available cover and it adopted formations suitable to that cover. It reconnoitered for defiladed routes of approach prior to the advance. It changed into a widely deployed formation at the latest minute permitted by the situation. It had not been necessary to resort to this earlier because the reconnoitered route of approach was sheltered and the situation was known.

The experience of the 3d Battalion was quite different. It

made no reconnaissance. It marched in column of squads, down an open road toward a position behind the front line, and it continued in this formation even after it had been warned that it could expect artillery fire. That this battalion was not severely punished during this stage of the operation speaks highly of its luck. Fortunately, the first salvos of the German artillery missed an excellent target and the battalion deployed. Whether it would have been better to deploy each company, but retain column of companies, and bear toward the shelter of the woods along the Ourcq, cannot be determined. The result of the actual deployment, made suddenly and without sufficient information having been given to subordinates, was inevitable. Units quickly lost direction and became intermingled. Before long the battalion had disintegrated into a confused body of men who, after heavy losses, finally scrambled into the woods along the Ourcq.

The great difference between the experiences of the 1st and 3d Battalions may be attributed to one thing: the 1st Battalion moved over ground that had been reconnoitered, taking pains to hide itself; the 3d Battalion moved in a conspicuous formation over ground that had not been reconnoitered.

✓   ✓   ✓

EXAMPLE 2. Early on the morning of August 22, 1914, the French 7th Division marched north through a heavy fog. Shortly after the march began, the leading elements of the division unexpectedly stumbled into the enemy near Ethe. A bloody and confused battle followed. During its course, the division commander ordered his rear brigade to attack in the direction of Belmont.

The situation was obscure. A few French troops were known to be along the north edge of the Jeune Bois, and the Germans, presumably, were still north of the Ton, where their artillery could be heard firing. Many German guns appeared to be in action and their fire seemed to be placed on the north slopes of the Jeune Bois. Since observation was lacking, it was apparent that the German artillery was unable to fire effectively except on the hilltops south of the Ton and on the slopes near that stream. Although these facts were few, they were significant. Let us see

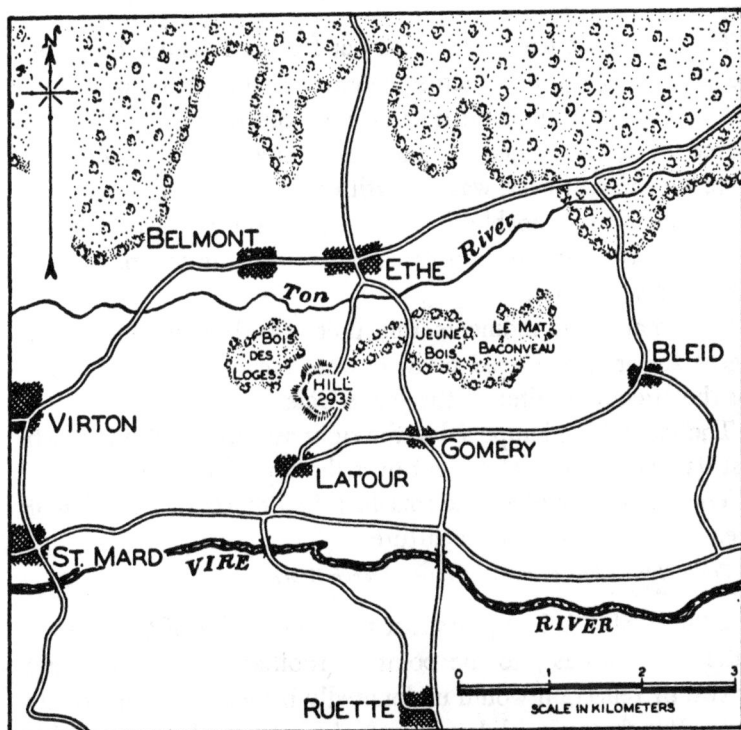

Example 2

how they were used in the planned attack on Belmont.

Four battalions of the rear brigade were ordered to move forward and jump off for Belmont from the northern edge of the Bois des Loges and the Jeune Bois. Two battalions were to be in assault and two in support.

The left assault battalion, commanded by Major Signorino, arrived at Gomery in route column where it received its attack order. Although Major Signorino knew nothing of the situation to his front and had only a 1:200,000 road map, he at once deployed his battalion, with two companies leading and two following. Each company deployed its four platoons in the same way.

Thereupon the battalion struck out for the Bois des Loges as the crow flies—straight across country. In its path stood Hill 293, but the battalion did not swerve. Straight up the hill it moved. When it reached the top it must have made the Germans gasp, for there, if ever, was the artilleryman's idea of a magnificent target. It is probable that most of the seventy-two German guns that were in position cracked down in unison on Major Signorino's battalion.

In a matter of moments this unit was literally blown to pieces and its bewildered suvivors were racing in wild disorder for the friendly shelter of the Jeune Bois.

The same thing happened to the right assault battalion, which lost its bearings and also went over the top of Hill 293.

The German artillery had smashed the French attack before it even reached its line of departure.

From "Ethe," by Colonel A. Grasset, French Army.

DISCUSSION. It appears that the commander of this French battalion was hasty to the point of foolhardiness. A moment or two of reflection would undoubtedly have averted this costly error. But the major didn't reflect; the moment he received his orders he placed his battalion in the formation that French regulations approved and set off for his objective.

Now in some cases a formation like this may be desirable for an advance under artillery fire. If there is no cover, for example, we will unquestionably want to spread out. But in this instance the terrain seems to indicate a movement south of Hill 293. Here a covered route of approach was available, a route that could be followed in a more compact formation—probably in column of companies, with security detachments ahead and on the flanks. Such a formation would have insured both protection and control. The formation actually adopted not only precluded the use of the covered route of approach but resulted in the battalion advancing over the only part of the terrain that the German artillery could effectively shell.

✶   ✶   ✶

EXAMPLE 3. By August 29, 1914, the German 4th Guard Regiment had crossed the Oise and its leading elements had reached Rû Marin. On this day the regiment was ordered to attack southward with one battalion in assault. It was definitely prescribed that this attack, which was part of a general advance by the Guard Corps, should pass east of le Sourd.

The colonel of the 4th Guards ordered his 1st Battalion to take over the assault rôle. In his order, he pointed out the east edge of Rû des Fontaines, which he mistook for le Sourd. Not much was known of the enemy except that he had been retreating rapidly before the German advance and that a few of his troops had been encountered north of Rû Marin.

The attack of the 1st Battalion jumped off at 11:45 a.m., by which time the 2d Guard Regiment, on the right, had already captured le Sourd. However, a few French troops still remained in Rû des Fontaines.

The 1st Battalion of the 4th Guards, which had only three companies available, deployed the 1st and 3d Companies in assault with the 2d following behind the center. Two platoons of the 6th Company (2d Battalion) joined the 1st Battalion instead of rejoining their own organization.

The 1st Company on the right, with all three platoons abreast directed its advance against the eastern corner of Rû des Fontaines. The 3d Company guided on the 1st. As the 1st Company neared the village it was attracted by rifle fire from the southwest and obliqued in that direction. All of the 3d Company obliqued with it, except one platoon which pushed on toward a knoll 400 meters east of the town where a small French detachment had been seen. A small gap was thus created in the front of the 3d Company. The 2d Company and the two platoons of the 6th Company immediately moved forward and filled this gap. Thus the entire battalion was deployed in one long skirmish line.

The 7th Company of the 2d Battalion, with a platoon of machine guns, was south of Rû Marin. One or two wounded men who had returned to that place reported that the French were attacking with dense lines of skirmishers and that a terrific fight was raging. The 7th Company and the machine gunners rushed forward at once, covered 1,500 yards without stopping and, exhausted and out of breath, mingled with the firing line southeast of Rû des Fontaines.

The French elements evacuated their advance position and the Germans moved forward almost without opposition until they encountered the main French position on the high ground near and north of les Bouleaux. In the face of heavy small-arms and artillery fire, the battalion pushed on. It was without artillery support, had no reserves, and all its units were intermingled. Its advance was held up with heavy losses 500 yards from the French position.

From the article by Lieutenant Colonel Koeltz, French Army, in "La Revue d'Infanterie," June, 1927.

DISCUSSION. Here 900 to 1,000 men were engaged to throw back a few observation elements. The German battalion split up. The reserves hastened to the firing line. False information reached the rear, and portions of another battalion rushed to the rescue. Units became intermingled. Then, in these unfavorable circumstances, the real resistance was encountered. Premature deployment had resulted in a blow in the air.

These errors were not committed by untrained troops but by the German Guard, a *corps d'élite* commanded by hand-picked officers.

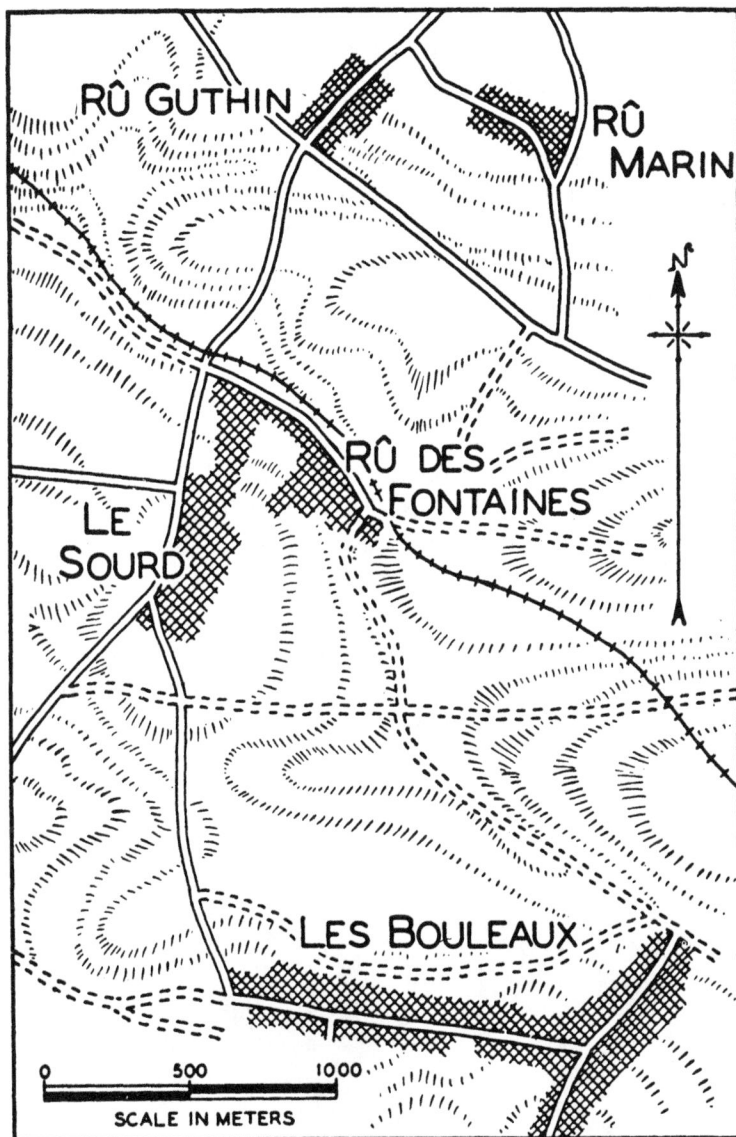

Example 3

CONCLUSION. The formation for the approach march should be elastic, readily lending itself to maneuver. Above all it should reduce both the visibility and the vulnerability of the unit.

The situation and the terrain will dictate whether or not the approach march will be made on or off roads and trails. Generally it will be made along ravines, slopes, and low portions of the terrain, as these avenues provide more cover than conspicuous hilltops and ridges. In open warfare the enemy will not have artillery and ammunition to maintain a constant interdiction of these covered areas.

The approach march should be secured either by advance guards or by units already engaged, and should be made over ground that has been thoroughly reconnoitered. Its object is to place troops close to their attack objective in good condition, with good morale, and with minimum losses. There is no formation which of itself can accomplish this.

The best way to avoid losses is to avoid being seen. The terrain itself will indicate the most suitable formation that can be employed without sacrificing control. Reconnaissance will enable the leader to read these indications.

Chapter XXI: *Soft-Spot Tactics*

In an attack reserves should be used to exploit a success rather than to redeem a failure.

THE ATTACK by infiltration, or soft-spot tactics, endeavors to push rapidly through the weak parts of the enemy position, avoiding or temporarily masking the strong parts. The small groups that filter through unite beyond the resistance. The strong points are then gradually reduced by action from the front, flanks and rear.

An initial breach made in the enemy position must be widened and deepened. This advance within the hostile lines is most difficult. The situation will be confused. Some units will have advanced much farther than others. Higher commanders will seldom know just where the smaller units are; therefore, close support by the artillery will either be impossible or largely ineffective. Such conditions demand the utmost in aggressive leadership on the part of the commanders of small units.

It is risky to drive through a gap without trying to widen it. Sufficient reserves to exploit the success cannot be pushed through a bottle neck. On the other hand, if the advance is halted while the breach is exploited laterally, time is lost, and the enemy is afforded an opportunity to reform on positions in rear and limit the success. As a rule some compromise must be adopted between lateral and forward exploitation.

Usually a rapid advance in its own zone is the most effective assistance a unit can render its neighbor. By so doing, it drives past the flanks of enemy groups that are still resisting, thereby making it possible to attack these groups in flank and rear.

If, however, a rifle company is having great difficulty in advancing in its own zone while its neighbor is pushing forward rapidly, it will often be advantageous to move the bulk of the

company, or at least its maneuvering elements, into the adjacent
zone and fight beside the company which has advanced. These
elements then have the option of advancing or attacking in
flank the resistance which has been impeding the assault elements of the company. Similarly, an infantry unit may, and
frequently should, fire into the zone of adjacent units, for boundaries are intended to be a help and a convenience, not a
hindrance. On the other hand, the commander must be certain
that this fire does not endanger neighboring troops.

Captain Liddell Hart, the British writer, has termed infiltration tactics "the expanding torrent system of attack." He writes:

> If we watch a torrent bearing down on each successive bank or earthen
> dam in its path, we see that it first beats against the obstacle, feel-
> ing and testing it at all points.
>
> Eventually it finds a small crack at some point. Through this crack
> pour the first driblets of water and rush straight on.
>
> The pent-up water on each side is drawn towards the breach. It swirls
> through and around the flanks of the breach, wearing away the
> earth on each side and so widening the gap.
>
> Simultaneously the water behind pours straight through the breach,
> between the side eddies which are wearing away the flanks.
>
> Directly it has passed through it expands to widen once more the on-
> rush of the torrent. Thus as the water pours through in ever in-
> creasing volume, the onrush of the torrent swells to its original
> proportions, leaving in turn each crumbling obstacle behind it.

Captain Liddell Hart suggests that the breach must be widened in proportion as the penetration is deepened, by progressive
steps from platoon to brigade. He propounds the following
procedure:

(1) The forward sub-unit, which finds or makes a breach in
any of the enemy's positions, should go through and push ahead
so long as it is backed up by the maneuver body of the unit.

(2) The forward units on its flanks who are held up should
send their maneuver bodies towards and through the gap. These
will attack the enemy in flank, destroy his resistance and so
widen the gap.

(3) Meanwhile the units in rear press through the gap and deploy (expand) to take over the frontage and lead the advance in place of the temporarily held-up units.

(4) The held-up units, as soon as they have accounted for the enemy opposing them, follow on as maneuver units to support the new forward units.

𝟙   𝟙   𝟙

EXAMPLE 1. On October 12, 1918, the French 12th Infantry attacked to the northeast with its 1st and 2d Battalions in assault (the 2d on the right). Diagonally across the regiment's front ran a strongly-held and heavily-wired German trench sited along a commanding ridge. Two lesser crests lay between the trench and the Seboncourt—Bernoville road, but otherwise there was slight cover.

Both forward battalions placed two companies in assault and attached two machine guns to each. Four machine guns were moved to positions near each reserve company. Each assault company advanced with two platoons in assault and two in support.

The 7th Company, which was closest to the Germans, became heavily engaged before the other units. Although it reached the German position, it was thrown out by a counter-attack and suffered such heavy losses that it was temporarily eliminated as a combat unit. The remaining three companies reached the last crest west of the German trench, where they were quickly pinned to the ground by heavy fire.

At this juncture a few men noted a threshing machine near the point where the Seboncourt—Grougis road crossed the trench and promptly converged on it to take advantage of the slight cover it offered. From their dangerous position behind the thresher, a lieutenant and a sergeant saw that the entanglement across the road was made up of portable wire. Here was an opportunity and both men were quick to seize it. They raced forward and succeeded in clearing away the wire at this point before the defenders picked them off. Nearby elements of the 5th Company saw the gap, rushed for it, broke through, and cleared a short stretch of the German trench on each side.

This group then continued the advance, leaving only five or six men to keep the gap open. These men were given a French machine gun and a captured German machine gun and ordered to fire to the north in order to assist the 1st Battalion.

Meanwhile the captain of the 3d Company, who had noted this success, brought up his two machine guns and opened fire with them. Since his assault platoons were pinned to the ground, he sent a runner to the leader of his right support platoon with a message directing him to move under cover of the crest toward the thresher, enter the German position and attack northward along the German trench. The runner was killed before he reached his destination.

Fortunately the platoon leader in question, acting on his own initiative, decided to make the very movement ordered. His platoon passed through the breach, turned north, took the defenders of the trench in flank and rear, and captured two machine guns and 50 prisoners. The assault platoons of the 3d Company then advanced, and captured all of the trench in their zone. This action allowed the 2d Company to capture the position in its front soon afterward.

From an article by Major P. Janet, French Army, in "La Revue d'Infanterie," November, 1926.

DISCUSSION. The mechanism of infiltration tactics finds a clear illustration here. A few men get a foothold in the enemy position. Most of them push forward. But the gap is small, so some men are left to keep it open, to widen it and to assist adjacent units by fire. In this case six men were left behind with two machine guns to neutralize the flanks of nearby enemy posts.

The assault platoons of the 3d Company were pinned down; they couldn't move. The company commander decided to use a support platoon—where? Not in his own zone where the attack was failing; had he done so he would probably have done nothing more than swell the casualty list. Instead, he ordered the platoon to move into his neighbor's zone, to the gap, to the

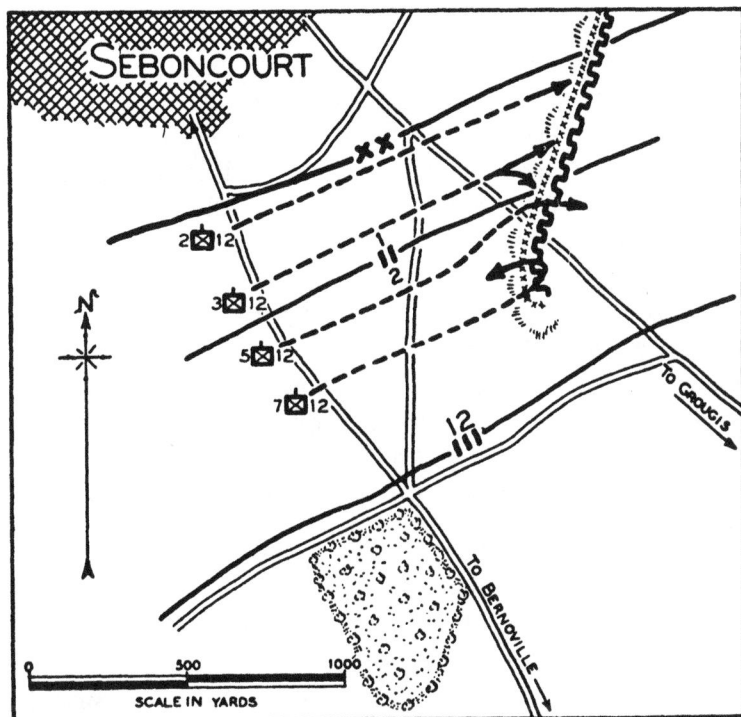

Example 1

weak point, while he used a small base of fire to occupy the enemy and pin him down during the movement.

It is interesting to learn that the lieutenant did the very thing his captain desired, although the order never reached him. He moved out of his zone, penetrated the hostile position and exploited the success laterally. As a result of this one small gap being widened, the entire hostile position was soon captured on a two-battalion front.

In this case the exploitation was almost entirely lateral, which was probably due to the virtual elimination of the 7th Company and the extremely heavy casualties in the 5th.

✓   ✓   ✓

EXAMPLE 2. The British 1st Division took part on September 25, 1915, in the Battle of Loos. The 2d Brigade, attacking on the right, was thrown back and failed to reach the German position. On the left, the left elements of the 1st Brigade were successful, captured the German front line, and pushed on.

The 2d Brigade, using fresh troops, renewed its attack. This renewed effort also broke down with heavy losses. The 3d Brigade (British divisions contained 3 brigades each of 4 battalions) and a force of two battalions, known as Green's Force, still remained at the disposal of the division commander. Green's Force was ordered to make another frontal assault on the left of the 2d Brigade, while elements of the 3d Brigade advanced north of it through the break in the German defenses near la Haie Copse.

Green's Force, attacking with one battalion on each side of the Lone Tree, was soon brought to a halt.

The leading battalion of the 3d Brigade lost direction, bore off to the right, joined Green's Force and was involved in its repulse. Let us see what happened to the next unit, the 2d Welch Battalion.

With two companies in assault and two in support, it moved in extended order over open ground for a mile. It was unobserved. The German front line was found to be completely deserted. No trace of the battalion supposed to precede the Welch could be found, so after advancing a short distance within the German position, the battalion commander changed direction to the right front toward a point where the exposed right flank of the 1st Brigade was believed to rest. This movement led the battalion in rear of the enemy trenches south of the Bois Carré, opposite which Green's Force and the 2d Brigade were held up. A number of Germans manned the reverse side of their trench and opened fire. The Welch kept moving forward.

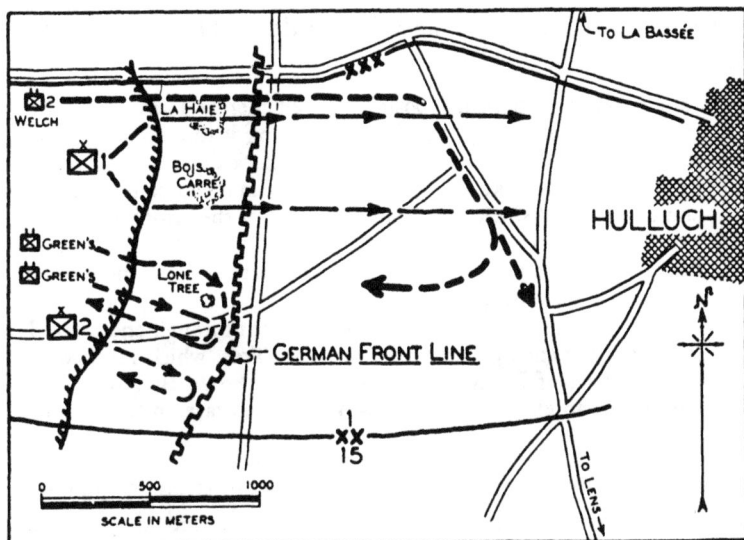

Example 2

Suddenly, fire from a portion of the trench ceased and a German officer appeared with an extemporized white flag. He was followed by 5 other officers and 160 men. This group came forward and surrendered.

The Welch moved on and halted on the Lens—la Bassée road southwest of Hulluch, where they were on the right flank of the 1st Brigade. From this point one company was sent against the remaining Germans still holding up Green's Force and the 2d Brigade. Threatened in rear by this company, the remaining German elements consisting of more than 400 men of the 157th Regiment surrendered.

The 2d Brigade and Green's Force were now free to advance.

By 5:20 p.m. they had reached the Lens road and had linked up with elements of the 15th Division on the right.

From "Military Operations, France and Belgium," Volume II, (British Official History of the Great War).

DISCUSSION. In discussing the Battle of Loos the British official history states:

> An attack on an entrenched position is not merely a matter of the commander making a good plan and getting it thoroughly understood and rehearsed. Once released, an attack does not roll on to its appointed end like a pageant or play. Innumerable unforeseen and unrehearsed situations, apart from loss of the actors by casualties, begin at once to occur. Troops must be led, and there must be leaders in every rank, and in the latter part of 1915 these leaders were in the making.
>
> The leading of the 2d Welch after it had broken through and arrived in rear of the enemy's trenches near Lone Tree, which resulted in the surrender of Ritter's force and enabled the 2d Brigade to advance, was an exhibition of initiative only too rare on the 25th of September.

The achievement of this one battalion compared to that of the four or five battalions that repeatedly dashed themselves against the German wire, is striking. Battalion after battalion attacked, only to prove a little more thoroughly that a frontal assault against wire and machine guns produces nothing but casualties—and a few medals for bravery among the survivors. All of these battalions, except the 2d Welch, were engaged where the original attack had failed, and in the same way. The barbed wire that stopped the first attack stopped the later ones just as effectively.

The 2d Welch, however, were used not where there had been failure, but where there had been success. They went through the narrow gap that had been created in the German front, then bore to the right, spread out and gained contact on the flank with the troops that had made the gap. A broad front of attack was again built up and the breach that had been created in the British line by the failure of the 2d Brigade was covered.

This one battalion accomplished what the 2d Brigade, assisted by three other battalions, had failed to do. The Welch pushed where the pushing was good. Thus, three years before the phrase and the idea became so prevalent, this battalion demonstrated the attack by infiltration.

✓ ✓ ✓

EXAMPLE 3. On August 8, 1918, "the black day of the German Army," the French 42d Division attacked southeast. On its left were Canadians; on its right the French 37th Division. The 42d used three assault battalions initially. From left to right these were: the 2d Battalion of the 94th Infantry; the 3d Battalion of the 94th Infantry; the 8th Chasseur Battalion.

The attack was launched at 4:20 a.m. The 2d Battalion of the 94th made a rapid advance along the left boundary of the division. In the early stages of the attack it saw no sign of the Canadians.

On the right, both the 8th Chasseurs and the 37th Division were held up in front of the Bois de Moreuil.

The center assault battalion of the 42d Division (the 3d Battalion of the 94th Infantry) attacked with the 9th Company on the right and the 10th on the left. Both companies had machine guns attached. The 11th Company followed the 10th.

As the 9th Company neared the Bois de Moreuil it came under fire and fell into disorder. Most of the men took cover facing the wood. The 10th Company advanced somewhat farther but was eventually held up by fire from the front and right front. The Germans were located in the woods and in the trench shown in the sketch.

The battalion commander caused mortar and machine-gun fire to be placed on the points from which the resistance seemed to come, but still the 9th and 10th Companies were unable to advance. Meanwhile, the battalion had lost the rolling barrage and a large gap had opened between it and the 2d Battalion on the left, which had swept victoriously on.

At this time the captain of the 11th Company (battalion reserve) took action on his own initiative. Taking advantage of the rapid advance of the 2d Battalion, he moved to the left of the 10th Company, found cover on the slopes of the Andréa Ravine and succeeded in reaching the trench to his front. There were no Germans in that part of the trench. Thereupon he sent one platoon to the right to attack generally along the trench. With the rest of the company he continued the forward movement through the woods toward the Gretchen Ravine.

The platoon that attacked laterally along the trench was successful. Its action enabled the 10th Company to advance, and between this company and the platoon ten machine guns and fifty prisoners were taken.

Meanwhile, the bulk of the 11th Company, moving by small groups and individuals, had reached the Gretchen Ravine and reformed. A Stokes mortar was pounding the northeast corner of the Bois de Moreuil where enemy machine guns had been firing. In addition, machine guns of the 2d Battalion were enfilading the southeast edge of the wood in order to assist the 3d Battalion. Taking advantage of these fires, the 11th Company attacked and captured the northeast corner of the wood.

While this was going on, the 10th Company had moved through the wood, swerved to the southwest and now came up on the right of the 11th Company. The 9th Company reorganized and later arrived in rear of the 10th and 11th Companies.

German resistance in the Bois de Moreuil broke down after the 11th Company captured the northeast corner of the wood and the 8th Chasseurs were enabled to advance and mop up.

The road running along the southeast edge of the Bois de Moreuil had been designated as an intermediate objective where the barrage would halt for a short time. The advance from this objective was resumed by all assault elements of the 42d Division in good order and on time.

On this day the 42d Division captured 2,500 German prisoners; its own losses were small.

From "Infanterie en Bataille," by Major Bouchacourt, French Army.

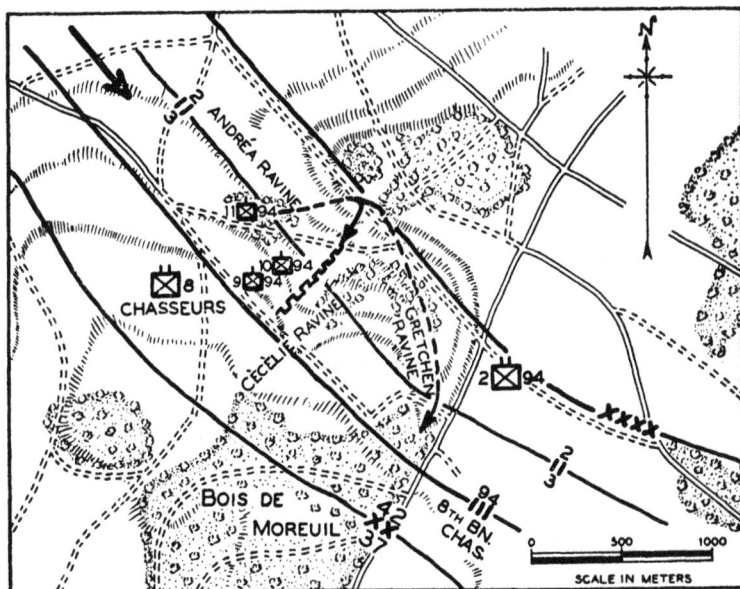

Example 3

DISCUSSION. The operations of the 11th Company furnish an excellent example of the "expanding torrent." The 2d Battalion had driven a hole in the enemy position—a deep, narrow breach. The 3d Battalion was held up but its reserve, the 11th Company, having more freedom of movement than the assault units, executed a maneuver.

Preferably this should have been ordered by the battalion commander. As it turned out, his subordinate recognized the opportunity and acted on his own initiative. By good luck there was coördination of effort. The battalion commander had caused certain localities to be covered by his machine guns and his Stokes mortar, and this fire facilitated the movement of the 11th Company.

It advanced on the left where there was cover, and where the attack of the 2d Battalion had swept the path clear. It reached a position abreast of the Germans who were holding up the 10th Company. No other troops being immediately available, the 11th Company employed one platoon to widen the breach while the remainder of the company pushed on to catch up with the 2d Battalion, thereby extending the front of attack. The 10th Company, thanks to this assistance, was now able to advance; it pushed on and became the right assault company instead of the left. The 9th Company was in such confusion that it could no longer be continued in assault. Accordingly, it was reorganized and moved forward as the battalion reserve. Thus the battalion was enabled to resume the advance along its entire front on time.

This action graphically demonstrates the concept of infiltration.

✓   ✓   ✓

EXAMPLE 4. On October 17, 1918, the French 12th Infantry attacked to the northeast toward Marchavenne. The attack, supported by considerable artillery, jumped off at dawn.

The 12th Infantry formed a provisional battalion of its depleted 2d and 3d Battalions and used this force as an assault unit. Its total in effectives came to about seven officers and 250 men. These men had been attacking for days and were close to the point of exhaustion. The battalion commander himself had little confidence in the success of the attack. On the other hand, the three company commanders were experienced, were close personal friends, and had the confidence of their men.

The battalion formed for attack with the company of Lieutenant Biard on the north and that of Captain Equios on the south. Lieutenant Brouste's company was held in battalion reserve.

A heavy fog covered the ground as the attack began. The French overran the German main line of resistance some 500 yards in front of the line of departure and pushed on. The Biard company, advancing rapidly, veered to the right and, without realizing it, crossed in front of Captain Equios' company.

The fog began to lift and as it did the Biard company came under heavy fire from a German redoubt (R). Lieutenant Biard sized the situation up, decided to envelop the redoubt from the

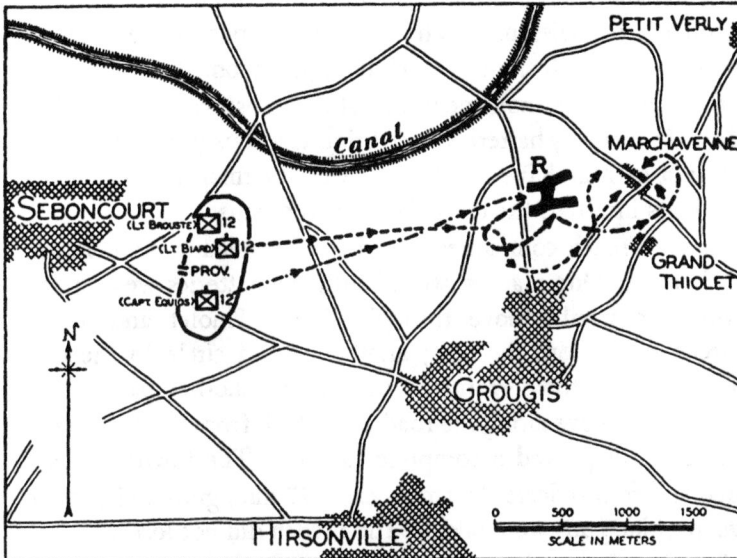

Example 4

south, and quickly swung his company in that direction. This movement was unnoticed by the Germans who were holding Grougis and the company reached the north edge of that village without meeting any resistance. To the northeast, toward Marchavenne, Lieutenant Biard heard artillery firing. He also noted that the Brouste company had followed his movement. He had received no word from the battalion commander and had no idea of the location of any troops on the battlefield except the two companies with him.

Lieutenant Biard now changed his plan. He decided to attack Marchavenne instead of the redoubt. Half concealed by the thinning fog, the company filtered through the orchards north of Grougis a man at a time. When they reached the Grougis—Petit-Verly road they turned northeast and followed the roadside ditches toward Marchavenne. The Brouste company conformed to this movement.

Lieutenant Biard sent out his scouts and, in addition, made a personal reconnaissance. The fog was almost gone. Grand Thiolet—a little cluster of farm buildings—loomed up 300 yards to the right. The movement was still unobserved by the Germans. Two enemy batteries were firing vigorously from orchards just west of Marchavenne. Nearby were German machine guns with belts inserted; the crews lay near the guns.

As the French companies closed up, Lieutenant Biard issued brief orders: One platoon would rush the batteries west of the town; one would move through Grand Thiolet and attack Marchavenne from the east; another would circle to the east and attack the town from the north; and another part of the force would move along the road and attack from the southwest.

The attack proved a complete surprise. The town was captured and four officers, 150 men, eight 77-mm. guns and twenty-five machine guns were taken. The French did not lose a man.

Shortly afterward the Equios company came up. This company had also stumbled into the redoubt at R and been nailed to the ground by fire. Fortunately, French artillery fire had opened up on the redoubt, and this enabled Captain Equios to pull back rear elements of his company and reorganize. While engaged in this he learned that the rest of the battalion, which he had been looking for on his left, had pushed far ahead on his right. He therefore utilized his reorganized elements to envelop the redoubt from the south and southeast. The redoubt fell, its defenders fleeing to the northeast. Captain Equios then continued the advance, rejoined his battalion, and assisted in organizing Marchavenne for defense. Counter-attacks were repulsed. Later, other French units arrived.

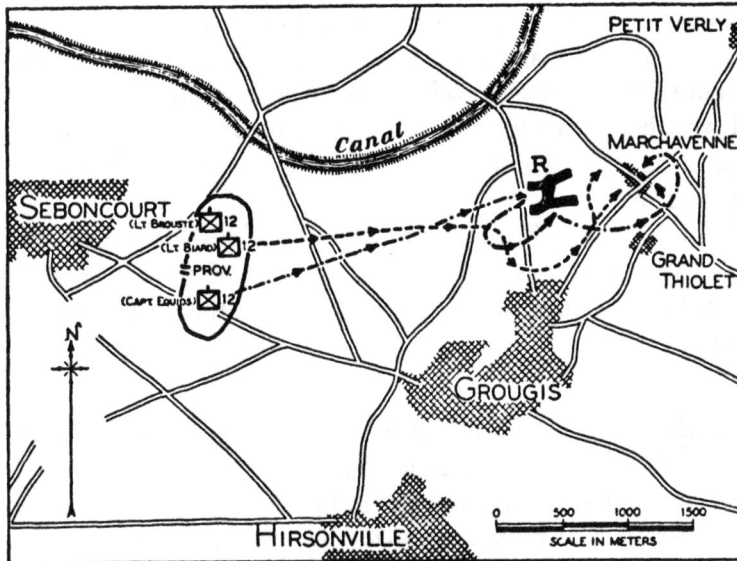

Example 4

The provisional battalion's bag of prisoners during the day exceeded its effective strength. Its losses were less than 60 men.

From an article by Major P. Janet, French Army, in "La Revue d'Infanterie," December, 1926.

DISCUSSION. Most of the success of this battalion must be attributed to the surprise it gained through the use of infiltration tactics.

The Biard company found a gap in the hostile defense—a soft spot. It saw that reserves were following, so it pushed through the gap. The Brouste company followed. Movement through the gap was on a narrow front, one man at a time. The movement continued unobserved until near Marchavenne. Here the companies spread out again to attack. Surprise was achieved by the care taken to avoid hostile observation and by the direction of the attack on Marchavenne.

There are things to criticize in the operation. The battalion commander exercised no control; he had no idea what was going on. Lieutenant Biard, after finding his gap, either did not try to notify or did not succeed in notifying his battalion commander of what he was about to do. Moreover, both assault companies lost direction early in the attack and also lost contact with units on the flanks.

Nevertheless, when all things are considered, the attack of this battalion stands as one more example of a master effort furnished by troops who have almost reached the limit of moral and physical endurance.

❧   ❧   ❧

CONCLUSION. The combat within the enemy position gives infantry its great hour. It is then that infantry is largely on its own; it must use its own fires to the utmost advantage while it maneuvers. It must neutralize and turn enemy resistances, infiltrate and inundate the enemy position. It is the hour of small assaults from the front, the flanks, the rear.

Fire action in the direction of progression will be difficult except for the elements of leading echelons and for curved-trajectory weapons. But machine guns with their flat trajectory will have excellent opportunities for lateral neutralization.

Successful maneuvers in such difficult circumstances demand an elasticity of mind, a lively intelligence and quick, sure decisions on the part of small-unit commanders. They also demand infantry that has been trained to maneuver. In war, troops will do only what they have learned in peace; at least this is true in the early days of a war.

No rule can be laid down that will state in what manner and to what extent a breach should be exploited. It would seem desirable for small infantry units to devote most of their strength to pushing forward and broadening the front of attack to its original dimensions. Direct action by a few men from flanks and rear against enemy resistance will often be decisive due to the moral effect. This was the case in two of the examples noted: the 2d Welch Battalion and the 11th Company of the French 94th Infantry. However, each case must be solved on its merits.

By using reserves where a success has been obtained, we oppose our strength to enemy weakness. If we employ reserves to redeem the failure of assault units and commit them in the same manner and in the same place as those assault units, we will frequently strike the very part of the hostile position that has already been proved the strongest. For instance, on August 7, 1915, at the Dardanelles, the Australians flung their reserves into battle over the same ground and in the same maneuver used by their terribly defeated assault units. Of that action the Australian official history has this to say:

> For the annihilation of line after line at The Nek the local command was chiefly responsible. Although at such crises in a great battle firm action must be taken, sometimes regardless of cost, there could be no valid reason for flinging away the later lines after the first had utterly failed.
>
> It is doubtful if there exists in the records of the A.I.F. [Australian Imperial Force] one instance in which, after one attacking party had been signally defeated, a second, sent after it, succeeded without some radical change having been effected in the plan or the conditions.

To sum up, then, we may say that to succeed we must go fast and to go fast we must go where the going is good.

Chapter XXII: *Battle Reconnaissance*

Infantry commanders of all grades are responsible for continuous reconnaissance.

DURING combat, leaders always seek information that will answer such questions as: "Does the enemy occupy those woods?" "Where is Company B?" "Is that hill held by the enemy?" "Where is my left assault company?" "I see hostile movement to my right front—what does it mean?" Usually, answers to such questions will be obtained by reconnaissance—reconnaissance to determine not only the enemy situation but the situation of our own troops as well.

The subordinate infantry commander has at his disposal only one sure means by which he may secure timely and vital information—infantry patrols. A well organized and properly conducted infantry patrol may operate successfully in spite of unfavorable weather, poor visibility, and difficult terrain.

Successful patrolling demands the highest of soldierly virtues. Therefore, the selection of personnel for an important patrol must not be a perfunctory affair. The men should be carefully selected and only the intelligent, the physically fit and the stout of heart should be considered. One careless or stupid individual may bring about the death or capture of the entire patrol or cause it to fail in its mission. The moron, the weakling and the timid have no place in this hazardous and exacting duty.

In the scheme of continuous reconnaissance, reconnaissance by the commander plays an important part. Personal observation, coupled with accurate information from other sources, enables him to make correct deductions from the past, prepares him to act promptly and effectively in the present, and permits him to anticipate the future.

EXAMPLE 1. For two days the U. S. 47th Infantry, in conjunction with other troops, had made a determined effort to establish a bridge-head across the Vesle near St. Thibaut. Actually, the 2d Battalion had effected a crossing early on the

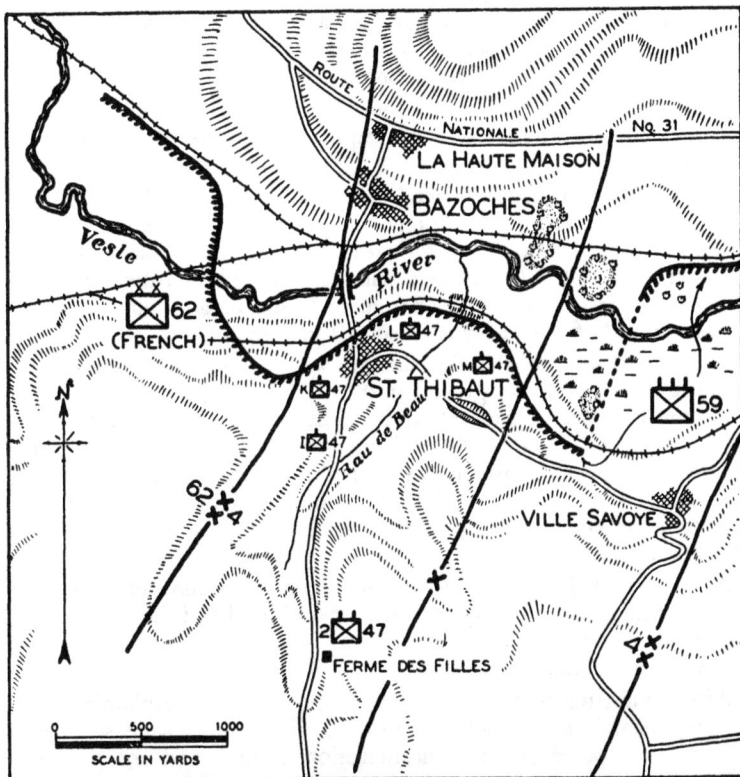

Example 1

morning of August 7, 1918, but it had been subjected to such terrific punishment that it was no longer capable of effective offensive action. It was therefore ordered to withdraw to the vicinity of the Ferme des Filles.

In the events that followed this withdrawal, patrols from the

3d Battalion of the 47th Infantry played an important part. The battalion commander tells what happened in the following paragraphs:

During the early evening of August 9, the 2d Battalion withdrew. This move left the 3d Battalion holding all of the 7th Brigade front along the narrow-gauge railway embankment south of the river. Contact was established with the 59th Infantry on the right and the French 62d Division on the left.

Although the day of August 10 was quiet compared with the three previous days, there was some sniping and a little artillery fire on St. Thibaut.

About 4:00 p.m. the regimental commander informed the battalion commander that a reliable report from the aviation indicated that the enemy had evacuated the area to the front and was hurriedly retreating to the Aisne River. He then directed the battalion commander to take up an advance-guard formation and move at once in pursuit of the enemy until contact had been gained.

The colonel was told that the battalion was now in close contact with the enemy and that ground north of the Vesle could be gained only by a well-organized attack. The colonel insisted upon the reliability of the information he had received, and pointed out the embarrassment it would entail if the enemy slipped away undetected. It took a great deal of talking to convince him that there were yet enough of the enemy to the front to stop an advance-guard march.

As a result of the discussion with the regimental commander, the 3d Battalion was directed to send out patrols and to follow them up with the battalion if the enemy was found to have evacuated the area to the immediate front.

After conferring with the company commanders and explaining the regimental commander's instructions, five patrols were selected, each composed of one noncommissioned officer and one private.

These men were selected for their fitness for reconnaissance-patrol work. They were equipped only with pistols, gas masks, and canteens. They were assembled before dark at points where the area to be covered could be seen. Their instructions were to cross the Vesle, penetrate to the high ground north of the Route Nationale, and find out whether or not the enemy had evacuated the area to the front. They were further instructed to report to the battalion command post immediately after completing their reconnaissance. These patrols were distributed along the front at five different points. The area to be covered extended from the St. Thibaut—

Bazoches road (the route of the left patrol) to a point more than 1,000 yards east of St. Thibaut.

Company commanders were ordered to start the patrols as soon as it was dark enough to hide their movement.

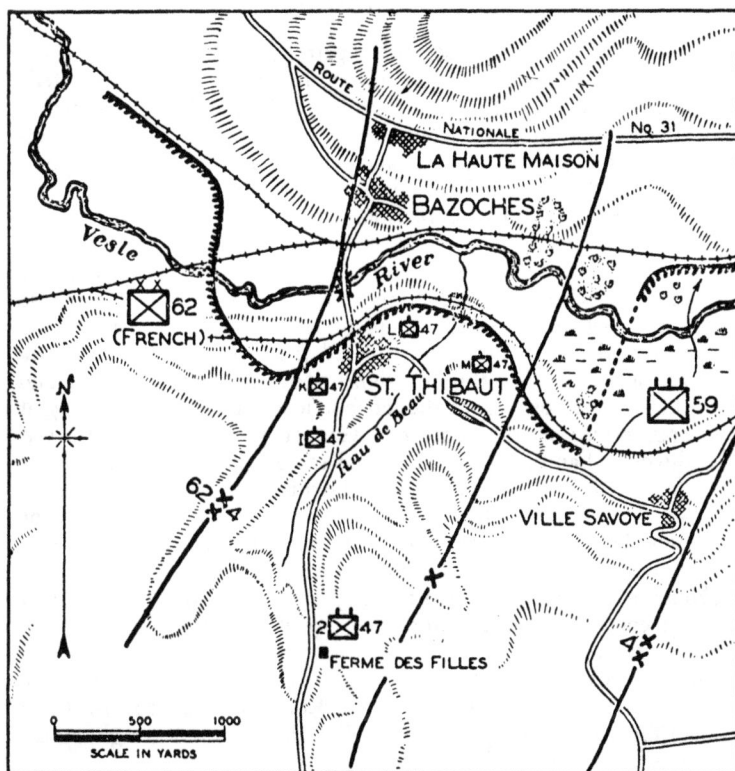

Example 1

In the meantime each company was told to be ready to move out, if the reported evacuation was indeed a fact.

About 10:00 p.m. two of the patrols which had tried to cross the Vesle at and near Bazoches, reported back with information that this town was held by the enemy. This word was transmitted promptly to regimental headquarters.

Between 10:00 p.m. and 11:00 p.m. two other patrols reported that they were unable to cross the river because of the enemy on the opposite bank. The leaders of these patrols said that they had remained on the river bank for some time observing the movements of the enemy on the other side. The enemy, they said, appeared to be concentrating troops just north of the river, particularly in a patch of woods just north of the railway and about 800 yards east of Bazoches.

About midnight one member of the patrol from Company M, whose route was on the extreme right, reported in. He was very excited; in his hand he had a Luger pistol and the shoulder strap from a German uniform. He reported that by working well into the sector of the 59th Infantry, he and his corporal had reached a point about 300 yards south of the Route Nationale and about 1,000 yards east of la Haute Maison. Here they stopped because of enemy traffic on the road. He stated that while they were lying in wait, they had seen the Germans unload some sort of weapons on small wheels and move them south toward the river. He also stated that several small groups of enemy soldiers came in along this road and turned south toward the river. As the returning patrol was passing through some woods north of the river and about 400 yards west of the left boundary of the 59th Infantry, it encountered a large number of German soldiers. The patrol was discovered and fired on. There was some fighting at close quarters during which the private killed a German from whom he took the shoulder strap and the pistol. The corporal was shot through the neck, but made his way into the lines of the 59th Infantry where he had been left for first-aid treatment.

From the information gained by the patrols it was quite evident that the enemy was not retiring. Actually, it looked as if he intended to attack.

This information was transmitted immediately to the regimental commander by runner and telephone. Runners were also dispatched to the 59th Infantry and to the French with messages giving the substance of the information.

Early the next morning the enemy launched an attack against the 3rd Battalion which was easily and quickly repulsed.

From the personal experience monograph of Captain Hurley E. Fuller, who commanded the 3d Battalion of the 47th Infantry.

DISCUSSION. This example is an excellent illustration of the effective employment of small infantry patrols in battle reconnaissance.

The location and activities of the enemy had to be discovered at once. Patrols were the surest and quickest agency that could get this information. Not one patrol but five were ordered out; this increased the chances of success and insured coverage of the entire front. The patrols were of minimum strength and made up of specially selected men. Each patrol had a definite mission and a well-defined objective—the Route Nationale—which could be easily located even at night. Each patrol was shown during daylight the area over which it was to operate. Their equipment is also worth noting, particularly, the substitution of pistols for rifles.

The fact that only one patrol actually reached the objective is unimportant. All patrols brought back valuable information. Those that were unable to cross the river brought back conclusive evidence that the enemy was still in position in considerable force and that no withdrawal was in progress. Moreover, the information gained by two of these patrols, together with the report of the one which did succeed in crossing, made it clear that, far from contemplating a withdrawal, the enemy was about to attack.

ꞁ ꞁ ꞁ

EXAMPLE 2. On March 22, 1918, the German 229th Reserve Infantry attacked to the west. After driving forward a considerable distance, the attack was brought to a halt near Saulcourt. Since it appeared that the British intended to stand and make a fight here, the Germans decided to find out where the enemy would offer the most resistance before they resumed the attack. The regimental commander promptly dispatched a patrol to determine the location of the enemy's new main line of resistance. This patrol consisted of a lieutenant, an ensign as second in command, one light machine-gun squad and one rifle squad. Machine-gun and minenwerfer fires from the regiment were to assist the patrol.

The patrol moved forward about 11:30 a.m. As it neared A (shown on sketch) it came under fire from a machine gun and suffered two casualties, one being the leader. The ensign then took charge and, not wishing to become involved in a fight, withdrew the patrol to the rear. This action was facilitated by the covering minenwerfer fire which was placed on the machine gun near A.

After a 500-meter detour the patrol again crawled forward and near B surprised and captured two enemy sentries. It then moved a short distance south to an old trench which it followed until it came under heavy fire from the direction of C. The patrol leader now halted the advance, got out his map, and showed his men just where they were and where he wanted them to go. He then ordered them to fall back, individually, some 300 meters, then move south across the road and assemble near the road junction at D. This was done. Meanwhile, hostile fire continued on the area that had been vacated.

From D the patrol leader saw that the British held Saulcourt, but it did not appear that the town was occupied in force. He noted that British outposts were stationed directly east of the town, but did not appear to extend far to the southeast, since he could locate no enemy near D. Having satisfied himself on these points, he then moved his patrol to the small wood at E, taking great pains to avoid hostile observation.

From E he saw only small British detachments along the southeast edge of Saulcourt, but 600 yards west of the town he saw strong hostile forces digging in. Their south flank did not extend far beyond Saulcourt.

The patrol leader immediately led his patrol back to the regiment. It had been gone two hours. The leader reported that Saulcourt was held by a British outpost, that the main line of resistance was 600 yards in rear, and that there seemed to be a gap in the British defenses south of the town.

Based on this report, the division to which the 229th belonged attacked without delay, making its main effort on the south. The attack succeeded with slight losses.

From an article in "Kriegskunst im Wort und Bild," 1928.

DISCUSSION. The article from which this example was taken attributes a large part of this successful attack to the lead-

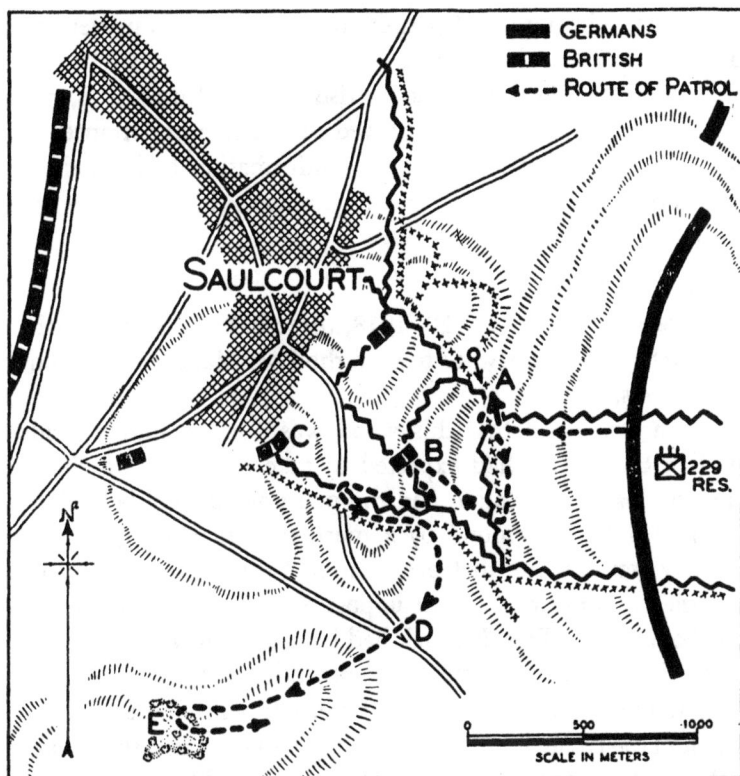

Example 2

ing of this one patrol. The paragraph of the German infantry regulations with which the article dealt says:

> Reconnaissance may never be omitted during battle. No difficulties of terrain and no exhaustion of troops or leaders should cause it to be neglected.

> Careful reconnaissance requires time, but unless the information acquired reaches the commander in time to be acted upon, the reconnaissance is valueless.

The patrol in this example was led with vigor and determination. When it encountered resistance it moved back and tried elsewhere; it did this several times. It did not become involved in a useless fight nor did it permit enemy outposts to prevent it from accomplishing its mission.

The fact that there were no British near and east of E, although negative information, proved of decisive importance.

Finally, the patrol leader got his information back in time for it to be acted upon. That is a requirement that can never be repeated too often.

*   *   *

EXAMPLE 3. On July 20, 1918, three battalions of French Chasseurs attacked eastward toward the Bois Manuet in column of battalions.

It soon developed that this wood was not the lightly held objective the French had expected to take so easily. In short order the leading battalion and the one immediately behind it were nailed to the ground by a murderous machine-gun fire. So heavy was this fire that even liaison between companies of the same battalion was almost impossible. There was no question about it—the French attack had been definitely checked.

Now just about this time the commander of the reserve battalion moved forward to acquaint himself with the situation. He found the commander of the leading battalion in a shell hole on the crest northeast of Rassy. This officer had been wounded and could give little information beyond the fact that his entire battalion seemed to be pinned down and that the enemy resistance from the Bois Manuet was very strong. One of his companies had gone astray.

It appeared that if any advance were to be made it would have to be made by the reserve battalion.

The commander of the reserve battalion continued his reconnaissance. To the north he discovered a slight depression and what appeared to be a covered approach leading toward the

Bois de Latilly. Nearby crests were swept by enemy fire but, so far as he was able to determine, no fire reached this approach. He therefore concluded that it was possible to advance by this

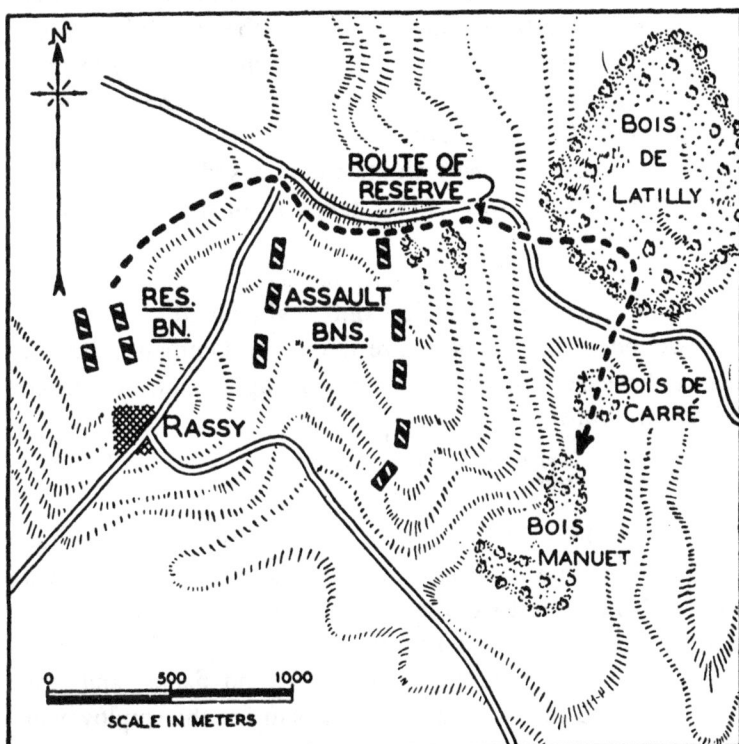

Example 3

route and decided to order his battalion forward. To cover his advance and to be sure he made no mistake, he ordered a number of small patrols to move over the selected route. These were to be followed at a considerable distance by half the battalion. Meanwhile he had made all necessary arrangements for covering fire on the enemy.

The patrols reconnoitered the route and found it protected

from hostile fire. The battalion commander followed near the head of his half-battalion which moved in single file. When this force reached the southern edge of the Bois de Latilly, a patrol which had been sent to the east edge of this wood reported that it had found there the missing company of the assault battalion. The battalion commander at once ordered this company to provide security to the east and then sent back for the remainder of the battalion. Upon its arrival he established a base of fire perpendicular to the enemy front, and attacked southward.

The Bois Manuet was quickly taken from its defenders—a fresh German battalion.

While the casualties in the original assault battalions were heavy, the reserve battalion lost only eight killed and twenty-three wounded during the entire day. The German battalion seems to have been almost destroyed in its fight against the three French battalions.

From Infantry Conferences at l'École Supérieure de Guerre, by Lieutenant Colonel Touchon, French Army.

DISCUSSION. This is an excellent illustration of the value of personal reconnaissance by the commander. Going in turn to each of the assault battalions, the commander of the reserve battalion gained first-hand information of the situation, obtained a good view of the terrain to the front and flanks, and was thereby enabled to formulate a sound plan for the employment of his unit.

Having formulated a plan and selected a tentative route of advance (which he had personally discovered), he ordered small patrols to precede his battalion as reconnaissance and covering groups. As a result of his own reconnaissance, he was more than reasonably certain that the route selected was suitable for his advance, but he took the additional precaution of sending forward patrols.

The success of the maneuver may be directly attributed to the careful reconnaissance made by this battalion commander.

EXAMPLE 4. On July 15, 1918, the Germans struck southward across the Marne at the U. S. 3d Division. The German plan
of attack called for the 47th Infantry to remain in division reserve until the 6th Grenadiers had cleared the south bank in
the vicinity of Mézy. The 47th would then cross.

The 1st Battalion of the 47th Infantry reached its assembly
position north of the Marne after suffering relatively heavy
losses from American artillery fire. Extracts from its report on
subsequent operations follow:

> The 1st Battalion, which was to be the first unit of the regiment to
> cross the Marne . . . assembled at 5:00 a.m. to march to bridge
> L-1. Its effectives at this time numbered 11 officers, 49 noncom-
> missioned officers and 244 men (these figures include the 1st
> Machine-Gun Company).
>
> The battalion staff, the 4th Company, part of the 3d Company, and
> the 1st Machine-Gun Company then proceeded to the Marne and
> crossed by bridge L-1. The 1st and 2d Companies and the rest
> of the 3d Company had been seriously delayed by heavy enemy fire
> and did not follow until much later. . . .
>
> Since the enemy's infantry did not contest the passage of the river
> and since the division had ordered the 6th Grenadier Regiment
> to clear the village of Mézy and the woods south of bridge L-1,
> the battalion advanced in route column. Still moving in this for-
> mation the battalion plunged into a wheat field a short distance
> south of the Marne. Its leading elements had penetrated about
> 200 meters into the high wheat, when they were suddenly taken
> under heavy and highly effective rifle and machine-gun fire from
> the direction of the Mézy—Mont-St. Père road and from the
> woods south of L-1.
>
> It not yet being daylight and the fog still prevailing, the position of
> the enemy could not be definitely determined. But in spite of the
> low visibility the battalion immediately met with heavy losses. The
> 4th Company, which was the foremost unit, suffered especially.
> On account of the high wheat, the men were only able to fire
> from the standing position; and whoever raised his head above
> the wheat was almost always hit.
>
> All six guns of the machine-gun company immediately assumed the
> highest possible firing position and opened fire. But the enemy
> was apparently well dug in . . . and the wheat too high even
> for the highest firing position of the machine guns. Therefore no

effect was obtained, despite the concentrated fire and the liberal expenditure of ammunition. Within a few minutes one man of the machine-gun company had been killed and eight wounded. . . .

A further advance was useless without the support of escort artillery and trench mortars which were not on hand. The attack of the battalion gradually slackened and finally came to a standstill, since the men, even when crawling, were hit by enemy riflemen posted in trees.

In these circumstances, the machine-gun company could no longer hold its ground. Accordingly it withdrew . . . and took up a new position close to the southern bank of the river. But here, too, no fire could be delivered owing to the high wheat. Since it was absolutely essential that something be done, the company retreated to the high ground on the north bank which permitted commanding fire. But low visibility still prevailed, and nothing could be seen from here either.

Meanwhile the 3d and 4th Companies suffered heavily from rifle and machine-gun fire and finally even from rifle grenades and shrapnel. The battalion commander, who was at the head of the battalion, now crawled back to report to the regiment and ask for auxiliary weapons. These weapons . . . could not be brought up. . . .

Finally all men of the 3d and 4th Companies who could crawl back did so and took up position on the north bank of the Marne. The adjutant having been killed and the battalion commander and orderly officer wounded, details of the subsequent action of the battalion can not be determined.

Elements of the 1st and 2d Companies do not seem to have crossed the Marne. The report says the effective strength of the battalion at this time was reduced to that of a small company.

Let us now turn to the 2d Battalion of the 47th which was dug in north of bridge L-1, and see what part it played in this attack. Early in the morning it supported the advance of the 1st Battalion by fire from the north bank. At 9:45 a.m. it received orders to cross the Marne by bridge U-1 (assigned to the 398th Infantry) and flank the machine-gun nests at the railway embankment and in the woods north of the railway. Here is this battalion's account of what followed:

Personal reconnaissance by the commander of the 2d Battalion showed that U-1 could not be reached under cover, and that a march to that point would probably cause inexcusable losses in view of the

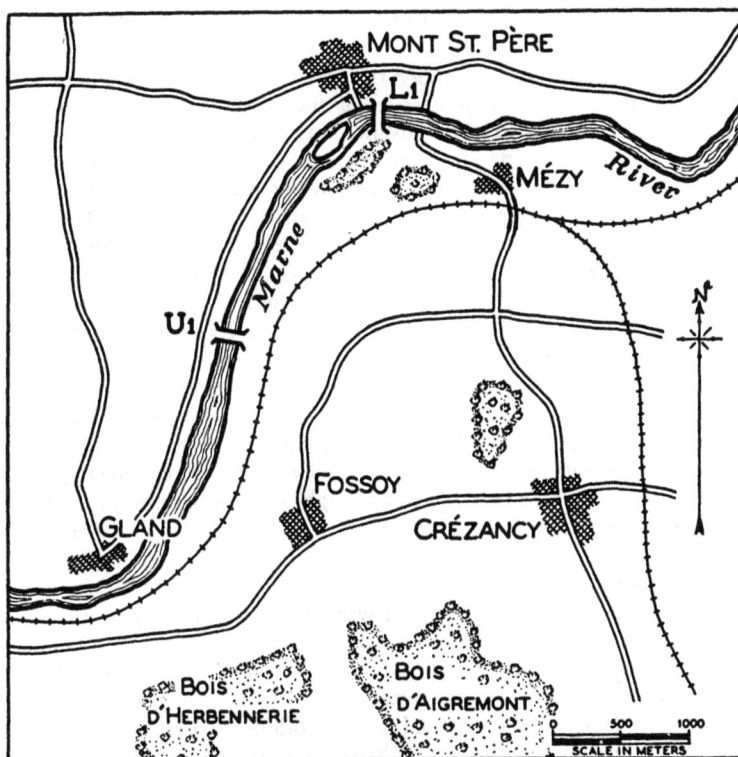

Example 4

well-directed fire of the French artillery. The battalion therefore
decided to cross at L-1, and obtaining permission from the regiment to do this, assembled its units and crossed in the following
order: 8th, 7th and 5th Companies, two platoons of the machine-
gun company, 6th Company, one platoon of the machine-gun
company. The 8th Company extended to the left on the southern bank and opened fire on Mézy and the edge of the wood. The
7th Company followed and extended to the right. Both companies
attempted to advance, but at once came under heavy rifle and
machine-gun fire.

A patrol under the command of Lieutenant Hoolman now succeeded
in gaining contact with the 398th Infantry on the right and an

NCO patrol was sent out to establish liaison with the 6th Grenadiers on the left.

The 6th Company now extended the front to the right, overwhelmed the enemy and took possession of the foremost wooded section (just south of L-1). The advance was made under heavy enemy shell fire. The battalion then attacked the next wooded section. Here it was taken under machine-gun fire at close range but . . . succeeded in carrying the wood and dispersing the enemy. It then took the railway embankment and the terrain immediately south of it, and connected up with the 398th Infantry on the right. This done, it reported that it had reached its objective and asked whether it should continue to advance and whether it could expect support and extension to the left.

Patrols were sent out to the south and to the east. Sergeant Hentschke in command of a small patrol advanced to a point east of Fossoy, found the terrain free from enemy troops and saw a German skirmish line enter Herbennerie Wood. This patrol took several prisoners, destroyed a field piece and a light machine gun, and brought back two badly wounded grenadiers. It also found that Mézy was not occupied by the enemy.

The battalion was now informed by the regiment that no further support could be given. A patrol was again sent to Mézy to protect the left flank. It was fired on. The hostile group, which was not particularly strong, was dispersed by a platoon of the 6th Company, but at considerable cost.

Since no contact could be gained with the 6th Grenadiers, close liaison was maintained with the 398th Infantry, and dispositions for the night were agreed upon.

On the morning of July 16 this battalion, acting in accordance with orders issued during the night, withdrew to the north bank of the Marne without suffering any loss in the movement.

The report of the commander of the 3d Battalion of the 47th Infantry tells why the 2d Battalion commander considered it impracticable to make the crossing at U-1 as ordered on July 15. According to the map it appeared possible to cross at U-1. The order from higher authority specified that the 2d Battalion, followed by the 3d, would move under cover of the woods from its present position to bridge U-1. The 3d Battalion report states:

The entire slope west of the Mont-St. Père—Gland road was shown

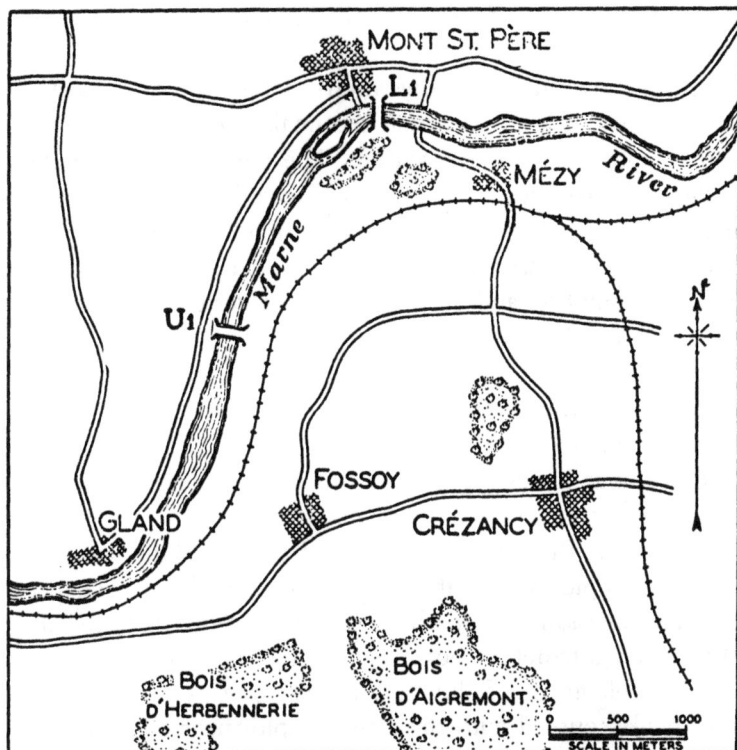

Example 4

on the map as wooded, while in reality it was completely bare and could be observed at all points by the enemy. Moreover, the road leading from Mont-St. Père to U-1 was under heavy artillery fire.

The 3d Battalion commander also made a personal reconnaissance, and in addition sent out an officer patrol to investigate the situation before he acted on the order to cross at U-1. He reached the same conclusion as the commander of the 2d Battalion.

From the battle report of the 47th Infantry.

DISCUSSION. These reports afford an interesting comparison of the separate advance of two battalions over the same ground on the same day.

From the account of the operations of the 1st Battalion it is apparent that little or no actual reconnaissance was attempted on the south bank of the Marne. The battalion commander undoubtedly assumed that the 6th Grenadier Regiment held the ground to his front and would furnish ample protection for his crossing. The assumption was logical but, after all, it was only an assumption and should have been verified. As it happened, the 6th Grenadiers had been virtually annihilated.

The subsequent actions of the 1st Battalion furnished the realization of the machine gunner's dream—to catch troops in route column at close range.

The ruinous losses suffered by this battalion are wholly attributable to a lack of proper reconnaissance.

By contrast, the actions of the 2d Battalion stand out as a shining example of how it should have been done. The personal reconnaissance of the battalion commander disclosed the folly of an attempted movement to the U-1 crossing. The prompt deployment of the battalion as soon as it gained the south bank, coupled with the active employment of reconnaissance and contact patrols, minimized losses and prepared the way for an effective attack.

ɾ   ɾ   ɾ

EXAMPLE 5. During the Meuse-Argonne offensive the U. S. 26th Infantry, part of the 1st Division, relieved troops of the 35th Division along the general line indicated on the sketch. The regiment was in contact with hostile patrols but the location of the enemy's main defensive position was unknown.

Before daybreak on October 2, front-line battalion commanders received an oral order to penetrate the enemy screen to their front with strong combat patrols and locate the enemy's defensive position. This order, which originated at corps head-

quarters, was based upon a report from the French that the
Germans had withdrawn.

In compliance with this order, the commander of the right-

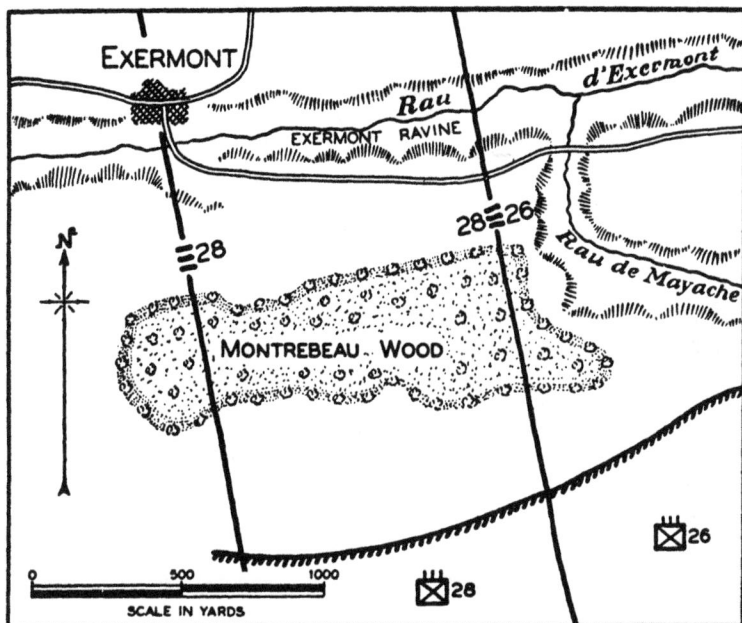

Example 5

flank battalion sent forward a patrol of two officers and 70 men.
Anxiety for the safety of the patrol caused him to include a
corporal and private from the signal detachment with a breast
reel and a telephone.

Of the two officers and 70 men who set out, only one officer
and twelve men returned. What happened is best described in
the personal diary of the surviving officer.

The patrol left battalion headquarters about one hour before sunrise
and advanced in double file to the line of outguards. At the line
of outguards it deployed in two waves, the first wave as skirmishers, the second in squad columns about 50 feet in rear. The fog

was thick. The two officers marched between the skirmish line and the line of squad columns.

When the patrol had advanced about a half-kilometer, it was fired on by several machine guns from Montrebeau Wood. Lieutenant X ordered the patrol to double-time to a draw just ahead of us. We advanced at a run to the Rau de Mayache and up the crest of the hill on the other side. Several men fell; we saw nothing to fire at. At this point the patrol was stopped by machine-gun fire from the left, the left-rear, and from across the Exermont Ravine. Suddenly a nest of two guns about 40 yards in front of us opened up. Lieutenant X, the patrol leader, was killed, so were a number of men who tried to rush the nest. It was finally put out and two Boches killed. Fire was so heavy that we had to dig in where we were. Men were falling on all sides.

At this time Corporal Y cut the telephone in. I got the battalion commander and told him what a mess we were in. He said to hold where we were. The fire from the woods to our left-rear became so heavy that I sent Corporal Z and six men to work their way against it. They succeeded in putting out one light machine gun and reported the woods heavily held.

About one hour later some 30 Boches were discovered immediately to our rear. Part of the patrol faced about. Just then we saw Captain A coming forward with a part of his outfit and the Boches withdrew.

About 1:00 p.m. orders were received to withdraw to the line of outguards. We had about 20 men left who were deployed on a front of 200 yards. I managed to get 12 survivors back to the line of outguards and reported my arrival to the battalion commander.

From the personal experience monograph of Major Barnwell R. Legge, who commanded a battalion of the 26th Infantry.

✓   ✓   ✓

The losses suffered by this patrol are appalling. Indeed, had the battalion commander not thought to include the little signal detachment there would probably have been no survivors left to tell the tale. In that event the patrol would have failed in its mission and its sacrifice been useless.

All along the front, American patrols drove through the enemy screen, took their losses and came back with vital information. Major Legge sums up their work in this statement:

> Although the cost was great, the patrols had accomplished their mission: information was now available to lay the barrage for the initial attack.

✓ ✓ ✓

CONCLUSION. It is not likely that infantry leaders will ever find an adequate substitute for the infantry patrol. Through it and through it alone is the small unit able to find timely answers to the myriad questions that arise in battle. The higher echelons are primarily concerned with the larger point of view; to them the problems that confront the battalion and the company are microscopic. But even when they do receive information of vital interest to the smaller front-line units, it seldom reaches those units in time to be of value.

There are no two ways about it—patrols are the eyes of the small infantry unit. Sometimes these patrols will discover just where the enemy is and just what he is doing. This, of course, is information of the highest value. But more often than not, they will bring in only negative information; they will report that the enemy is *not* in such-and-such a place and is *not* doing this, that, or the other thing. To the intelligent leader, information of this type is frequently of the greatest importance and he will impress that fact on his patrols.

As for the leader himself, he must never lose sight of the value of patrols nor allow this important duty to degenerate into a routine, slipshod, you-do-it-sergeant affair.

Since the success of a battalion, a regiment, or even a division, will frequently depend on the conduct of one small patrol, patrols must be hand-picked, carefully instructed, and given a clear, definite mission. These three things play a vital part in the borderland between success and failure.

When to send out patrols, their number and their strength, are matters that must be determined by the situation. Of course, there is such a thing as over-patrolling; sometimes a reconnaissance enthusiast will exhaust his command through incessant, unwise, and unnecessary patrolling. This error, though serious, is rare. Usually it is a question of under-patrolling. In this connection, the old saying is a good guide: "When it is apparent from the situation that patrolling is unnecessary, send out patrols anyway."

Chapter XXIII: *Counter-Orders*

Rapid changes in a situation often require rapid changes in decisions. Therefore counter-orders will be frequent and should be accepted as normal incidents of battle.

ONCE MADE, a decision should not be changed except for weighty reasons. Infantry commanders, however, are constantly confronted with changes in the situation that demand new schemes of maneuver and consequently new orders. With such kaleidoscopic suddenness does the situation veer and shift that it is not unusual for a subordinate unit to be ordered to intitiate a certain line of action only to have the order countermanded before the action has gotten under way.

When counter-orders do occur it becomes a paramount duty of all leaders to curb irritation and the instinctive tendency to criticize. Success in combat is certainly not rendered more likely by the muttered criticisms of junior officers—criticisms which rapidly and seriously affect the moral tone of a command.

Responsibility for changing a mission rests squarely with the commander. When the march of events has invalidated his original assignment he must of necessity take the new situation into account. Behind every counter-order there is usually a valid reason. If we are able to adopt the French proverb, "To understand all is to forgive all," we shall meet changing orders with greater equanimity.

ⴼ　　ⴼ　　ⴼ

EXAMPLE 1. On September 5, 1914, the 2d Company of the 57th Infantry, part of the 14th Division, which in turn was part of the German Second Army, made a long march to the south in pursuit of the retiring French. The 14th Division, on the right of the army, passed east of Montmirail.

The 2d Company crossed the Petit Morin and spent the night in a small village south of the river. At daylight, September 6, heavy cannonading was heard to the south. But instead of marching toward the sound of the guns, the 14th Division turned about and moved to the north.

Consternation spread through the ranks of the 2d Company. The men could not find out why they were required to march to the rear. They had never done so before. About noon word passed that the division was in army reserve. A little later the column halted along the main road from Château-Thierry /to Fontenelle. Good spirits soon returned, for the men felt that the battle must be going well if the reserve was allowed to rest. At dusk the sound of artillery firing died down.

In the early morning of the following day, September 7, these troops made a short march into a wood near Artonges. There they encountered badly damaged supply wagons returning from the front. The drivers told of a German retreat, of heavy casualties, of defeat. The men again became apprehensive.

At 8:00 a.m. the 2d Company marched to Villenoyenne and began digging in. The situation was baffling. They had been driving the French to the south. Suddenly they had marched to the north with ominous rumors of a German defeat. Now the whole division was digging in facing to the west. Where could the First Army be? Leaders sensed a certain anxiety among the men.

At 11:00 a.m. orders arrived directing that intrenchment cease and that the division start a forced march on Fromentières to the east. The march was long and difficult. Again and again the column had to cross long trains of ammunition and supply wagons going to and from the front.

At 1:00 p.m. the column was halted, although it had not yet reached Fromentières. Orders had been received to countermarch on Artonges. These bewildering changes reacted badly on the men. It appeared to them that the higher commanders were unable to decide on any course of action.

Artonges was finally reached at 5:00 p.m. Officers and men sat about discussing the events of the day, trying to deduce their meaning. At 8:00 p.m. the command was informed that the French had penetrated the left wing of the army and that during the night the reserve would march to their assistance without rest and without regard for march casualties.

It was very dark when this forced march began. Part of the

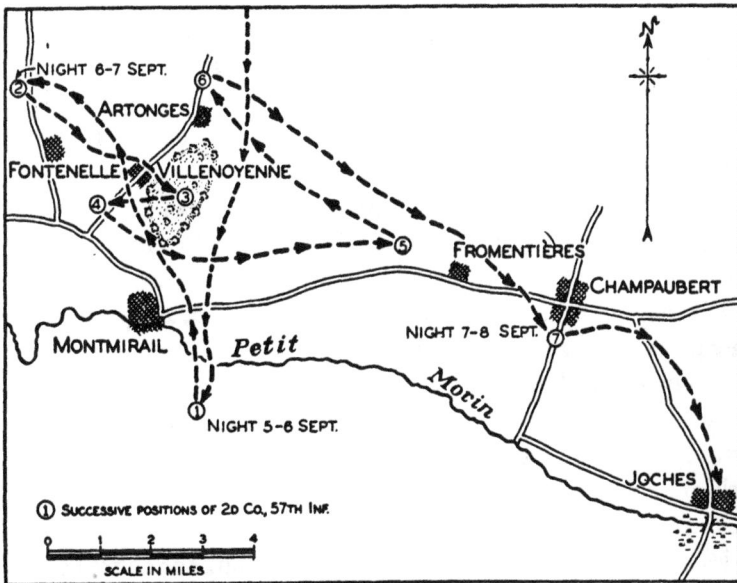

Example 1

route led across country. Once more the direction of march was east. The impression gained headway among the troops that the battle was going badly. At 1:00 p.m. on September 8 the reserve reached its destination near Champaubert. The men dropped to the ground in the sleep of exhaustion. In three hours they were aroused. They had expected to attack at daylight; instead they continued the march to the east. No one knew why. Arriving at Joches definite orders were finally received to attack to the south.

Now let us consider the reasons for these movements. The German Second Army and the First Army on its right were directed to execute a wheel to the west. The left or east wing of the First Army was, on September 5, farther advanced to the south than the Second Army. Therefore, if the wheel were to be made, the right or west element of the Second Army (the VII Corps consisting of the 13th and 14th Divisions) was superfluous at the front at that time. Consequently it was designated as army reserve and ordered to move north to Montmirail.

On September 6 all corps marching to the south were engaged in heavy fighting. The 14th Division remained in army reserve. A French attack from the direction of Paris against its right flank had caused the First Army (on the night of September 2) to shift troops from south of the Marne to the north to meet the threat to its flank. Thus the 14th Division heard rumors of defeat.

The gap resulting between the two armies, being protected only by cavalry, was a weak spot. It was obvious, therefore, that the right flank of the Second Army would have to be refused. Only the left wing would continue the attack. In this plan the 14th Division, situated behind the right wing, was allotted the task of securing the right flank. Accordingly we saw it digging in, facing west.

Meanwhile a desperate battle had begun along the entire army front. No decision was reached. Reports of the situation in front of the gap between the First and Second Armies did not appear critical at this time. The army commander naturally wanted his reserve centrally located. Hence the march to Fromentières.

In the meantime new messages reached the army which forced it to guard its right flank. The 14th Division again marched back to the threatened right wing.

On the evening of September 7 fresh intelligence indicated that the French had penetrated between two corps of the Second Army. The only available reserve had to make that difficult night march. Later the situation cleared up and the danger to this particular portion of the front disappeared.

On the morning of September 8 it was thought that a weak point had been located in the hostile front. Owing to the situation on the right flank it was imperative that a decision be reached promptly. Hence the troops of the army reserve were awakened after three hours' sleep, marched farther to the east and ordered to attack.

From the personal experience monograph of Captain Adolf von Schell, who commanded the 2d Company of the 57th Infantry.

DISCUSSION. There is no question that these apparently aimless marches affected the fighting capacity of the troops. Undoubtedly morale suffered. Perhaps the army commander changed his mind too often. Perhaps he jumped at conclusions too quickly as reports filtered in. But regardless of whether or not each of the decisions was best, each move corresponded to a definite conception of the situation. They were not the result of a commander's whims but an honest effort to meet the situation as understood at army headquarters.

Such counter-orders are virulent irritants, but leaders, by precept and by example, may do much to instill calmness and fortitude in accepting these inevitabilities of war.

1   1   1

EXAMPLE 2. During the early days of the Meuse-Argonne offensive the U. S. 30th Infantry (3d Division) was held in the Bois de Hesse in corps reserve. The men lived in shell holes with little or no protection from the unending rains.

For two consecutive days order followed order with weary monotony—"be prepared to move at a moment's notice." Finally, at 9:00 p.m. the night of September 29-30, an order was received directing that packs be rolled and that the regiment be held in readiness for an immediate move. After a two-hour wait in a torrential rain, a new order arrived stating that no move would be made that night, and that men would be permitted to pitch tents.

One hour later, at midnight, a third order was received directing the battalions to be ready to move in thirty minutes. The movement actually took place at 3:30 a.m.

From the personal experience monograph of Major Turner M. Chambliss, who commanded the 2d Battalion of the 30th Infantry.

DISCUSSION Frequent changes of orders seriously affect morale. Men lose confidence in their superiors. "Order—counter-order—disorder" is more than a pungent expression. Pointless vacillation, whether by the lieutenant commanding a platoon or the general commanding an army, cannot be too vigorously condemned. Only the exigencies of a changing or obscure situation can justify the serious effects of the counter-order.

In this instance the apparent indecision was probably the result of varying information concerning the situation of the 79th Division. The 3d Division relieved the 79th on September 30, *making a daylight relief,* upon the receipt of information which indicated, or which was interpreted to indicate, that the situation of the 79th was critical.

✓ ✓ ✓

EXAMPLE 3. The 82d Reserve Regiment, part of the main body of the German 22d Reserve Division, marched south toward the Marne on September 5, 1914. It was part of the IV Reserve Corps which had been assigned the mission of protecting the flank of the German First Army from the direction of Paris.

About noon the troops were going into bivouac in accordance with their orders when a counter-order arrived directing the column to march west to Penchard. A short time later firing was heard to the west.

The 7th Reserve Division, north of the 22d, had become en-

gaged with the French near Monthyon. The 22d was ordered
to advance in echelon on its left. Accordingly, on reaching
Penchard, the leading elements of the 22d Division turned
northwest toward Monthyon.

The French were reported in the vicinity of Iverny and le-

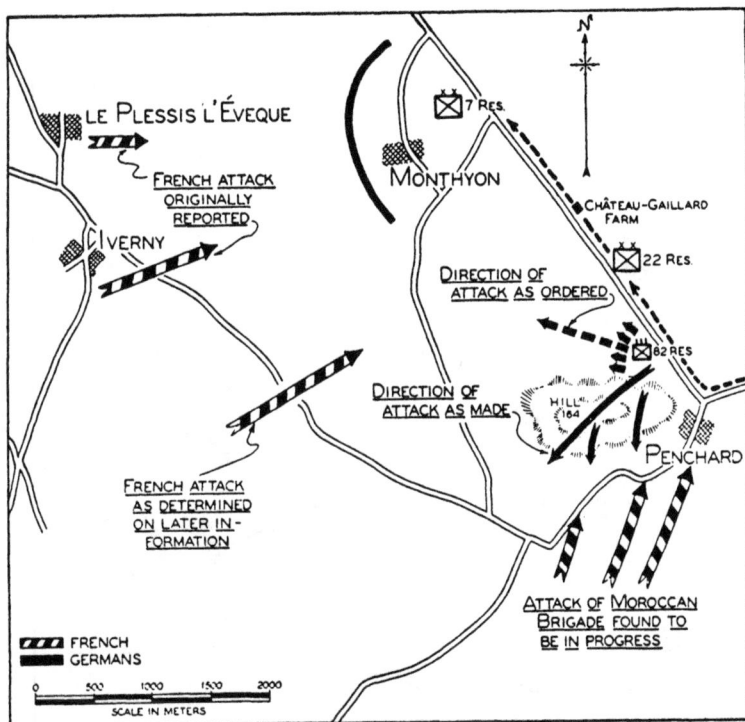

Example 3

Plessis-l'Evêque. The 7th Reserve Division, whose units were
deployed and considerably intermingled, was near Monthyon.
The 82d Reserve Regiment was still near Penchard when a hostile
advance was noted driving from the south of Iverny toward
Château-Gaillard. This threatened to take in flank the 7th and
22d Divisions which were moving on Monthyon.

The 82d Reserve Regiment had been ordered by the division commander to attack at once in the direction of le-Plessis-l'Evêque. The regiment was deploying under cover of the valley northwest of Penchard. Orders had been issued, plans had been made, and officers were studying the terrain to the northwest.

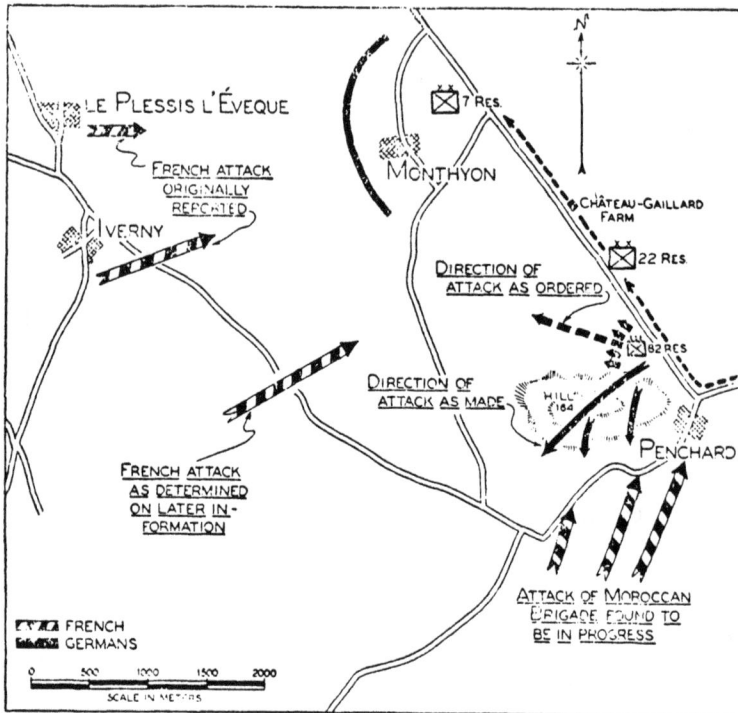

Example 3

Then just as the regimental commander was about to launch the northwest attack he learned that strong hostile elements were advancing from the west on Penchard and Hill 164. Violent firing was heard to the west and southwest.

The regimental commander promptly abandoned the objective and direction of attack assigned him. He caused his entire regiment to face to the southwest and attack straight over Hill 164.

The 82d reached the south and west slopes of Hill 164 as the Moroccan brigade entered Penchard from the southwest. Some leading elements of the Moroccans had already reached the slopes south of Penchard and were approaching Hill 164. Others, having reached Penchard, opened fire on the German trains that congested the road, and caused a panic. The 82d Reserve Regiment took the Moroccans in flank and rear, re-established the situation and drove the enemy back.

From the account by Lieutenant Colonel Koeltz, French Army, in "La Revue d'Infanterie," October, 1930.

DISCUSSION. Here we have a case where an infantry commander who was ordered to do one thing, disobeyed, and did something entirely different. He was ordered to attack to the northwest and take a French attack in flank. Instead he attacked to the southwest.

He took the responsibility of disobeying a definite order because he realized that the order had been given in ignorance of the existing situation. He felt sure that he was doing what his superior would want him to do, and that there was no time to ask for instructions.

The troops, of course, received numerous counter-orders. "We are going to halt for the night." "No, we march to the west—why to the west?" "We are to attack to the northwest." "No, we attack to the southwest."

The counter-order directing the turn to the west and continuation of the march just as the troops were going into their announced bivouacs, was the result of a decision by the corps commander, General von Gronau, who had the mission of protecting the right flank of the First Army from the dangerous direction of Paris. The situation was obscure and General von Gronau ordered an attack to clear it up. He struck the Sixth Army of General Maunoury as it moved forward to get into position for a decisive attack on September 6.

The counter-order issued by the commander of the 82d Reserve Regiment to attack to the south and southwest, instead of to the northwest as the regiment was preparing to do, was based on information received after the first attack order was issued.

Had the 82d blindly followed its original orders the Moroccan brigade might well have secured Penchard and Hill 164, thereby taking both the 7th and 22d Reserve Divisions in flank and rear.

In both cases counter-orders were the manifestation, not of vacillation, but of aggressive leadership of a high type.

✓   ✓   ✓

CONCLUSION. It is an error to think that counter-orders indicate a lack of resolution. Many of them, probably most of them, result from the obscurity of war. In mobile warfare we know the situation will invariably be vague. As information filters in to the higher commanders, changes in dispositions will be required. The information on which these changes are based will seldom reach the lower units at the time. They will read about it in a book after the war. Counter-orders, therefore, should be regarded as normal, accepted cheerfully, and passed downward with an air of confidence.

Chapter XXIV: *Action and Morale*

Action, physical and mental, is an efficacious antidote for battlefield nervousness.

A SOLDIER pinned to the ground by hostile fire, with no form of activity to divert his thought from the whistling death about him, soon develops an overwhelming sense of inferiority. He feels alone and deserted. He feels unable to protect himself. With nothing to do but wait and with nothing to think about but the immediate danger that surrounds him, his nerves rapidly reach the breaking point. Inactivity, therefore, constitutes a most serious danger to his morale.

By diverting the attention of the soldier through some simple mental or physical expedient, this nervous tension may be materially reduced. The leader, by thinking objectively himself and by causing his men to perform tasks involving thought and movement, may successfully combat the intense mental strain of battle. So too will simple, matter-of-fact actions by a commander tend to instill in the men a sense of confidence and security.

1   1   1

EXAMPLE 1. On August 22, 1914, the 6th Company of the French 116th Infantry attacked over open ground toward the little town of Maissin. Although the men were in their first fight and were obviously nervous, they drove steadily forward under a galling machine-gun fire. Finally they reached a wheat field on the crest near Maissin where the enemy's rifles and machine guns definitely brought the company to a halt. The instant a man lifted his head a spray of bullets cracked ominously through the wheat.

But where was this enemy? That was a question that no man in the 6th Company could answer. Although they had made their advance under a harassing fire and although they were now nailed to the ground, they had yet to see a single enemy target. In fact, the company could not even tell where the fire was coming from. Bit by bit, nerves stretched toward the breaking point; the situation on the crest grew electric.

And then the company commander saw two or three Germans near the edge of Maissin. Immediately he ordered his company to open fire on the outskirts of the town—*each man to fire only six rounds.*

The company opened up with a will. One soldier near the captain fired his six shots with the greatest deliberation. Then, with the empty cartridge cases in his hand, he turned and asked: "Captain, shall we save the empties or throw them away?"

The crisis had passed and the company was again well in hand. Their subsequent attack succeeded.

From "The Battle of Ardennes," by Major Pugens, French Army.

DISCUSSION. The captain saw that his men were becoming dangerously tense. They were in their first fight. They had been advancing under enemy fire and were pinned to the ground with no good target before them.

He wanted to give them something to do, something that would occupy their minds. He did not want them to dig in for that might stop the attack; furthermore, such a procedure was at variance with the French ideas of 1914. The two or three Germans seen near Maissin did not present a target which warranted the expenditure of much ammunition; therefore, the company commander did not permit his men to fire at will. Instead, to settle their nerves, he ordered them to fire by counted cartridges. This gave each man a task on which he had to focus his attention and at the same time reasserted the control of the leader.

The incident of the soldier and the empty cases shows that the company commander succeeded in his aim. He had prescribed a first-rate sedative.

EXAMPLE 2. In August, 1916, German reinforcements were rushed to the assistance of the Austrians who had been thrown far to the rear by General Brussilov's pile-driver offensive. Shortly after the Germans put in their appearance several of their units were ordered to move forward and occupy a reserve position. Austrian noncommissioned officers were detailed as guides. One of the German companies, led by its Austrian guide, moved forward under cover of darkness and eventually reached a large shed. Here it was halted and the men slept until morning.

When dawn broke the company commander found that this shed was located about 200 meters from an Austrian battery and therefore was very likely to suffer from Russian artillery fire. He had just sized up this situation when he looked up and saw a Russian observation balloon hovering to his front. In spite of the all-too-apparent danger, he felt that the situation as a whole demanded that the presence of the Germans remain a secret. He therefore decided to keep his men hidden in the shed until the balloon went down.

Almost immediately the Russians began to shell the Austrian battery. One out of every three or four rounds fell short, striking near the shed. The company commander noticed that his men were becoming increasingly nervous. Some of them on excuses of one sort or another, tried to obtain permission to leave the shed. When the captain did not allow this, the men lapsed into a sullen silence; not a word was spoken. Minute by minute the tension grew. The company commander saw that action of some sort was necessary. Therefore, he called the company barber, sat down with his back to the Russian fire, and directed the barber to cut his hair. He had the most unpleasant haircut of his life, but the effect on the men, however, was splendid. They felt that if their company commander could sit down quietly and let his hair be cut the situation could not be as bad as they had imagined. Conversation started up; soon a few jokes were cracked and before long some of the men began to play cards. After that no one paid any attention to the shells. Even when two men were wounded by shell fire, the morale of the company was not noticeably affected.

From a lecture by Captain Adolf von Schell, German Army, at The Infantry School.

DISCUSSION. In discussing this and other incidents of a similar nature, Captain von Schell stresses the importance of causing the individual soldier to do something. He says:

> As soon as a soldier does something, he becomes master of the situation. . . . When men have been on the defensive for a long time, send out patrols even if there be no special reason for patrols. The patrols instill a sense of self-confidence and superiority. Inactivity and waiting undermine morale and rub nerves raw.

✓　✓　✓

EXAMPLE 3. On August 22, 1914, the French 7th Division, advancing in route column, suddenly encountered Germans near Ethe moving south and west. The French had not expected any serious engagement that day.

The battle opened at close range in a pea-soup fog. In the murk and obscurity units soon became intermingled and disorganized. Neither side knew anything of the situation. Perhaps that should be amended, for the French did know one thing: they knew that everywhere they went they met Germans.

The 11th Company of the French 103d Infantry had been one of the first units to blunder into the unsuspected enemy. It had fought hard but without any idea of what was going on. Later in the morning, when the fog began to lift, this company could find no other French units. But, for that matter, they were unable to locate the enemy either.

Bullets cracked about them from several directions, but no one had any idea where they came from. The enemy seemed to have vanished into thin air. This company, in its first fight, felt completely isolated.

The company commander tried to determine his objectives and locate targets while death struck around him. His company had already suffered appreciable losses, including several platoon and section leaders. Finally, he noted a wood about 1,000 yards away and decided that it might harbor some Germans. Accordingly he ordered his company to open fire on it.

He did not expect any physical effect from this long-range fire directed against the edge of a wood. Indeed, he didn't even know whether or not the enemy was in the wood. He opened fire for one reason—to quiet the nerves of his men.

A little later other French troops deployed along a crest near the 11th Company. These men had scarcely deployed before the ubiquitous enemy blasted their front with violent rifle and machine-gun fire and at the same time struck them in rear with a furious cannonade. These new arrivals lost little time in staging a withdrawal. The crest was not healthy.

The captain of the 11th Company saw this withdrawal, but since he had received no orders he held his company in its position. A bit later two German battalions assaulted the abandoned crest. Their attack broke down completely, due to the flanking fire of the 11th Company from one side and of two stray machine guns from the other.

The repulse of this attack probably exerted a decisive influence on the fight, for it kept a German brigade from taking a large part of the French 7th Division in flank and rear at a critical moment.

From "Ethe," by Colonel A. Grasset, French Army.

DISCUSSION. The unexpected situation in which the men of the 11th Company suddenly found themselves was undoubtedly nerve-wracking. The wise company commander, wishing to occupy their minds, ordered fire against a distant wood. Colonel Grasset emphasizes the fact that this fire was ordered primarily for its moral effect. Although he does not specifically set forth the resulting effect on the men, the events that followed speak eloquently.

This company, having been given a dose of soothing syrup, remained to face and *stop* an attack by two German battalions although the rest of the French had withdrawn. In so doing it played a decisive rôle in the fight of the 7th Division.

✓   ✓   ✓

EXAMPLE 4. At 4:35 a.m., July 18, 1918, Company D of the U. S. 16th Infantry jumped off in the Aisne-Marne offensive. At the outset it was a support company of an assault battalion. A few minutes before the scheduled hour of attack the Germans opened a violent bombardment which appeared to be directed at Company D. The troops were tired; they had undergone a difficult and fatiguing march to the front; the company commander and his men, facing this hostile bombardment, felt that the outlook was far from encouraging. Suddenly the American barrage opened!

> This American barrage was the most inspiring incident of five days of fighting [writes the company commander]. We who had been depressed and who had dreaded the formation of the company under the German barrage now jumped up and hurried to our places. It was a great relief to have something to do—the officers to supervise the formation and the men to get into their proper places.
>
> Many had been killed and wounded by the enemy's barrage. Several squads had to be reorganized while shells were still falling in the immediate vicinity.
>
> During the first part of the advance I was surprised to see every man smoking a cigarette. Then I heard someone call out, "Over the top with a cigarette!" I remembered, then, that the company had been issued a tobacco ration the previous evening and that I had cautioned them all to save one smoke, so each man could start "over the top with a cigarette." This gave the men something to think about during the first few minutes. The badinage that arose, while still under the barrage, relative to the comparative worth of several popular brands of cigarettes, proved that the idea was not without merit.

The advance continued. Losses in the company became increasingly heavy from artillery and long-range machine-gun fire.

> After several men of the company had been blown up by shells, I noticed that a spirit of uneasiness became dominant. Men stopped at the sinister whine of an approaching shell; ranks began to sag; the threat of the shells was uppermost in the minds of the troops.
>
> To divert their attention I decided to try some disciplinary measures of the drill field. I moved from front to rear, and by dint of vigorous whistle-blowing and considerable yelling, dressed up the lines. Whenever a man strayed out of formation I called to the platoon or section leader to dress his outfit. It was not long before each man was paying more attention to his place in line than to machine-gun bullets or shell fire. I noticed a good deal of talking among the men, accompanied by puzzled glances in my direction. I overheard such remarks as "Must think we're on the drill field," "What the hell's eating him?" etc.
>
> The company moved forward without faltering, even when a shell landed squarely on a column composed of a lieutenant and his platoon headquarters.

The attack progressed successfully and later Company D became engaged as an assault company. On July 19 the attack was continued. On this day, as Company D approached a slight rise northeast of Chaudun Farm, it encountered machine-gun fire from front and flanks. Here is what the company commander says:

> The machine-gun fire seemed to be coming from the wheatfield that crowned the rise, so I passed the word along the first line that the leading platoons were to charge toward the top of the hill. The orders miscarried somewhat for, as I jumped up, the entire company advanced. The machine-gun fire did not vary in its intensity and a few men fell. The support platoons advancing in squad columns had the misfortune, however, to have a shell land on a column in which a platoon leader was marching.
>
> The charge, which had started at a run, soon slowed down to a jog, due to the difficulty of climbing the incline over the slippery grass. The line was walking when the crest was reached. Still we heard the machine guns firing. They were farther to the front. We had now come under observation, and a few bursts in our ranks convinced me that our charge had been premature.

Now that the company was unable to advance, the company

commander found that both he and the men were becoming intensely nervous. He thereupon directed one platoon to dig in near the crest of the hill and took the remainder of the company about 100 yards to the rear and ordered them to dig in there.

> I found it was a great relief to be busy, so my striker and I dug a shelter in a new shell hole. I worked until I was wet with perspiration. The extreme nervousness which had seized me after our capture of the hilltop then left me.

> Shell fire continued on our position and casualties were numerous, although the company was now dug in below the surface of the ground. I found in my inspection trips, however, that the exercise had calmed the men to such an extent that they were joking about which platoon would receive the next enemy shell.

> *From the personal experience monograph of Major Leonard R. Boyd, who commanded Company D of the 16th Infantry.*

DISCUSSION. The incidents described in this example deal with measures taken by a company commander to reassure his men and allay their tension during critical periods of an action.

In each instance the remedy consisted of giving the men something to do and something other than their troubles and dangers to think about. It should be noted that at the time the company commander required his men to dress their lines in parade-ground fashion, the company was in support and not in assault. In this case the serious drawbacks that usually accompany rigidly dressed lines and columns, applied only to a limited extent. The company commander here considered that the moral effect on his men far outweighed the disadvantages inherent in an extreme regularity of formation. Says Major Boyd:

> The mental effort of the men to maintain alignment while under heavy fire, and their secret amusement at their leader's idiosyncracies, made the element of personal danger a secondary matter.

Major Boyd comments on the ineffectiveness of the rifle fire during the first few hours of the attack. Owing to excitement many men failed to set their sights; others set their sights and never used them; still others shut both eyes and jerked the trigger. He noted that later in the action the rifle fire was much steadier and far more effective.

> Movement [he states] applied to individuals will frequently afford a tense and apprehensive man a physical means of letting off steam. If the man is required to perform heavy labor, personal danger is readily forgotten. However, when shells are exploding near an unoccupied soldier he is unable to push back waves of fear. He crouches and waits; and for him the battle will probably degenerate into an unending series of "waits."

ꞷ ꞷ ꞷ

CONCLUSION. Until recently, armies fought in comparatively close order. Masses were held together by drill and by discipline. The enemy was in plain view. Now we usually struggle against an invisible enemy. We no longer fight in masses but in small groups—often as individuals. Therefore the psychological reaction of the individual is more important than ever before.

In war, the soldier is the instrument with which leaders must work. They must learn to play on his emotions—his loyalty, his courage, his vanity, his sense of humor, his esprit de corps, his weakness, his strength, his confidence, his trust. Although in the heat of battle there is no longer time to prepare soldiers for the violent impressions of war, there are, however, two simple means by which a leader may lessen tension: He can do something himself that will give the men a feeling of security; or he can order his men to do something that requires activity and attention.

Chapter XXV: *Night Attacks*

*Success in a night attack depends largely
upon direction, control, and surprise.*

THE THOUSAND-AND-ONE contingencies that an attack by night gives rise to must be foreseen and provided for. Especially must careful provision be made for maintaining direction, for preserving control and for insuring secrecy.

Owing to the power of modern armament, night attacks will probably be more frequent in future conflicts. Positions which infantry has failed to take by day may sometimes be successfully stormed by night. Particularly will darkness aid in the passage of areas that enemy fire denies by day.

Night attacks have their place but they are by no means a panacea for avoiding the difficulties of modern combat. They present many difficulties all their own. Imperfectly trained and partially disciplined troops will seldom succeed in these operations. Even seasoned veterans, led by experienced commanders, have often failed to overcome the dangers of the dark.

✦ ✦ ✦

EXAMPLE 1. During the opening days of the First Battle of the Marne, the German Fifth Army suffered so heavily from French artillery fire that its infantry was unable to close with the enemy. In order to come to grips, the army ordered a night attack on a twenty-kilometer front for the night of September 9-10. Portions of four corps participated. One of the units engaged in this action was the 30th Infantry of the German 34th Division.

On September 9 this regiment, which had just received a number of replacements, was in reserve near Bulainville. That afternoon the colonel received the division attack order. In this order the 30th Infantry was directed to launch its attack from the vicinity of Amblaincourt, which was believed to be occupied by the French. The small hill about 1,800 meters southwest of Issoncourt was assigned as the regimental objective.

Realizing that the Bunet stream would have to be crossed, the colonel promptly dispatched an officer patrol to reconnoiter for crossings. Before dark this patrol returned with the necessary information.

At nightfall the regimental commander assembled his officers and issued his order. The regiment would attack with the 2d and 3d Battalions abreast, the 2d on the right. The 1st Battalion would be in reserve. The 2d Battalion was to move forward along the west edge of Chanel Wood and then turn eastward following the south edge toward the objective. The 3d Battalion would move on the objective by guiding on the north edge of the wood. Weapons would not be loaded and there would be no firing. Silence was mandatory. Necessary commands would be transmitted in whispers. First-line battalions would advance "with units well in hand, preceded by a thick line of skirmishers."

By midnight the 30th Infantry and adjacent troops had reached attack positions north and west of Amblaincourt without alarming the French. Rain was falling. The advance began. As the leading elements neared Amblaincourt there was a sudden burst of firing. Immediately everyone rushed toward the town. There were no French there. In the confusion some straw piles nearby caught fire, revealing the milling Germans to the French, who actually occupied Chanel Wood and who promptly opened a heavy fire. The German assault units forthwith fell into the greatest disorder, and the 30th Infantry became intermingled with the 173d on its left.

In spite of the confusion and the heavy fire, most of the men of the 30th and some of the 173d pushed on toward the dark outline of the Chanel Wood. They crossed the Bunet, the water reaching to their breasts and sometimes to their necks. Emerging from the stream they charged the wood in one confused mass. They reached the edge and hand-to-hand fighting followed. German accounts state that an irregular fire came from all sides, that no one knew friend from foe. Neighboring units had lost direction and there were even men from other corps mingled with the troops of the 30th. About 2:30 a.m. the Germans were in possession of Chanel Wood, but their losses had been enormous. The history of the 30th Infantry says:

> The most complete disorder reigned after the incidents of Chanel Wood. Near Anglecourt Farm there were units of the 30th, 173d, 37th, 155th, and even Württemburgers (XIII Corps). Officers strove to organize at least squads or half-platoons, but the smallest group, as soon as formed, became lost in the obscurity. It was only along the southern edge of the Chanel Wood that sufficient order was reëstablished to continue the advance. . . .
>
> The 8th Company managed to push on and capture several cannon after a hand-to-hand fight with the gunners. Unfortuately, they had to withdraw soon afterward, having come under an intense fire from their own comrades.

At daybreak the 30th Infantry, completely intermingled with the 173d, held the line: northeast corner of Chanel Wood—Hill 309. Although ground had been gained, the attack was considered a failure.

On September 12 a German colonel who commanded a unit in the same division with the 30th Infantry, met the German Crown Prince, who commanded the Fifth Army, and asked permission to speak frankly regarding this attack. This being granted, he said, "Imperial Highness, one more night attack like that one and the Army will be forever demoralized."

From an article by Colonel Étienne, French Army, in "La Revue d'Infanterie," August, 1927.

DISCUSSION. The history of the 30th Infantry refers to this night as "St. Bartholomew's Eve." In the memory of the survivors, it was the most terrible of the entire war.

Although the incontestable bravery of the German troops achieved miracles, the action was doomed before it began.

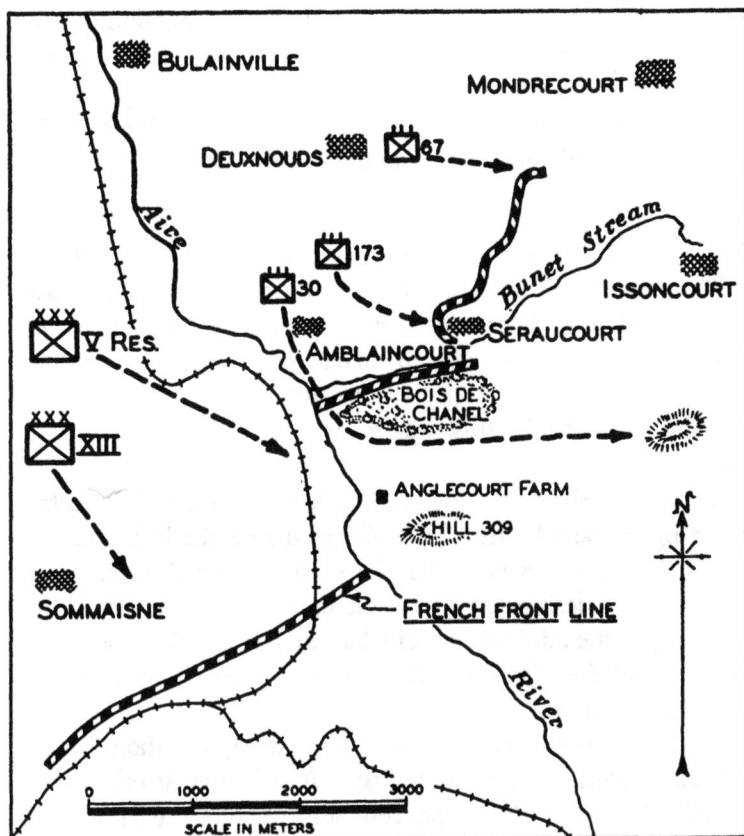

Example 1

Subordinate commanders were not given an opportunity for daylight reconnaissance. The infantry was not opposite its objective at the jump-off. The objective itself was more than 6,000 meters away with the intervening terrain unknown. As a crowning touch the regiment was ordered to execute an abrupt change of direction—this in the dead of night and at the height of the attack. To demand that the 30th Infantry, in a night attack, take Amblaincourt, capture Chanel Wood, then change direction and push on to a distant objective, meanwhile maintaining control, was more then demanding the impossible; it was presenting an unequivocal invitation to disaster.

By their very nature, night attacks should have limited objectives. The results may be exploited by day.

✓   ✓   ✓

EXAMPLE 2. On the night of October 6-7, 1914, the French 2d Battalion of Chasseurs moved by truck to Vrely, where it arrived at 7:00 a.m. There it was attached to the 138th Brigade. At 2:30 p.m. it was ordered to march on Rouvroy in order to participate in a night attack by the 138th Brigade. Another attack, coördinated with this, was to be launched from Bouchoir toward le Quesnoy.

The 138th Brigade planned to attack with the 254th Infantry on the right, the 2d Battalion of Chasseurs on the left, and the 251st Infantry in reserve. The dirt road between Rouvroy and Hill 101 was designated as the boundary between the 254th Infantry and the 2d Battalion of Chasseurs. The terrain between Rouvroy and Parvillers was flat and presented no difficulty to movement at night.

The 2d Chasseur Battalion was an élite organization. However, as a result of previous fighting, its effective strength had dwindled to about 150 men per company. Most of the battalion's six companies were commanded by noncommissioned officers.

At 5:45 p.m., with dark closing in, the battalion moved forward through Rouvroy. Not more than an hour had been available for reconnaissance. Information was vague. It was believed that Parvillers was held by the Germans.

The 2d Chasseurs formed for attack as follows: Two companies deployed in one long line of skirmishers, preceded by patrols. Four companies followed in second line. These four companies were abreast, each having two platoons leading and two following. Platoons were deployed in line of skirmishers. The distances ordered were:

150 meters from the patrol to the first line.

200 meters from the first line to the second line.

  50 meters between leading elements of second-line companies and their supports.

The machine-gun platoon was placed fifty meters behind the left of the third line.

Shortly after dark the battalion advanced on Parvillers. As the advance neared Hill 101, one of the patrols ran into an enemy outguard which promptly opened fire. Many of the French answered this fire without knowing what they were shooting at or why. Soon, firing became general.

The two leading companies halted. Instantly a cry of "Forward!" rang through the darkness and this was caught up and echoed by hundreds of voices. Abruptly the second-line companies rushed forward, charging pell-mell through the leading companies, one of which followed. A terrific uproar ensued, punctuated with shouting and cheering.

The rush reached a trench 250 meters northwest of Parvillers. The defenders had fled, leaving weapons and equipment, but the enemy farther in rear had been warned. Suddenly three 77-mm. cannon, 150 meters behind the trench, opened at point-blank range on the French. By the flashes, German artillerymen could be seen serving the guns. The French in front of the battery stopped, but those on the right closed in and captured the three pieces.

In great disorder the advance continued toward the village. As the French moved forward, their left flank came under fire of enemy machine guns located near the road junction 600 meters northeast of Parvillers. By this time all French units were hopelessly intermingled, several company and platoon commanders had become casualties and in many places the French, confused by the dark, were firing on their own troops. The attack wavered and stopped.

It was 11:00 p.m. With much difficulty noncommissioned officers rallied a few scattered groups and occupied the conquered trench. It was realized that further concerted action by the battalion was impossible.

Meanwhile, the right assault company, which had not followed the general movement, was still under partial control. The battalion commander ordered it to a central position 600 meters northeast of the trench to cover the withdrawal of the battalion. When the order to withdraw was given, voices, whistles and bugle calls were heard. Firing continued during the entire movement, but eventually the battalion managed to extricate itself and reform in rear of Rouvroy. It had suffered in the neighborhood of 300 casualties.

The entire French attack failed.

From an article by Lieutenant Colonel Jeze, French Army, in "La Revue d'Infanterie," June, 1924.

DISCUSSION. In this engagement the French solved the problem of direction but failed completely in the coëxisting problems of control and surprise.

As a matter of fact, the direction phase practically solved itself, for the roads paralleling the advance on Parvillers made any great loss of direction virtually impossible. Unfortunately, no kindly terrain feature could eliminate the remaining difficulties.

It was inevitable that this widely scattered formation should result in loss of control. At night, distances and intervals must be diminished and formations kept compact. In this instance, section columns or even larger groupings would unquestionably have gone a long way toward keeping the battalion in hand. Particularly was a compact formation mandatory here since most of the company and platoon leaders were noncommissioned officers with little or no experience.

The patrol that encountered the hostile outguard on Hill 101 should have closed with the bayonet without firing. It failed to do this, and firing soon became general. The usual results fol-

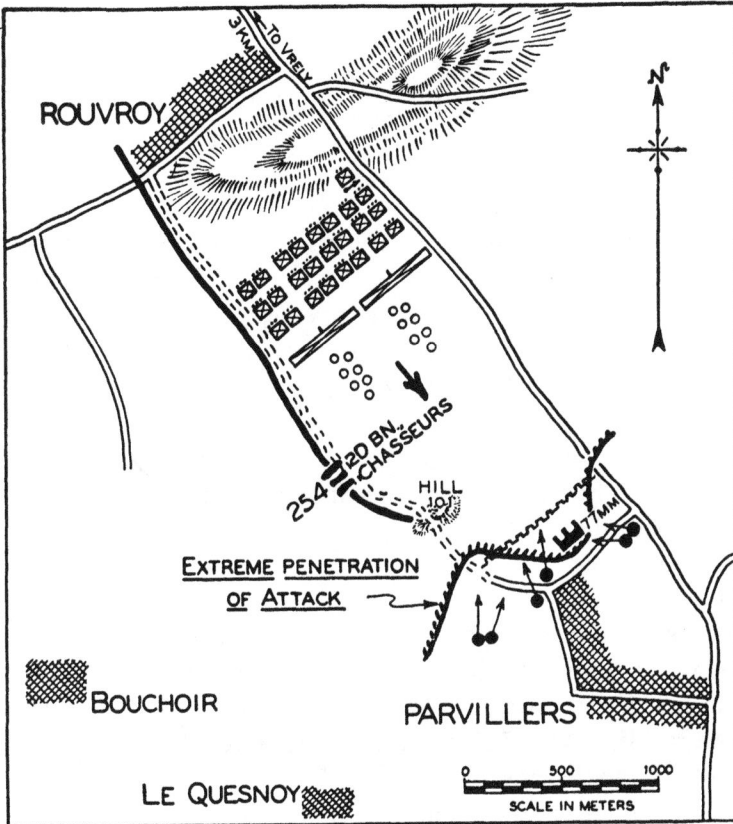

Example 2

lowed: once started, the firing could not be stopped; officers
were unable to get the leading elements to continue the advance; and the attacking units fired into their own troops.

The second-line companies, with due courage but with undue
cheering and firing, charged. The tumult, the firing and the on-
rush of hundreds of men from a distance gave the Germans
ample warning. It was an attack—an assault that had started
too far off. The French lines, revealed by their cheering, were

swept by machine-gun fire. In the utmost confusion the assault wavered to a halt.

Loss of control through a vicious formation, and loss of surprise through yelling and firing, had wrecked one more night attack.

᠇   ᠇   ᠇

EXAMPLE 3. On January 12, 1915, the French were attacking northward near Soissons. At 7:00 a.m. the 1st Battalion of the French 60th Infantry, which was in reserve, marched from Villeblain to Maast-et-Violaine where it arrived at 10:45 a.m. There it received an order to move back to Courmelles which it reached at 8:00 o'clock that night.

At Courmelles the battalion commander was told that his battalion and a battalion of the 44th Infantry would immediately move forward and retake Hill 132 which had just been captured by the Germans.

No large-scale maps were available and no one in the battalion knew the terrain or the exact location of the hostile positions. The order received by the battalion commander more than met the requirement of brevity: "Attack when you get close to Hill 132." The information he received was equally helpful: "The enemy is on Hill 132. He will shoot at you." Someone, however, was thoughtful enough to provide a guide to conduct the battalion to the French front line.

The two battalions cleared Courmelles at 8:30 p.m. and two hours later reached the Vauxrot Glass Works where they dropped packs. They now marched along the road in single file. Soon the guide turned off into a communication trench that was knee-deep in mud and blocked in several places by fallen trees. At these blocks the column was broken and the companies became disorganized. In consequence, considerable time had to be spent in reorganizing platoons when the front line was reached. It was 3:30 a.m. before the attack formation could be taken.

The 1st Battalion of the 60th Infantry was directed to form with two companies in assault and two in support, each company in column of platoons, and each platoon deployed in line of

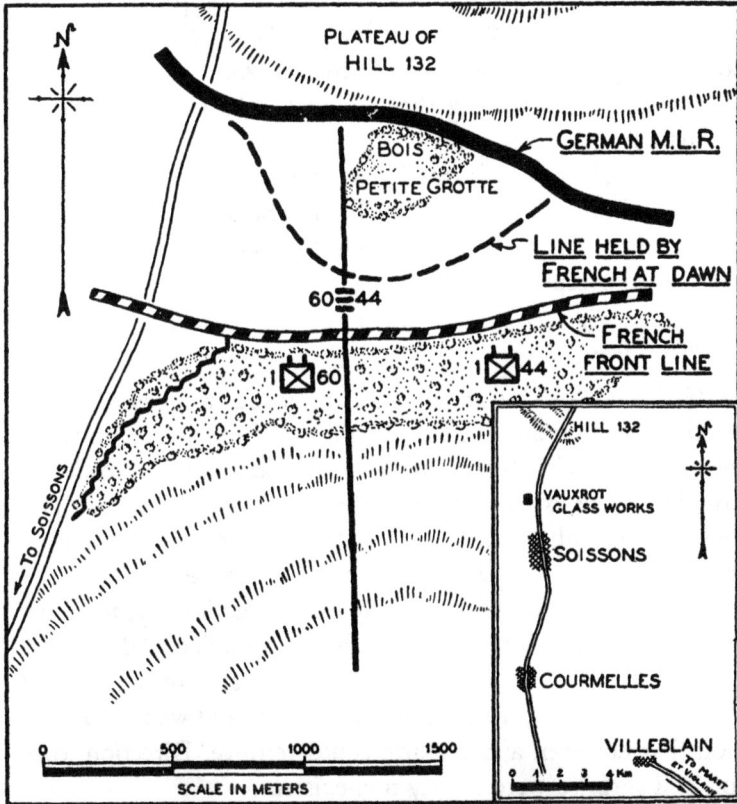

Example 3

skirmishers. When the company commanders attempted to form up they found that entire platoons were missing and that those on hand were badly intermingled and completely out of control. Voices were raised, commands shouted, and questions yelled back and forth in the darkness. Here and there matches were lit to check compasses. German flares became increasingly frequent.

At 4:00 a.m. the attack jumped off—but in places only. Firing began almost at once. The troops were poorly oriented. They did not know where to go or where to stop. There was no liaison. One assault company lost direction. The company behind it pushed on and the two became hopelessly intermingled. German artillery and machine guns opened a withering fire on the disorganized units, forcing them to halt, take cover, and wait for daylight.

At daybreak it was learned that the battalion of the 44th had jumped off at a slightly later hour. The attack of both battalions failed. The losses in the 1st Battalion of the 60th Infantry were exceptionally heavy.

From an article by Lieutenant Colonel Jeze, French Army, in "La Revue d'Infanterie," June, 1924.

DISCUSSION. This attack is a conspicuous tragedy of error. A deliberate effort at failure could not have been more thorough. The troops, having spent the day in marching and counter-marching, were exhausted when the attack was launched. The precipitation with which the battalion was engaged precluded proper preparation, particularly reconnaissance. Indeed, the troops were in the dark figuratively as well as literally, not even knowing the exact location of the hostile position. Add to this the lack of control at the jump-off, the unsuitable formation, the lighting of matches, the shouting and firing, and we have a situation that not even a Bonaparte could retrieve. Direction, control, and surprise were simply non-existent.

As Colonel Jeze concludes:

> In doing exactly the opposite of what was done, they would not have been far from realizing the most favorable condition for the success of the operation.

❧   ❧   ❧

EXAMPLE 4. On October 10, 1918, the 2d Battalion of the U. S. 30th Infantry was in reserve in the Bois de Cunel. On the

previous day, as an assault unit, it had reached the north edge
of the wood and was therefore somewhat familiar with the
terrain beyond.

Early on the 10th the 1st Battalion of the 30th Infantry had at-

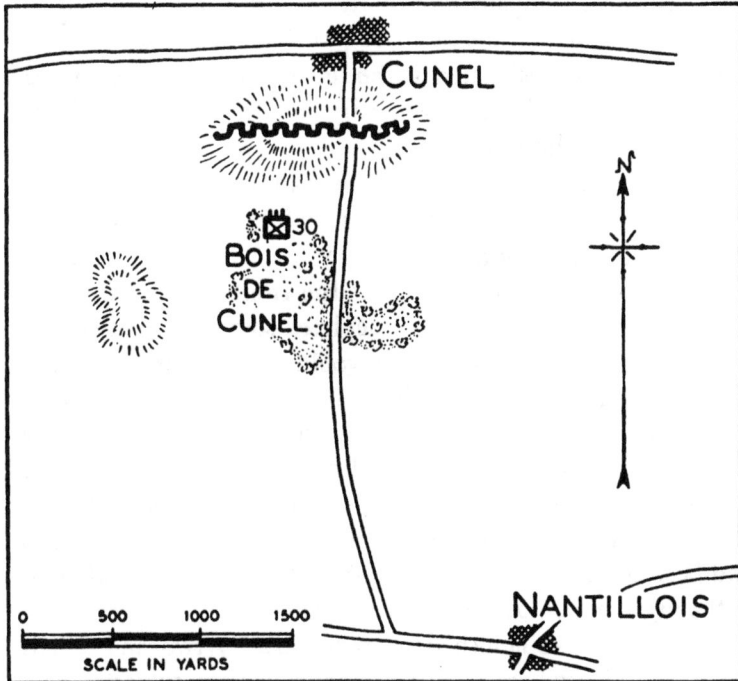

Example 4

tacked to the north, but after advancing a short distance had
been pinned to the ground in front of a German trench located
north of the Bois de Cunel. It was ordered to withdraw to the
woods, reorganize and resume the attack at 7:30 p.m., assisted
by a new artillery preparation. The withdrawal began shortly
after dark, but in the process the battalion became so disorganized that it was unable to launch the attack at the designated
hour.

Now since the division commander had ordered that the trench 800 yards north of the Bois de Cunel be taken on the 10th and since the 1st Battalion had failed to do this and was unable to make a second effort in time, the 2d Battalion of the 30th Infantry and one company of the 7th Infantry were directed to attack the hostile position at 10:00 p.m. The northwestern edge of the wood was designated as the line of departure for the 2d Battalion and the northeastern edge for the company. There would be no artillery support.

After all units were in place the battalion commander assembled his company commanders and explained the attack plan in detail. The battalion would attack with three companies in assault and one in reserve. Since the frontage was large and since all organizations had been depleted some forty per cent in previous fighting, each company would employ three platoons in assault and one in reserve. The assault platoons would deploy as skirmishers with intervals of two to five yards. The reserve company, formed in line of squad columns, would follow the center assault company at 100 yards. The machine-gun company attached to the battalion would remain in place until the enemy had been driven from the trench, then move forward and assist in the organization of the captured position.

The attack was launched on time. Exactly two and a half hours had elapsed since the Germans had been subjected to a heavy artillery preparation, following which the attack of the 1st Battalion had failed to materialize. When no attack followed this 7:30 p.m. bombardment, the Germans apparently concluded that the Americans would make no further effort that night.

The advance of the 2d Battalion was slow and cautious. Secrecy had been stressed. German flares went up frequently. Each time one began to illuminate an area, all men remained motionless, resuming their movement only when the flare died out. This method of advance was continued until the assault units were close to the hostile position. Finally the movement was discovered and machine-gun and rifle fire ripped into the assaulting units from front and flanks. But the Americans were now too close to be stopped. In a swift charge they closed with the enemy, overcame a determined resistance and captured part of the disputed trench. The Germans, however, still held portions of the trench on the flanks.

By this time every vestige of organization had disappeared. Many company, platoon and section leaders were casualties. The reserve company was completely intermingled with the assault companies. All was confusion. Immediate steps were taken to reorganize the battalion, while a message requesting reinforcements was sent to the regimental commander.

At 2:30 a.m. the battalion commander reported to the regimental command post. He informed the colonel that the 2d Battalion was now occupying the trench in the zone of the 30th Infantry and had established contact with the company from the 7th Infantry on the right, but that reinforcements were necessary on the left, where the enemy still held the trench in considerable force. One company was promptly dispatched to this dangerous flank and after severe fighting drove the enemy from his position.

At 6:00 a.m. the strength reports of the units that had made this attack showed the following effectives:

> Company E, 30th Infantry: 1 officer, 30 men.
> Company F, 30th Infantry: 40 men.
> Company G, 30th Infantry: 1 officer, 20 men.
> Company H, 30th Infantry: 1 officer, 27 men.
> Company G, 7th Infantry: 1 officer, 10 men.

Not all of the missing were casualties. Many men who could not be accounted for had merely lost their way in the darkness.

From the personal experience monograph of Major Turner M. Chambliss, who commanded the 2d Battalion of the 30th Infantry.

DISCUSSION. Here most of the conditions essential to the success of a night operation are evident:

The battalion knew the terrain.

It was close to its clearly defined line of departure.

It was placed opposite its objective.

The objective was limited and was unmistakable even in the dark.

The troops had not been engaged during the day and were therefore comparatively fresh.

Details of the attack were carefully explained by the battalion commander.

The movement was made in silence, great care being taken to avoid alarming the enemy.

The attack was made at a time when the Germans had concluded that no further effort would be made that night.

All of these factors made for success.

On the other hand, the extended formation contributed to the loss of control; and the subsequent confusion and intermingling of the reserve company with the assault units necessitated a call for help to clear up the situation on the left flank.

The figures giving the effective strength of units indicate the disorder which may attend even a successful night attack. True, the companies were depleted at the start but, even so, the small effective strength at the conclusion of the operation is striking.

ꭶ   ꭶ   ꭶ

EXAMPLE 5. Late in the afternoon of November 5, 1918, the French 123d Division, which had been attacking to the east, was stopped west of Esquehèries. The troops were on the verge of exhaustion, but despite this, the 12th Infantry, with the 1st Battalion of the 6th Infantry attached, was directed to prepare an attack to take Esquehèries without delay.

The colonel of the 12th Infantry issued orders for an attack at dark. The 2d Battalion was directed to attack the town from the west, encircle it on the north and seize the exits toward Petit Foucomme and la Voirie. The 3d Battalion was ordered to pass north of the 2d Battalion and hold the exits leading toward RJ 191 and le Nouvion. The 1st Battalion was told to

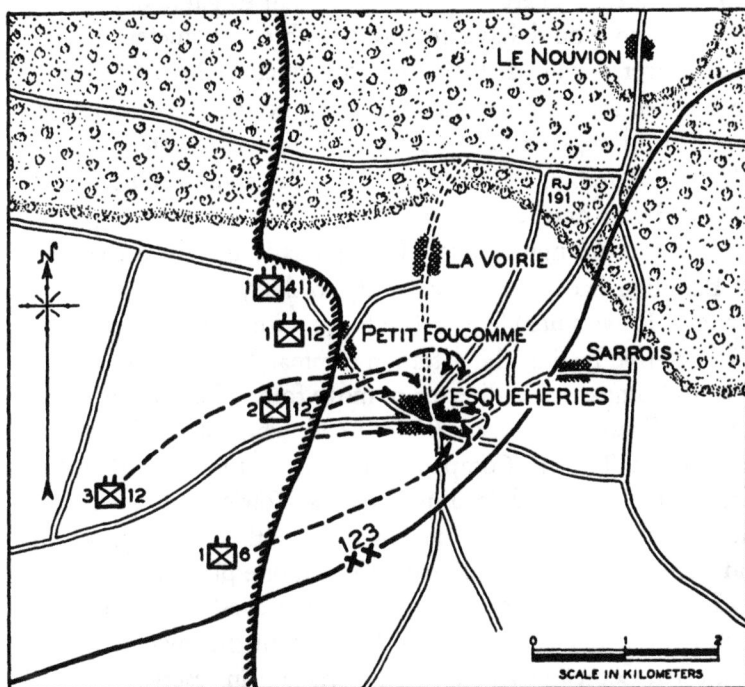

Example 5

push forward to the le Nouvion road and occupy a position where this road entered the forest. The 1st Battalion of the 6th Infantry was directed to seize the southern exits of Esquehèries and those leading toward Sarrois. After securing these exits the attacking battalions were then to strike toward the center of the town.

The commander of the 1st Battalion received this order at 8:00 p.m. and immediately sent for his company commanders.

At 9:00 p.m. none of them had yet reached the battalion command post. In the interim the battalion commander learned that the 1st Battalion of the 411th Infantry, on his left, had received no order to attack. The night was pitch dark and rain was falling in sheets. There was no road or trail to guide him to his objective; he would have to advance three kilometers across country over terrain that bristled with thick hedges. Considering his men incapable of such an effort, he requested authority to remain in position until daybreak. This was granted.

The 2d Battalion also received this order about 8:00 p.m. Its commander at once endeavored to get in touch with adjacent battalions to arrange details. He was finally informed that the 1st Battalion had received authority to delay its advance until daylight. He was unable to get in touch with any other unit.

Undeterred by this, the battalion commander issued his order. The 5th Company was directed to move forward until it reached the Petit Foucomme—Esquehèries Road, which it would follow to the town. The 6th Company was ordered to advance until it reached the dirt road leading from la Voirie to Esquehèries, then follow that road to the town. The 7th Company, which had been in reserve, was directed to send one platoon down the road that entered Esquehèries from the west. This platoon would attack and capture the western part of the town. The rest of the 7th Company was directed to remain in reserve.

The company commanders protested that their men were extremely fatigued, the rain heavy, the night dark, and the terrain unknown. The battalion commander was obdurate. He stated that the operation would be carried out according to his order and that the movement would start as soon as the 3d Battalion arrived.

At 11:00 p.m. the 10th Company of the 3d Battalion put in its appearance. Its commander stated that at the start of the movement it had been the rear company in the 3d Battalion column, but that now he had no idea where the remainder of the battalion was. After a further fruitless delay the commander of the 2d Battalion directed his companies to move to the attack without waiting for the 3d Battalion.

Shortly after the attack jumped off the remaining units of the

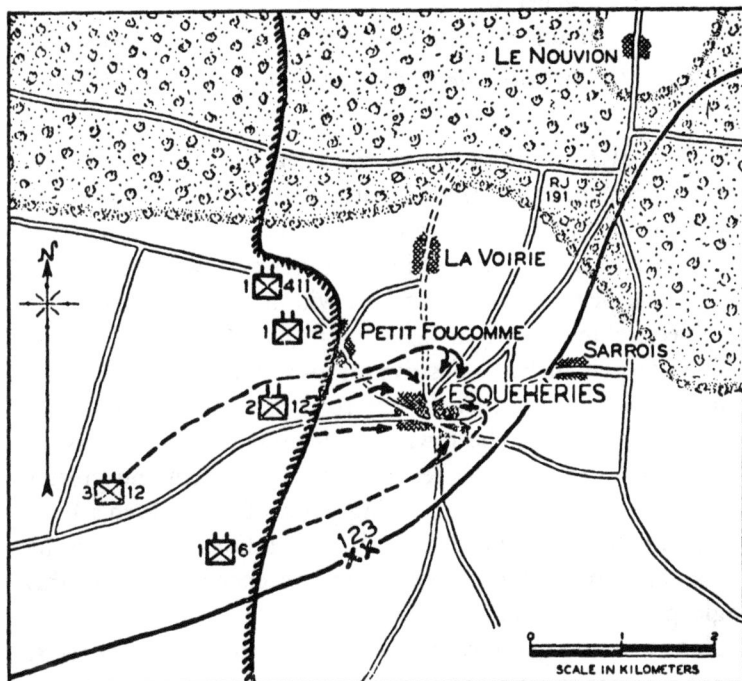

Example 5

3d Battalion arrived. The men were exhausted, the companies disorganized and the officers unoriented. The battalion commander thereupon decided to remain in position until dawn.

Meanwhile, the 2d Battalion had moved out at 1:00 a.m., much later than had been expected. Darkness and the heavy rain made the forward movement slow and difficult. The 5th and 6th Companies did not reach the north edge of the town until daylight. The 1st Battalion of the 6th Infantry encountered

similar difficulties and did not reach the southern exits until
5:00 a.m. However, the one platoon of the 7th Company which
had been ordered to attack from the west and which had a road
to guide on, advanced rapidly and captured the western part
of Esquehèries. When this happened the Germans evacuated the
entire town, leaving this one platoon in undisputed possession.

*From an article by Major P. Janet, French Army, in "La Revue d'Infanterie,"
April, 1928.*

DISCUSSION. The failure of the attempted encirclement of
Esquehèries is instructive. Four battalions were ordered to participate in the operation. So great were the difficulties that two
did not even make a start, while the other two, with the exception of one platoon, did not arrive within striking distance of
the objective until daylight.

This one platoon had a positive means by which it was enabled
to maintain direction, namely, the road that ran past its initial
position straight into the town. Other units, lacking points on
their routes that could be readily identified, spent the greater
part of the night in a disheartening game of Blind Man's Buff.

Again it is pointed out that of four battalions ordered to the
attack only one platoon closed with the enemy. And yet this
single platoon captured the objective.

This operation graphically demonstrates the following facts:
troops who are to take part in a night attack should be familiar
with the terrain; the ground should not present too many obstacles to movement; the troops should be close to and opposite
their objective; the axis of advance should be clearly marked and
unmistakable; and finally, the troops involved should be in good
physical condition and imbued with a high morale.

✦   ✦   ✦

EXAMPLE 6. On November 11, 1914, the French 121st Infantry was entrucked and moved to the north where a great
battle was in progress along the Yser River.

In three months of war the 121st Infantry had been both lucky and successful. Morale was excellent. As an added touch, many officers and noncommissioned officers, wounded in earlier fights, had recently returned to the regiment.

About noon the 121st arrived at Oostvleteren. Here it was

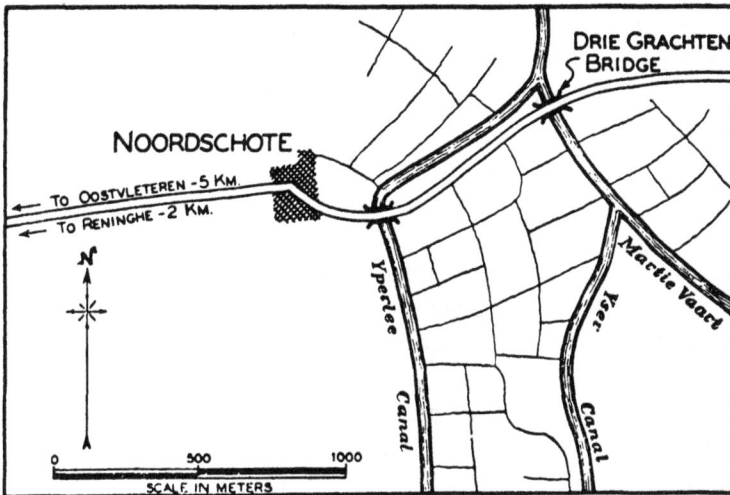

Example 6

directed to march to Reninghe where further orders would be issued.

At Reninghe at 4:00 p.m. a division commander informed the colonel:

> Your regiment is attached to my division. The Germans have crossed the Yser Canal between the Drie Grachten bridge and a point 800 meters south of it. There is nothing in front of Noordschote to prevent their rapid progress toward Reninghe.
>
> At 1:00 a.m. tonight the 121st will attack and drive the enemy over the Yser
>
> The XX Corps will be on your right and a regiment of Zouaves on your left. There is a gap between them. Their flanks are near the canal.

You will find the colonel of Zouaves at Noordschote.

Carry on without further orders.

The regimental commander designated the 2d Battalion, supported by a machine-gun platoon, to make the attack.

Noting from his map that the terrain between the Yser and Yperlee Canals appeared extremely difficult, the battalion commander determined to make a personal reconnaissance. Saddle horses having just arrived, he mounted all his company commanders and moved rapidly toward Noordschote. Finding no one there, the party climbed to the second story of a house and studied the terrain. Although dusk was closing in, enough light remained to show that the problem of reaching the Yser with troops at night would present grave difficulties. The intervening terrain was a quagmire, interlaced with small canals and large ditches, which would obviously make the maintenance of direction and control extremely difficult. No French units could be seen. Apparently there were some Germans near the Yser Canal.

Following the reconnaissance, the battalion commander issued an oral order for the attack. He directed the battalion to move forward without delay to Noordschote and to form by 11:30 p.m. along the Yperlee Canal with three companies abreast, their right 400 meters south of the Noordschote bridge, and their left just north of the Yperlee bend. Patrols would be sent out to seek liaison with units on the flanks. Reconnaissance of the canals directly to the front was limited to 200 meters in order not to alarm the enemy. Two companies were directed to search Noordschote for light material such as ladders and planks which could help them across canals.

At 12:15 a.m. the 8th Company would move out along the ditch 400 meters southeast of and parallel to the Noordschote—Drie Grachten Road and follow this ditch to the Yser.

The 6th Company, starting at 12:30 a.m., would at first follow the ditch just south of the road, then incline to the right and march on the junction of the Yser and the Martie Vaart.

The 5th Company, at 12:40 a.m., would follow the road, or the ditch just north of the road, and attack the Drie Grachten bridge.

The 7th Company and the machine guns were to remain east of Noordschote in reserve.

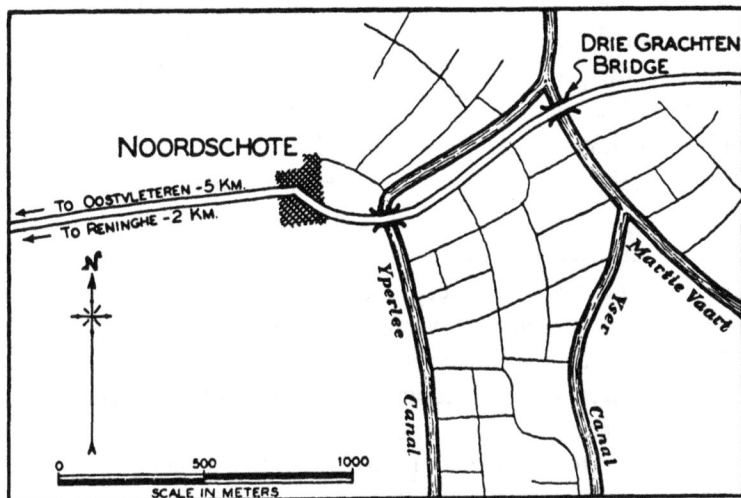

Example 6

The battalion commander further directed that there be no firing, that leading elements wear a white brassard, and that particular attention be paid to control—each company moving in a single column, preceded by an officer patrol.

About 6:30 p.m. the battalion started its march on Noordschote. In the meantime the battalion commander had reported the results of his reconnaissance and his plan for the attack to the regimental commander, who approved his dispositions but informed him that he was going to try to have the attack postponed twenty-four hours.

At 8:00 p.m. the battalion commander met the colonel of the Zouave regiment at Noordschote, which still appeared entirely deserted. The Zouave commander stated that he knew reinforcements were coming but not that a night attack was contemplated. He added that he could not furnish any guides who knew the terrain in question. There was no evidence of the XX Corps to the south.

The battalion reached Noordschote at 8:30 p.m. Efforts to find the commander of the front-line battalion of Zouaves on the left failed. However, the few Zouaves in the vicinity were notified of the proposed action of the 121st and told not to fire. A few tired soldiers of another unit were found just north of the Noordschote—Drie Grachten road, and their commander, a noncommissioned officer, was informed of the plan to attack. To questioning, he replied that he knew nothing of the terrain south of the road but believed that the water in the ditches would be about a meter deep. At 11:00 p.m. patrols reported that water in these ditches was breast high.

Just at this time an order was received countermanding the attack and directing the battalion merely to hold its ground. All companies were immediately notified.

At 11:10 p.m. a patrol reported that it had gained contact with the XX Corps to the south and found it in a state of complete confusion; no one there knew where any units were.

At 12:30 a.m. came a new counter-order directing the attack to be launched at 3:00 a.m. The battalion maintained all its previous arrangements with the exception of the times at which companies were to move.

The 8th Company moved forward at 2:15 a.m. At 2:30 a.m. the captain of this company reported that it was almost impossible to cross the canals. Several men had fallen in and were unable to climb out of the sticky mud. He added that in such conditions movement to the Yser would require several hours, that many men would be lost en route and that there would be no surprise. Having implicit confidence in this company commander and feeling that he would not exaggerate difficulties, the battalion commander immediately ordered:

The 8th Company will follow the 6th and on reaching the Yser, move
south to its objective.

The 6th Company moved out on the Noordschote—Drie
Grachten Road and followed it almost to the Yser before turn-

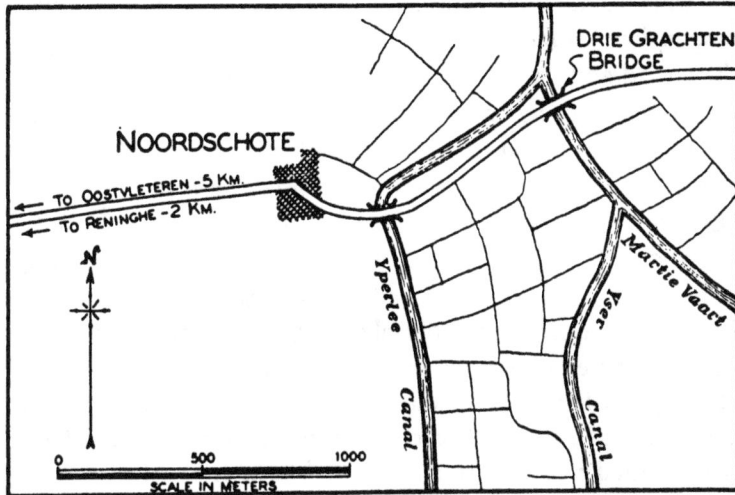

Example 6

ing south. A few minutes later the 8th Company followed the
6th. The 5th Company then moved by the same route to the Drie
Grachten bridge.

The attacks of all three companies succeeded.

The Germans, completely surprised, were thrown back over
the Yser without more than a shot or two being fired. The battalion captured 25 prisoners and suffered no losses.

*From an article by Lieutenant Colonel Baranger, French Army, in "La Revue
d'Infanterie," April, 1929.*

DISCUSSION. This attack succeeded despite conditions
which might easily have led to failure, such as fatigue of the
troops, the almost impassable state of the ground, the confused
situation of adjacent units, and the fact that the troops arrived

on the scene after dark.

Why did it succeed? *Direction! Control! Surprise!*

The column formation in which the advance was made facilitated control. Each company was preceded by an officer patrol; thus, when contact was first made, it was made by a group under a responsible leader.

The road and the Yser guided the troops to their desination. In the original order these companies were to advance abreast, each in a column and each following a specified ditch. When this was found to be impracticable, all used the road.

Extreme precautions were taken to obtain surprise. Despite the obvious desirability of ascertaining the state of the terrain, the battalion commander limited reconnaissance to 200 meters to the front in order to avoid alarming the enemy. In the advance he insisted on silence and prohibited firing.

Finally, the battalion consisted of good troops and determined leaders, and as a result of success in three months of war, a feeling of mutual trust and confidence had been established.

"The symphony in black was not known to this battalion," says Colonel Baranger.

✓ ✓ ✓

CONCLUSION. Night attacks can not be improvised; to have even a reasonable chance of success they must be planned and prepared down to the last foreseeable detail. Among the many things the leader must take into consideration in planning a night operation, the following are particularly important:

Night attacks should preferably be undertaken by fresh, well-trained troops in good physical condition. The troops must be under control at the start.

The objective should be well defined and easily recognized in the dark.

The units making the attack should be able to form opposite the objective and at no great distance from it.

Generally speaking, there can be no maneuver. Each attacking column must drive through to its objective without regard to the progress of adjacent units.

Routes of approach should be clearly defined and unmistakable in the dark.

Subordinate leaders should be given adequate opportunity for daylight reconnaissance.

The formation should facilitate the maintenance of direction and control. This means a column formation in the early stages and, as the enemy is approached, a line of small columns preceded by patrols. The skirmish line is undesirable.

A strong leader with a few determined men should head each column. A reliable officer or non-commissioned officer should bring up the rear.

Orders must be explicit. Every subordinate leader should know the objective; the compass direction of attack; the formations that are to be taken up; the exact mission of his unit; the signal for the assault; action in case the enemy is not surprised; locations of rallying points in the event the attack is repulsed; action upon carrying the enemy position; and the means of identifying friendly troops. Subordinate leaders should pass this information on to their men.

Secrecy and silence are essential. There must be no firing, no yelling, no smoking, no striking of matches. Absolute silence should be maintained until the attack erupts in the enemy works.

Night attacks are difficult operations. They are frequently the expression of a vigorous leadership which, regardless of difficulties, is determined to carry through to a successful conclusion. But despite the vigor of the leadership, these attacks will usually fail unless extreme attention be accorded that military trinity of the night: *direction, control, and surprise.*

Chapter XXVI: *Miracles*

Resolute action by a few determined men is often decisive.

TIME AND AGAIN, numbers have been overcome by courage and resolution. Sudden changes in a situation, so startling as to appear miraculous, have frequently been brought about by the action of small parties. There is an excellent reason for this.

The trials of battle are severe; troops are strained to the breaking point. At the crisis, any small incident may prove enough to turn the tide one way or the other. The enemy invariably has difficulties of which we are ignorant; to us, his situation may appear favorable while to him it may seem desperate. Only a slight extra effort on our part may be decisive.

Armies are not composed of map-problem units, but of human beings with all the hopes and fears that flesh is heir to. Some are natural leaders who can be relied upon to the limit. Some will become conveniently lost in battle. A large proportion will go with the majority, wherever the majority happens to be going, whether it be to the front or to the rear. Men in battle respond readily to any external stimulus—strong leadership or demoralizing influences.

Thus we sometimes see companies of 170 or 180 men reduced to fifty or sixty a few minutes after battle has begun. Such a company has not been reduced two-thirds by casualties; it has suffered, perhaps, but not in such heroic proportions. Every army contains men who will straggle at the first chance and at the first alarm flee to the rear, sowing disorder, and sometimes panic, in their wake. They tell harrowing tales of being the only survivors of actions in which they were not present, of lacking ammunition when they have not squeezed a trigger, and of having had no food for days.

A unit can be seriously weakened by the loss of a few strong characters. Such a unit, worn down by the ordeals of battle, is often not a match for a smaller but more determined force. We then have a battlefield miracle.

It is not the physical loss inflicted by the smaller force, although this may be appreciable, but the moral effect, which is decisive.

The familiar exploits of Sergeant York and Lieutenant Woodfill afford striking examples of what one or two individuals can accomplish in combat when resolute action is accompanied by tactical efficiency.

✓ ✓ ✓

EXAMPLE 1. On March 6, 1916, the German 38th Reserve Regiment attacked to the south. The 1st Battalion of the 38th Regiment was ordered to take the high ground south of the Forges Brook while the 2d Battalion of the 51st Reserve Regiment (on its left) took Forges.

The 4th Company, the left assault company of the 1st Battalion, reached the Forges Brook where it was held up by machine-gun fire from the village of Forges on its left flank. The 2d Battalion of the 51st was still engaged in a hard fight to the left-rear against the defenders of the village.

Sergeant Glodecks, with three men, was on the left flank and somewhat separated from the 4th Company. A few fruit trees afforded him concealment from the direction of Forges. By careful observation Glodecks discovered that the principal fire holding up the 4th Company came from a house southwest of Forges.

He briefly told the men with him what he had learned. He then told them that he had decided to infiltrate forward and take this house from the rear. At his command the men made a quick rush to the Forges Brook. They waded the icy, breast-deep stream, crawled forward past the house, turned to the left and prepared to attack. Their movement apparently had not been discovered.

At Glodecks' command the four threw grenades, then rushed the house from the east. They surprised and captured twenty Frenchmen. This allowed the 4th Company to advance.

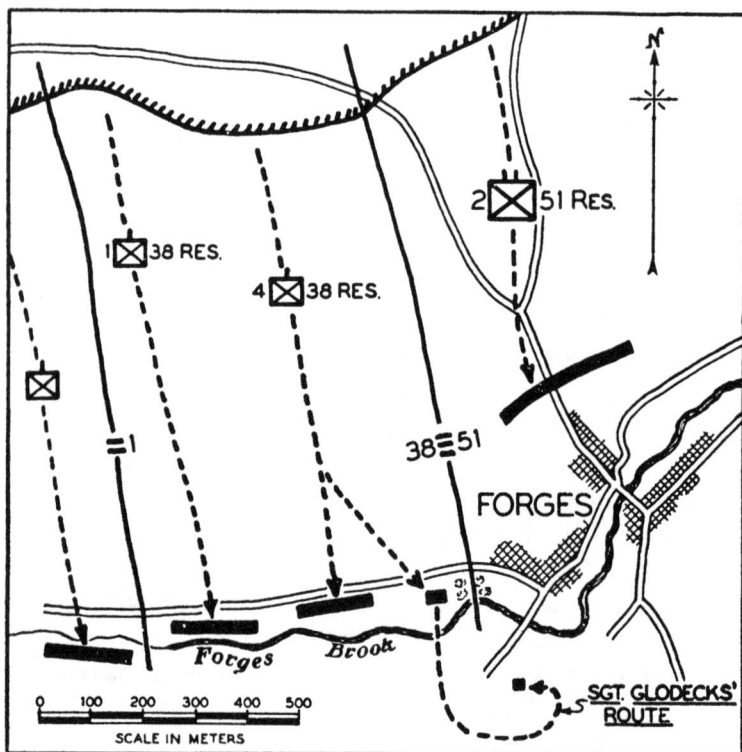

Example 1

Glodecks and his three men advanced northeast through Forges taking their prisoners with them. A party of eighteen Frenchmen was surprised and captured as a result of the unexpected direction of this small group's advance. Continuing through Forges, Glodecks' party took 130 more prisoners. This permitted the 2d Battalion of the 51st to capture the town.

From an article in "Kriegskunst im Wort und Bild," 1929.

✓   ✓   ✓

DISCUSSION. The moral effect of a sudden attack from the rear caused the French to give in at a time when they were offering stubborn resistance to an attack from the front. They had undergone hours of bombardment. They had faced a violent attack. Perhaps some of their natural leaders had become casualties. At any rate, their will to resist suddenly broke.

Why didn't the French laugh at the Germans and disarm them? There were enough Frenchmen, even unarmed, to have overpowered their German captors. Physically there was nothing to prevent it; morally there was much.

Evidently the German sergeant was a determined man. The account says he had the confidence of all the men in the company, and was known as a clear-thinking soldier. His three comrades were either men of the same caliber or, as is often the case, the determination of the sergeant had been contagious.

$$\textit{1} \quad \textit{1} \quad \textit{1}$$

EXAMPLE 2. On the afternoon of August 22, 1914, the situation of the French 7th Division appeared desperate. Its leading brigade (the 14th) in Ethe, was almost surrounded. Units were intermingled, casualties were heavy and the town was on fire. The French 13th Brigade was south of the Jeune Bois with Germans on three sides. German artillery on the heights north of Ethe ruled the battlefield and had cut communication between the two French brigades. A German force, estimated as a brigade, was assembled at Bleid, after having annihilated a flank-guard battalion of the French 13th Brigade. French artillery support had been ineffective.

Captain Bertin and his company of some eighty men were in the Bois de St. Leger where they had been cut off from the rest of the French. He decided to make a detour to rejoin his own troops. About 2:00 p.m. he reached the edge of the woods as shown on the sketch.

In front of him, at close range, he saw German batteries firing to the south. German local reserves were scattered over the terrain. Groups of German officers were observing the action in and around Ethe. The French company had not been seen. Bertin knew almost nothing of the general situation.

Captain Bertin and his company attacked. They captured two batteries, shot down horses and gunners, and pushed on toward the west—almost to the command post of the German 10th Division. Here a counter-attack by hastily gathered runners, engineers and infantry, led by the German artillery-brigade commander, finally dispersed the French company. Most of the French were killed or captured. Only a few managed to escape.

Let us now note what followed. The commander of the German 10th Division became worried about his left flank. The German 53d Brigade at Bleid belonged to another corps and there had been no communication between these troops and the 10th Division. Actually, the 14th Brigade in Ethe was almost at the mercy of the German 10th Division and the French 13th Brigade was about to begin a withdrawal to escape a threatened double envelopment.

Fortunately for the French, the commander of the German 10th Division did not realize this. He had received pessimistic reports concerning the unit on his right and now his left seemed to be threatened. For all he knew, the attack of Bertin's company might be the forerunner of a powerful French effort against his left flank. Late in the afternoon he ordered a withdrawal of the entire division to the woods north of Ethe. The French division escaped.

From "Ethe," by Colonel A. Grasset, French Army.

DISCUSSION. The commander of the German 10th Division did not realize the death-grip he had on the French. Pessimistic reports from corps, the death of the chief of staff at his side, heavy losses, and the failure of communication with the unit on his left contributed to his gloomy impression.

The psychological effect of Bertin's attack coming at this time undoubtedly played a great part in the German commander's decision to withdraw. Emerging from the forest, shooting down gunners and horses, pushing right up to the divisional command post, this company destroyed itself, but in so doing it probably saved the French 7th Division.

In this case the French captain could not realize how far-reaching his decision might be. He did not know the desperate situation of the French or the strength of the Germans. He was

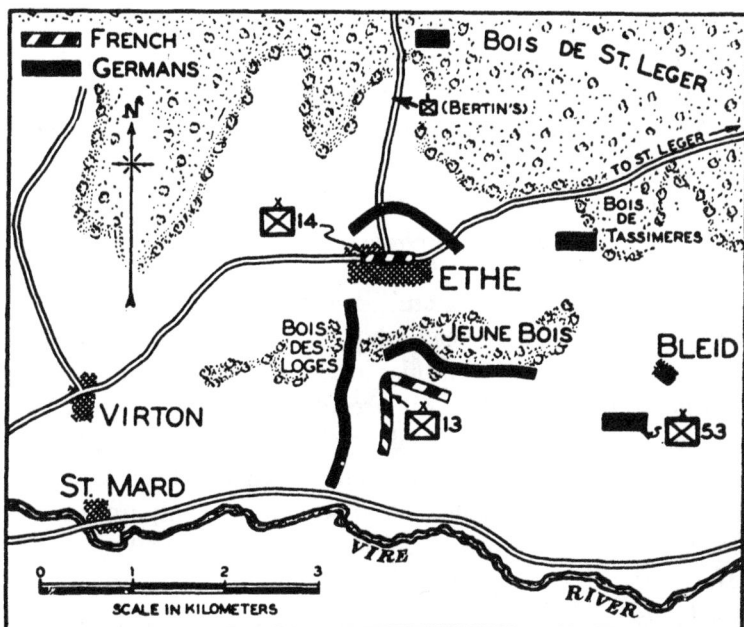

Example 2

alone and unsupported. He knew that the chances were against the ultimate escape of his company. Yet fortune offered him an opportunity to do a great deal of damage to the enemy and he did not hesitate to seize it.

✓ ✓ ✓

EXAMPLE 3. On July 31, 1918, the 1st Battalion of the U. S. 47th Infantry attacked northward near Sergy, with Company B on the right. During the attack, the unit to the right of the 1st Battalion was temporarily held up; this left the battalion's right flank exposed. At once this flank came under a murderous enfilade machine-gun fire and at the same time the enemy smashed at it with artillery fire from the right-front. The battalion was stopped in its tracks and casualties began to pile up. In the right platoon of Company B the platoon leader was killed and all the noncommissioned officers killed or wounded.

Private Walter Detrow saw the situation and immediately assumed command on the right of the company. Forthwith he led that part of the line forward in the face of heavy machine-gun fire. The company slowly fought its way forward, destroying machine-gun nests and their crews. By noon it had reached the road leading from Nesles to Fère-en-Tardenois.

From the personal experience monograph of Captain Jared I. Wood, Infantry, who commanded Company B, 47th Infantry.

DISCUSSION. The successful advance of Company B may be directly attributed to the leadership of Private Detrow. While he did not achieve a spectacular personal triumph, his action nevertheless multiplied the real strength of the Americans with him many times. His spirit and determination so inspired the rank and file that an officerless unit which had been shot to pieces under the deadly enfilade fire of machine guns, drove forward and destroyed those guns and their crews.

If an organization loses its commissioned and noncommissioned personnel it usually ceases to function as an effective combat unit. And yet, in this instance, the action of one private galvanized a moribund command and swept it forward to victory. Detrow, promoted to sergeant, was killed in action in October, 1918.

✓   ✓   ✓

EXAMPLE 4. The Germans attacked the British at Cambrai on November 30, 1917. The 2d Battalion of the 109th Infantry drove deep into the British position but was finally stopped a short distance east of Gonnelieu by British machine guns.

Brave attempts to push on failed. Squad and platoon leaders reported that the support of accompanying weapons and artillery was necessary if further progress was to be made. The regimental commander tried to get artillery fire but the British and Germans were too intermingled. Accordingly he arranged to resume the attack with the support of heavy machine guns and minenwerfers.

The 5th Company of the 110th Infantry, which had been following in reserve, was now pushed forward into the front line with orders to attack a machine-gun nest at A. The following arrangements had been made:

Two German heavy machine guns from positions near C sought to neutralize the British machine-gun nest at B. Artillery fired on another machine-gun nest located about 800 yards northwest of A. A minenwerfer in a shell hole at D fired on the nest at A.

Under cover of this fire the 5th Company attacked. Some elements went straight forward, while small groups tried to work around the flanks of the nest at A.

Sergeant Gersbach of the 5th Company led a squad on the right. Each time a minenwerfer burst on the British nest, Gersbach and his group made a short rush forward. Meanwhile, the German machine guns beat down the fire of the enemy nest at B and eventually silenced it. Gersbach and his group progressed slowly. Several men were hit, but the others, encouraged by the example of their leader, continued on. Meanwhile, a similar group was working around the left flank.

Gersbach finally reached a trench leading to the nest at A. With two or three men he turned to the left, attacked the nest with hand grenades, and captured it. The breach thus opened in the British defenses was widened, and the 109th Infantry continued its attack successfully. The fight for the nest at A lasted two hours.

From an article in "Kriegskunst im Wort und Bild," 1928, dealing with the historical basis of the German regulations.

DISCUSSION. The German article from which this example is taken deals with the continuation of the attack within a hostile position. In his discussion the author says: "The squad leader, supported by the fire of heavy infantry weapons and acting in conjunction with neighboring rifle and machine-gun squads, continues the attack from nest to nest, seeking always to strike the enemy resistance from the flank."

The article states that in the heat of battle the troops themselves discovered the suitable methods of carrying forward the attack within the hostile position. It emphasizes the necessity for coördination of effort, the support of minenwerfer and heavy machine guns to neutralize enemy nests, and then adds, "Success, however, was always brought about through the flanking action of courageous small groups."

This minor incident in a great battle illustrates four things. First, the difficulty of getting artillery support on the nearest enemy once the hostile position has been penetrated. Second, the action of the leader in coördinating his supporting weapons with his attacking riflemen. Third, the use of machine guns to neutralize the enemy on the flank and the use of curved-trajectory weapons to fire on the position being directly attacked. Fourth, the fact that such fights frequently develop slowly and last a long while.

Coördination is important, supporting fires are necessary, but above all there must be the determined leaders and the "courageous small groups."

CONCLUSION. One of these examples rivals the case of Sergeant York. Four men take more than 100 prisoners and decide a battalion combat. Another demonstrates the moral effect on the enemy of determined action by a group of men. A third illustrates the effect that the courage and intiative of one man may have on many. And one typical case portrays a brave enemy overcome by the flanking action of "courageous small groups." The first two examples are more striking in that one decided a battalion fight and the other may have saved an entire division. During the World War the last two, with slight variations, were reproduced hundreds of times.

Who can tell the ultimate effect of the courageous and resolute
action of one of these small groups? Occasionally the result on

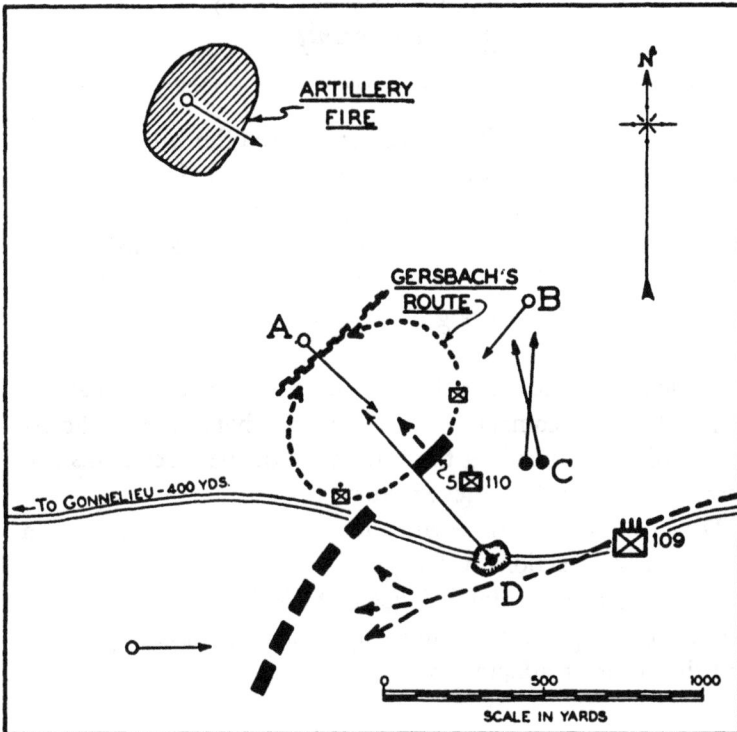

Example 4

the battle as a whole is clear-cut, and then we read of a battlefield
miracle. Were we able to examine all battles through a military
microscope it is probable that we would almost always find the
small seed of victory sowed by a determined leader and a handful of determined men.

Chapter XXVII: *Optimism and Tenacity*

Optimism and tenacity are attributes of great leadership.

BATTLE IMPRESSIONS tend to weaken the will of a commander. Casualties, confusion, reported failure, exaggerated stories of actual conditions, all batter at the rampart of his determination. He must consciously resist these onslaughts; he must deliberately take an optimistic view. Otherwise he, and his unit with him, will bog down in a mire of discouragement and despair.

Tenacity demands relentless pursuit of the end to be gained. Only a higher commander can relieve a subordinate of the responsibility of expending the full power of the force at his disposal in the effort to achieve victory.

Tenacity does not necessarily mean dogged persistence in a given course of action. A change of methods may be desirable. In the language of Marshal Foch, the will must be powerful without being pig-headed and stupid; it must have suppleness and the spirit of adaptation.

✓　　✓　　✓

EXAMPLE 1. At 8:00 a.m., October 15, 1918, the U. S. 61st Infantry, which had suffered heavily in previous fighting, attacked to the north in column of battalions with the Bois des Rappes as its objective.

About 9:00 a.m. the 1st Battalion (in assault) reached the northwestern edge of the Bois de la Pultière. Both flanks of this unit being exposed, the 3d Battalion, which had been in support, was moved to the right and abreast of the 1st. The capture of the Bois des Rappes, which was the real task, still lay ahead.

About noon Companies A, C, and D gained their final objective—the northwestern edge of the Bois des Rappes—and began to reorganize. Although victorious, this battalion had been literally shot to pieces. Companies A, C, and D, together could muster no more than seventy-five men. Company B could not be

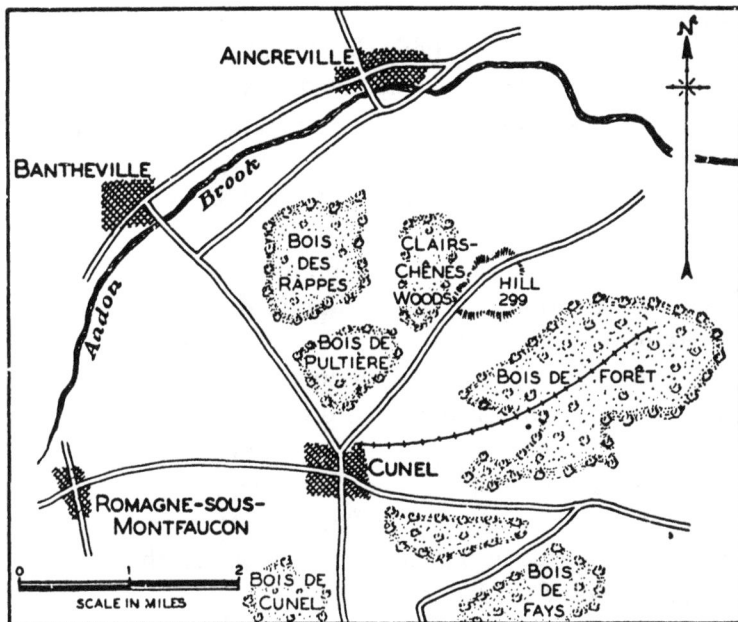

Example 1

located. While noncommissioned officers in command of companies struggled to effect a reorganization, American artillery blindly dropped shells on the remnant of this shattered battalion.

The 3d Battalion, upon the loss of its leader and three company commanders, had become completely disorganized and had been passed through by the 2d Battalion.

Liaison between assault elements and the regimental command post failed. No information reached the regimental commander throughout the morning save from the wounded. These stated that although the Bois des Rappes had been entered, the attack had been stopped and artillery support was necessary to break the hostile resistance.

Some time later a staff officer of the 3d Battalion, unnerved by the terrific casualties, arrived at the regimental C.P. in a state bordering on collapse. He gave the colonel what appeared to be the first authentic information. He reported that his battalion commander and three company commanders were casualties, that the battalion itself had been practically annihilated, and that the few survivors were retreating in confusion.

Without verifying this disheartening news, the colonel immediately went to the brigade command post and repeated it. Although this report created the impression that the entire 61st Infantry was retreating in disorder, the brigade commander none-the-less directed that the troops be reorganized and pushed back to the north edge of the Bois des Rappes.

By this time, however, rumors of disaster had reached the division commander. Acting upon these rumors, he promptly countermanded the order of his brigadier, directed that no further advance be made into the Bois des Rappes that day, and ordered the brigade to organize its front line on the northern edge of the Bois de la Pultière.

Pursuant to this order the 1st and 2d Battalions withdrew, abandoning positions which had been won at great sacrifice. Some days later the Bois des Rappes was retaken at the cost of many lives.

From the personal experience monograph of Captain Merritt E. Olmstead, Infantry.

DISCUSSION. This example dramatically illustrates the error into which commanders may fall if they base their estimate of the situation upon the reports of wounded and shaken men who filter to the rear. Such men are naturally discouraged. Frequently they come from a point where things are going badly and they assume that the same conditions exist everywhere. Moreover, they are prone to justify their own action in abandoning the fight by painting a dismal picture of disaster.

In this example a great contrast existed between the actual situation and that which was reported to higher commanders. The division and brigade commanders believed that the entire 61st Infantry was a broken and beaten unit, retreating in confusion. Actually, the 1st Battalion was on its final objective, battered and disorganized—but victorious—and the comparatively fresh 2d Battalion had passed through the 3d in order to continue the attack. Unquestionably the 3d Battalion was in a state of great confusion and undoubtedly some of its men were retiring, but even if the entire battalion had been withdrawing it would not have compromised the situation, for it had been passed through and was no longer in assault. No crisis existed that would have precluded its reassembly and reorganization.

True, the situation had its unfavorable aspects, but the fact remains that success was at hand. Some of the higher commanders, however, could see only the black side of the picture.

There are three points in this illustration worthy of categorical emphasis. First, a subordinate should not add to the troubles of his superior by indulging in unduly pessimistic reports. The situation as known should be accurately and exactly reported without any pessimistic assumptions or opinions.

Second, when discouraging information is received, particularly if it comes from wounded men or stragglers, it should be materially discounted. In no case should it be taken at its face value without corroboration.

Third, it may always be safely assumed that the enemy is also in difficulty. We know that in this engagement the Germans were in great disorder and confusion. The fact that the depleted 1st Battalion held its position all day, not withdrawing until nightfall was, in itself, indicative of the fact that the enemy had been fought to a standstill.

EXAMPLE 2. At 7:00 a.m., October 20, 1918, troops of the U. S. 3d Division attacked the Clairs-Chênes Woods. Their division had been in the front line for approximately three weeks and during this period had suffered enormous casualties. The troops had reached a point verging on exhaustion. Although their repeated attacks had met with some slight success they had won no striking victory.

The attacking force on October 20 comprised the 1st and 3d Battalions of the 7th Infantry (which were consolidated and organized as a provisional company of 301 men), two companies of the 6th Engineers, and one company of the 4th Infantry. The attack penetrated Clairs-Chênes Woods and, at about 8:15 a.m., the advanced elements reported that they had reached the northern edge of the wood. These leading troops were numerically weak and were not closely followed by supporting units. Those Germans who still remained in the woods were quick to take advantage of this and soon succeeded in working their way around the flanks and filtering through the sparsely held American line. A confused and obscure situation resulted. After hard fighting some of the Americans of the support units began to withdraw.

To all appearances the attack had failed and reports to that effect reached the commanding officer of the 7th Infantry. Assembling all available men in the vicinity—150 all told—and personally taking command of this nondescript detachment, he counter-attacked into Clairs-Chênes Woods. Despite severe losses from machine guns and minenwerfers, this party gained the northern edge of the woods and joined the few remaining men of the advanced elements. Three German officers and 112 men were taken prisoners and the Clairs-Chênes Woods passed definitely and finally into American hands.

The next day this aggressive officer was placed in command of an operation directed against Hill 299. At noon the depleted 7th Infantry, Company E of the 4th Infantry, one battalion of the 38th Infantry, three companies of the 6th Engineers, and a few machine guns—all that was available of the spent 3d Division—moved to the attack.

The disputed hill fell, but almost coincident with the moment of success—when all available infantry had been committed to the action—word came in that the enemy, driving from the northeastern edge of the Bois des Rappes, were attacking Clairs-Chênes.

Some of the troops holding this hard-won wood withdrew. Streaming back to the 7th Infantry command post in the northern edge of the Bois de la Pultière, they reported that the Germans were attacking in force and that the line had been broken.

All available troops having been committed, the commanding officer of the 7th Infantry, with three members of his staff and sixteen runners and signalmen, moved forward at once, picking up a few stragglers on the way. "Come on, now, we're going back to the front," he called. "We're going to get the old line back again."

Under shell fire the little party continued its advance until it reached the point where the attack was reported. Here it captured a small German patrol but found no evidence of the strong hostile attack that had been reported.

From "History of the 3d Division."

DISCUSSION. The commanding officer of the 7th Infantry displayed marked resolution in the operations on these two days. On the first day, after a brief initial success, the bulk of his force failed. The attack had become disorganized. Men were moving to the rear individually. A commander lacking in tenacity would, in all probability, have contented himself by sending back a report of failure supported by sundry and assorted reasons. But this leader gathered a small detachment, made one last effort, and succeeded.

At the crisis of the operation on the second day the situation again seemed desperate. Men were streaming to the rear. A strong German attack was reported to be striking toward the flank of the 7th Infantry. There were no troops to meet it. Again rising to the emergency, this same energetic officer, with his

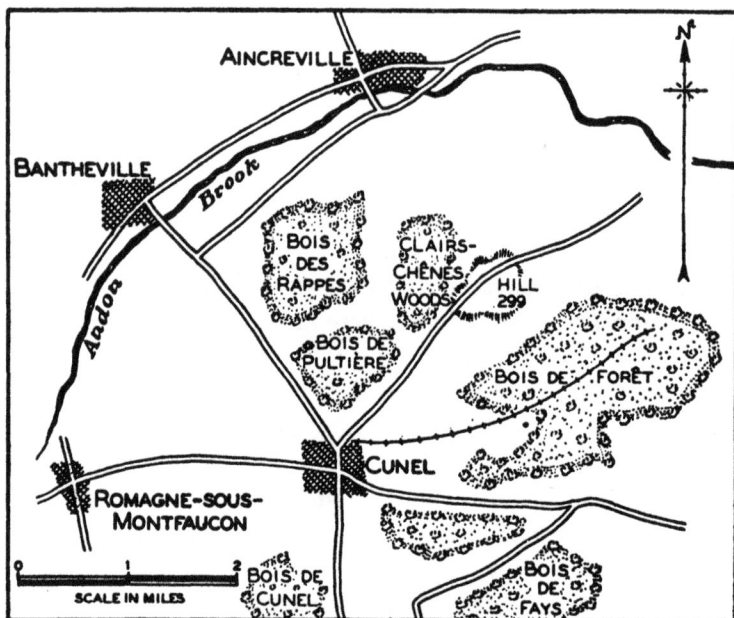

Example 2

staff and a handful of runners, moved forward to the threatened locality. There he found the situation far less critical than it had been painted. The few men with the colonel were sufficient to restore it. The point is this: had not some troops moved forward, had not this leader imparted his own courage and optimism to the men, the position might well have been lost.

This example portrays a commendable reaction to pessimistic reports. The commanding officer did not accept them blindly and send back word of defeat and disaster; neither did he ignore them. Instead, he investigated at the head of a small improvised force and in each instance this proved sufficient to restore the situation.

✓   ✓   ✓

EXAMPLE 3. On October 2, 1918, elements of the U. S. 77th Division attacked northward in the Argonne Forest. A force under the command of Major Charles W. Whittlesey, consisting of headquarters scouts and runners of the 1st and 2d Battalions of the 308th Infantry, Companies A, B, C, E, G and H of the 308th Infantry, two platoons of Companies C and D of the 306th Machine-Gun Battalion, and Company K of the 307th Infantry, reached its objective east of the Moulin de Charlevaux. Company K of the 307th Infantry joined the command after the objective had been reached.

Neighboring units and supporting troops had been stopped far short of the line reached by Major Whittlesey. The Germans quickly seized this opportunity to work their way behind this isolated unit and cut its communications with American troops to the rear. This force—known to history as the Lost Battalion—was cut off and surrounded. It had only one day's ration for four companies.

Upon reaching his objective, Major Whittlesey had organized for defense. Enemy artillery shelled the position. This ceased after a time and trench-mortar fire followed. An attempt to establish contact with the rear failing, the situation was reported by pigeon message and the force disposed for all-around defense.

The following message was then sent to all company and detachment commanders:

> Our mission is to hold this position at all cost. Have this understood by every man in the command.

Fire from enemy machine guns and trench mortars continued. About 3:00 p.m. the next day (October 3) the Germans launched a frontal attack supported by fire from the flanks and rear. The leading assailants got close enough to throw grenades, but the attack failed. About 5:00 p.m. another attack came from both flanks. This too was repulsed but with heavy American losses.

By way of medical assistance the Americans had three Medical Corps enlisted men; no medical officer had accompanied the out-

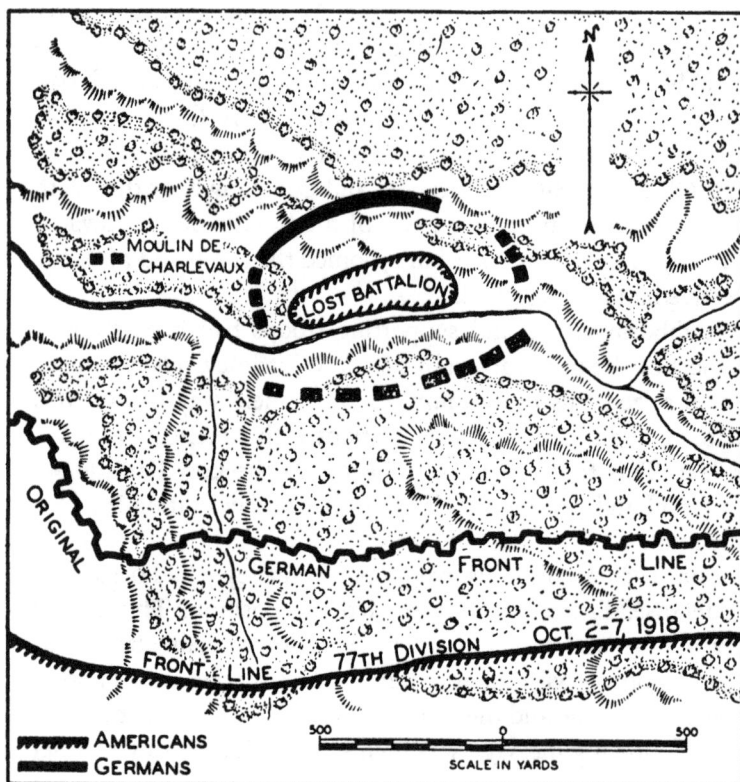

Example 3

fit. All dressings and first-aid bandages were exhausted on the night of the 3d.

Daylight of October 4 found the men tired and hungry. All, especially the wounded, had suffered bitterly from the cold during the night. More enemy trench mortars went into position and opened a steady fire, causing heavy casualties. Scouts reported that the Germans were all around the position in large numbers. No word from the rear had been received. Again the situation was reported by pigeon message.

During the afternoon of the 4th an American barrage, starting in the south, swept forward and settled down on the position, causing more losses. German trench mortars added their shells. At this time the last pigeon was released with a message giving the location of the force and stating that American artillery was placing a barrage on it.

American planes flew over the position and were fired on by the Germans. About 5:00 p.m. a new German attack was repulsed. Water was being obtained from a muddy stream along the ravine below the position. Often a canteen of water cost a casualty, for the enemy had laid guns to cover the stream. Guards were therefore posted to keep men from going to the stream during daylight. A chilly rain the night of the 4th added to the discomfort.

About 9:00 p.m. a German surprise attack failed. The wounded were now in terrible condition and, like the rest of the force, were without food.

Indications of American attacks from the south had been noted, but no relief came. Actually, several battalions of the 77th Division had been almost wiped out in valiant but vain efforts to reach the Lost Battalion.

During the afternoon of October 5, French artillery located to the southwest opened a heavy fire on the position. The Germans waited until the French fire lifted and then launched another attack which the Americans again stopped.

Shortly after this, American airplanes attempted to drop packages in the position but their aim was bad and the packages fell in the German lines. The men realized that this was an effort to get food to them.

Bandages for the wounded were now being taken from the

dead; even wrap-leggins were used. It became increasingly difficult to get water.

On the morning of October 6 the enemy's rifles and machine
guns started early and his trench mortars again took up their
pounding. Another American airplane came over and dropped
packages, but again they fell in the German lines. Soon afterward there were signs that the Germans were forming for
another attack, but this was broken up by American artillery
fire.

During the afternoon of October 6 a murderous machine-gun
barrage plastered the position and took a heavy toll. This was
immediately followed by an attack which, though beaten off,
added to the roll of dead and wounded.

By this time ammunition was running low. But despite everything, courage and morale remained high. The men were determined to fight to a finish.

About noon on the 7th another attack was repulsed. At 4:00
p.m. enemy firing ceased. From the left flank an American soldier
appeared limping toward the position. He carried a long stick
with a piece of white cloth tied to it. This soldier had been captured while attempting to obtain a package of food dropped
by the airplanes. He brought a letter from the German commander, neatly typewritten in English.

SIR:

The bearer of this present, Private ———— has been taken prisoner
by us. He refused to give the German intelligence officer any answer to his questions, and is quite an honorable fellow, doing
honor to his Fatherland in the strictest sense of the word.

He has been charged against his will, believing he is doing wrong to
his country, to carry forward this present letter to the officer in
charge of the battalion of the 77th Division, with the purpose to
recommend this commander to surrender with his forces, as it
would be quite useless to resist any more, in view of the present
conditions.

The suffering of your wounded men can be heard over here in the
German lines, and we are appealing to your humane sentiments
to stop. A white flag shown by one of your men will tell us that

you agree with these conditions. Please treat Private ———— as an honorable man. He is quite a soldier. We envy you.

Major Whittlesey made no reply, oral or written. He ordered two white airplane panels which were being displayed to be taken in at once. Nothing white was to show on the hillside.

The fiercest attack of the siege followed. Wounded men dragged themselves to the firing line, and those who could not fire loaded rifles. The enemy used flame throwers in this attack, and nearly took the position. But finally he was driven off.

At dusk on the 7th it seemed impossible to hold out. Only two machine guns were left of the original nine. No gunners remained to man them. Ammunition was almost exhausted. The next attack would have to be met with the bayonet. There had been no food since the morning of October 3d. The water obtained was slimy and bad. Still these men were willing to fight on.

That night the enemy withdrew and American troops arrived soon afterward. One hundred and ninety-four (194) men out of the 700 that jumped off on the morning of October 2 were able to walk out of the position. Many of these were wounded.

Despite the desperate situation and the hardships, the morale of the Lost Battalion had not been broken. Inspired by their leader, the men were determined to fight to a finish.

From the personal experience monograph of Captain Nelson M. Holderman, who at the time commanded Company K of the 307th Infantry.

✓   ✓   ✓

EXAMPLE 4. On the afternoon of August 22, 1914, the French were engaged with the Germans in the Belgian Ardennes. It had been a meeting engagement, or rather several meeting engagements—division against division and corps against corps —without much connection between the various combats.

Late in the afternoon, five separate French commanders made pessimistic decisions based on reports of what had happened to troops other than their own. In each case, the actual situation and action taken by the Germans did not correspond to the fears of the French commanders. In each case the French decisions hurt the French. They occurred in five adjacent columns, each decision being a separate one, and each made at approximately the same hour.

The commander of the 7th French Division at Ethe, finding his division cut in two and fearing that he was about to be enveloped on both flanks, withdrew the rear elements of his division, leaving the advanced elements to their fate. The forward half, although engaged against superior numbers, fought so well that the Germans withdrew at dark.

On the left of the French 7th Division was the 8th. This unit had been surprised early that morning in the fog near Virton. Confused fighting followed. The corps commander, charged with protecting the flank of the more advanced unit on his left, sud denly decided that he would do this very well from a position in rear and forthwith ordered a withdrawal. His troops however, were hotly engaged and a large part never received the order. At dusk, assisted by troops of an adjacent division, these uninformed soldiers attacked and captured the German front line. Previous decisions prevented exploitation.

Elements of the French II Corps were engaged against the flank of the Germans fighting the French 8th Division. Late in the afternoon a strong attack was about to be delivered, but was called off because a few Germans were seen on the north flank. Actually, these Germans were merely a few stragglers who had become lost in the confusion of battle. Had the French gone through with their attack they would have found no enemy on their flank.

Going to the left, we find the French 3d Colonial Division, late that afternoon, cut in two; half of it north of the unfordable Semoy, half of it south. The north half, with both flanks being enveloped by superior German forces, was in a desperate plight. At this point the 2d Division of the Colonial Corps arrived and found itself in position to take one of the German pincers in flank and rear. So far the Germans here had enjoyed a numerical superiority. Now the tables were about to be turned—a French victory, or at least a draw, was within sight. But the vision faded, for at the crucial moment the corps commander halted the attack and took up a defensive attitude. Pessimistic reports from his left column (the 5th Colonial Brigade) and from units on his flanks had undermined his resolution. For this irresolution of their corps commander the 3d Colonial Division paid a heavy price—the destruction of that half of the division north of the Semoy.

Let us see what had happened to the 5th Colonial Brigade (left column of the 3d Colonial Division). This unit had struck head-on into the flank of the German XVIII Reserve Corps at Neufchâteau. Although it had been terribly hammered and driven back, it had fought so hard that by 5:00 p.m. the German attack had been stopped, and the enemy had decided to quit for the night. The Germans thought they were facing at least a division, possibly a corps. Nevertheless, the French brigade commander sent back word that he was withdrawing after a hard fight. This caused the French corps commander to suspend his attack near Rossignol. The 5th Brigade, however, seems to have had a temporary change of heart. Its withdrawal was made later, and largely as a result of reports that the XII Corps on its left had been engaged and that elements were withdrawing.

As a matter of fact, the XII Corps had met little opposition and at the time was even considering launching a pursuit. During the night it withdrew due to the situation of units on its flanks.

From the accounts "Ethe," "Virton," and "Neufchâteau," by Colonel A. Grasset, French Army; "The Genesis of Neufchâteau," by Major Pugens, French Army; and French official documents.

✦   ✦   ✦

CONCLUSION. In the case of the Lost Battalion we see a

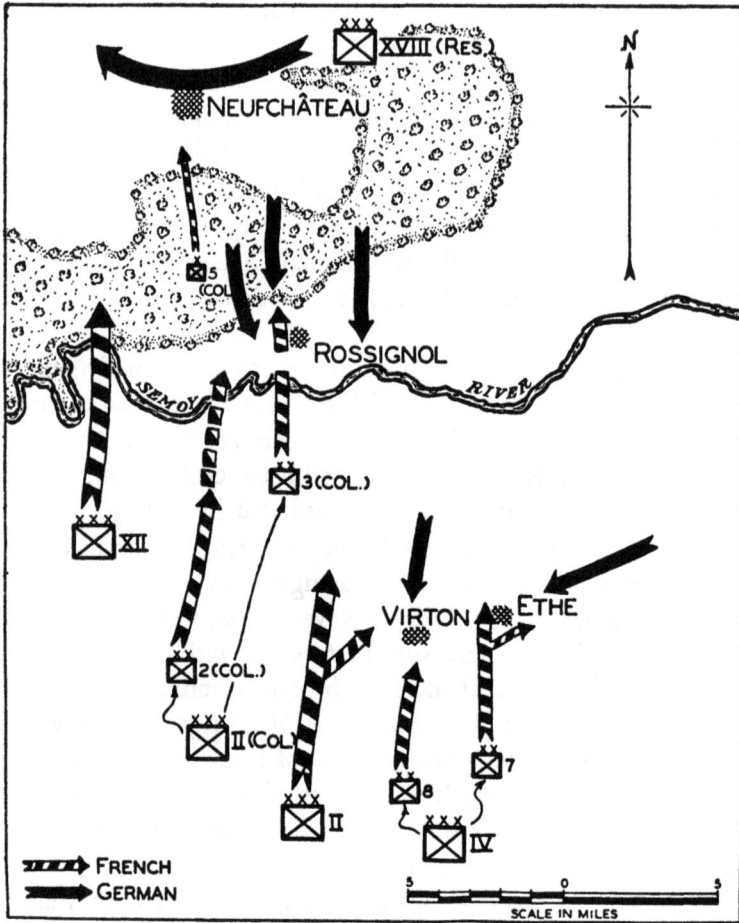

Example 4

marvelous record of endurance, a soldierly acceptance of conditions and a determination to accomplish its mission. Of the examples quoted, this is the only one in which rumors of disaster and exaggerated stories and reports do not figure. Had the battalion commander and his subordinate leaders shown even a momentary weakness, that weakness would have been reflected in their men. But there was no weakness in those leaders or in the men they led. The story of their fortitude and tenacity will always live.

The other examples show the action of leaders when confronted with pessimistic reports. Where such reports were accepted at full value, the result is frequently disaster.

Consider the battles of Magdhaba and Rafa, in which the British defeated the Turks. In each case the British commander made the decision to break off the fight. In each case before the order could reach the front line the victory was won.

At Magdhaba it appears that a large portion of the credit should go to General Cox, who commanded the 1st Australian Light Horse. When he received the order to retire he turned on the staff officer who brought it and shouted, "Take that damned thing away and let me see it for the first time in half an hour." Half an hour later victory was assured.

Scharnhorst, when consulted in regard to the appointment of Blücher to high command in the Prussian Army, asked:

> Is it not the manner in which the leaders carry out the task of command, of impressing their resolution in the hearts of others, that makes them warriors, far more than all other aptitudes or faculties which theory may expect of them?

INDEX

INDEX TO PUBLICATIONS QUOTED

INDEX TO UNITS

GEOGRAPHICAL INDEX